D0284269

BOOKS BY CAROL DE CHELLIS HILL

THE ELEVEN MILLION MILE HIGH DANCER

LET'S FALL IN LOVE

SUBSISTENCE, U.S.A.

AN UNMARRIED WOMAN

JEREMIAH 8:20

CAROL DE CHELLIS HILL

HENRY JAMES' MIDNIGHT SONG

POSEIDON PRESS
NEW YORK LONDON TORONTO
SYDNEY TOKYO SINGAPORE

POSEIDON PRESS

SIMON & SCHUSTER BUILDING
ROCKEFELLER CENTER
1230 AVENUE OF THE AMERICAS
NEW YORK, NEW YORK 10020

THIS BOOK IS A WORK OF FICTION. NAMES, CHARACTERS, PLACES AND INCIDENTS ARE
EITHER PRODUCTS OF THE AUTHOR'S IMAGINATION OR ARE USED FICTITIOUSLY. ANY
RESEMBLANCE TO ACTUAL EVENTS OR LOCALES OR PERSONS, LIVING OR DEAD, IS ENTIRELY
COINCIDENTAL.

COPYRIGHT © 1993 BY CAROL HILL

ALL RIGHTS RESERVED
INCLUDING THE RIGHT OF REPRODUCTION
IN WHOLE OR IN PART IN ANY FORM.

POSEIDON PRESS IS A REGISTERED TRADEMARK
OF SIMON & SCHUSTER INC.

POSEIDON PRESS COLOPHON IS A TRADEMARK
OF SIMON & SCHUSTER INC.

DESIGNED BY KAROLINA HARRIS
MANUFACTURED IN THE UNITED STATES OF AMERICA

10 9 8 7 6 5 4 3 2 1

LIBRARY OF CONGRESS CATALOGING IN PUBLICATION DATA
HILL, CAROL DE CHELLIS.
  HENRY JAMES' MIDNIGHT SONG / CAROL DE CHELLIS HILL.
    P. CM.
  1. JAMES, HENRY, 1843–1916—FICTION. 2. FREUD, SIGMUND, 1856–1939—
FICTION. 3. AUTHORS, AMERICAN—AUSTRIA—VIENNA—FICTION. 4. PSYCHOANALYSTS—
AUSTRIA—VIENNA—FICTION. 5. VIENNA (AUSTRIA)—FICTION. I. TITLE.
PS3558.I3846H46 1993
  813'.54—dc20   93-11135
                                                              CIP
ISBN: 0-671-75575-7

THE "BEATRICE PALMATO" FRAGMENT THAT APPEARED IN R. W. B. LEWIS'S BIOGRAPHY OF
EDITH WHARTON, EDITH WHARTON (HARPER & ROW, 1975), IS REPRINTED BY PERMISSION OF
THE AUTHOR AND THE WATKINS/LOOMIS AGENCY.

A PICNIC IN LINDLEY WOOD, C. 1895, APPEARS COURTESY OF B. T. BATSFORD LTD.,
LONDON.

ACKNOWLEDGMENTS

The willing readers, and kibitzers, among my friends and family are here heartfully thanked for their much needed support and their generosity in reading time. I would especially like to thank Bradley Albert, Tamara Follini, Carol Mack and Tom Weyr for their thoughtful and inspired editorial critiques, not all of which I had the wisdom to incorporate. I'd also like to thank Susan Margolis, Liz Darhansoff, Irene Skolnick, and Anne Freedgood for their help and encouragement. Sandra Davis Randle did a heroic job of retyping a complex and unreadable manuscript. I very much appreciate the work of my most remarkable copy editor, Melinda Mousouris, and of course my editor and publisher extraordinaire, Ann Patty. And a very special thanks, as always, to my husband, Jerry Albert.

To The Memory of My Maternal Grandmother
Margaret Traynor Ward McCaffrey
1889–1915

and

To My Mother
Margaret McCaffrey De Chellis Morrison
1910–1986

Bearers of the Golden Winds

THE MUSHROOM FEAST

CONTENTS

Certain authors, speaking of their works, say, "My book," "My commentary," "My history," and so on. They would do better to say "Our book," "Our commentary," "Our history," etc., because there is in them usually more of other people's than their own.

PASCAL
Pensées

O man! Take heed!
What saith deep midnight's voice indeed?
"I slept my sleep—
From deepest dream I've woke, and plead—
The world is deep,
And deeper than the day could read..."

NIETZSCHE
Thus Spoke Zarathustra

PART I
THE BEAST

1

"Look out, Sigmund!" Oskar grabbed his friend's coat sleeve as the two young doctors emerged from the Vienna medical school building and attempted to cross the Waehringstrasse. The coach and four black horses wheeled suddenly around as Oskar jerked Sigmund back and, without halting, the horses sped off in another direction. "My god!" Sigmund said, stunned, as Oskar helped him up and he wiped himself off. "They nearly had you," Oskar said grimly.

At that moment, in the early morning light, the sun was just staining the sky pink, lighting up all of the Ringstrasse. When they looked up again they saw the coach and four magnificent black horses with bells all a-clamor racing at full tilt toward them. The coachman flailed the horses directly at them, and then as if receiving another order, whirled the team around, and they sped off down another street, the wheels spinning precariously in the wet snow. From the carriage window, a tiny gloved hand, covered in pink kid and studded with pearls and shining stones ("Diamonds, I thought surely, such glitter," Oskar said later)—a tiny hand appeared in the carriage window, and as if in a wave, threw a small blue letter that blossomed in the air, the pages opening to land on the wet snow.

"For us, it seems!" Oskar said to Sigmund and ran to the blue letter, which was blown again and danced precariously on pointed end, just before it blew away, just out of reach. Sigmund watched the coach disappear into the city.

"Was it deliberate, or was she simply ridding herself of the letter?" Sigmund thought. It was an odd place to dispose of a letter. Except the lady, he had seen as the coach turned, had been passionately engaged with a gentleman. The letter, he suspected, had been thrown out in an effort to keep it from the one whose fervid embraces she had been enjoying. He wondered, were the advances unwelcome? Perhaps the lady was well known. Perhaps the gentleman. Perhaps it was a question of scandal. Perhaps not . . . And yet, surely, she had seen them. Or not? Or someone else, for certainly the coachman, upon seeing them, had changed the path of the horses.

"Look at this!" Oskar said, coming up to him with the note, and reading the tiny inked handwriting.

"It has a signature?" Sigmund asked.

"Just this," Oskar said, handing him the second page of the letter.

"Help me," it read.

She had thrown it out the window. Blue tissue papers, billet-doux as the French had it, letters, recordings of those places that had tormented her, carving shapes into her life while they themselves remained invisible. Evidence of memories. Thoughts, if not acts, wrapped into those thin blue lines, crying now, like lost wild animals, for her to open the chest and let them out, let them in.

She ran to her room slamming the door and threw herself into the pitch blackness where she lay sobbing uncontrollably on the bed. The mattress heaved with her agitation, her moans and sobs rising in the darkness to drift through the thick draperies out the window cracks, stealing now thin and muted into the streets of Vienna where they would drift, those sobs and whispers, in and out of every inhalation on the street that morning. Shopkeepers just arriving in their homburg hats, bending and unlocking their stores would raise their heads suddenly like dogs sniffing the air, what was it? Something sensed. Something known, but barely perceived, as the scientists would say later. Not too much later. It would not be long now, before the sobs and paroxysms of that one female heart would begin their expansion and contraction, in and out of the breaths and minds of generations of Viennese. Those cries, those sobs, that distraught woman uttered in the dark, the mysteries of that darkness were about to be known to the world.

The two young doctors continued down the street, talking quickly, and with great excitement, about the work being done with hysterics in Paris.

Editor's Note

That was the first page of the manuscript, which broke off abruptly, so you can imagine my curiosity, heightened, no doubt by the peculiar circumstances of its arrival.

I should begin by saying that at first the entire matter struck me as absurd, if not histrionic, and there was absolutely no indication of the very serious nature of what I was about to enter into. When a package is delivered on a dark and stormy night to an old house hidden in the woods, anyone, most especially a reader of books, is immediately suspicious. But that is precisely what happened. I had rented the rather small cottage near the Maine coast for a vacation. I was to have it for several months during which time I was attempting to complete a treatise on medieval mysticism that I had been working on for some time. I personally have no belief or faith whatsoever in anything supernatural, or even transcendent for that matter, and so I thought myself eminently qualified for the difficult task of elucidating mystic states. I was deep in my studies, and at first I thought that perhaps overwork had begun to affect my mind; that the long hours and the solitude had made me subject to the visions or hallucinations brought about not infrequently by lack of food and/or solitude in the very mystics I was reading. But in fact I did have food; I have little or no interest in self-abnegation and very little tolerance for it. How then shall I explain the events of that evening? I shall not. But I shall describe them.

The wind had been howling for hours, and when I first looked out the windows of my small abode there was clearly nothing to be seen but the clashing of trees and branches against the glass. Then, quite distinctly, I was certain I heard a kind of steady, rhythmic knocking at my front door. This frightened me at first as the house is deep in a thick wood, at the end of a long, and in very wet weather, impassable drive. I heard the knocking again and I froze. No robber would brave that trail; it would take an entirely different sort of determination to make that journey this night. I immediately turned on the small radio I kept on the table; perhaps some inmate had escaped from the state prison many miles away. I was by now convinced what I heard was indeed a knocking.

The radio broadcast was full of static and I kept turning the dials but could not discover a station that would bring me news. The knocking occurred again.

I do not keep a gun on the premises. I turned the lights out in the front hall so I could not be seen and I approached the glass windows framing the door. Through the pane I could see a bundle of some sort on the step. I looked carefully through the glass and then, on impulse, I opened the door and snatched the package inside, and just as I did so it seemed to me, although I realized later this was impossible, that I saw a large, rather awkward shape disappearing into the woods. A thin maroon line trailed behind it, swirling into the gravel beyond the porch. Torrents of water were washing over the stones, and the blood, for I knew that is what it must be, was fast disappearing.

I slammed the door immediately and locked it. I then ran to the back door and made sure it was fastened as well. At the time, being a person committed to reason, I ascribed the hallucination to nerves, a fit caused by solitude and the storm. This was, I firmly believed, the only possible cause for my alarm. The package, I assumed, simply must have been left prior to the storm by a delivery service and I had failed to notice it. There was no other explanation.

My curiosity about the package was very strong. I took it into the kitchen where, I confess, I got out a long butcher knife I hadn't used in some time, sharpened it, and laid it next to the package. My anxiety was considerable as I tore open the outer wrapping, my hand on the handle of the butcher knife the entire while, ready to pounce if neces- sary on whatever might spring from the wrapping.

The wrapping itself was elaborate, fastened by a series of knots that I got through only with great difficulty. The twine appeared thin, but it proved extremely difficult to break. After several minutes I was perspir- ing as much from anxiety as from effort, and it was with enormous relief when the first wrappings finally fell away that I spied a high square package. It suggested nothing so much as a manuscript, which, I soon discovered, is precisely what it was. When I had cut through the second layer, it fell away and I opened the strange binding to see the title page of the manuscript written in a fine, firm hand: *Henry James' Midnight Song.*

I saw then that there was a paper, written in a very different hand, attached to the manuscript underneath the title page and it was headed "Letter of Explanation." This was an equally curious document and one which I found difficult to evaluate. The letter, signed by a professor at the University of Vienna whom I didn't know, claimed that the document before me was discovered only a few months ago, having been confis- cated he believed during Hitler's Anschluss in Vienna. I did not know if that meant the manuscript had been written just prior to the Anschluss and never reached publication or if it had been written contemporane- ously with the times it described and simply never published. This matter became most difficult to decide, as there were various complexi- ties involved in attempting to ascertain when it was written and by whom. It was clear it had been sent to me because of my credentials as a scholar. As part of my work on medieval mysticism, I was known as an expert in deciphering handwriting. It is essential to medieval work as there are so many hands, all of them unique and difficult. My exper- tise in this matter led to a secondary interest and a considerable reputa- tion in the history of pseudonymous writing.

When I attempted to contact the professor from Vienna, however, I discovered to my total consternation that the professor was himself pseudonymous. I could never determine from whence this manuscript came.

Upon my first reading I thought, quite frankly, that it had to be a hoax of some sort. Surely if there had ever been such a murder, and the suspects had included Sigmund Freud, Henry James, and Edith Wharton, it is highly unlikely it could have been "hidden from history." Yet at the same time the book produced some nagging doubts. After all, it has only recently been established that the distinguished analyst Dr. Carl Jung, did have an affair with one of his earliest patients, the young Sabina Spielrein, whom he did, at least, cure. This material was suppressed for many years from any public records. So it is not inconceivable that more material has been suppressed. Unfortunately the Freud archives will not be opened until the end of this century.

Much curiosity about Freud centers on the speculation as to whether he had a sexual relationship with his sister-in-law Minna Bernays, who lived in the Freud household. Some scholars have gone so far as to suggest that Minna was pregnant by Freud and went for an abortion at his insistence. In a less constrained century than our own of course, such matters would not seem so pressing. Until they are proven, however, I personally remain full of doubt. Of the Countess von Gerzl and Inspector LeBlanc and the American family, the Mains, there remain no records.

I initially thought this was, without question, a work of fiction. For although all of the events occurred between 1890 and 1910, the chronology is select, and confused. For example, there is no mention of the assassination of Empress Elizabeth, by an Italian anarchist in Sarajevo, in 1898. And on occasion events in 1905 precede those in 1900 and so on. Alice James died in 1892, well before the Dreyfus trial. I thought possibly this kind of transposition was an effort to show that chronology is simply another arbitrary order and that the importance of themes supersedes their sequence. Perhaps the author was of the conviction that cause and effect do not propel history. If David Hume's famous billiard ball rolls *before* the cue stick hits it, one certainly cannot say that the cue stick *caused* the ball to roll.

The fact remains we do not know who authored the remarkable story you are about to read. There is no record other than this one. Whether it was originally written in English or was a translation I leave to the reader to decide.

I cannot hazard an opinion as to when the manuscript was written. It has the odd quality of seeming to have been written in the midst of the events, yet at the same time it telescopes events in the way that can only be done in *retrospect*. The way that we say "during the sixties, this was the climate," is not something we can say when we are in fact *in* the sixties; it is only in perspective that a time takes on a general character.

This is the kind of telescoping that usually happens over a long period of time, when one is trying, for example, to recall childhood events, and Uncle Henry's birthday party when one was four becomes attached, for complex reasons, to the memory of another celebration at a different age. It is a commonplace of family memory, for one member to say, "Do you remember that time at the lake when Raymond ate the clams?"; and for another to say, "Oh no, we weren't at the lake then, we were at the sea, and it wasn't Raymond, but Lawrence." What actually happened eventually becomes clear, but often over a difficult, knotty course of disentanglement.

It was this curious aspect of the manuscript which led me to think that perhaps it had been written many years after these events had passed. The author in that case would have to be, I daresay, the sister of Cecily Main, of whom there is no trace whatsoever, except perhaps this rather curious one: a fingerprint, in ink, is left on one of the pages near the end of the manuscript. I intend to locate the police files in Vienna regarding this incident, where I hope to find her print, so I would know for certain that this manuscript has at least passed through her hand.

It has even occurred to me that the manuscript was originally sent to me, not only because of the difficulties in distinguishing the handwriting, but also because of the confessional nature of the document. For it is related partially by a narrator known only as "I," or "Cecily's sister," and the confession of this the narrator proves central to solving the mystery. I use the word *confession* because of the complicit nature of crime, if you accept the argument that her witness requires she speak or she remain complicit. Or was this authorial confusion deliberate— to cast, in some subtle way, aspersions on the very nature of the

"I"? To cast a medieval spell, as it were, over the personal nature of the "I"?

At the same time events commingle, there are curious inversions. Edith Wharton's affair with Morton Fullerton did not occur until almost ten years after Freud's *Interpretation of Dreams* was published. Yet in the manuscript they appear simultaneous, the way they might in a dream, or nightmare. As there is simply no proof as to the identity of the author of the manuscript, it has also occurred to me that perhaps there was no single author but rather a multifaceted group of individuals who, living in a certain time and place, met with astonishing force the limitation of their individual histories by condensing, as it were, their disparate selves into one being and representing each of their combined lives as one individual voice. This, my colleagues have remarked, is an overly prolix way of saying that perhaps there is such a thing as the "voice of an age." This would also account for the juncture of occurrences which we know are *chronologically impossible.*

There are, finally, strange twists of memory in this document. For a memory of an event, cannot, strictly speaking, *precede* the event, although psychoanalytically it must be said, certain re-pressed memories can predispose the mind so that the event which *is* re-membered is "standing in" for some earlier event; and becomes then, an event that took place, actually, prior to its own moment. This is particularly true of course in the case of trauma.

It is important to reflect upon the circumstances in which these events took place. Turn of the century Vienna was a city of remarkable, almost unprecedented vitality in the arts and sciences. New techniques flourished: among painters such as Oskar Kokoschka and Gustav Klimt, architects and designers, Kolomon Moser and Adolf Loos, and composers Arnold Schoenberg and Gustav Mahler, all of whom became world famous.

Discoveries in science were momentous: Einstein's theory of relativity was first published in 1905, followed by Ernst Mach's theory of sensation[1] which was, some say, the beginning of the disappearance of the self, at least conceptually. Yet, it was also a time of the "finding of the self"; for it marked in the work of Freud, especially, the founding of a science of the mind—psychology.

It was also a period of overcrowding, inadequate housing, and competing cultures, as thousands of Europeans of all races and nationalities poured into Vienna, a collision of what we would now call "competing ethnic groups." Assimilation versus separateness was hotly debated. Anti-Semitism, particularly in that city, where Jews were prominent in all aspects of civic life, and both valued and reviled, was strong. In France as well, expressions of anti-Semitism soared during the Alfred Dreyfus case. There were three stages, the first trial in 1894, which resulted in his conviction, the second in 1899, and his acquittal in 1906. This case had a tremendous impact not only on French society but on Jewish awareness throughout Europe. Theodor Herzl, who covered the trial for a Viennese newspaper, was the founder of the Zionist movement. He lived in Vienna and published the first call for the Jews to have their own country in a pamphlet called *The Jewish State* in 1896.

It was a time of discord and discovery. German feminism and Austrian feminism were just beginning. One can say that it was a time of both a tremendous artistic flowering and a dangerous political divisiveness that we are still attempting to understand today.

As I read the manuscript, I began to believe it was in some ways extremely reliable. The nagging thought would consistently occur that possibly such a murder as is described here *did* in fact take place, and it was only my acceptance of recorded history that prevented me from embracing such a possibility. And I am sympathetic myself to Henry James' observation that fiction is just the other side of history. And then, of course, there is the provocative idea that historians cannot in ordinary circumstances document what takes place in the *minds* of individuals.

---

[1] Mach's book and theory had a tremendous impact not only on the Viennese but on all developments in philosophy. *The Analysis of Sensations and the Relations between the Physical and Psychical,* first published in 1886 and reissued in 1900, posited a fluctuating and uncertain identity and dismissed the stable self as a "useless hypothesis." The ego, he claimed, is only a complex of sensory percepts.

They can only document events, and merely attempt to deduce thought from action.

Or, is it absurd? Are the murder and the events surrounding it the working of an overwrought imagination? This manuscript does not deduce but stakes a claim to the dreams and fantasies of its individuals in history. To what extent do the undreamed dreams, so to speak, of an individual determine his actions? What arrogance on the part of this narrator would dare to believe that he or she knows? That arrogance surely suggests the work of a novelist. And yet, this story seems to be an eyewitness account. It is not infrequently the author himself or herself that persuaded me of this, although the issue of personality or *persona* of this so-called document is so complex it is not possible to address all aspects of it here. The author's motives are concealed, baffling, and I must say, on occasion, inspired. I will add that the impressionist technique, the small swatches of color here and there combining finally to form a coherent image, was for me rather effective.

Under ordinary circumstances the principles of clarity and consistency would demand that an editor delete any material that does not "fit" into the manuscript. I have found it necessary to modify and at moments suspend my usual practices in this case. I have allowed to remain occasional partial sketches of persons and fragments of thought, because they seemed in some way to be part of this remarkable account, although I confess that their precise purpose was not at all clear to me until I had put down the last page and stared out the window for what seemed a very long time.

PROFESSOR THEO. RYDEWORT

2

In Vienna: at 19 Berggasse, three shots rang out. Blood spilled across the figure in the worn Persian carpet.

Black horses galloped, black angels in the night, hooves striking fire, like flint against stone, across the cobblestoned streets, pulling the swaying coach.

"Faster, faster," the voice implored the coachman as the woman, moaning, buried her bloodied face in the handkerchief. Red blots seeped through the fine white cloth. She turned to look at him. Her eyes rolled upwards in pain.

"Hurry, please, I beg you," the gentleman roared, his head hanging outside the coach door as the coachman whipped the horses into a final frenzy, and then, on the far turn, the wheels tipped and the woman screamed as blood poured through her handkerchief like water into a cup.

In Vienna black horses galloped, foam speckling their necks, breathing the breath of demons—frozen clouds of white—and in Paris the Police Special Inspector, Maurice Cheval LeBlanc, slowly opened first one eye, then the other. This was how the Inspector woke up. He raised himself up on one elbow, drenched in sweat. They kept calling him to Vienna—and he knew that he had to go—a series of unsolved murders—but he had been delayed. Delayed. Delayed, he told them, by grief and mourning. He and Gustav the painter had been out drinking all night, desperate and hopeless over the death of the young girl, Elise. Now something had awakened him. Listening and looking about the room, he realized it was only a thought. He searched for it, but all evidence had left him now, and he turned to attempt to go back to sleep. It was three o'clock in the morning, and he was badly hung over, with sadness and absinthe. He had befriended the girl. She had wanted to be a painter, instead of a model, and she had been crushed to death on the steps of the Beaux Arts Institute. A riot, they said. They didn't admit women, they said. The crowd had gotten out of hand.

''NIETZSCHE says,'' the artist slurred, drunk and inconsolable over the death of the girl, "he has said insanity is uncommon among individuals and the rule in a group." He moaned and fell onto the table. His friend shook him. "Gustav, Gustav, come on." It was time to take him home.

Insanity? Yes. In groups. There seemed to be a lot of that. It was tragic, about that girl. It was dangerous. It is always dangerous for a woman to be *ahead* of her time. The smart woman, he would have told her, only stays *abreast* of it. She made a fine model. Why should she want to paint? He roused his friend to a standing position and began the long walk home, Gustav draped over his shoulder as they made their way through the streets.

He must read him, this Nietzsche. Everyone was talking about him. Gustav most of all. "He doesn't say man is irrational," Gustav had said, "he just says he is not rational." Was this so brilliant? the Inspector wondered. He sighed. Well he would read him, the man who said God was dead. Gustav said that although God was dead the soul lived on and that Nietzsche was concerned with the drive to believe. "Nietzsche says it is religions," Gustav expounded, "that are destroying the world. He asks the important question: Why is there such a drive to believe? Why must there always be something?"

Maurice shrugged and shifted Gustav to his other shoulder. Then he paused, facing the stone steps that led to the painter's garret. All these philosophers, all these questions, religion, women, violence. What would become of it all? He didn't know. He knew of course why people had a drive to believe. He thought

Nietzsche must know that. He felt Gustav's weight begin to slip on the third step. "Come on, Gustav, wake up, wake up, walk," he urged and felt some life revive in the body slung across his shoulder. Gustav moaned. We go up the stairs, the Inspector thought, only because we think there is something at the top. You didn't have to be a philosopher to know that. Every baker knew that. You do not open the oven if you think the bread has disappeared.

The Inspector shivered suddenly in the cold morning mist. He could feel it still, the unthought thought, hovering there, affecting him even as he slept, that strange, menacing sense of something rising from his consciousness and stealing towards him, inexorably, like the draft from under a sill. They had called him to Vienna and he did not want to go. He was sick with mourning for the girl, and he loathed that city.

In Vienna, black horses galloped, black angels in the night pulling the swaying coach, and in Paris, on the Ile Saint-Louis late at night, the doctor recalled his newest patient.

‘‘I am the Countess Bettina von Gerzl and I do not want to lead a tragic life," the woman had announced. "I have come here to avoid it." She stood in her mauve silk dress, with her parasol held sternly beside her, the folds gathered at the top, like petals on a flower. Her voice trembled when she made this announcement.

The doctor leaned forward in his chair, as if to get a better look at her. But he could see her quite clearly. It was as if her very fragility drew him forward. Like the moon pulling the water, he found himself rising toward this fragile creature, intrigued, sensing in the strange combination of her intention and her posture, in the determination of that unyielding back, that there was more in store for him in this case, with this particular patient, than he had been allowed before.

"Come in . . . sit down," he said, gesturing toward a chair.

"I speak quite as well standing," she said, but she moved then, just a little inside the door. She was a striking woman—her eyes were so unusual—yellow, honey-colored eyes with a light that was most disturbing, a kind of glittery light, with a startling white iris. She reminded him of paintings he had once seen. Of tigers.

She paused to swirl her magenta and white parasol, like a top on the floor, then stopped abruptly and snapped it shut. She moved across the room sweeping her hat off with one hand, trailing plumes and feathers of pink, mauve, and black, and tossed it onto a chair. Then she looked a moment at the sofa and said, "I know all about this treatment. Since you are not about to make love to me, I want you to cure me."

By then she had moved to the couch and laid herself languorously down. Before she could explain her compulsion, the doctor had some indication, for he saw at once that her fingers flew to her throat. He watched as she unbuttoned her dress, her fingers rapidly unlatching the small champagne-colored silk-covered buttons with a practiced, rhythmic ease until she had almost undone the entire bodice. Then suddenly, like a harpist plucking the wrong string, she cried out, and looked at him, horrified, her fingers stopped and then slowly began their rolling ascent. "I design dresses," she said. "Secretly. In an atelier attached to my house."

The doctor sat quietly in the chair, smoking. He did not usually see patients in Paris, but she had insisted on seeing him immediately and said she must return to Vienna. She had also agreed to return from Vienna to Paris for a second visit this week. At first he said nothing. As he watched her he found himself thinking about her parasol. He had seen the pretty, beautifully dressed aristocratic ladies walking by the Seine twirling parasols like that. The parasols were always open, so pink and white and pretty, and on some of them he had read, "Down With the Jews."

He paced to the windows and looked out. He wondered now if, in fact, the Countess would keep her next appointment.

In Vienna black horses galloped, black angels in the night, the carriage careening dangerously as the rain began, a fresh torrent striking suddenly with a thunderous clash, flashes of lightning illuminating the streets, the houses, the red stained handkerchief, the terrified woman's face, the streets heavy with mist, and the man crying again and again, "Hurry, hurry, you must hurry," as Emma Eckstein[1] passed slowly to the floor, blood pouring from her nose, like water into a cup.

The report on the latest female body was on the police captain's desk. At least this body was intact. It was believed to be a suicide from a gunshot wound. He read:

> It is only to be accounted for by the smallness of the projectile, and to some extent, also, perhaps, by the slight force which it possessed. The projectile must have been about the size of a pea (5 millimeters in diameter), judging from an unused bullet which was found. The width of the track of the wound in the brain (anteriorly 12, posteriorly 18 millimeters), is therefore quite out of proportion to the width of the aperture of entrance in the integument (3 millimeters), and in the bone (6 to 8 millimeters), and also to the projectile. There can, therefore, be no doubt that the track of the wound in the brain was originally much narrower, and that the width which it finally attained was due to the increasing effusion of blood. The symptoms, therefore, of compression of the brain gradually developed as the extravasation increased.

In Vienna, the murderer cut carefully: separating flesh from bone.

3

In Vienna black horses galloped and Martha Freud awoke with a start at the sound of a carriage on the cobblestone street outside her window. In the darkness she groped toward the space beside her in the bed. It was empty. Sigi was gone. Her heart began to pound, not from

[1] This is, of course, the infamous Emma Eckstein whose nose symptoms were mistakenly attributed by Freud to hysteria. Freud's colleague, Dr. Wilhelm Fliess, operated on Emma and left, by accident, a wad of cotton in her nose. This caused further bleeding and infection, which Freud continued to attribute to hysteria. Freud's passionate attachment to Fliess during this period clouded his judgment. Upon discovery of Fliess' error, Freud "covered it up" publicly but expressed great anger and disappointment to Fliess personally.

fear but from fury. Oh, of course, she *knew*—he was on one of those night calls from one of his patients, that baroness again. Anytime she called, Sigi just up and went. She lit a candle on the bedside and got into her robe, her fingers drumming against her chest, as they always did when she was angry. The baroness was maddening—she seemed to get ill *only* during the night. Then she would send her coachmen, and Sigi always went. Always.

She moved to the window and seeing the rain driving in under the sill, slammed it angrily. Damn that woman, sending for him at all hours of the night, and he, Sigi, oh—how had he explained it to her? —it was a new science, experimental, the baroness was suffering, he had to help her, *only he could help her.*

She listened. Doors opening, closing, the sound of feet. She felt a slight alarm. Probably just Minna, she thought, with irritation. Minna and her damned insomnia—Minna always up and making endless pots of camomile tea, pacing about in that insomniac way. She wrapped her shawl about her and made her way to the door. Then she heard *something.* Perhaps it wasn't only Minna. She pulled her shawl tightly around her and in the dark, cold hallway, holding the candle before her, realized how much she dreaded running into her sister—Minna with her whining concern, her clucking insinuation, "Oh is Sigi gone *again?*" Martha's cheeks flamed red at the thought, and then she was fully awake. How foolish of her, to think Sigi was with the baroness . . . she had quite forgotten, in her excitement, that he was away in Paris.

4

In Vienna six horses galloped, black angels in the night, the foam flecking their necks, and . . .

Emperor Franz Josef walked the floor. Was it too strong to say, that the women of Vienna were dying? By their own hand, or perhaps victims of a madman? Suicides and murders were rampant. Why were women killing themselves? Wealthy women, married women, poor women, prostitutes. The reports of these suicides were amazing. And the rumors of murders were feeding the anti-Semites. One murder, or twelve, it was increasingly hard to tell. He had finally agreed to send for that policeman from Paris.

5

Elmsville, U.S.A.

The day we found out about Vienna, Mama, Papa and I were having breakfast when a great commotion occurred outside. Timothy, my brother, rushed from upstairs out the door, and when we raced after him we saw a crowd surrounding a woman on top of, of all things, a bicycle! I had seen bicycles only three times before and I had never seen a woman riding one.

When I saw who the woman on top of the bicycle *was,* I heard Mother gasp at precisely the same moment, "Oh no! It's Ida!"

Ida is my aunt. She is a suffragette who goes to rallies and causes riots, according to Mother. According to Father she never had enough love as a child. She is beautiful and knows how to dance, although Cecily, who spies on everyone, says she cries a lot at night. Mother thinks this is because she goes about without a corset, which Mother finds shocking. Aunt Ida has said that her mission in life is to free her sisters from their chains. Everyone except me smirks at this and thinks it is melodramatic, but I have been paying close attention, even though, strictly speaking, I am not allowed to pay close attention to these matters, and I do not think it is melodramatic at all.

Mother and Aunt Ida do not get along. Mother is always saying Aunt Ida thinks too much and that girls who do wind up unhappy. So when she hears Aunt Ida has been crying, she says she knows she is right. Although I am not sure. Mother never cries, and I think sometimes she is unhappy, too.

She was certainly unhappy this morning when she saw Aunt Ida on that bicycle. Ida did look splendid in her green and white striped bicycling shirt with the huge balloon sleeves and that bifurcated *skirt* that parted as she pedaled. As she moved her foot downward, the bicycle moved forward; then she increased the speed and stopped! And then she turned around! It was all quite breathtaking, and I thought that this must be what Aunt Ida meant when she said women must become *emancipated,* although she had told me all along that the Underwood typewriter machine was going to do it, because women could get jobs and be independent. But now I think it must be this bicycle. Mother turned and ran into the house declaring something about "the mortifications of the separation," by which she meant, I knew, Aunt Ida's separated *skirt.* Father came down the steps smiling, stroking his mustache and saying, well, well, well.

Now everyone was in the street and some women, such as Mrs. Saunders, had even rushed out with their aprons on, to see Aunt Ida, holding on to her straw hat with one hand and driving the bicycle with *only her other hand,* as she went up and down the street, even making circles without falling down. I knew my sister Cecily would die, simply die, that such an extraordinary and extravagant thing had occurred in Elmsville and involved our own Aunt Ida, and I had seen it and *she* had missed it!

When we returned to the breakfast table, we had our next excitement of the day. As Mary was serving the raspberries we had picked yesterday, Father said he had an announcement to make, and with a big smile he told us he had been given a rare opportunity to supervise a banking enterprise in Austria, and not only was Timothy going to Vienna to medical school, but we were all going to live in Vienna! I was thrilled, and all the more because *I* knew before my sister Cecily. But the excitement fell away when mother almost immediately said, "I think we should talk about this in the *library,* Frederick." Father looked extremely dismayed because Mother never said they should talk in the library, Frederick, except in matters of gravest importance or if someone had just died.

Nonetheless I couldn't wait to tell Cecily, who was away at grandmother's but would return that evening.

By dinner time I was no longer certain we were going to Vienna as there had been many meetings in and out of the library with Mother and Father and even Timothy, although I was not allowed in. When I looked into the study I saw Timothy looking very forlorn. He was standing next to Father's desk, and I saw at just that moment the afternoon sun lighting up the painting of the Countess behind Father's desk.

The Countess von Gerzl was Father's cousin, and she was very beautiful, although Aunt Ida said she looked like a wild tiger, her eyes were so yellow. When it arrived the painting was considered altogether shocking, and Mr. Partridge, a portrait artist, had been hired (although I was not to know) to place a white lace border on the dress so that the Countess' bosom was more covered up. Cecily had said it was rather like planting a row of flowers along the edge of a walk, and Timothy said it was nothing to be ashamed of.

Timothy is bold and speaks of medical things. He wants to study medicine in Vienna, and so he is very upset with Mother's being very upset. When he saw me he said he "didn't want to discuss it," so that I eagerly awaited Cecily's return home, as I knew she would find out everything, because no matter how many times people tell her not to ask questions and she ought not to know, she finds some way to get them to say things they never meant to.

Cecily arrived home at 5 o'clock, and after she had gone to change I slipped up the stairs and apprised her of all that had happened.

Mother was upset, Cecily said, because Vienna was full of absolutely scandalous things, not the least of which was our cousin, the beautiful Countess with yellow eyes, whose name was Bettina, but whom Mother referred to as That Woman. That Woman had offered us her house, but Mother was refusing, because of the scandal, even to stay for a fortnight, and that was why Mother and Father were in the library.

Cecily told me that Vienna was an extremely interesting and wicked place, both of which words actually meant the same things to Cecily, and she said she heard Timothy say to Father that there was a doctor there, a doctor Timothy wanted to study with, a doctor about whom everyone was talking. Aunt Ida also knew about this doctor and had mentioned his name two weeks ago when Father's friend, the famous writer Henry James, had come visiting and had told Aunt Ida (whom Mr. James liked rather a lot I thought) about his sick sister Alice.

Timothy and Aunt Ida had spent the entire morning we went picking apples in the orchard talking about Mr. James' sister Alice who had some dreadful malady that none of the doctors could help. I overheard at some point Aunt Ida mention the *"fan da sea clay"* syndrome and I felt very silly because my French is not good, and although I eventually learned to spell it *"fin de siècle"* I kept thinking of it as something you got from sea clay. Apparently fan da sea clay happens when the century ends, Aunt Ida said, but it made Father very angry and he said he had no idea how a normally intelligent person could subscribe to such an idea. I myself was rather entranced with fan da sea clay sickness since we were close to the end of the century or the beginning and I thought that possibly at times I had quite a dreadful case of it myself, as Aunt Ida said it meant you worried a lot. Aunt Ida said she had heard from a very respected friend, who was not eccentric as Father charged, but simply a historian who said that societies underwent terrible uncertainties when centuries were ending, or beginning, or anyway turning, and when Aunt Ida told Father this he said, "Societies undergo uncertainties all the time," and wanted to hear no more of it.

So we were not, strictly speaking, allowed to speak of fan da sea clay at the dinner table, and Aunt Ida had been told not to speak of such unscientific matters in our company as "the girls are too suggestible." Aunt Ida then dropped that subject and proposed her favorite cure for female ills: work.

Aunt Ida told Mr. James she would like to interview his sister Alice, as she was certain gainful employment was the *surest* cure for maladies of that sort. I thought that Mr. James was quite charmed by my Aunt Ida, but he did seem a trifle wearied when Aunt Ida would go on and on about emancipation and work outside the home. She told Mr. James that hundreds of women had been saved from "lives of no importance" by the Underwood typewriting machine and that he should urge his ailing sister to take it up at *once*. Aunt Ida assured Mr. James again and again that liberation was possible for his sister, but she finally realized after hours of apple picking, in which Mr. James was always, at Cecily's insistence, helping her up and down the ladders and taking such a *lot* of time, that Mr. James' sister Alice would *not* consider being saved by the Underwood.

Then Timothy told Mr. James about the doctor in Vienna who had treated the wife of his chemistry professor for a nervous disorder—for it was "nerves, no doubt about it, nerves" Timothy said, as if he was a doctor *already*—and Mr. James wrote the doctor's name and address down. Cecily wasn't sure, but she thought his name was Dr. Floyd. And when Mother heard of this she said that Timothy could not study with Doctor Floyd because there was talk of scandal, and Father said, why don't we meet him? All kinds of respectable people went to him, Father said. He'd heard even the Prince of Wales, and there was nothing scandalous about it. People told him their dreams, and he wasn't a witch doctor or soothsayer or anything like that, but Father said it was very strange because people got better, very sick people, by telling him *stories!* At least that was how it sounded, and Timothy said later it couldn't be, that it had to be *hypnosis.* I didn't know what hypnosis was, but later Cecily told me it was something like witches did, putting spells on you.

In Vienna black horses galloped, black angels in the night. They flew through narrow cobblestoned streets, the white foam glowing on their necks, the breath from their nostrils making smoke plumes in the air, hooves clattering as the wooden wheels of the carriage slipped dangerously around corners, through the gaslit streets, curtained with fog and a light rain, while behind them a young girl, panting with fatigue and desperation, cried, "Wait!", knowing she would lose them any moment as they pulled off into the mist. And then she saw the back door of the carriage slide open on the curve and the huge black box slid out, fell and rested on its side. The lid fell off, and two men in capes appeared quickly from the alley. A lightning flash lit up the street, and the young girl, whom we shall call Clarice, ran through the torrent to the box. An empty coffin now filling with rain lay before her. She fell across the box, groping into its empty, aimless corners. "Papa . . . Papa," but there was nothing.

That was how the police lieutenant found her, a young woman in a night dress, soaked through, so that every contour of her figure showed, her hair spilled around her like seaweed. He picked her up from a dead faint in the cobblestoned street, covered her quickly with his coat, and brought her to the station.

"You must have been dreaming," the police lieutenant said to her.

She was very beautiful, with blue ribbons wound around her wet and streaming hair.

When he notified her mother, she said the girl was distraught. The father had died three years ago.

In Paris, the Inspector slowly opened one eye, then the other. Above him, Violette swayed.

That girl, Violette wondered . . . he must be dreaming about that girl, the one who was killed in the riot. The one who wanted to be a painter, not a model. Everyone had told her the times were not right for a woman to become an artist. Posing was respectable, to a degree. But *not* painting. Such a pretty, vivacious girl, too. Elise—what was her name? He was different these last weeks. Was it the death of the girl? For weeks now they had been summoning him to Vienna. And he made no preparation to go. She saw him now, waking as if from sleep.

Vienna—he didn't want to go there. When they called him to Vienna, he kept having dreams about horses. It must be *Die Valkyrie,* he thought. He had seen *Die Valkyrie* at Bayreuth, and he had been much affected. He could swear he heard them now—the Valkyrie and their horses bearing the slain heroes from the field.

He felt pinned down by memories that hovered over his consciousness like birds above their prey. He dreamt of vultures, falcons, winged creatures of attack. He read Baudelaire, and felt worse. His doctor said he was suffering from mourning Elise. Violette, who was jealous, said he was overworked. How could he mourn the girl so? He had never slept with her.

The Inspector knew he was gradually losing that line to his determination, his will that had held him steady for so long. His will, under assault from he knew not what, was trailing now, like a loose line in the water, bobbing, sinking, bobbing, attracting nothing, waiting simply, in time, to sink. He did not care. He could not rouse his passion for anything. Not even his work. He could not think. He was not there. He did not want to be there.

Violette, hovering over his fever, saw that the sweating had stopped. Perhaps. Perhaps he was getting better. His doctor said a few more days. She knew now whatever it was, was more than the girl; this fever seemed to cut right to the marrow of the man.

6

Vienna

In minutes the storm had risen to a fury, relentlessly banging a door as Martha entered the kitchen. The clock read two A.M., and the banging grew louder.

"Minna!" she said, dismayed. Her sister was seated at the kitchen table, looking very déshabilée. Her breasts spilled from her night dress, her skin was pink and glowing, and there was a strange, surprised smile on her face.

"Martha, whatever are you doing up?" Minna said, looking totally astonished. Then she added quickly, "Of course, it must be so hard for you with Sigi away." She stood there, gathering her blue robe tightly up around her throat. Martha saw Minna's large, ugly, blue ring she'd bought somewhere, with her penchant for antiques, gleaming in the light from the lamp. She'd told Martha stubbornly it was a rare sapphire; Martha knew it was colored glass.

"Good heavens!" Martha jumped at the loud sound which sounded like a shot, and Minna leaped and spilled her tea as she ran out of the room. Martha called out, "Minna, wait!" as she bent to wipe the brown puddle from the floor, but Minna had disappeared into the morning dark.

Then Minna heard the horses, the high whinnying, it sounded as if there was a team of them, and then two more shots, and she screamed when she heard the great clattering as the coach sped away and she raced back into the room, her face pale.

"Call the police," Minna gasped, and Martha, startled, ran into the dark room to call the police and saw it lying face up on the floor. She reeled back, thinking, "the children," and ran upstairs into Anna's room where she saw her sleeping safely, and then to Martin's room, and was relieved they were safe. Then the clattering horses were gone, and there was only the sound of her fiercely beating heart. The children had not awakened, so Martha quickly locked the doors and slipped back down to the kitchen, where she found Minna looking drawn and shaken, barely able to stand. She thought for only a split second, for she was fond of her sister, very fond when in fact she was not feeling jealous—she was jealous of Minna a lot lately—for a split second she thought triumphantly and competitively, "Humph, Minna never could stand the sight of blood. No use at all in an emergency." But only for a second; before she looked again into the parlor and saw the bloody body wasn't there!

Minna was holding her head in her hands and moaning, so Martha led her to a chair, soothing her and turning to pour tea. As she raised the pot from the stove, she heard the whinnying again, the horses were back! She held the kettle poised in midair as she heard sliding sounds, the doors banging open, and felt her entire arm begin to tremble.

"The gun." Minna's eyes were wild as she ran to open the cabinet with the rifle. Martha, her heart pounding in her ears, went quickly to the telephone and turned to see Minna, rifle poised, staggering toward the parlor.

Minna thought Martha needed a sedative. Martha thought Minna was *in extremis*. Minna, without Martha knowing it, went to the cabinet and took a package of the special herbs she'd gotten, and poured, all of it, into the tea. Martha tasted the tea and found it odd. She wondered where Minna had got *this* tea.

7

WHERE MINNA
GOT THE TEA

As Minna climbed the small narrow stairway above the dressmaker's shop, she smelled the unmistakable scent of roses. She heard voices, a door close, and saw a most beautiful woman coming towards her, who carried the fragrance of roses all about her, and whose hat and dress were made entirely of lace, the most exquisite ivory lace Minna had ever seen, which followed the contours of her body in a highly suggestive way. Her hat, swirling with white goose and cockatoo feathers, almost covered the side of her face. But when the woman raised her head, just as she passed Minna, the beauty of her face and the kind, curious look in her startling yellow eyes made Minna flinch.

"I see that Didi has another customer," the woman in the lace hat said and smiled.

"I, uh yes," Minna stammered. She did not wish to be observed going up these stairs. "I am picking up a dress." She hated lying. Didi was a dressmaker as well, of course, but no one went to her for that. Or hardly anyone.

"Of course," the beautiful woman said, smiling, and continued on her way.

But when Minna got to Didi's door and rang the bell, Didi knew by the expression on her face she had not come for a dress.

"Please," Minna said, "the herbs. I understand you have a way. To . . . to help forget."

Minna had expected Didi to be an old woman. Didi was not old. She was rather bright and cheerful. She let Minna into the parlor which Minna noted was filled with figurines and vases. Rose-colored tablecloths were flung over the furniture. The rugs were worn and patched. It was a pleasant, strange place.

"Fr. Gerhardt has sent me," Minna said, "I, I want an herb that makes you forget."

"Please," Didi said smiling, "please have a seat. You seem very nervous."

Minna did not like to be told this.

"No, no, I'm fine, I'm just in a hurry." She kept glancing over her shoulder at the doorway. "I must have the herb. Do you have it?"

"I have an herb," Didi said. "It is very strong. It will make you weak for a few days. Then you will begin to forget. You must then take it every three days for two months. By then, you will have forgotten."

"Will I forget everything?" Minna said.

"Not everything, but a lot. I cannot be sure," Didi said. "It is a risk you take." She excused herself and returned to the kitchen. In a while she brought out a tray with steaming cups of hot water.

"You should think carefully about this before you do it."

"If I should choose in the future to remember, can I regain the memory?" Minna asked.

Didi looked very stern. "Sometimes it is possible. But it is difficult.

You should think carefully about this decision. Why don't you come another day?"

"No," Minna said. "It brings me no harm, is that not correct?"

"The harm it brings is in the forgetting," Didi said. "That is all."

"Fr. Gerhardt said you had an herb for everything. That you helped her with her pregnancy, when the doctors refused."

Didi shrugged. "Sometimes I can help. If it is not too late."

"I want to take that herb," Minna said. "Is this it, this tea?"

Didi shook her head. "No, the tea is to help you to relax. For your pleasure. Have some."

Minna eagerly reached for the tea and sipped it. "May I have the herb now?" she said.

"Yes," Didi said, "but I want you to wait until tomorrow. Then you can come back. You must be *certain*. I will prepare it for you in the kitchen. And you must know that it is very expensive."

Minna was aghast at the price, but she hesitated only a moment. "I must have it, at any cost," she said. She implored Didi. She told her that she was certain, very certain, and reluctantly the woman, shaking her head, went into the kitchen to prepare it.

It was not long before Didi returned, carrying a small tray. Didi said, "The herb will make you very drowsy and then very very silly. You will act drunk for about half an hour. Then you will be fine. You have until four o'clock before anyone else arrives."

Minna relaxed a moment and then took the tea. She leaned back on the chair.

Once in her coach the woman smelling of roses, who was the Countess Bettina von Gerzl, realized she had forgotten her glove. She had taken it off and placed it on the window ledge while staring out at the traffic passing below. She turned abruptly to her coachman, "Please turn around at once."

She climbed the stairs and began knocking at the door. Didi answered and when she saw it was the Countess let her in, putting a finger to her lips.

"Someone is sleeping," she said, nodding at Minna who indeed appeared to be sleeping.

The Countess whispered, "My glove," and proceeded to the window sill. It wasn't there, so she and Didi searched the small apartment, during which time Minna sat up, as if in a dream, and began to giggle. Didi explained to the Countess, "It is the herbs." The Countess nodded knowingly.

"Here it is," she cried, seizing the glove from under a small table in the dim hallway. She had to pass through the sitting room again, and Minna called out to her, "That is such a lovely gown. Did you buy it in Paris?"

The Countess, surprised, turned. "Why, yes. It is from Worth," she said.

"So pleased to meet you," Minna said, standing up. "Let me introduce myself. I am Frau Professor Freud,"[1] and she stood up to her full height as if this was the most marvelous thing in the world.

"How do you do, delighted to meet you," the Countess said, her face paling only a little, "and now you must excuse me. My carriage is waiting."

The Countess wondered if it were possible this was her doctor's wife. She would have to mention it. Didi in the meantime attempted to get Minna to sit, but she was extremely restless and talkative, so that Didi had no choice but to sit and converse. After about fifteen minutes the herb's second effect began to set in. As she saw Minna fight the sleep, she helped her to a chair, and in a few minutes Minna was sleeping.

Didi checked her watch. The herb was working more quickly than usual. She expected Minna to wake up in a few hours, and the process of the amnesia would begin. The Countess was discreet so there was no harm, Didi thought, that Minna had offered her name. Although she did promise anonymity to her clients, and this made her a bit uncomfortable. Still, no harm in the Countess knowing this, surely. No harm at all.

Minna woke up slowly and said to Didi, "Oh, I must have fallen asleep." She seemed puzzled. "I, I'm so tired."

Didi said, "I gave you the herbs. To help you forget. Here are the rest, two months' worth."

"Oh yes, of course," Minna said, "I suppose they're starting to work,

---

[1] It is odd that Minna said she was Frau Freud, instead of Fräulein Bernays. However, it is true that in London, after Martha's death she introduced herself this way.

of course. Thank you. But, but I still remember the, the other thing," she said, pausing with consternation near the door.

"It will fade quickly," Didi said, and she saw the look on Minna's face. They come, Didi thought, to forget something they cannot bear to remember nor bear to forget.

She did not like giving this herb.

8

Minna thought Martha needed a sedative. Martha thought Minna was *in extremis*. The storm thrashing, the doors banging, the horses whinnying—it had been a *most* upsetting night. Minna poured the herb, generously, into the tea. When Minna put her head down for a moment, Martha, turning to the stove, put three shots of schnapps into the pot as well. "Drink this," Martha said, handing it to Minna. "Only if you will," Minna said. "We are both distraught." "I am *not* distraught," said Martha, who was.

"But I will have tea." Martha poured a large cup and drank it, thinking the schnapps had improved it immensely.

Minna drank hers gratefully; the herb, she thought, had made the tea quite pleasant.

Martha thought the expression now on Minna's face was very strange indeed. It rather embarrassed her. Almost a look of what one could call *wantonness*. She wondered what it was that was always keeping Minna up.

After the tea, Martha felt very sleepy, and dragged herself toward the sofa. She collapsed there and dreamt she heard someone rapping on the door. Then they entered, with a knife, and Martha woke up with a shout.

In Paris, the doctor slept, dreaming the dreams that would bring him fame. Not everything he dreamed would be reported in his books. He was a man who had a remarkable courage for self-disclosure. But he did not disclose everything.

T H E Y were in a hotel room, the wallpaper was streaked with rust. He watched her getting dressed. He watched her walk toward the door. He watched her hand poised on the knob. The blue stone gleamed in the light. He saw her open the door, begin to step through it, and then, hesitant, retreat and close it. He heard the lock click.

"Sigmund," she said, "we cannot go on." He saw her lower lip quivering.

Outside he heard the rain, but dimly, as if in sleep. He lay back on the bed and looked up at the ceiling. A crack had appeared, and the paint, like fungus on a tree in the wood, had furled back, and through the crack, water seeped. A drop fell on his foot.

"I detest being bourgeois," she said, "I detest it. I have no respect for the bourgeoisie, none. I detest their morals, their false values, their hypocrisy." She made this speech to no one, he observed. Only to the door. "But I cannot go on with this."

"If the only reason is your guilt, you should dispense with it. I believe you can. I believe, too, that is your only reason. But perhaps there are others, others you have not told me."

"I tell you everything!" Now she no longer spoke to the door but to Sigmund, who lay upon the bed smoking, his foot beneath the sheet, damp in one spot from the falling rain.

"You tell me as much as you know," he said quietly. "But we both know that is not everything." He was hoping she would not cry. He desperately did not want her to cry. He did not want her to be tortured. He wanted it to be simple, to go on the way it was, as before.

"If we stop, this time we stop forever," he said. He saw her face turn pale. "It is the only way. It is my responsibility. I was not firm before." He saw her face at the edge of the bed, now contorted in pain as she bent to the ice-white coverlet and ripped it with her hand. Then she put it in her mouth as if to chew it, or to stifle a scream. Suddenly she threw herself into a standing position and with a savage glance once again opened the door and this time ran out.

He looked at his watch. And then he lay there some time, smoking. The rain continued to drip on his foot. He made no effort to move it. He felt another drop on his head. The ceiling was bleeding, bleeding memories into his brain. How many hours, how many afternoons had he loved her here? The drops were reminders of the failures of time, of time to recall all the times. His memory grew duller as he attempted the effort. He could remember now, at this moment, only her face in anguish at the side of the white starched coverlet as she attempted to draw it into her mouth, rocking there for a moment, like a hungry and desperate child.

The drops continued and his memory faded, of that afternoon and of all the other afternoons, of when it had begun and when it had ended, if it ever ended, even when it ended, all these times began to fade, farther and farther with each falling drop, driving it down so deep he didn't know what hour it was, only that it was dark outside, and drops were falling on his hair. The pillowcase and his foot were soaked.

9

Where oh where is Gertrude Van de Vere?
Her hand is in the sandbox
And her toes are over there.

The Inspector read the latest telegram from Captain Heinrich Voll with some alarm. All these women being murdered in Vienna, and all they'd found so far were the notes, and four severed toes and a hand. The notes were compiled, unfortunately, rather than handwritten. Composed letter by letter and pasted together to form these rhymes. He shuddered and broke out into a sweat. He didn't understand—it must be the remains of the fever. He had dealt with crimes like this before. This time he found it took everything in him to confront it.

He didn't want to go, but the Viennese seemed relentless in their pursuit of him. He read the new telegram again and felt his hand, as if it belonged to another, brush against the top of his hair. It started even there, the subtle manner in which everything that was normally close and integral to himself began to fall apart under the weight of his

Vienna associations. His own hand floated now, across the crest of his hair, like that of a total stranger.

Murders and suicides. All women. Some bodies turning up whole, some in parts, some with accompanying rhyme. Shot at, cut up, bloodied to a pulp. Were the suicides really suicides? Why were some of the murdered women dismembered and some not? Was it the work of one, or many? He sighed a sigh of exhaustion.

He pushed the telegram back across his desk. He was ill. Unfit. They must find someone else. He was not the one for this job.

10

Edith Wharton, in the Paris house she kept on rue de Varenne, was surprised that the baroness von Tulow had sent her a book. Mrs. Wharton did not like the baroness von Tulow, after all, and was certain that she had given this gift now, in the hopes of securing an invitation to one of Mrs. Wharton's salons. Mrs. Wharton's reputation was rapidly spreading throughout Paris. Little did she know, Edith scoffed, that the baroness' fate had been sealed during that horrid afternoon at Doctor Jean-Martin Charcot's. She had mistakenly anticipated that the baroness was a serious woman who shared Edith's own interest in scientific matters. And she knew, too, that she had thought on occasion that she should be making more of an effort to make women friends. The few she had had criticized her for this. But the afternoon had been a disaster.

As soon as Edith had settled herself next to the baroness, who was giggling uncontrollably behind her fan, she experienced a momentary sensation of regret. The baroness, eyeing her at tea, had said, "If you are interested in science then of course you must come to Charcot's." Edith had heard of the amazing wizard of hysteria and been only mildly curious. The baroness, pressing her, had said that Charcot was demonstrating the very next afternoon and she must of course come.

They had not been there very long, she remembered, when the baroness, upon witnessing one of the *hystériques* faint over the arm of Charcot, had burst into such giggles that she had to absent herself from the room, and Edith sensed her mistake. And then! As if that were not enough! Her cheeks burned suddenly at the thought of the baroness' tasteless efforts at attempting to introduce her to that disgusting doctor from Vienna. Just thinking of it now Edith felt the sea of nausea that had swept through her.

''HE'S the one," she had said pointing to him, "the one with the beard." The baroness leaning forward, had whispered into her ear, "You know he has published the most shocking theory," and Edith had said, "I'm not easily shocked," but she had been then, had nearly reeled off the chair when she heard it. "He says that fathers seduce their children," the baroness has tittered, "All of them—perverts, fathers and grandfathers. Can you imagine?" The baroness' voice had reached a crescendo of high nervous laughter. The words seemed to reverberate. "Fathers and grandfathers, can you imagine such things?"

The words had undone her, and in a sudden moment, Edith felt her disaffection turn to hatred. She hated, suddenly, everything about this woman, from her fashionable clothes to her silly voice and her superficial mind. *Everything.*

"It is absurd," Edith had said, as the baroness assessed her reaction with those envious, competitive eyes. She knew the baroness was trying to shock her. She knew there were men like this, but she thought, it was really the exclusive province of women— this competitiveness and jealousy that emerged in a particularly vicious way. As if they were desperate to know everything about you, to "understand" you, only so they could demolish you.

She had heard these women, overheard them, more than once, behind doors talking about her, "I don't know how a woman like that, could ever write of love." More giggles, "Oh, she is fashionable, she has no..." more giggles, and then quickly, sometimes in French, sometimes in German as if she were not totally competent to understand either, "This is why Lily Bart is such a Lily—a virgin," and more laughter.

The scene came back to her now, as she tore into the wrapping around the book. Freud or Freund or froid or fraud, Edith Wharton didn't know which, but to think that so-called doctor had given public lectures on such a subject! Suddenly she felt a great agitation and stormed into the kitchen for some water. She forgot momentarily what she was doing. Oh yes, the book. She returned to the living room, trying not to think about that afternoon.

THE baroness had turned, surprised then to see that Edith Wharton was not directly behind her. Edith had gone to her car, cheeks burning with former humiliations and then, suddenly, she felt the flush in her skin turn to one of pride. She turned and climbed into the front seat, taking the wheel from her astonished chauffeur and waved to the baroness, who imagined that she, Edith Wharton, knew nothing of women's things.

Edith thought of Fullerton. Of all she did know, and glancing back with the thrill of victory, she now knew what other women knew. Morton Fullerton had given her that. She knew the revelries of the bed. She knew a woman's power. She waved with a toss of her hand, no longer prisoner to their superior, knowing smirks. They still would never speak to her of "womanly" things. She knew this. And she did not care. She was an expert on art, history, and literary matters, and there were many men she knew who said that she was one of the few women who could join the men in after-dinner conversations. She knew about politics, affairs of the mind, and had, she felt, a good grasp of philosophy. These were the important things, she told herself, pressing her foot on the pedal and feeling the speed increase. She loved the feeling of the wind on her face; damn what they said about florid complexions.

The afternoon seemed long ago; not less than a month's time, and now here was the baroness offering a book. She opened the package with apprehension, fearful it was something by the Viennese doctor. And to *think* that Henry was actually seeing him. A total charlatan! The thought of this upset her again as she tore at the wrapping. She was relieved to see the title revealed: *Etiquette for Automobiles* and opened the book. She had indeed heard of the author, an Englishwoman, Miss Dorothy Levitt, an avid automobile woman who had recently set the world record for women of ninety-one miles an hour, and was forever being fined for breaking the twelve-mile-an-hour speed limit, an impulse to which Mrs. Wharton was definitely sympathetic. Her eye fell to a paragraph entitled "Automobile Fashion":

> Under no circumstances must you wear lace or fluffy adjuncts to your toilette, if you do, you will regret them before you have driven half a dozen miles. Tweed, frieze, or homespun lined with "Jaeger" or fur. For summer, the ideal coat is of cream serge, which does not crease like silk, alpaca, or linen. A cloth cap to match the tweed should be pinned securely, and over it, put a crêpe de Chine veil of length a-plenty.... In a little drawer in the motor car is the secret of the dainty motoriste. In its recesses put clean gloves, veil, and handkerchief, powder puff, pins, hair pins and a handmirror ...

Then her attention was caught by another sentence, "If you are to drive alone, it is advisable to carry a small revolver. I have an automatic Colt and find it easy to handle as there is practically no recoil—a great consideration for a woman...."[1] Well, she'd heard this recommendation before. And she did often drive the Panhard without the aid of her chauffeur.[2] Always a hand mirror and a small revolver. Well, one never did know. She had bought one actually, precisely for that purpose. It was silver, with a handle of mother of pearl. Quite elegant. She was packing to meet Fullerton in Vienna. She may as well pack it in.

11

Sabina Spielrein hurried away from Dr. Freud's house. It was a terrible driving rain. She had pounded on the door, yet no one answered. Dr. Freud would certainly not refuse to answer his door in

---

[1] This is in fact precisely the wording from such a book. Miss Levitt was famous, apparently, for having driven from London to Warwick and back in a day in a four-cylinder Gladiator.

[2] This is an odd detail, as a literary colleague who read this manuscript informed me that he believed this was the first he had ever learned that Mrs. Wharton, a motoring enthusiast, had actually driven her own car.

the night. If no one was there, why had she seen a light? A neighbor on the street had told her that afternoon that perhaps he was still in Paris. Was he really still there? He had never answered her letter. Did he want nothing to do with her?

She had written Dr. Freud a second letter explaining her circumstances. To the first one he had replied that she was "suffering from fantasy." The second one he hadn't answered at all. His condescension rankled her. It made her furious.

Sabina continued walking. It was a dangerous hour to be out, she knew, but she could not sleep tonight. Soon she would come to the Danube Canal. She hurried, pulling her cloak close and glancing carefully around her. A woman had to have her wits about her in this half-light, and a walking cane as well. She grasped the smooth, round knob of the silver cane beneath her coat. The walking cleared her mind. She had had such a terrible row with Carl, just this morning, and she'd gone to Dr. Freud, she knew, to do him further damage. She was bitterly ashamed now. She should understand, if anyone should, the great difficulty in curbing impulses. She resolved, even in her pain, that she must be generous enough to help Carl, with the assistance of Dr. Freud. Carl needed help; he had saved her once, now she must not hate him, she must not hate him, she must save him.

The wind gathering at her back had a real bite to it, a tremendous chill had come into the air, and as she walked, she saw the rain was thickening, turning to sleet. The wind by the water was too strong to press on, so she turned. Tears stung her face. She would not see him —Dr. Carl Jung—her doctor, her friend, her lover—tonight. He had told her that tonight his wife was arriving in Vienna. He must take her to dinner. After the terrible row, Sabina relented. Of course. He had a wife. She understood.

Sabina saw ahead of her the glowing light of a cafe. She opened the door to take refuge from the storm, and she had only taken two steps inside when she saw them. Her body went rigid as she stared, and a hurrying couple impatiently shoved past her. They tossed Sabina about in the vestibule like a leaf on the wind. He had told her he had to be with his wife—he had told her that, the good doctor Jung—her lover. He had risen from her bed that morning, caressing her thighs, nuzzling the soft round rise of her belly, kissing her breasts, and now here he was, right in front of her, with a woman who was *not* his wife.

Sabina stood there stunned as she watched him press his lips to the upraised face of the young and very pretty girl. At that moment the girl turned and seemed to look directly at Sabina, looked at her without seeing, her bright dark eyes and the wet mouth—an actress. She was an actress for certain—in public display with the doctor. His hands reached forward again and the young girl turned her lips to them. His hands caressed her hair, his adoring eyes gazed at her upturned face, now with a light that glanced like bullets from the girl's hair to Sabina's heart. She reeled from the sight, turned to reach the door, and heaving it open, threw herself into the mercy of the wind. An overwhelming sensation had shaken her body so violently she could barely stumble toward the street. Then she was convulsed in sobs—a *fool,* a *fool*—she had been a *fool.*

She had believed him, pitied him. She buried her face, awash with tears and snow, into her muff, as she plunged through the snow and wind to the street.

12

The two men hasten to the edge of the Danube, struggling with the corpse, which is wrapped tightly.

"Look out," says the first one, who is bearded and ugly and has a missing front tooth.

"Shhh," says the second one, well-dressed and extremely nervous. There is still time before daylight. The wrapped body is in a sack, and they drag it through the thick mud, which is turning firmer now with the sudden cold.

The well-dressed man comes forward, reties the sack and rolls it, pushing it with his foot into the river. It is necessary once it is in shallow water to step in, through the thin ice at the edges, in order to place his foot upon the head and shove it out into the swiftly moving currents. Then he turns and taking the small velvet pouch from his coat, opens it. He sees the gleaming eye of the thief who has assisted him and changes his mind.

"That will be all," he says, handing the thief two crowns. The suspicious look lingers. He reaches into his purse. "It's robbery for this, here you are!" He hands him ten crowns, which the thief looks at greedily.

"Bring me that horse and go," the gentleman says.

The thief, shrugging, goes up the hill to the coach. The well-dressed man watches. The second lead horse is a problem. The first man unharnesses it and leads it down to the gentleman with a rope halter and no saddle. The horse halts, halfway down the bank. The man whips the horse, and the horse rears and turns, freeing the rope and flies off into the night.

The well-dressed man runs up the embankment and raises his cane.

"Fool!" he cries and lunges into the empty air. The thief is gone, away, up the hill, lashing away at the coach and five.

The man with the cane is horseless. But determined. Determined to mislead all inquiries. He opens the pouch and throws the rings, the brooch, and the necklace up the shore. He reaches into his pocket for the letter, reassuring himself it is there, and walks quickly back to town. It is a good hour's walk, but he can still make it before daybreak and leave the letter where he intends.

As he walks, he notices it is colder, and that the rain is beginning to turn to snow . . .

13

Sabina struggles on, wishing she might die. She has opened her coat, hoping to freeze, as the wind swirls around her. She doesn't care, she doesn't care, she doesn't. . . .

She looks up . . . she hears something . . . the city is quiet except for the sound of the wind and her sobbing. She hears hooves, and then around the corner through the snow come five black horses, running wild without a coach, five *abreast* galloping down the Rossauerlaende. Behind them, running on foot, is a coachman yelling and snapping his huge wet whip. The horses are running and skidding and then, at the coachman's voice and the crack of the whip, she sees them move into formation, running now around the Ringstrasse, the coachman lagging far behind, farther and farther behind them in the snow, yelling, "Whoa, whoa, whoa," as the horses pull around a far curve, still in formation, and disappear.

Sabina pauses, feeling weak . . . strange . . . the horses. Her chest aches, as if someone had ripped it open. He has hurt her. The rush of sobs clutches her again; cutting off her air, collapsing her chest; her breath comes in short gasps, tears sweeping through her eyes, the storm whipping her hair into her face, slashing her as she attempts to walk down the streets of Vienna like a normal woman, an unhappy woman, a woman who might have had a fight with her lover, a sniffling woman, but not *this;* and she feels the heave of emotion within her so strong that it sends her crashing against the lamp post, a strangled cry echoing from her throat. *Let me die, oh, God, please, I beg you, let me die.*

14

The Inspector looked up from the bench in the square. The trees were astir with rain and increasing wind. He felt someone move beside him. It was Violette.

"You must come away," she said. "They have telegraphed for you again from Vienna. There has been another one." He heard her only dimly. She pressed her hand into his and he felt her small cool fingers fold over his palm. He could say no more and felt her cheek then against his, and the cool press of her lips. He did not know why it should be, in the moment of his grief, when he wanted nothing more than to feel *nothing,* he should feel, in addition to unrelenting pain, the straining presence of her lips against his cheek. Violette drew away, the kiss, like the wind, passing into the rain—lowered darkness within him.

15

Edith Wharton climbed into the automobile, flung her fur boa across her neck, adjusted her enormous motoring hat with the veils securely tied, rose up, pulled down her motoring coat, wiped off her goggles, and pressing the pedal all the way to the floor, roared off in a cloud of dust that shocked even the most cosmopolitan Parisians. They were barely getting used to the automobile, but to see the American lady writer driving and the zeal with which she attained the highest speeds caused the most sympathetic of them to profoundly re-examine the American presence in Paris.

Edith Wharton was frantic to get to the train station. She had thirteen minutes. She took the corner on two wheels, her luggage sliding around and her bag almost out the door, and then the car righted itself until she took another. She must get to Vienna, she must. And no one must know. Why? To rendezvous with Morton Fullerton at the Hotel Wandl. He had gone to Vienna with Mr. Herzl, whom he'd met while covering the Dreyfus trial. Mr. Herzl had a plan to solve the problem of the Jews. Edith Wharton had not thought greatly about the Jews. Some of them, the best of them, were quite amusing. And, Henry always said, remarkably intelligent. Of course Berenson was a Jew, but Berenson was an exception to absolutely everything so far as she knew. She herself thought that probably there was nothing so terrible about Jews, but in Paris now, because of Dreyfus, they seemed to be *such* a problem. And in Vienna as well. They were, she often thought, both at the very center of the society and on its periphery. Simply everyone who was in charge of anything seemed to be Jewish—the banks, the newspapers, the shopkeepers, even the musicians! But she did not dwell on this. She had to make this train, get to Vienna and back before the weekend.

Her heart was pounding as she took her bag from the car and strode rapidly towards the station. Her cheeks flushed at the thought of Fullerton and the enormity of her desire. She was struck by the almost unbearable intensity of her feelings, always when she was with him, about to see him, or leaving him.

She remembered how the blue sky that morning had seized her like an embrace, the shining vividness, a kind of hovering blue, at once sharp and soft. The sky seemed to be coming and going and her thoughts with it, as if the color blue were a feeling, with all its contradiction and complexity, that somehow this vivid opacity, this translucent grandeur that was both the light and the blue, this uplifting spirit had invaded her so that she felt herself flying there, hanging just above the earth and the slip slip clip of her heels on the walk was just her way, a kind of occasional reminder that there was a surface she was gliding across, a surface that ran beneath her no longer for support but simply as an aspect of the landscape.

She did not know how she had come to this point in her life. She knew she had been desperate for love, and Fullerton, seeing this, had opened her heart. The surprising part was she did not feel like a fool. With Fullerton's reputation as a ladies' man, she might easily. But his passion was such that when he loved her, she knew she owned him entirely and, she suspected, in a way he'd never experienced before.

She looked at her watch. She had three minutes.

16

In Edith Wharton's Paris house, Henry James was in the bath, reading a dreadful pot-boiler:

> Anna, the beautiful and enchanting Anna, whose years scarce numbered seventeen, had known the exquisite pain and pleasures of a secret love; and, in the simple innocence of an unsuspecting mind, had given her heart, her soul, her all to a—*Stranger.*"[1]

He hid it when he heard them knocking on his door with dinner. It was disgusting, lurid trash, shilling-shockers they once called them.

---

[1] This is actually an anonymous nineteenth-century tale entitled *The Ruins of the Abbey of Fitz-Martin.*

He found himself quite fascinated. Edith wouldn't be back until tomorrow. She was in Vienna he knew, with Fullerton, although he was not supposed to know. He was looking forward to an entire evening in which to sink himself into the excesses of this abominable stuff. It excited his mind, to his chagrin, to read about murders. Fact or fancy, it didn't matter. He traded off pot-boilers with evenings spent reading "Great Unsolved Murders"—of London or Paris or wherever. He found it most compelling.

17

Through the cold and the wind Sabina felt her feet and hands go numb. She lost all sense of time as the blizzard howled around her, snow piling up as she stumbled again and again. Each time it was harder to raise herself from the ground.

It seemed only moments later that the strange figure appeared through the snow. Illuminated by the lamp, a well-dressed man was walking her way. Clearly he had no awareness of her. He stumbled over her boot and looked up, seeming to come to his senses for a moment at seeing her lying there. He stared blindly at her and then turned to pick up his cane. As he bent over, a small heavy object fell from the bundle in his arms and landed on Sabina's neck. This startled her. Under the street lamp she saw the cane with the satyr's shining silver face inches from her in the snow. Her eyes opened and flickered, and she saw clearly the gun, the cane, his ring. Then she knew nothing as he struck her and shoved her with the side of his boot and left her for dead in the snow.

18

The Countess Bettina von Gerzl, called by many the most beautiful woman in Vienna, did not feel beautiful this dawn. She sat in her coach looking out through the driving snow feeling the pain in her chest. She wanted to cry, but she could not. She had gone to the marquis to persuade him to give her money for her lover, Philippe, who had been arrested in Paris with the anarchists. But the marquis had, in his cruel intuitive way, nearly exposed her. Of course, she had been a naive fool, she saw now, to support the anarchists. How could she have imagined there would be no violence? It was Philippe; she knew he could persuade her to do anything. She laughed loudly, and suddenly, surprising herself, fighting her tears. "You are so beautiful," they said to her. Did they know she had a lover she detested?

Her hands clenched the strap on the side of the coach as she tried to regain her composure. She looked out through the coach's window and saw the storm was fierce. Thoughts of the evening's incident flew through her mind as she repeated again and again, "I must resist this, I must conquer this, I must, I must." The marquis had approached her, and, it seemed, within minutes he instinctively knew. They had met only once before, and there in the midst of the crowded ballroom he put his hand in a too familiar way upon her shoulder. He smelled of sex as he bent toward her and began, to her shame, to excite her by kissing her cheek, then her ear, then her neck. He saw, in a moment, that she was helpless in it, and he let his hand fall down her neck in a most insinuating way as the Countess Bettina von Gerzl stood, dazzling and bejeweled, unable to move her feet or her arms, an old, familiar torment keeping her rooted in rapt excitement, in utter humiliation as if the most disgusting, odious, repellent serpent were crawling over her, and she in a kind of unwilled, hypnotic surrender allowed this even as her mind fought, valiantly if impotently, unable to call out to protest, to run, to fight back, stung by his power and her shame.

It was Karl Kraus[1] standing nearby who had unwittingly saved her. He had thought, she imagined, that she had too much breeding to be able to dodge the amorous intentions of the drunken marquis, and spinning around he had walked over, taken her by the arm, as if breaking a spell, and said to the marquis, "I must speak with Bettina

[1] Kraus, a brilliant and angry journalist who founded his own publication *The Torch* (*Die Faeckel*) in 1890, where he ridiculed and exposed the pomposity of contemporary Viennese morals, seems to have remained a devoted admirer of the Countess throughout the phases of his career.

now." He was shocked, she knew, when the person he had called "the most beautiful and courageous woman in Vienna" had run from him onto the balcony and collapsed in grief he was completely unprepared for. Kraus had stood there awkwardly, asking her what was wrong, helpless at her pain, which she revealed only by the rhythmic rocking of her body as her hands gripped the balustrade.

Only now did the Countess, alone in her carriage, feel that she could at last begin to recover herself. It was a long and arduous fight that she felt she continually lost. She could fight her husband to the death if need be, she could hold her own in any argument or circumstance save one: If a strange man approached her and touched her, she was under a sudden, inexplicable compulsion. She became both very excited and yet paralyzed, spellbound to submit to whatever he demanded. So far the doctors had been of no help. She had gone to this new one in Paris in utter desperation. "There is no cause to feel shame," he had told her, "the reasons for this usually lie in early childhood, in a seduction that occurred at a time when a child cannot be held responsible for her responses." She heard his voice now, soothing her, and then the surprising information, "Unfortunately it is highly likely in such cases that these episodes will continue to reoccur in a disguised form, until we can bring the original memory from the unconscious, where it is repressed, to your conscious mind."

And then he had asked her simply to say anything that came into her mind, which struck her as the strangest thing. But she did it.

She was so preoccupied with these thoughts that at first she did not see the body. It was only *after* she passed something lying in the swirling snow by the street lamp that she realized the figure must be a woman. Leaning forward, she ordered the horses to stop at once. "Back there," she cried to the coachman, and through the blizzard she made her way to the prostrate form. Bending down, the Countess felt the young woman's warm breath on her cheek. She reached for the hands, one nearly frozen, and the other still warm inside a beautiful ermine muff. And then she saw the blood, dried, on the side of the girl's head.

"Quickly, bring the brandy, *quickly,*" she cried to the coachman as she bent down rubbing snow onto the girl's frozen hand. The cut or blow had been stopped by the cold. The Countess furiously shook the near-lifeless girl and began tapping and rubbing her face, first on one side, then the other.

"Here," she urged the coachman, who returned with the brandy, "rub her hands like this," which he did as she continued to massage and slap the unconscious girl. The girl's eyes opened, but revealed a dull, dead gaze. The Countess was shouting at her. "Get up! You must wake up! You must try! Drink this." And then the Countess shook the girl fiercely.

"Drink this. You must," the Countess said as the girl coughed and sputtered, and she poured more brandy into her.

"Help me," she said to the coachman, and the two of them half dragged her into the coach. It was only when she saw the girl's muff had fallen and went to retrieve it that the Countess saw the cane. A strange silver-topped cane with some kind of carved head, nearly covered by the snow. She picked it up and climbed back into the coach.

By the time they reached the house the girl was gaining consciousness. She seemed now to be aware and looked utterly startled. The Countess watched her with concern. She leaned forward with relief and stroking Sabina's face, said, "Fortune follows you. A little longer and my efforts would have been in vain."

"I . . . I've been in the snow," Sabina said, dazed.

The Countess grasped her hands. "You were nearly frozen. You had collapsed. You will come home with me now and I will see that you are taken care of."

Sabina felt very strange, light-headed, as if her hands were not moving. The woman opposite her seemed to move in and out of focus in strange undulations. Sabina was entranced by her voice and her face. She was wearing a white fur hat and coat, and her red-gold hair spilled around her like light from an angel.

Sabina felt warm and sleepy. As she began to fall asleep she heard the clattering sounds of those horses again—those black horses with the phantom coach she'd seen, and then she saw nothing and her head fell back as she dreamt of deep, warm snow.

19

Paris

There were dreams, he thought, and there were memories. Sometimes there were dreams so as not to have memories, or to have rememoried the memory, and that morning, for just a moment Sigmund Freud was not at all certain what it had been. A flash of intuition, or recall, he could not be sure, but he had awakened to the sound of horses, and the sound of carriage wheels askew. And then he saw it, as immediate as that moment when he and Oskar were crossing the Waehringstrasse: a coach and four and a blue note dancing, blowing across the stones.

It was sheer coincidence, but it unnerved him, the next morning to discover the letter on his desk forwarded to him from the Spielrein woman, was also blue. It must mean, he knew, on some level, he felt her allegations about Jung might be true. But he didn't want to face it.

And he knew he didn't.

20

Maurice," she said softly to him. The sweating had stopped now. She wiped his forehead. The doctor had said the crisis was passed. There would be no further threat from the pneumonia. "They have sent another telegram. From Vienna. It is urgent." His eyes brightened when he said, "Tell them I cannot come. I will tell them myself . . . tomorrow." He had tried to get up. In one more day perhaps he could make it. Perhaps. He would try. Then the night sky, black and endless, rolled up on the horizon and spread over the green hills of his dreaming like an inverted sunrise, a blackness that filled the sky pushing the red to its edges, a darkness coming, like the light, from below.

21

The Countess leaned back in the coach now, finally relaxing. She thought the girl would survive, whoever she was. But why was she out alone in that storm? And the blow on her head? The girl had no memory of it. Women of her class did not go about unescorted at night, unless in despair. A jilted lover she suspected. Well she was fortunate, and the Countess was glad. It had taken her mind off more troubling matters. She had work to carry out in Paris. And she must catch the 4 A.M. train.

She had become very concerned about the Dreyfus affair. There was no question in her mind but that he had been framed despite the fact that the famous detective, Bertillon, had identified the handwriting as that of Dreyfus. There were others too who had their doubts. She would be dining at the pro-Dreyfusards' tomorrow night, at Rosa Fitz-James'.[1] She was worried also, at her position with Philippe. She wanted to turn her efforts toward helping Dreyfus and did not need to be involved with the anarchists at this point. But Philippe had manipulated her in a way that seemed to her quite dangerous. In any event, she now had one possible recourse. Her friend, Annette, a feminist and a radical, had told her she had an important friend in the police department, an Inspector, M. LeBlanc, who could be trusted. She was shocked when Annette told her she had a friend who kept the dossiers. Most unusual. She would have to find him, but she would have to be careful. And she did want to return to that doctor. He had given her, briefly, some hope. So preoccupied was she with her thoughts in this way, the Countess failed to notice the lone figure who,

---

[1] It is unclear whether this is the first or second Dreyfus trial. The Dreyfus affair had broken up salons all over Paris as the pro-Dreyfusards and the anti-Dreyfusards would not speak to each other. This was dramatically true in the case of Rosa Fitz-James who was both Jewish and a Dreyfus supporter and whose husband was not.

witnessing her rescue of the young woman, had climbed aboard her carriage and was dismounting now, as she entered her courtyard, to reclaim what might reveal him.

22

THE CROSSING

We had arrived at Le Havre a day too early due to the decision on the captain's part not to stop at Southampton first, because of very bad sea conditions and the warnings of a storm.

Father was extremely anxious to get to Vienna and was distressed at having to make altogether new arrangements. Nonetheless he had done it, and we were now jostling along in the carriage within hours of the Countess' house.

I must finally have fallen asleep as well because I woke up suddenly when I heard Aunt Ida exclaim, "Oh, we must be here but what dreadful weather!" and I felt the coach lurch and saw rain driving against the windows. Mother and Father were huddled up under blankets opposite, and Aunt Ida was peering out one side of the coach and Cecily out the other.

"Oh look," Cecily said, grabbing my arm, "look there..." and I looked and I heard them both at the same time, five black horses, manes flying in the night, flying through the sleet and snow with the harness and traces and no coach behind them. "Look it's just as we *imagined*," Cecily said, "I cannot believe it."

"Oh," I was startled, as I watched the horses turn in a large circle and proceed, their hooves stamping into the clouds of snow, down another street. As they fled through the gathering mist I grabbed Cecily's arm and said, "Look again, there's only five." Cecily started, "Five...yes,...oh well," she said leaning back, and as only Cecily could and only Cecily would, within a minute she was fast asleep again.

"Don't let her sleep," Mother admonished me, "we are within minutes of the Countess' house," at which Cecily, who was not asleep after all, sat up. "Already?" she said. "Cecily," Father said impatiently, "we have been traveling for days."

"Oh I know, but it is so early in the morning. Will she be expecting us?"

"I wired," Father said with great weariness just as our coach drew up in front of a magnificent house with high arched windows and beautiful castlelike turrets rising on both sides. The rain was turning to snow and billowing around the coach as the coachman opened the doors. A servant had run down from the house with a cart of sorts, and the other servant was ushering Mother and Father up the stairway. Cecily and I were looking about as much as possible in the early morning light and the blowing wet snow. Aunt Ida and Timothy were supervising the rest of the luggage; I heard them arguing behind us as we hurried up the walk. Mother and Father had disappeared inside the door, which had closed and opened again when we arrived, and as it did, we stepped into a grand and beautiful hallway ablaze with light. As the servants took my coat, I looked up the stairs and I saw a woman who was clearly the housekeeper. She looked very startled but she quickly descended the stair and said, "How do you do? The Countess has just gone off to Paris. You were not expected until Thursday."

23

As I climbed the magnificent staircase in the Countess' house, I saw my brother Timothy Main pass a mirror and lean into it to adjust his hat with navy trim and admire his new suit, his bright blue eyes and his straw-colored hair. I could see he thought he was quite American-looking, if one didn't count the Indians and slaves as Aunt Ida always said one must do. I knew Timothy wanted to be as American as possible and to have American thoughts. Worthy thoughts. But I also knew he didn't. Cecily had shown me the utterly shocking and fascinating drawings in his medical book and the pictures from his magazines that were not medical at all. It was a magazine that showed ladies and men with electric belts that could stimulate their private parts, and on the same page was an article about the horrible things that happened to young girls whose parents allowed them to go to college and smoke.

Timothy leaned over into the mirror, thinking he thought all the time about sex, and love, and dying. And occasionally baseball. But more, actually, about sex and love and dying and the seizure that gripped his heart when he saw a certain girl walk a certain way in a certain dress. Perhaps the worst of it, he thought, adjusting his blue cravat, was that he did not feel wicked. Not in the least. Not a bit wicked for any of this, whereas he was certain that anyone else would have felt wicked, at least somewhat. For he thought wicked feelings unprofitable as well as unpleasurable. And he had concluded that he would enjoy his pursuit of the study of medicine in Vienna. And sex and love and death among other things.

24

It was morning at Vienna's Wandl Hotel, and Edith Wharton was getting dressed. Fullerton had left, as he had to return on an early train for the Dreyfus trial, and had kissed her sleepily one last time, just before dawn.

Now, as she slipped her stockings over her legs she shivered. It was perfectly extraordinary, this new body that his love had given her. It was as if her sensitivity were so exquisite now that she almost could not withstand the pleasure of it. Even now, mere stockings seemed to roll up her skin like a voluptuous caress. There were moments when she thought perhaps she might be losing her mind.

And then, she would feel the tears, as if the only things that were driving her mad were her happiness and her desire. What is life? she thought, looking into the mirror at her reflection, and who is this woman? Could this woman, radiant, happy, above all, *happy,* could that woman *there,* be she? Could this woman in a hotel room with her lover possibly be the Edith Jones who had married Teddy Wharton and was indeed still married to him? That Edith Jones had never known *this* body, or this joy.

She slipped the chemise over her shoulders, and as she thought of Fullerton and their evening together, a torrent of yearning welled up inside her. It alarmed her now, and she sank back onto the sheets, feeling the feverish desire roll over her, feeling exposed, out of control, as if her reaching center wet with yearning was like a mouth to the sky, searching for eternity, reaching in one long sucking pulling for that source, while beneath her and below her, her buttocks trembled, feeling sundered, searched too, every orifice yearning for his touch, her body shaking with a desire that rolled up and down her spine through the center of her belly, her breasts aching now, as she touched them, aching for *his* touch.

Reeling, barely able to walk, she mustered herself to find the dignity to complete getting dressed, to leave her room and climb down the stairs, nodding to people, composing herself until she got outside where, looking at the trees, instead of feeling expected relief, she was rushed into a new madness, a pagan trick. It seemed all at once her entire being slipped as she walked down the drive, across the lawn, waving away the coachmen, trying to gather herself, she felt it, this new demon returned and whistling now, like a tiny tornado, in a spin of passion and glee was tearing up the great front lawn, slipping beneath her skirt and drilling into the very center of her, ripping away all dignity, all grandeur leaving in its wake this basic primal *thing,* this animal joy. She could not look at anything now, not even the grass, without this excitement. There was nowhere to go. She knew she could not hear music, lest she feel the color rise in her cheeks, and she dared not enter a coffee house, because she knew that even the taste of tea across her lips would arouse her more, that the extreme sensitivity into which she had passed had converted her entire body into a teeming erotic chamber. It had even invaded her mind. Her thoughts had gone baroque.

She collapsed on a park bench holding her hands against the wood hearing the pounding of her heart and tried to pull herself together. "Now, Edith," she heard herself say. "Now Edith," but it was no use. At that moment of full rapture, the Edith she hailed was totally gone.

25

At the police station, the captain's horses clattered off at a great gallop while his aide, Lieutenant Ludwig Stekal, reviewed the quandary.

A murder had occurred at 19 Berggasse sometime during the night. Two women, alone in a house. The children sleeping. Lieutenant Ludwig Stekal had been sent to the scene this morning. An attractive woman, Dr. Freud's wife, had swooned into his arms.

"When did it happen?" he asked as he tried to revive her.

"During the night," she said gasping, lying in his arms as he bent close to her face, slapping it gently, so gently as to be almost a caress.

When he entered the living room he was astonished to see that one of his superiors had already preceded him, for the rug was bloody but the body itself was not there.

"Oh," he said, "so you have already reported this?"

"No," she said, her eyes wild with fright and something more. "No one was here." She leaned for consolation against his chest.

"Well, who took the body then?" he said.

"I do not know," she said in a whisper as she fell against him, and she fainted again.

Another taller woman appeared in a shawl. "We heard shots," she said.

"Who are you?" he asked.

"I am her sister," she said. "She said she heard the gun."

"And where is the good doctor?" he asked.

"The doctor is away," the sister said, letting her eyes fall demurely to the ground, "for a while."

"Ah," said Stekal, and then "oh." It was most disconcerting: a murder without a body, a body left, so to speak, for them to discover. Then there was the warmth and fullness of her breasts against him, for she had swooned in a most peculiar way so that the full weight of her body leaned into his chest. As if to add further to his mortification, he felt a leap in his groin. Blushing, he felt her stir as he attempted to lead her to a chair, but she only leaned harder into him, pressing now, full tilt against his groin. Even through those skirts she would be aware. He prayed she did not recover from the faint, although in truth he could not guarantee precisely how unconscious she was. So he dragged her across the blood-stained floor. There was a couch at one side of the room, and while the sister went to the door, he laid her on the couch, and then, who could say how? he either slipped or lost his balance or she pulled him down, which is how it appeared to him, so that his full weight and most especially his groin was pressed against her, and he heard her moan as the captain entered the room.

"Ludwig!" the captain boomed.

Stekal disentangled himself. Mercifully she appeared to stay in a faint. Blushing bright red, he saluted the captain and said, "She swooned, sir, and I laid her down and fell." The captain's eyes crackled like fire. "What has happened here? Tell me at once!"

"I, I do not know, sir," Ludwig replied. "It is most alarming. There is no corpse for this murder."

"Then who has removed the corpse?" the captain asked. He wiped his brow. Minna entered and offered him a cool glass of water even as he caught the distrust in her eyes.

Stekal advised him that in addition to the problem of where the body had gone was the problem of what kind of body had it been. For the two ladies, one recovered now, were not of one mind. It appeared that they both heard the gun, but one heard one shot, and the other heard four. Both were quite positive about it. They were both in agreement that they had seen the body, a murder had occurred, or perhaps a suicide—although since the body was missing, a suicide could not practically be entertained—and both had heard a commotion at the back door. At the back, one sister said she saw a coach and five clattering away into the foggy night. Something in Lieutenant Stekal tingled when she said this; he felt the hairs on the back of his neck rise.

"At what time, Frl. Bernays?" the captain asked politely.

"It was three," she said, "for I heard the church chime."

"Would it not have been a coach and six?"

"No," she said. "I noticed it was five. The second lead horse harness was there, but there was no horse. No, it was a coach and five."

There was a pause of silence in which all of them thought it was indeed a night for spirits; not only had the murderer and the corpse been spirited away but the second lead horse as well.

Bearing in mind the remote possibility that the perpetrator could have planned to have a horse unleashed at the back door for him to place the body upon and spirit it away, they could simply conclude that the sister-in-law had not been seeing well.

The captain and Stekal went for a walk. They concluded there were too many things missing. The horse was missing from his harness. The body was missing from where it had been slain. The doctor was missing, and worst of all, any reasonable explanation was also missing.

That was the first of the difficulties. The second was perhaps even more serious. The sister insisted that the murdered person was a woman, and the wife protested that the murdered person was a man. The Vienna police were expert at dealing in discrepancies among witnesses, but the sex was something they always agreed upon.

Stekal looked perplexed. He saw the captain was upset. He knew they had been told to wait for the Inspector, who, if things had gone properly would have been here now. But they had received several telegrams advising them that the Inspector would be delayed. And now they had another murder.

The Inspector, the captain knew, would not arrive until the next night on the Paris–Vienna Express. He had been detained by the death of a student. A riot at the Beaux Arts Institute. An unfortunate thing. But still, the captain thought, it served her right, a woman wanting to be an artist. A certain portion of the female population had gone quite mad, the captain concluded. He himself thought that it had to do with the bicycle. It allowed them too much freedom. Independent movement of the limbs. He sighed. That was the beginning of untold dangers. Next he mused, they'd be taking off their corsets. So no wonder a young woman like that got crushed in a riot. It was in all the papers.

Still nothing so bad as here. Twenty women in less than three years, some of them chopped up. And now the rumors. The recent rumors threatened to put the city into a crisis. Rumors were mounting that these women who were being murdered were the victims of ritual murders by the Jews. And now this; a woman murdered in a Jewish doctor's house. The emperor was a staunch protector of the Jews, but it was to the advantage of Karl Lueger, the mayor, to fan the fires of the anti-Semites who had elected him. They had now locked horns, Lueger and the emperor, over the bodies of the dead women. The city was on the verge of hysteria. If it got any worse, Voll mused, this famous Inspector would be walking into an absolute blood bath.

26

Edith Wharton knew that Henry would hate her for it, but she felt that something must be done. She must do whatever possible to re-lease him from the thrall, which she felt was the proper word, of that total fakir, Dr. Freud. Why Henry had not been the same ever since he'd been to see him. She stood now in Vienna, before 19 Berggasse, her purse held firmly in her hand, and rapped the knocker sharply.

The door opened at once, and the woman standing there seemed startled.

"I am Edith Wharton," she said, pushing the woman aside and strode into the room before she turned and said, "I am here to see Dr. Freud."

The woman seemed pale, Edith noticed.

"The doctor is away," she said weakly, her hand on her head. "Did you have an appointment? He told everyone . . ." Her voice drifted off and then she became extremely agitated.

"Come come," said Mrs. Wharton, "don't dissimulate. I can assure you," she said, patting her large handbag, "the doctor will find my visit most profitable."

"The doctor is not here," Martha said, returning. "He is in Paris." Mrs. Wharton noticed the woman had large, fearful eyes and her cheeks were sunken.

"Then I'll just wait until he returns," Mrs. Wharton said, and to Martha's horror Mrs. Wharton sat down, on the seat right in front of the blood spot! Mrs. Wharton's foot went tap tap tap just on the border of it, and Martha grabbed the edge of the table and tried not to swoon. Had she seen it? Hadn't she seen it? They had telephoned Sigi and wakened him from sleep. He was annoyed and told them their fearful imaginations were aroused by the storm. He told them not to report it to the police, not to speak to any reporters, and of course, to cover up the blood spot from Emma Eckstein's nose.

Tap tap tap . . . Horrified, Martha watched Edith Wharton's toe circle the edge of the blood spot. "I believe I hear the kettle, I'll fetch some tea," Martha said. Fearful and in danger of succumbing to the vapors, she escaped at once into the kitchen. Edith Wharton decided to investigate.

She saw the guest book on the table that read APPOINTMENTS. Examining it, she saw there was nothing, absolutely nothing for the day. Boldly and defiantly she scrawled her name in her hand, noting the time was 9:05, and then retired to her seat. Whatever was taking the woman so long? He was probably back there whispering. She opened her bag to check her cash. She was so concerned about Henry's agitation and nervousness that she had determined it was necessary to buy the doctor off, and she was prepared to pay. As she looked into her bag, she saw the handgun and the mirror which she had removed from the glove compartment of the Panhard at the station. She lifted the gun out, and placed it on the table, then the mirror, and then the wad of cash. She counted it out again. She would try half at first. A matter of negotiation. As Martha returned with the tray of tea, Edith was just picking up the revolver to replace it in her bag. Martha stopped dead in the middle of the room. Her mouth dropped open and her terrified eyes held Edith's as she dropped the loaded tray. She screamed and fainted. The teapot broke. The gun clattered to the floor. Edith stood up and said, "Oh dear." Another woman entered, crying out, "What has happened! What has happened!"

"Really," Edith said, "she's simply fainted for no reason at all, but she did look very unwell. Where's the doctor, surely he will come out of hiding to assist his wife?" she said.

"He is in Paris," the other woman said, slapping the face of the fainted one. "Who are you?"

"Here," Edith said, never without smelling salts, although why she didn't know, whisking them under Martha's nose, who soon took to a fit of coughing. In minutes, all was well, or as well as it could be. Edith could hear one of them calming the fainted one, who was whispering in the kitchen. Edith was now convinced the doctor really wasn't there;

perhaps in Paris as they said, but she found the two of them very high strung, so she busied herself gathering her things back into her purse and let herself out, politely, but in something of a huff. She would find him, soon enough.

27

People had told the Inspector he was condemned by excess—excess of food, excess of drink, excess of feeling. He only knew now he wanted to be drunk; although drink was making him ill, he wanted that, too, to be ill beyond all consolation. Tonight, he barely knew where the chair was, simply under him somewhere as he made an effort to rise and make his way through the cafe, amid the blurring voices, faces, entreaties, jokes. He needed to get to the toilet. He had just managed to stand, grasping the back of the bar chair with one hand, when he felt the hush of anticipation, and then the cold sobering snap of a messenger's heels, as he turned and felt, as much as saw, a figure blazing with gold medallions and feathers. A royal courier appearing out of the mist at a Montmartre bar.

"Inspector Maurice Cheval LeBlanc?" he demanded.

The Inspector barely nodded as the scroll of paper was put into his palm. He suddenly noticed Violette next to him. What was it that he couldn't bear—her scent, or the scent of nearness? It threatened to engulf him, and he steadied himself with one hand on the chair.

"Maurice," he heard her say, "Maurice . . . from Vienna." He heard her reading the scroll and he knew he was lost now, "By the order of the Emperor Franz Josef of Austria, you are respectfully requested to appear . . ." He heard no more. He had told them they should call on Gross, Hans Gross, a brilliant criminologist, who lived in Graz. They said Gross was traveling and unavailable. Why then, he telegrammed, not Bertillon if they must have a Frenchman? Bertillon, he was informed, was too busy with Dreyfus to come now. It was a difficult series of murders. The fear was that there was perhaps more than one man, one killer. Lives were in danger. Especially women's. He must come. He sent excuses. He became ill. And now there was no avoiding it.

"By Order of the Emperor." He thought about this. Why in God's name was the *emperor* becoming involved in a question of murder?

28

Where oh where is Gertrude Van de Vere?
Her hand is in the dustbin
And her leg is over there.

Captain Voll pushed aside the latest murderer's note and opened the telegram from the renowned Paris inspector who had finally agreed to arrive on Wednesday's train.

"Regarding 19 Berggasse, begin at once," the Inspector's telegram read, "to interrogate all witnesses to the latest incident. Draw up a list of all visitors to 19 Berggasse within two weeks before the event. Examine and interrogate them as to the purposes of their visits. This is the only hope we have of establishing a motive."

The police captain stroked his red moustache and read the telegram slowly once again. Well, he had drawn up a list of visitors of sorts. He had torn it, actually stolen it, just that morning from one of the doctor's appointment books when Frl. Bernays, the sister-in-law, whom he found both an exciting and a formidable presence, had briefly turned her back. Fortunately the maid, whose name was Irina, had posed no problem to his entry, as she was hopelessly incompetent and, he thought, perhaps a little mad. But Frl. Bernays had barred his way so he had no choice but to steal it. He looked now at the pilfered appointment list he held in his hand: It was dated a week before the murder.

Wednesday, 22 February, 10:00 A.M., Dr. Carl Jung regarding his patient Sabina Spielrein. Extremely agitated.
Wednesday, 22 February, 1:00 P.M., Sabina Spielrein regarding Dr. Jung. Extremely agitated, full of fantasy regarding her doctor.

Thursday, 23 February, 10:00 A.M., Emma Eckstein regarding Dr. Fliess'
operation on her nose. Still hysterical.

Thursday, 23 February, 2:00 P.M., Wilhelm Fliess, regarding Emma
Eckstein. Discuss sexual periodicity.

Henry James, re: Alice James

Wednesday, 28 February, 4 P.M., M.

There were several dates without *any* notations. And then the most
cryptic entry of all: simply H.R.H. It couldn't be what it looked like,
surely. It couldn't be His Royal Highness, could it?

H.R.H. and some other woman's name—it looked like "Ida Bauer"[1]
—without notations, or he assumed the notations were elsewhere. He
would leave that to the Inspector. Nonetheless it was odd that of all
those leading the list, each was followed by the name of a person who
had come after them, who was coming regarding the preceding person. Most unusual. And he suspected in some way significant. Still,
there were others. Many others. Neighbors, passersby.

"Interrogate *everyone*," the Inspector wrote firmly. "There are those
who do not *know* that they are witnesses." Now what did he mean by
that? the captain wondered. Would he have to interrogate everyone
who *might have been a witness?* How indeed would he know?

The police captain stood now opposite 19 Berggasse and nervously
paced the walk wondering who indeed would be the witness they
required.

29

Henry was reading:

Poor Anna shrank from the angry glances of the enraged Knight; despair
and anguish seized her soul. The Stranger never came; he had forgotten

[1] Ida Bauer was the name of Freud's patient who became known as "Dora." She was
treated by Freud in 1900, and returned for treatment in 1901, at which time she was
refused. Freud did not publish the case until 1905, when he acknowledged he had failed
to account for transference, as well as to confront her strong homosexual love for her
father's girlfriend and had insisted instead on her repressed desire for a man, Herr K.

his solemn vows, neglected his promise, and abandoned her to her fate. Whither could she fly? How was she to avoid the choice of miseries that equally pursued her? Either she must perjure her soul to false oaths, or meet the dreadful alternative of a parent's dire malediction. —Oh! whither, lost and wretched Anna! canst thou fly?

Henry tore himself away from the book, even though he did want to go on. It made him positively shudder, no literary aspect whatsoever, still he couldn't stay away from it. He would resume reading in the morning, and hoped really quite fervently that she didn't die on the steps before he awakened.

30

Really, Henry, whatever is taking you so long," Edith Wharton said under her breath. It wasn't like Henry to be writing at this hour. She was extremely perplexed at how very *odd* Henry had become these last weeks, ever since that woman died in Venice. And going to that terrible doctor Freud had only made him worse. All that talk about the supernatural. And William goading him on about psychical research. It wasn't good; he was writing too many ghost stories, and was not himself at *all*. She was especially irritated at the thought that anything might go wrong this evening because the table looked so lovely tonight, and they expected two of her most distinguished and favorite guests: Paul Bourget and his wife. Bourget was bringing along a young writer, someone with whom he was quite impressed, although he had published very little. Marcel Proust was his name, and Bourget was convinced he had promise. She had asked to see his work. Henry had apparently read something and concurred with Bourget about the talent. "However," he had said to Edith, "he goes on endlessly with the *finest* nuances. I mean simply on and *on*" and Edith thought it was the oddest thing for Henry of all people to be making that particular criticism. Perhaps, she thought with a sigh, we are only alert to our own foibles in others.

31

The next morning the Inspector, with Violette in attendance, got dressed and went out to a cafe.

He put down his coffee cup and sighed. He was in the habit of feeling strong, of taking early morning walks, and drinking his coffee black, and was unhappy at the fatigue he still sensed in his own body as he looked out through the sooty windows of the cafe. He could barely see the street lamps, still burning although it was early morning. Perhaps the dulled glass was a blessing. If you could see far enough, the old men said, you could see into the future. He had no interest in seeing the future. It brought him pain.

He was waiting that morning for the young boy Pierre to return with the Vienna papers, and he heard him now as the door into the cafe banged. He opened the *Neue Freie Presse* first, unsurprised to see the news about the Dreyfus trial. He admired Theodor Herzl who was covering the trial, but didn't pause to read him. He was looking for an item about what had happened at 19 Berggasse. If the emperor was now involved he imagined the active Vienna censors were at work keeping it out of the papers. He flipped through and saw no signs of it. But as he scanned the paper, another story arrested his attention:

The child was wearing a dark blue jacket in the latest French style, with a white ascot, trimmed in the finest lace from Belgium. Her green velvet skirt was trimmed with two rows of gay red flowers, one row of large, followed by one of small blossoms, which struck a dramatic balance with the red blood in her hair.

The slash of red blood, which ran from her skull down across the bruised forehead, spilling onto the white ascot and onto the skirt, ended in a perfect large red circle, which echoed the tiny red flowers beneath it. Three fingers on the left hand were broken, and there was evidence, the police said, that the child had been sexually abused.

The guardians of the child, Sophie and Leonard Oberkampf, have been charged with murder. Today Sophie appeared outside the courthouse in a lovely yellow afternoon calling dress, and Leonard in a handsome black velvet frock coat. They denied all charges, although they did acknowledge that the child was a foundling, and it had recently been discovered that she was the daughter of Jews.

The Inspector put down his copy of the *Neue Freie Presse* and his coffee as well. The Jews, the Jews, it always came down to a question of the Jews. He didn't know for a moment which it was that disgusted him more—the crime itself or that peculiarly Viennese way of reporting it. He thought that the Viennese, in so many ways an accomplished people, could on occasion regard even the grossest death as an aesthetic event, simply another aspect of theater, and murder itself as an interesting diversion, a kind of twisted art.

He noticed this because it struck him that in a man of his profession, all the training and exposure to the beatings and rapes he encountered daily were still not enough, even after twenty years, to prevent him from a sober despair at each new encounter. This made him think again about Vienna. The city of his childhood. He hated the thought of going there and all that it held for him. A beautiful city, damned by his dreams. It made him ill. But he would go. The fever was gone, and he was prepared. But first, he would pay a visit to the doctor, Dr. Freud.

32

There was a tremendous buzz in the courtroom as Theodor Herzl, Paris correspondent for Vienna's *Neue Freie Presse,* entered the courtroom of the Dreyfus trial and took his familiar seat on the bench toward the rear. There were several correspondents for European papers seated in the row. Morton Fullerton of the London *Times* nodded politely and moved some papers aside to make room for Herzl, who he noted was wearing a very well tailored suit that morning, navy with a faint pinstripe. The aroma of spices arose from Herzl. Fullerton thought he would ask him where he purchased his cologne—and his suit.

To Fullerton that was one of the joys of being in Paris—the clothes. Although he was endeavoring to pay prime attention to the Dreyfus affair—which he recognized was becoming an even bigger story than he had originally thought, he had difficulty in removing his concentration from the subject of attire. He was still contemplating the purchase of a hat he had seen that morning in the hatter's, a homburg they were calling it. It had appeared in Germany and gotten voguish because that overweight English aristocrat Prince Edward VII had taken a liking to it. Fullerton had tried on the homburg, which was black and made of excellent silky wool, and thought he looked rather dashing himself. It complemented so perfectly what he was wearing this morning, a rather too boldly patterned pin stripe, a navy-blue and green striped tie, and white gaiters snapped over black leather boots. His high opinion of himself was confirmed by the admiring glances he elicited from even the most modest lady when he smiled and tipped his hat in a certain way.

He had not, of course, had much time to spend with ladies since he had taken up his pursuit of Mrs. Wharton. She was not as attractive as he would have liked, but her conversation was brilliant, and the possibility of seducing her had proved a remarkable challenge, to say the least. He found himself thinking of and seeing Mrs. Wharton much more than he had originally anticipated. It was a pursuit he had expected would go slowly, and it had. She was an extremely conservative married woman, a miserably married woman, he knew, so that finally after months of talking and walking and—on this he prided himself— a superb orchestration of flirtation, he was relieved when there occurred a sudden release of her affections, and they had plunged into a passionate affair. Her passion had actually moved him, not an altogether easy thing to do. It made him think there must be something in a slow start that heightens the excitement. The woman had never had a lover before, and her response was most extraordinary. But then, Fullerton thought happily, he was such an extraordinary fellow himself, especially when it came to women. He smiled at this idea as he heard the people in the row behind him settle in and a man mumbling that he had seen Captain Dreyfus the day before and he didn't look troubled enough to be innocent.

"It's a sinister frame. Zola knows," Herzl said to him, scanning his own report. "He is unswervingly loyal to the army and they're pinning others' treachery on him."

Fullerton shrugged. Although he was covering the trial for the London *Times,* he was only remotely interested. He was thinking about his meeting in Vienna with Mrs. Wharton. She had made him realize once again what a remarkable lover he was. He had found it impressive that she had gone all the way to Vienna to meet him there, but he did not actually think too much about it. Fullerton attempted now to turn his full attention to Herzl, whom he admired, but thought that on political issues, he was something of a fool.

"The Jewish issue is always there," Herzl said, "raised or lowered. Still the lieutenant isn't helping." He added almost as an afterthought a key element in the case, "It's a pity the French feel so passionate about the army." It was some minutes later when Herzl whispered, "I must tell you of my plan." But Fullerton was preoccupied. A handsome woman in a lace hat and a lace dress, an utterly astonishing dress that seemed at first glance to run over her naked skin but was in fact attached to yards of champagne silk, had just hustled down the aisle of the courtroom and onto a bench, trying as she did so to lift her veil, and as she turned imperceptibly, she acknowledged Fullerton, whose breath had stopped at the sight of her.

The judge entered the courtroom. There was a stir. The woman in the lace dress rose to adjust her skirts and glanced directly at Morton Fullerton. His heart froze. Never would he forget those eyes. Yellow eyes, the color of burning topaz. He had met her once, at a soirée in Vienna.

33

No one understood, least of all the Inspector himself, why his grieving for the young art student Elise had made him so dramatically ill. He forced himself out now, for a walk, in some effort to accumulate a fatigue in his muscles that would allow him finally to sleep. While his fever was gone he still was restless. He pushed on through the light rain and fog.

It was early evening and he had walked as far as the Bois de Boulogne when he heard a noise in the brush; he paused, and then recognized the sounds of lovers. He sat for quite a while on a bench, seeing nothing before his eyes but the brief flickering of escaping light, back and forth behind the clouds. Elise was dead, so now, why now the thoughts of his mother?

"I'll see you, I'll send for you, darling," he could hear her quite suddenly now, his mother, the last time he saw her she was blowing kisses, her plum-feathered hat and her white gloves waving, vanishing in the oval window of the carriage. Thoughts of her long gone rose now through the mist as if it were she, and not Elise, who had caused his woe. His chest contracted as he thought of this, small seizures crowded his heart. He tried to sigh, no air. He felt he had swallowed a cage. He tried to breathe and felt the cage again.

Eventually he rose, and turned, this time walking more slowly back the way he had come. That was when he saw the lovers emerge from the thicket. He saw only the back of the lady, but was startled to see she was so elegantly dressed. It was unusual for an aristocrat to be so boldly compromised. She was adjusting her clothes and there were twigs adhering to the back of her dress. His eye was caught by her magenta gloves arranging the plumes on her hat. He recognized the man. He was a rogue.

PART II

MEANWHILE...

1

TWO MONTHS EARLIER, ACROSS THE SEA THE FOLLOWING EVENTS TRANSPIRED

It was a surprise when we learned that Mr. James was coming to visit once again, and I thought it was possibly because of Aunt Ida, although she did not seem too excited, but it was quite clear that Cecily was. Father was very agitated about the table being set exactly right because Mr. James was bringing as his guest a very famous woman writer, a Mrs. Wharton, and Father wanted to be certain that someone had read her books, and was relieved that Cecily and Aunt Ida had each read at least one. Everyone had heard of Mrs. Wharton and there was going to be quite a to-do. I imagined that Cecily would spend all of her time trying to impress that lady, but I turned out to be quite wrong.

Mrs. Wharton had a most imposing presence and was very fashionable. She had on an elegant brown velvet coat and a long string of pearls. Her dress was yellow and had a small bustle in the back. It seemed that Edie, the maid, had known about her somehow, which I will get to later, and it was a relief apparently to Mother that Mrs. Wharton didn't recognize Edie. Mrs. Wharton had altogether much too imperious an air for me to feel at all comfortable around her. The dinner was very strange because Mrs. Wharton seemed to address almost all of her remarks to Father and to Mr. James. I also noticed something that I had observed during the day of the apple picking, which was that Cecily seemed to take on a different character in the presence of Mr. James. She seemed quite beside herself, and this expressed itself in a most extraordinary quality of animation and vital-ity. Not that Cecily was not always quite animated indeed, but in his presence I noticed what could only be called a kind of fever of en-chantment that seemed to rise into her cheeks, making her almost black eyes very bright. Her whites were very white and her eyes were also, not exactly slanted, but rather oval and her cheeks were so pink, and the entire effect was of a very gay, laughing and blushing creature. But she was not blushing, nor do I think I had ever seen Cecily blush. She was quite *agitated,* and Mr. James himself was most engaged, even I could tell that. For he seemed to direct most of his questions to Cecily and seemed almost to resent it when anyone except Mrs. Whar-ton interrupted.

I couldn't hear all of what they were saying, but I could see Mother casting her eyes about in that direction with some concern and some puzzlement, and once she even said, "Now, Cecily, you must allow Mr. James to finish his dinner and not be asking so many questions," to which Cecily had given Mother quite an awful look, but Mr. James said quickly, "Oh no, please, I quite enjoy the questions, indeed," and he bent his head again as Cecily went on in what I thought was quite a serious mode for her, somehow. The expression on her face was the kind of intense, studied look she would get when she was desper-ately trying to learn something difficult.

I had also seen, although I was not to talk about it, Cecily with a similar expression on her face when she was studying Grandfather's anatomy books. It had created quite a scandal when Mother and Father found the books under Cecily's bed. There had been a most terrible row about it, but Grandfather of all people had come to Cecily's rescue and insisted to Mother and Father that she be answered questions she had about "the human body." Aunt Ida had been chosen as the one who would convey the information from Grandfather to Cecily, and the way it was arranged was that Cecily could read the anatomy books one hour each week and then would submit written questions to Grandfather, who would confer with Aunt Ida, and then Aunt Ida would bring the answers to Cecily. This routine had gone on now for some time, although Mother had sworn us all to secrecy that no one outside the family could know of this, and Timothy was forbidden to speak to Cecily on the subject at all.

After dinner when we retired to the drawing room I became quite intrigued with the conversation between Cecily and Mr. James. Aunt Ida, too, had been drawn into it, and I thought that Mr. James rather fancied Aunt Ida but was making his more obvious attentions towards Cecily so as to avoid any embarrassment of anyone actually knowing this.

Aunt Ida had drawn her chair near, and I thought perhaps she was as interested in Mr. James as he in her. Cecily at any rate was going on about how she thought it would be so thrilling, so simply thrilling to be character in a novel, and she said, suddenly turning to Mr. James, "And wouldn't you like it yourself, finally to actually be in someone's story? Now wouldn't you?"

"Why no," Mr. James said, paling visibly, "no, not at all, quite the contrary." He put his finger around the inside of his collar and seemed suddenly to be quite pink. Father noticed this and went to the veranda to open the door for some air. But Cecily was not about to drop the subject.

"I don't mean," she was careful to say, "there could ever be anyone *equal* to you, I mean you are such a fine writer yourself, but perhaps someone sympathetic . . . someone who . . ."

"No, no, my dear," Mr. James interrupted, quickly picking up his napkin and pressing it carefully about his lips as if to seal some thought he was about to utter, "I mean it is something that would be a challenge beyond the most talented of inventors and recorders, for I lead a very quiet life, you see, and there would not be much to tell."

"Well," Cecily said, "they could make up something just to add a little flavor to it, don't you think?" She smiled at him so sweetly it appeared for a moment he had forgotten what he heard, for his face froze, just for an instant between what I thought might be horror and the pleasure of listening to anything Cecily had to say in her most charming way, and then his face took on life, only it reversed its first horrified expression and moved to one of amusement.

"Make it up, you say?" his eyes positively crinkled at the ends. "You mean invent a life for me?" He had put down his fork and looked at Cecily as if he could only marvel at her, and I don't know, of course, but he continued to look thoughtfully off into space while coffee was served, and I suspected that he was contemplating that very possibility, wondering who might ever conceive of such a task.

Mr. James said he was quite all right, but I thought actually he wasn't. He seemed to want to change the subject rather quickly, which finally Cecily did, but only after she had gone on for some time about various female characters in novels she had read. I noticed she avoided mentioning anything by Mr. James. I knew that when the apple picking was done, Cecily, who was normally not so interested in novels, had gone straight to the library and taken out almost everything that Mr. James had written. Although she had a tremendous interest in Grandfather's anatomy books up until this point in life, I would have to say that Cecily could be described as a very curious and bold and difficult, but quite whimsical creature. She seemed interested mostly in boys and bows and her hair and whether she would get what she wanted when she pointed it out to Father in the store.

Suffice it to say that for the few weeks after Mr. James' first visit Cecily stayed in her room, reading. Mother forbade her to bring books to the table, so Cecily would disappear soon after dinner to read again.

Mother at first thought she had the anatomy books up there in her room, but Aunt Ida assured her this was not the case.

It made me uncomfortable because I had always been the "bookish" one, and I sensed in Cecily some quality that I lacked. It seemed that Cecily was reading with a passion to discover something that would save her from the fate that even then, perhaps, she knew she was destined to suffer.

I was thinking all of these things when I suddenly heard Cecily say to Mr. James, "I do not think you should have sent Isabel back to Rome and Mr. Osmond. It was a dreadful thing to do."

Mr. James seemed quite taken aback. He coughed and then said something quite complicated about the characters and the plot working together, and I think he used the word *believable*. It was meant to silence Cecily, but it didn't at all. "But it was *you* that did it. I would have believed something else. You might have saved her. I don't think you really understood her very well. She *was* fond of kissing," she added. At that point Mrs. Wharton turned around. She had clearly been listening and cast a very intense look at Cecily. Perhaps it was because of this look, I don't know what prompted her, but suddenly Mrs. Wharton said something to Cecily that upset her; Cecily only said, "No, I think not." Perhaps she'd asked Cecily if she wanted to be Lily Bart, for *The House of Mirth* was quite a famous book indeed, but Cecily never told me.

The conversation was interrupted at this point by Mary with cordials, which was just as well, and we didn't return to it until the very moment that Mr. James and Mrs. Wharton were leaving, when Mrs. Wharton turned, and Cecily said: "I, I'm saying that in a way it is the only way to be alive. I mean to finally really, really live." Cecily's voice had taken on an altogether different tone, a rather alarming one at that.

"But surely you don't mean this," Mrs. Wharton said, suddenly looking very uneasy.

"But I *do,*" Cecily said, looking very distraught and turning to Mr. James. She grabbed him suddenly by the arm. *"You* understand, don't you? You *must."* She was beseeching him so earnestly he stepped back several paces.

"Why yes," he said to her, frowning, "I believe I do. We can talk about this more at another time. Now I am quite exhausted, and the carriage is here, and Mrs. Wharton and I must drive to the station this evening."

Clearly Cecily was holding back tears. This was a very awkward moment until Mrs. Wharton, trying to save it, said, "I'm certain you will be quite satisfied with who you are, in life, eventually." I thought this remark would end the new discussion with Cecily, but unfortunately it didn't, as Cecily said curtly, "That is not my point, that is not what I was saying at all."

Edith said nothing to Henry for some time as the coachman drove them from the house. Then she spoke:

"It's so strange, about that girl."

There was a pause.

"Cecily, you mean," said Henry James, although he knew precisely who she meant.

"Why . . . yes," Edith said, "I mean it is ever so *odd."*

Henry didn't want to think about its being odd.

"I suppose it's like any young girl, it's the same as wanting to be an actress, don't you think?" he said uneasily.

"But it *isn't,* Henry, it's quite different. I've never heard of such a thing, really. It is quite remarkable."

Henry said nothing. He felt suddenly most uncomfortable.

"Think of it, Henry, imagine that you feel you can only be alive if you become a character in a book, that you can't live otherwise, that your entire existence is without merit, that you have to be *written,* that is; it's not a literary ambition at all, it is the *strangest* sort of ambition . . . wouldn't you agree?"

"Why . . . yes . . . no . . . oh, I don't know," he said with dismissive irritation. He didn't know why she pressed on about it so. He really didn't want to think about it. He didn't want to think about understanding it either, but he did. It wasn't something *he'd* ever wanted, good God.

The thought that he might after all be described by someone else's sentences provoked a chill in his bones. He would never want it, never choose it. It offended him to think that someone, anyone might dare to describe the inner working of his mind. Or the outer garments he wore. Or anything at all.

In the click of the carriage wheels, in the lurching of the harness, the stamping of the horses' feet, the thoughts obsessed him. Who would do such a thing? Had he not contained himself, expressed himself, described himself in every comma, semicolon, and period of every sentence he had *ever* inscribed? Was he not in fact contained in every pause and pronouncement of each and every word and phrase? Who would attempt to describe him in words other than his own? To think that some part of his very selfness might escape into the hands of others to peer at and invade the very presence he took such pains to describe himself, to limit, yes, limit and enclose what any other intelligence save his own could know about his soul; to think one could be violated in this way depressed him, and, suddenly, looking at Edith Wharton in the cab, the occasional light cast from a street lamp illuminating her face, the fact that she had brought such a subject to his mind filled him with a ferocity that surprised him: perhaps she herself had thought of putting him into her books. At that moment, for that thought, he hated her.[1]

And then he thought of Constance Fenimore Woolson,[2] and he felt his fist clench in his hand.

---

[1] It is not possible to know whether James was thinking about the character of Selden in *The House of Mirth.* Scholars have suggested he has something of James about him.

[2] Constance Fenimore Woolson was an American writer who had a close friendship with James. She was a spinster and it is believed she was infatuated with James. A character in one of her stories is modeled on James. She died in Venice, in a suicide, it is believed, by falling from a second-story window. James rushed to Venice upon hearing the news and burned all of his letters to her. James addressed her as "Fenimore."

MISS Woolson awaited him. He saw her standing on the quay as the gondolier skillfully moved the boat across the Grand Canal. The church of Santa Maria della Salute was glimmering in the early sunlight as he approached. He sighed. A certain sense of fatigue had possessed him of late. He was very glad to be meeting her. He found her company most diverting.

Miss Woolson nervously paced the steps lining the canal, the water lapping against the stones now green and grey in the light. It was a cloudy day, but there was promise in it, so she did not know why, until she looked down at her new black boots, she shivered so. The boots were gleaming with wet.

"Now how have I done this?" she wondered, stamping her foot and raising her head just in time to see Henry James seated in the front of the gondola, his white shirt impeccable, his cravat just so, and his tweed suit looking as if it were picked up from the tailor, although she knew differently. It was clear to her that Mr. James did not have a very large fortune at all, but she was irritated now, at her wet foot, feeling she could not detain him in order to change her shoes, finding it so, well, gentlemanly that he had offered to pick her up in his gondola, although it did mean coming all the way across the canal. And it was only one foot, although it was cold, and she would soon forget about it, for they were to go this morning to see the Caravaggios, and Mr. James was so considerate, so charming, so very special a friend.

The boatman drew up alongside the steps, the boat nestled neatly against the stone, as if there were no waves, and Mr. James and the boatman offered both hands at once. Mr. James, touching her hand, her elbow, helped her down into the boat and before she knew, the gondolier had turned the front of the gondola once again into the Canal, Miss Woolson now seated beside Mr. James. As they began to talk, an immediate kind of tension occurred between them, at once intense, and almost formal, but in it could be heard Miss Woolson pleading, feeling her way for she felt his interest in her so acute, felt that she was, it was true, forty, but she was very nice, very considerate, most sensitive, extremely well educated, and they did like the same things, and he was most attentive and a bachelor, such things were not unheard of, and they did spend almost every day together, and would you spend so much time with a woman if you did not entertain some thought of marrying her? Some thought? She smiled at him now, and he looked at her warmly and she felt the hope start up in her again, for he looked at her, well, warmly, she would say, although not quite as warmly as she would have liked.

2

Apparently Mrs. Wharton and Mr. James had gone off to her home in the Berkshires, a place she called The Mount. I had overheard them making elaborate preparations to be brought to the train and Mrs. Wharton saying something about how she "wished she had her beloved Panhard," which was an automobile she had recently purchased in Paris. I asked Father why it was that her car was in Paris if she lived here, and he said that actually she lived there for the most part, although her husband lived *here*. As luck would have it, earlier that afternoon both Cecily and I had overheard the downstairs maid, Edie, telling mother that Mrs. Wharton's husband Teddy was a terrible drunk and some sort of awful whispering that we would not have heard had we not been in the pantry where we happened to be and then just stayed, it is true, in order to hear more, but that anyway Mrs. Wharton was very unhappy and got very ill around him, something called depressions, and had to go to the clinic in Philadelphia, which is where Edie had once worked and so she knew the entire story. Edie was not a mean person at all, and I was surprised to hear her gossip in this way, except I thought she was actually quite sympathetic to Mrs. Wharton, who was not a person to inspire sympathy.

She was a rather grand woman I thought, for someone who went to hospitals. And she was impatient, and rather to the point, not at all graceful, or soft, or anything like that, and I saw that she absolutely wanted nothing to do with Aunt Ida. I could tell that right away. And so could Aunt Ida. She was not the kind of person one thought one could *like* too easily, although Cecily said the book about Lily Bart, which was *The House of Mirth,* showed that one had to be a kind person to even *think* of writing it, so then I wasn't so sure. But there was something that quite intrigued me about Mrs. Wharton, and not only that she was such a grand lady to be a writer, and that she was famous as well, but that a lady of such *sweep* should ever go to the hospital for depressions, which Edie said was a terrible feeling in which no one ever wanted to live, was so mystifying to me that I could not quite stop thinking of it.

3

What Cecily said made Henry James wonder now if anyone ever would actually have anything to say about *him?* It rather intrigued him, the brief moments when he looked up on his library shelf and dared to think that someone, sometime, hopefully, he thought, a man of erudition and good will, might write a book about him, Henry James. He looked at the library shelf and it seemed to glow. Sheer poppycock and nonsense to be sure, yet how elevating in a way to think it might be *true.* He permitted himself the conceit of imagining a book, one entire book devoted to a study of his work. Maybe, he thought wistfully, it would even have gold letters. If it was about his *work,* he thought he would actually be quite pleased. It was the other suggestion that annoyed him.

That night before preparing for bed, Henry James lit a long candle; Edith was not fond of electricity, and it was not yet available in her new home here in Lenox, Massachusetts. He was planning to return to London in a day's time, and from there, on to the Continent. He took up one of the long letters from Fenimore. It was particularly disturbing to him to read her letter now, and he did not know exactly why he was reading it again. He knew only that he wanted to bury himself in the sound of her sentences, her hesitations, the coy way she flirted with him, to insinuate his full attention into every nuance of those words, to ferret out from this evidence her real feelings towards him.

As he made the effort, he felt the perspiration begin to creep up the back of his neck and soon encase his entire head. He felt it must be fever coming on and went to his small suitcase for a tonic he had procured in England, Dr. Seligman's Compound, which he found useful for many occasions. He was altogether dismayed by the label, which had a lady holding her hand to her head, appearing to faint backwards into a group of rosebushes. It was after the tonic—and he would later ascribe these thoughts to it—that, as if in a dream, as he lay there, he saw young Cecily, in a white dress with a pink ribbon and violets gathered on the side at her waist, enter the room and sit down in the chair opposite him. She seemed, as she turned those large dark eyes toward him, to be imploring him to help her in some way. She had come to ask him something, to grant a reality to her she could not grant herself, a reality without which she believed she could not live.

"I should so like it if you would," she said quietly to him.

"Well, really," he heard himself as if from another planet, "I shall have to think about it. Such an unusual request. I've not had it before."

"But surely you've thought of it. Of me."

"No. It hadn't struck me, actually. I like to start with characters I think of myself, you know. Zola might be more open to suggestions, perhaps you should visit him. You admire him, you told me."

"Oh ever so much," she said laughing with that gay, girlish delightful laugh she had, seeming to bubble with amusement at the sheer pleasure of being alive, "but I shouldn't want to be in his stories. They are ever so improper, and the places one should have to go, no, I don't think I would like it at *all*."

"Try Tolstoy," he wanted to say. "The Russian countryside is good for your health. Countless young women, pale from all sorts of causes, have found refreshment there." But he could not say anything. He had fallen quite asleep, and his last thoughts as his eyes closed were that he ought to say something but he couldn't, and he heard her tiptoeing slowly out of the room.

4

My sister Cecily, soft and pink, slept in the bed beside me. Her dark curls spread out across the pillow in swirls, coiled and shining, and in her hand, barely grasped, was a pencil. Across her feet lay the map of Europe, Austria just now, pinned by her knee. I was awake early, for I was excited by the news of the journey. I had barely slept at all. Cecily had been up later than permitted, writing down corrections, as she saw it in my diary, which contained my "fancies," about Vienna. In my excitement I had started to write a story, which I often did (although Mother disapproved of this most terribly), and Cecily reading it had stamped her feet and told everyone it was *too* romantic. This surprised me as I thought nothing could ever be too much of *anything* for Cecily. But I was in for a surprise.

5

THE CROSSING

Aunt Ida was reading a book by Frederick Engels, which a lady visitor had pressed upon her as we were leaving.

If you are going to Austria, and you are among the Germans, you had better read Engels, the lady said. And also someone named Marx.

So Aunt Ida read aloud from Engels every night at dinner, and Father said she was so genuinely excited he hadn't the heart to stop her. It so happened that one night she stopped herself.

It had been rainy and windy all day, and the ship had pitched most uncomfortably, so there were not many people in the dining room. Most people were sick in their beds, and the ones who were in the dining room were very quiet. When Aunt Ida began to read, her voice, which was very strong and passionate, was louder than usual, and I do not know if she had read these passages already or she just discovered them as she was reading, but Aunt Ida's strong, authoritative voice booming across the dining hall produced an effect I shall never forget:

> . . . And therefore we conclude [said Aunt Ida speaking for Mr. Engels] that marriage is responsible for the circumstances that have caused the historical downfall of all females of the species.

It was as if an explosion had gone off. All I heard Mother do was give a small intake of breath, a kind of uhhhh. Then her face went red, bright red.

"Well," Aunt Ida said, putting the book down, not really knowing, I think, what else to do. She smacked it shut in a very satisfying way.

"He is certainly the kind of thinker who gives you something to think about," she said, looking about the entire ship's dining room with her very bright smile, the blue tassels on her hat swinging as she turned. It is too much, Mother had said about the tassels, as she often said about Aunt Ida, and this time I thought she was probably right. Everyone had stopped eating. They stared at us, their cups, forks, knives poised in midair, as if, Cecily said later, Aunt Ida was *scandalous.*

"All she did was *read* it," Cecily said later. "It's the silliest thing I've ever heard, I'm just amazed they take it all so seriously." She was flouncing out of her pink dress and attempting to climb into her blue one.

"Whyever are you changing?" I asked her, annoyed. "It's only ten o'clock in the morning."

"I have nothing else to do," she said.

"You could read or study," I said, and to my surprise she replied, "You know, I just might." She had that mischievous look on her face again. "I think I must read more by this Mr. Engels. Perhaps," she said, her eyes twinkling, "*I* can read aloud tonight." I held my breath at such boldness, and then the two of us could contain it no longer and collapsed on the bed, shrieking with laughter, especially at the way that woman, Lady Dunbarton, at the next table had started choking on her soup and coughing and coughing, and she was so mean, and her face was so funny, and everyone was fussing so with their There, there, theres, and their Oh dear, dear, dears, and everyone positively glaring at Aunt Ida as if it was her fault she'd choked on her soup. Why, that was at least five minutes later, unless, as Cecily said in her wicked way, she'd been holding the soup in her mouth with her cheeks out the entire five minutes, in which case she deserved to choke on it.

But there was quite a fuss, and in the midst of it one of the waiters slipped on something and fell on the floor, and all the dishes fell on top of him, and still everyone turned and looked at Aunt Ida, and Cecily and I looked at each other, and she grabbed my hand under the table, and we couldn't help it, we just giggled into our napkins with Mother's eyes rolling around the room while she kept saying, "Girls, girls, girls . . . Please, Frederick, *do* something." But it was no use. And I thought I would simply expire of laughter, and finally Father had to lead the two of us out of the dining room onto the deck to get some air, but the laughter still didn't stop for what seemed like hours, and by then it was really hurting my stomach horribly, and Timothy didn't help at all. He just stood round like a brother, looking *positively* disgusted, and said, "I can't *wait* to be on land. They've gone giddy."

6

Mama was sending a telegram from the ship to the hotel in Paris. She said she had worked out an arrangement with Papa that we would stay at "that woman's house" in Vienna for only one month, and Papa had agreed. Mama was very good at working out arrangements. She felt very strongly that there must be *understandings,* a word that she used a lot. She and Aunt Ida had an "understanding," which I know was only reluctantly agreed to by Aunt Ida, that Mama must approve any books Aunt Ida gave us to read. I think the way Aunt Ida worked this out was that she didn't always tell Mama exactly what was in the book.

The latest book she had given us just before sailing was *Mother Right* by Bachofen[1] which she told mother was a history book. Which it was. But it was a history which said that originally women ruled society, and that only women could invent wealth. Aunt Ida would never have suggested we refrain from telling the truth, but when Mother asked me about it, I told her it was a very good history book, and when she asked Cecily, Cecily said there were early drawings of very interesting fashions, and Aunt Ida shot her a look and I knew wanted to throttle her, because if Mother ever saw the fashions in the book she would faint dead away. The women in the book wore necklaces and earrings and their bodies were half-naked.

---

[1] J. J. Bachofen was popular at the time and one of the first anthropologists to suggest a "female" origin of the species. He cites the Lycians, who were described as matriarchal by Herodotus. Today most readers would find him a bit overreaching.

Aunt Ida said that was because they were in a hot climate, and it was necessary to take their clothes off or they would die of the heat, and Cecily said it looked very jungly in there, weren't they afraid of poison ivy? and Aunt Ida said no, they were more worried about the heat.

7

There were several evenings at sea when we had perfectly charming dinners, as Mother said. That is, no one said anything to offend anyone and Cecily and I had got control of our giggles. But the next-to-last evening before we were to arrive, the English lady with whom Aunt Ida had struck up an acquaintance came over to our table after dessert positively aflutter with excitement.

"What is it?" Father asked her, finally attempting to understand her talk about Parliament in Vienna and a particular American writer. And finally between her talk and Aunt Ida's questions it became clear that she was talking about the wild politics of Vienna.

"The Parliament is an absolute circus," she said to Father, "I can't imagine how you'll all survive. Although," she added, "the Viennese are charming, and brilliant. The music is wonderful, the theater is fabulous, the art is inventive—but the politics, oh the politics. Why it is enough to send an Englishman mad, I tell you. They are a very paradoxical people. But your Mr. Twain, he does an excellent job of summing them up."

"I thought," Aunt Ida intervened, "although I do not know, of course, but I understand from good sources that the one thing the Viennese hate is to be summed up, to have anyone say or write anything about them that says, Oh the Viennese are this, or that. That in fact it is almost impossible ever to say exactly what a Viennese is."

"Well," Timothy quipped, " 'paradoxical' pretty nearly covers everything, so that can't be objected to," and everyone thought this was silly but apt, and then Father abruptly changed the subject. But not before the lady offered to bring round the magazine with the dispatch by

Mark Twain. Aunt Ida accepted immediately, as she and Father would find it important to read it. But Father said with some annoyance that he had read it already before we'd left America, and he excused himself somewhat abruptly and told Aunt Ida he would give it to her himself and told the lady politely and most definitely not to bring Mr. Twain's article round at all.

Of course Cecily and I by now were determined to read it as well and over the course of the next day we managed to get hold of it. We found it in the deck chair where Aunt Ida had left it. Or actually, what we got hold of was a rather official-looking envelope which was addressed to Father and had stamps on it and had in it the magazine which Aunt Ida had been reading. I was most curious about this Mr. Twain and wondered if we might meet him in Vienna, although Cecily said no, couldn't I tell because Father was quite annoyed about the article and said something about that "Jewish business again." When we finally opened it up and started to read, it was quite late and the ship was pitching awfully and the candle kept going out, at which point Cecily said it was very confusing and boring, and if Vienna was like that she didn't want to go at *all,* and she kept falling asleep and finally lay back under the covers, but I read on and on far into the night about this place that seemed almost like a fairy tale except it was real.

That night I dreamt of circuses and kings, and toward morning I had a terrifying dream that lions were loose and eating everyone up. Although Timothy always seemed to be interested in *dreams* he wasn't interested in my dream at all and simply said it was from eating too much dessert or possibly due to the motion of the sea. I personally thought that Timothy was overly aware of the motion of the sea as he had spent the entire morning with the camera he had gotten as a graduation present and it kept rolling so he couldn't get any pictures and I was glad.

Later that morning I went to look for Aunt Ida, who had a book on dreams and symbols, and she told me she would look it up because she thought it was very special. And I felt better immediately. I thought the nicest thing about Aunt Ida was that she was the kind of person who wanted to ride bicycles and would read about science and marriage and Lenin and yet she always knew the silly things that made you feel better like how to interpret dreams and tea leaves.

8

Captain Voll was extremely upset this morning. The emperor? Why the emperor? How had such a thing happened that now the emperor wanted to be told of every aspect of the investigation? "Keep it out of the papers," he had ordered Voll. Of course, Berggasse would be kept quiet. He would do what was necessary. But rumors of Jewish ritual murder were rampant. Two Jews were badly beaten just off the Lindenstrasse last night. He knew that the emperor had sent for Count Badeni[1] early this morning.

[1] Badeni, who was Prime Minister in 1897, was sympathetic to the Jewish cause in Vienna. He persuaded the emperor, who was no enthusiast of Lueger, not to confirm him for mayor. This had the unfortunate side effect of requiring a new election of the city council, which added four more seats for anti-Semites. The anti-Semites combined with various political parties during the late nineteenth century and the liberals were finally defeated. The complexity of anti-Semitism can be seen in special studies of the period, most notably Steven Beller, *The Jews of Vienna,* and P. G. Pulzer, *The Rise of Political Anti-Semitism in Germany and Austria.* Mark Twain's account, in *Harper's* which Aunt Ida read on the crossing, gives some indication of the total bedlam that reigned in parliament.

PART III
THE
WOMAN
IN THE
DANUBE

1

The morning light had come and gone on the Danube now, and the river, covered with snow, lay like a soft satin ribbon, still beneath the moon. The snow sparkled in a fine powdery mist that rose like confetti as the winds swirled down from the mountains into the freezing valley. The sudden, icy drop had turned the days of rain into a blizzard of sleet and ice. The wayfarers who dared this way on foot moved in slow, snow-covered processions, like parades of frosted shrouds. White coaches and horses, manes frozen with ice, sought shelter in inns along the way. At the river's edge, travelers were stopped in their journeys.

That night, when the storm had cleared, a few intrepid walkers ventured forth. Along the previously snow-clouded trail, the clarity of the skies seemed to them now a benign presence—the sparkling light, the white round moon just above the horizon, and the night, brilliant with stars in a blue-black sky. The travelers reassured, returned to their inns, full of laughter and good spirits, shaking the snow from their shoes. That night they slept, safe in their beds, secure in the thoughts of clear bright days ahead. Yet beneath and within this frozen beauty, another tale unfurled. Sparkling, still and cold, the river's surface gave no clue to the story it held hostage as the water plunged on, taking with it, far, far down, an unseen body to the sea.

The coarse sack was tied at the head and feet, and yet that night, by chance, an opening occurred, and through this tear, like jewels from a pocket, six stones fell, unweighting the murderer's plan. The corpse, now freed, floated upwards in its long solemn passage. And then the night grew bitter, the wind howled forth again, snapping the trees from their roots; the ice on the river burst into a new thickness. And the wind bore down, hurling the trees, shattering the branches. Amputated trunks, grotesque and tilted, lay by the river's edge. Piling higher and higher, stick upon stone, the dam awaited the shrouded tide. Hours passed. Deep down beneath the ice, the body traveled on, the feet, still tied, moved past, and then the legs as well, until the torso slipped beneath two limbs, which, falling, held her prey.

But nature, unlike society, did not permit such easy confiscation of its own; a new surge swelled the river then, sweeping the branches from their spot, ripping the shroud as well. And into this rip long blonde hairs escaped. Tendrils flailing, fine filaments spewed forth, unwinding, sprawling upwards like a vine, meshing with weeds and grass and decaying roots until they hit the ice, and held; freezing to the spot. Firm proof now, locked just beneath the surface, waiting, only waiting, for the thaw.

2

Perhaps it wasn't too late. Martha and Minna pulled and pushed until the big chair covered the spot. It was heavy and they were both sweating.

"I think the chair looks much better there," Martha said.

"Oh yes," Minna said. She still had a wild look in her eye.

3

In Paris Henry James swung his legs over the side of the bed. As his feet hit the cold floor, he instantly drew them back, shivering.

As much as he admired the fine woodworking in the walls of the downstairs room in Edith Wharton's house on the rue de Varenne, at this moment he regretted his equal enthusiasm for the travertine marble floors. They were mercilessly cold. It was still dark, and he realized at once that he had awakened in a dream. Ever since his return from America, *and* Constance Fenimore Woolson's death, he had been unable to sleep. Upon news of her dying, he had rushed to Venice and reclaimed any insinuating evidence. Yet he could not rest. He felt the old fear rise up in him again. Then he felt his nightshirt. It was soaked.

He yanked it off and realized for a shocked moment that he had absolutely no clothes on. He fell back instantly beneath the covers, trembling. It was so embarrassing to him somehow to be lying there with *nothing* on, even though he knew no one could possibly see through the roof. Not even God. He imagined sometimes, as if he were a child, God's gaze penetrating the roof, the ceiling, through all the covers, focusing on Henry's own naked body, and necessarily, therefore, on its most exposed point. There was a terrible wind whistling through the house now. Then he remembered.

There were screams elsewhere in the house last night. He had been awakened by them just after midnight. He could see the clock by the candle he'd lit, and he'd heard Edith, he was sure, screaming. The servant assured him that it was nothing, that everything would be all right. A short time after that, his own cries had awakened the servants again. Even in the dark, his face burned at the thought. He knew, of course, why he was upset. It was the murder. He had constant thoughts about the murder. Surely no one would find out. Not even the maid knew. At least he didn't think so. And the gardener wouldn't find the body because he'd put it in the trash. So he was safe. It was of no consequence. But now, now the nightmares.

All because of that dreadful Dr. Freud and his endless questions. He looked at the clock and then again to the windows. It was a very cloudy day and not as early as he had thought. He lay back in his bed and reached for his trousers. He would have to get dressed under the covers. It was undignified, but it was also very cold.

He had told that doctor he had come about his sister Alice. He had meant only to discuss Alice, Alice and her maladies, to see if the doctor would see her, and then the doctor had started with all those questions. Dreadful questions, he thought. And now he was having those dreams again. Dreams about Fenimore. And Italy. And *the murder.* He had quite forgotten about the murder, or at least he thought he had forgotten, but now, the nightmares.

In the midst of that thought, he realized he had another dilemma. His behind was cold. He desperately wanted to get the pants on, but· as he was lying on his back, he found it difficult to raise his rump sufficiently to pull the pants up over it. He realized he would have to roll over in the bed, under the covers, and then jackknife his behind up under the coverlet and pull the pants up and over his rear side while his face lay nearly suffocating in the pillow.

He was pleased when he finally managed to do just that. Once the pants were on, he managed to sit up, drop the covers, and pull on his sweater. Now, dressed, he threw back the coverlet and placed his legs on the floor where his feet, like a pianist's hands at the keyboard, moved an octave on his left, then on his right, to find his shoes.

He knew that he must hurry because the indomitable Edith would be awake early, sitting in bed scratching away at her writing on the huge tablet. How she worked! He really couldn't imagine sitting there in *bed* for three or four hours every morning tossing your manuscript pages onto the floor, where the maid—good heavens, the maid— picked them up and scurried into the next room to bring them to the typist. He wondered if he could ever make as much from his writing as Edith did if he had the abandon to toss the papers on the floor and send them off to the typist. And then the thought vanished. Of course, he could entertain such a thought only if he wanted to be *common*— not that Edith was actually a common writer, but, hers wasn't the same as his own work, absolutely no comparison, he had to acknowledge that. And besides, he'd rather taken to his new dictation method.

He planned to be out early in order to go and see Dr. Freud again.

He didn't want to run into Edith. She totally disapproved of Freud. He'd wind up telling her more than he intended. There was something about indomitable women; he always ended up entrusting confidences to them, something he didn't want to do.

He wondered now if he should ever have listened to that seemingly wonderful American woman, Miss Ida Main, who had recommended the doctor in the first place. He had been dulled, he felt, by the enchantress of the day. That utterly charming young girl Cecily, with a bold and impetuous spirit that boded nothing but great difficulties, had captivated him for hours as they went apple picking. Then in the evening, as he strolled about the veranda with Miss Ida Main, he found her conversation most radical, and stimulating. He saw at once that she was one of those women—the French were now calling them suffragettes—whom he tried to avoid at all costs. Ever since he'd written *The Bostonians* they told him he had put them in a terrible light. Yet there was nothing strident in Ida Main's manner, and her conversation was most *dramatic* and often inspired. He remembered standing in the shadow of a large hemlock that overhung the porch, as she told him of a theory of history by a Professor Bachofen, an anthropologist who had scientifically documented that women, once a powerful military species, living in hordes, had actually ruled the earth. His eyes rolled at the thought of these Amazon women. He didn't know whether he was fascinated or appalled, but it gave him a rather peculiar feeling, even now when he thought of it, almost what he might be given to call, if he hadn't been so shocked, a kind of visceral pleasure.

Then he caught and held his breath. He heard a step and feared it might be Edith Wharton on the stair.

4

I believe I met your wife in Vienna," the Countess, lying on the couch, said to Dr. Freud.

He raised his brows.

"She was at this herbalist I go to, for certain treatments."

"My wife does not go to herbalists," he said, "so it was not she. But tell me your thoughts."

"I thought I overheard Didi saying it was an herb for making you forget."

"Is it possible you *imagined* this?" he said.

"No—well, it is possible."

"Is there something connected to this event that you would like to forget, such as that I have a wife?"

The Countess grimaced. He flattered himself, she thought, and went on to her next thought.

5

Henry James stood across the street from the apartment house on the Ile Saint-Louis where the doctor was staying. He had watched the woman with the pink and white parasol enter only an hour before. He checked his watch and began to pace up and down the street. This time he knew he had evaded Mrs. Wharton. He looked up at the door again. The Viennese doctor was visiting Paris for only two weeks now, they said. Henry James began to perspire and took his gloves off. When the woman left, he was determined to cross the street and go in there.

He began to pace. The impact of what he had done seized him anew every day. He thought he understood the criminal mind now more clearly than ever before. He felt that same prickling sensation at the bottom of his spine just thinking of what he'd done, he felt the warm neck in the palm of his hand, and he was shocked at the pleasure the memory brought him—to imagine that he, who had begun to feel he had no access to *actions,* had simply responded, taken the action, quite literally, into his hands, had become, for a brief instant, an animal yielding to its most primitive impulse. It thrilled him to think of it. To act, to engage physically, had been transforming. It had shocked him. He had felt vigorous, alive, as if silencing forever all of his oppressors in one swift move. An energy had moved him almost to song. And then later, he had been shocked, ashamed, chagrined; he'd realized what he had done to a helpless animal.

He knew he had always been drawn to murder of course. Crimes of passion. But only as an observer. The case of Madeleine Smith had first intrigued him as a child. Clearly a murder, and *she* got off. And properly so. Of course, to think of a crime of passion was ludicrous in comparison to this small single act... of mercy, one might say, or could say, couldn't one? He thought the creature was dying, struggling, yes, that must have been it. He reached up and ran his index finger around the inside of his collar. It seemed intolerably tight to him all of a sudden. He looked at his watch again. The woman had been in there a good long time. Perhaps it was *her* first visit. He remembered his, in Vienna . . .

'' I have come to see you," Henry James said, "concerning the matter of my sister."

The doctor looked at him so intensely that James was taken aback.

"She has suffered for some time from exhaustion, from weakness, from invalidism, is quite ill, and Dr. Marlowe in America recommended you see her. I thought perhaps I should meet with you myself, before you, that is, if you did agree to, see her yourself."

He suddenly felt strange and awkward. The startling notion occurred to him that he was shy. The doctor studied him, he thought, rather than looked at him in a normal way, then motioned him to a chair, and very professionally took up a long piece of paper and a pen.

"Your sister's age?" Henry winced. He did not wish to be interrogated; he had come to speak.

"Oh, twenty-three," he said.

"Tell me about your mother and your father."

Henry was startled. "Tell *you?* They were fine people, of course. My father was a great scholar, in some ways a difficult man to be sure. I have, however, come about my sister and . . ."

"It is important for me to have as much information about the family as possible. Let us begin with your father." The doctor's voice had lowered. He had seen something. Henry, sensing this and resenting it, drew himself up to his fullest, most formal posture and began to relate some telling and hopefully flattering anecdotes about his father. He had not got far when he found it rather more difficult than he had thought. To his considerable annoyance, the doctor kept asking about events in *his childhood.* He could not, indeed, keep his mind focused on the reason he had come, and he was beginning to think that perhaps he should not recommend Alice to the doctor at all, when in the midst of a rather difficult story he was telling about William, how William up until that year had always been the superior one, and how . . .

The doctor interrupted, "I think you loved your father very much," and this expression, just then, so softly put, completely, and to his utter astonishment, undid him. To his immense shame tears fell from his eyes, and he had to retrieve his handkerchief.

Throughout this display, the doctor said nothing. The silence wrapped around Henry like an excruciating chain. He thought his chest would burst, and this wretch, this medical fraud, sat there, enjoying, he was certain, *enjoying his humiliation.*

"I really must leave, I am quite overcome, so sorry to have taken your time," Henry said, standing, wiping his eyes, voice trembling, and the doctor, pushing his chair back quickly— Henry noted again what a small man he was—said, "You should not be ashamed to weep for your father. A child who does not feel loved *must* weep." This, to his chagrin, made the chain seize him further; the room began to reel.

"Sit down, here," the doctor ordered. To his surprise, he obeyed as the room spun into blackness.

And now the doctor was in Paris.

Of course he did not want to come. But here he was now, pacing up and down outside the large doors to the building courtyard on the Quai de Bourbon, clutching the piece of paper and watching the movements of visitors. He was undecided: he would do this for Alice's sake; he would do nothing for Alice's sake. He ventured down a side street, paused in front of the house and then returned. He did this three times.

Should he go in there, or shouldn't he? He must, if only to clear this matter once and for all, persuade the doctor that . . . He felt a trembling in his body, and as he stepped into the street, he recalled the painful ending of his last visit, remembered those red walls as he recovered from his faint.

W H E N he opened his eyes, he saw the doctor sitting quietly, smoking his cigar. He sat up. "I am so sorry," he said, "I—I must have collapsed from weakness . . . my journey . . . the water . . ."

"You do not recall what you have said to me?" the doctor asked, looking at him in that strange way he had. Eyes so dark they seemed to pierce into you. Yet he had been kind when James had felt faint.

"Why, no," Henry James said, wonderingly. "I . . . I have no recall of having spoken to you at all."

The doctor looked at him sharply.

"Does the word *vastation* mean anything to you at all?" the doctor said. Henry felt the blood leave his face. What had he said, what *had* he said—he must have been delirious.

"You told me," the doctor said, "about your father. The word you used was vastation."

"Yes . . . my—my father . . . I must have told you my father . . . suffered at times . . . from great despair. . . . He called such times, his 'vastations.' "

Henry felt tired. He had never felt so tired. He slumped against the chair.

"You are tired," the doctor said. "The recollection of these episodes with your father has been exhausting for you. Perhaps we can continue another time. Perhaps you would prefer that."

"No!" Henry said at once and too sharply. "That is, I see no need for *me* to come again . . . I am asking you to treat my sister. I—I have no need for a doctor. I am in good health."

"You complained you did not sleep, when you fainted," the doctor said. "You mentioned, when describing your sister, that she was fatigued, but you remarked she did not suffer with her stomach the way you did, although, you also stated you had been to a physician, and there was no organic cause for your difficulties in eating. It is possible that both your insomnia and your dyspepsia are nervous disorders which have their origins in some disturbing memory you have of your father that has been pushed away, that you do not wish to recall. It is my belief that if you can recall it, with my help, we can *remove* the memory, we can eliminate the dyspepsia and the insomnia with it."

Henry listened to him, almost speechless for once. Did this man really think he was going to discuss his most personal feelings with him, a total stranger? From the expectant look on the doctor's face, he apparently did.

"I see," James said, recovering and smoothing his gloves. "That is, of course, very interesting. However, I really think I am fine. Quite fine. If you would like to know more about my sister, if it is in some way critical to your decision about whether to accept her or not, I will be happy to supply you with more information, although perhaps another time. I am not feeling too strong. I have just got back from Venice, changes in the water often make me weak."

"You mentioned Venice while you were faint," the doctor said.

Henry felt the skin stretch taunt across the back of his neck. "I did? While I slept?" A brief flurry of panic went through him. "Did you hypnotize me, is that it, have you . . . ?"

"No!" the doctor said firmly.

"What did I say? I insist you tell me what I said!" He had, in his excitement, jumped up and grabbed the doctor by the lapel. This was so uncharacteristic he found himself staring at the startled doctor's face as he himself stared at his own hand upon the lapel.

"I—I beg your pardon," he said, immediately releasing the lapel. "It—it was most disturbing. A friend, a close friend, has died."

"Miss Woolson," the doctor said, "I believe you said her name was Miss Constance Fenimore Woolson."

Henry James looked at him, stricken. Fenimore. He had told him about Fenimore! Henry sat down on the couch again, perspiration coating his hands, his neck, his brow. He could see her now, dancing in the air before him; he could feel the sweat seeping through his shirt, thought, in fact, that the cold sweating furnace of his body would burst through his tweed jacket and leave a large spot, drenched, across his back.

"You *must* tell me what I said. I was quite delirious . . . I, it was most disturbing . . ." He had taken the handkerchief now, wiped his brow, and, the doctor noted, was twisting it and untwisting it mindlessly in his hands.

"You called her name," the doctor said, "Fenimore . . . Fenimore . . . forgive me, you said." Henry leaned forward, tensed, as the doctor, having turned away from him, stood with his back to him, in front of a window, until Henry could stand the tension no more and said, "What else—did I say *anything else?*" His voice sounded loud in his ears. The sun had come out and was getting stronger now.

"Yes," the doctor said, turning, the light from behind casting a weird shadow on his face. At that moment, his beard black and pointed, he looked to James like Lucifer as he said, "Yes, you said she was dead. That you had killed her."

6

"Another woman reported missing," Lieutenant Stekal said to Captain Voll, "a French dressmaker, Mme. Pacquin. Looks like another suicide, a drowning. They found her jewelry by the shore. What's strange is it's the same shop where a mannequin left a note saying she'd returned to Paris, but Madame never accepted that; was very upset, she believed the girl had met with foul play."

"Are you sure it's the same shop?" Voll asked.

"Yes," Stekal replied. "I remember Mme. Pacquin came here herself and reported it. She was concerned about the girl. And now *she's* gone."

"She came *here?* How is it you didn't tell me this?" Captain Voll demanded.

Stekal was surprised at the irritation in his voice. "It was just a routine missing person. We get so many. . . . I filed a report, I saw no need to mention it."

"I see," Captain Voll said. "Did she ask you anything else? Mme. Pacquin?"

Stekal furrowed his brow, "No, sir." He felt somewhat sheepish about this. She had actually asked to speak to the captain, but as he wasn't in, Stekal decided he was perfectly capable of making a report.

"Well we'll look into it of course," Voll said.

He returned to the Freud case. He noted that the group of visitors to Freud's house that week included that strange Jew he'd heard about —Herzl was his name, and he was planning on doing something with baptizing all the Jews in St. Stephens.[1] Herzl lived not far from Freud. Voll thumbed though the diary wondering if there was any evidence of an earlier visit.

7

The Inspector was thinking.

Due to his illness the Inspector had been unable to confront Dr. Freud directly and had required his aide, Lieutenant Cuvée, to visit him and advise him of events. He had expected the doctor to express, at the very least, shock and dismay at such a dramatic series of occurrences in his own home. Instead, he refused to be interviewed. Cuvée had come to the Inspector's bedside, twirling the dark blue policeman's hat in his hand in an agitated manner.

"Well, did you see him?"

"Yes," replied Lieutenant Cuvée, looking extremely uncomfortable.

"And?"

"Most uncooperative."

---

[1] Prior to Herzl's publication of *Der Judenstadt: An Attempt at a Modern Solution to the Jewish Question,* he formulated some strange solutions to the "Jewish question." These solutions ranged from a recommendation for fighting duels, to a proposal for a mass baptism of all the Jews, to be held in St. Stephen's cathedral. Such proposals were indicative not only of Herzl's naiveté, but of the difficult dilemmas facing an assimilated Jewish intellectual living and working in Paris and Vienna. It is important to note that Herzl was desperately trying to eliminate "difference"—especially for his *children's* generation. Herzl exempted himself from the baptism plan. It is important to remember that assimilated Jews themselves felt enormously "different" from the poorer Jewish immigrants flooding in from Galicia, who were known as the "Ostjuden."

"What did he say?" asked the Inspector.

"He said it was quite ridiculous. He said it was all nonsense. He denied there was a murder at all," said Lieutenant Cuvée, looking up in astonishment. "He said that all of them, the women—were suffering from hysteria."

It was a strange case, this one; one which required rather unorthodox procedures. Although Captain Voll had been cooperative, the Inspector felt frustrated by this failure to locate a body. In any event, he was drawing up a list of suspects in his own mind and Freud was first among them. It was easy enough to take the train to Vienna, commit the murder, and return to Paris. It struck him as a very meaningful coincidence that the doctor had dismissed his housemaid for precisely those two days. The day before and the day after the murder.

The Inspector believed it best that he take this Dr. Freud by surprise. He was going to a party this evening at Dr. Charcot's, and he planned to confront him there. In the morning he would travel to Vienna. He looked uneasily in the mirror as Violette straightened his jacket and he caught the look in her eyes. Her look of longing moved him, not to pride, but to overwhelming feelings of inadequacy. Violette knew she was beaming with joy as she looked at him. Such a fine figure of a man, she sighed to herself, and tonight so elegant. And he was hers.

Or, as hers as he might be for the moment or as long as he might stay. He had told her that he loved her but that it was a fault in his nature, or a limitation of his character, that he loved many women and always had. That he would not under any condition confine himself solely to her affections had been his brief from the beginning. And yet, Violette mused, it was not as if he were a flirt. And he had lived with her now for over two years. But she knew the time would come when he would, as he said, find it necessary to move on. She tried not to think of it as she brushed down his lapel.

"You are not well enough, but I know you wish to go," she said.

"I am well enough," he replied. "It is important. He will not be expecting me, and a surprise interview provides the best information."

"Well," she said, "you look very elegant."

"I invited you to join me."

She shook her head. "I wouldn't know how to talk to those people," she said quietly. The Inspector picked up his cape with the white silk lining and threw it over his arm.

As he eased himself into the hall he ran straight into Marie-Thérèse, who was nursing her baby on the stair.

"Ho!" he said, "I nearly stepped on the two of you. Why are you out here?"

"It is so cold in my apartment," Marie-Thérèse said. "There is a driving wind." The Inspector saw she was wrapped in blankets.

"Well, go inside," he said, pointing to Violette's apartment.

"I . . ." She looked up at him. "No, you cannot."

"I can," he said to her. "Go inside." He turned and unlocked the door. "Go," he said, shooing her in. Her large eyes looked at him. "I am so grateful," she said. "I do not understand why you work for the police."

The Inspector shrugged. "No one else will hire me." Violette had come to the door. "Do not worry," he said to her. "Good night."

He was touched by their concern. They were worried about his reputation. He had been brought before the police tribunal only months ago on a long list of charges, courtesy of his enemy, M. Dumas, and that vile little priest, Boudoin.

Dumas had with great officiousness and drama read off a list of the "heinous crimes" committed by the Inspector. The crimes included corresponding—and the word was meaningfully enunciated—with prostitutes, cavorting with lesbians, having coffee with anarchist-socialists, fraternizing with homosexuals and communists, and committing a host of other indiscretions. The Inspector's reply to the horrified faces of the jury was, "He forgot to mention that I am also invited to the best parties in Paris," and he gave a little bow.

Of course, that infuriated Dumas and Boudoin all the more. It was a sore point with Dumas, who had social pretensions, that the Inspector managed to mingle with all of the artists and low-lifes (as he would have it), of Montmartre, and at the same time be invited into the most exclusive salons on the rue St. Honoré.

Thinking of this the Inspector walked toward the cab, enjoying the play of light from the street lamps on the thinly falling snow. He concluded that he had handled the tribunal well. "An investigation depends on information," he had said simply. "The more people one knows, and trusts, the more information one has. Murders are committed in societies. One has to know the society. Whatever I do, I do because it is necessary."

"Is there no limit to what is necessary?" asked Leroux, a particularly hostile questioner.

"No limit," said the Inspector without hesitation.

"But surely there are societies," said Leroux, "to which even the Inspector has no access? For example, unless you have the habit of dressing as a female, which as far as I can tell you have not so far exhibited, you might finally have met your match if there were a murder in a harem."

"Short of supplying services to the sheik," the Inspector had replied with a little bow, "I can assure you I would do whatever was necessary to solve the crime." His boldness had caused great laughter and the inquiry, which had begun with much scandal, eventually faded.

The Inspector had been to Charcot's house many times before. He had met in the course of the years every celebrity who was part of Parisian life or whoever might be visiting it. This included the grand dukes of Russia, Cardinal Lavigerie, his own prefect, Lépine, Cernvishci, the art collector. And there was always a host of political leaders as well as artists, architects, and writers.

As for Charcot's "afternoons," the Inspector had seen the same demonstrations too many times not to suspect the *hystériques* of pretending. The glee with which they snapped up pieces of coal in their mouths upon being told they were chocolate, the way Isabel, the most reliable one, always bent over backward in the famous "*arc-en-ciel*," which excited the gentlemen no end, and then lifted her skirts to an alarming height when thrown a glove, which she imagined was a snake, seemed to him rehearsed.

He had no doubt that some of the girls were genuinely disturbed, as much by the constant hypnotic suggestion as anything else. Many of them were hypnotized dozens of times a day, bewildered by absurd suggestions. He had seen them crawl on all fours on the floor, barking like dogs, and then rise to "turn into pigeons," flapping their arms as if trying to fly. He suspected Charcot had once been a serious man, but fame, as always in the Inspector's view, had seriously imperiled his original mission. He no longer went to the hospital at all, he saw his patients in his magnificent study at home. And he still—at this the Inspector snorted to himself—resorted to binding women up in the ridiculous "ovarian belts," which allegedly enabled a woman to control her own hysteria.

Charcot was convinced that pressure on the ovaries would start an hysterical attack and also end one, and the belts were allegedly to help a woman control the attacks. The Inspector had walked out once when watching a demonstration involving a young girl whose breasts were being massaged as an example of being both the cause and the cure of her hysterical outburst. The ladies had tittered and hid behind their fans, and the gentlemen had watched the way they watched in private houses or in clubs. The Inspector was furious; this had nothing to do with medicine or science. Clearly the girl was ill and she was being used for entertainment. The next day he sternly recommended to Charcot that he limit his audience to medical students, but Charcot had only smiled and said, "The public has a right to know."

Tonight as the Inspector entered Charcot's glittering salon, he scanned the faces to see who was there. He noted with some amusement that most of the beautiful women of the right bank had gathered appropriately on his right, while the beautiful women of the left bank were on his left. He noted that the only women who appeared from the latter were actresses, so there were far fewer women on the left.

The ladies of the right bank paused for a moment, wine glasses in the air, faces turned toward the door expectantly. As they saw him, each face lit up.

"*Enchanté, ma chérie,*" he said as he kissed hands and cheeks and bowed. He moved through the women like electricity through a wire. It was as if he had touched each of them, and they had come alive. This was precisely what the Countess von Gerzl thought as she watched him move through the room.

"*Bonsoir,*" said the Inspector, at first to all and then softly, quietly, glowingly to each one. Their heads tilted forward, their heads tilted back, some faces bent down, others threw their eyes to the sky showing new expanses of neck, but it was clear that someone special had entered. The Inspector murmured as he bent to kiss hands, *"Enchanté, madame, bonsoir,"* his eyes raising occasionally to meet the very special ones in a very special gaze.

"Really," said the Countess de Noailles, who was *not* one of them, "it is said that the Inspector is utterly fatal to women." This was said with a mixture of envy and regret as, alas, the Inspector had never been "fatal" to her. She had been bolder than she ever dared be with anyone, and the Inspector had positively but politely ignored her.

The gossip was that the Inspector's father was a baron, but the Inspector had renounced the title after his father's death, sold off the land holdings in France and Austria, lived off the money and invested the rest. "His mother was a Jewess," people said with a mixture of curiosity and critique. She was a beautiful, well-educated woman who had married the baron when she was only sixteen and died mysteriously when only twenty-five. Some said the Inspector had invested a considerable portion of his funds with the Jewish merchants. Others said he invested it in the fur industry in America, where apparently even *women* were wearing furs. Thus the Inspector spoke French, Italian, English, and German, all expertly. He was extremely well educated, so it was to everyone's surprise that he accepted a special appointment to the Paris police department and in a short period of time (some said it was because he read some stories appearing in the *Strand* magazine about a man called Sherlock Holmes), established such a reputation for ingenuity that people claimed there had never been a crime the Inspector could not solve.

"I'd like to meet this Dr. Freud," the Inspector said, coming up to Dr. Charcot. "Has he arrived yet this evening?"

"Oh yes, a charming fellow, quite a wit, but too serious, a pity. It seems a problem arose just minutes ago." Charcot looked disappointed. "I saw you arrive and told him I wanted him to meet you, that you were a brilliant psychologist yourself, but he felt unwell, and left just minutes after you arrived."

This annoyed the Inspector and increased his determination to interrogate Freud. It was only moments until a beautiful baroness touched his arm and asked if he intended to dance with her. As he whirled onto the floor, he was for one of the few moments in his life utterly innocent of a pair of yellow eyes that were following him with more than casual interest.

8

Edith decided to confront Henry on his walk through the Jardins du Luxembourg. She ran straight up to him as he paced up and down with a totally preoccupied air. Upon seeing her, he seemed to flush and then hustle—positively hustle—her away from the spot, his hand firmly under her elbow as she turned her head once again to get a clear impression of the house fixed in her mind. What was Henry hiding? Who was in that house?

"There is a charming little tea room I've discovered not far away I do so want to show you," he said, speaking quickly. "Whatever are you doing here? I know you've been at *Les Quatres Vents* buying books again. I was there just moments ago." He spoke with such nervous urgency that she stopped him in the street.

She turned to him suddenly. "Henry, if you are ill, I am your friend. You must tell me. You can always stay in my house as long as need be. You *know* that. There is no reason for you to return to London next week."

"Oh," he paled and looked stricken, "but I *must.* That is," he paused, having revealed too much, she thought. "I simply *must.*"

When they had seated themselves in the tea room and ordered, Edith peered slowly over the edge of her cup at Henry. There he was again, staring into space.

"You may as well know," she said, "I am very concerned about you and I can't keep a secret from you any longer. I went to see that terrible Dr. Freud, and I . . ."

She got no farther.

"What!" he said. His cup dropped to the floor with a crash. He leapt up as if there were fire all around him. "Oh my," he said. "Oh dear, did he tell you anything? Oh my." He was sweating *profusely.*

"He wasn't in," she said.

Henry turned to her, "He told you *nothing,* are you certain?" His eyes had a glaze over them. It frightened her.

"Nothing," she said, pulling back. "Henry, I really think you should stay on rather than return to London. You need the *rest.*"

"It is very kind, most generous to offer, and you know how much I would love to stay," he said, "but I have some pressing matters in London . . ."

"What pressing matters?" It was a bit rude of her, she reflected later, to press the matter so, but his vagueness and constant apprehension were driving her mad. "Well, what is it?" she said, as surprised as he by her persistence. "Henry! I must speak! Something is disturbing you and . . ."

He turned on his heel and walked out. She was stunned. He had never before walked out on her in the middle of a conversation.

Later, at home, as she was stoking the fire, she began to realize that he had no sense he had walked out in the middle of a conversation. He had meant simply to get away from the question, from her, from restraint of any sort. Something was haunting him and he was not about to tell her what it was.

9

As the judge pounded the gavel for a adjournment and Fullerton leapt like a gazelle toward the front of the room in order, Herzl was certain, to attend to the lady in the lace dress who had glanced his way several times, Herzl saw the note that dropped from Fullerton's pocket. It was blowing toward the rear of the room. He excused himself hurriedly and raced for it. It must, he thought, be another one of those letters from the woman called Katharine.

He walked quickly down the street and into a small cafe, sat down, and unfolded the crisp pages and smelled the heady perfume. Compulsively he read the lines, his heart imagining the letter was addressed to him:

My dearest Morton,

How I long for you. Now that the news is out, I cannot but tell you all the years I have lived with this love flooding my heart, my soul, my mind. I have been reckless with desire. How wrong I thought it was! What mishappen creature must I be to feel such disgusting things for you. But they are not disgusting, they are the true unbridled passions of my soul. They are my true self, and they wait now only for you and your return. Oh, write to me, I implore you. Any news at all will vanquish the desperate neediness of my soul. I cannot believe the news! I am saved at last!

He stopped reading and glanced about him in the cafe. He was most embarrassed at the thought that anyone, particularly Fullerton, might have witnessed this. What news did the woman have of Fullerton, he wondered? Not, he hoped for her, that he was a reliable or honorable man. He was *not*. Of this Herzl was sure.

He glanced around once more and saw Inspector LeBlanc, but his eyes were on the table in front of him. Herzl breathed a sigh of relief; the Inspector was engrossed. What, Herzl asked himself, was he *studying* so carefully?

When Amboise in the police division had returned the sketch of Dr. Freud, the Inspector had recognized the face at once. He had actually spoken to the man at one of Charcot's "afternoons." He remembered it clearly now.

It was just after one such a performance that he had met Dr. Freud in the vestibule. He remembered his impression—ambitious, charming, and very witty. And something else, something incalculable, a kind of demonic drive that could, if given the proper occasion, or so the Inspector thought at the time, produce a startling success. He had seen nothing in that brief encounter to suggest a criminal mind. Freud was driven but not desperate, an important difference. Perhaps all the difference in the end.

He reached into his pocket and pulled out one of his favorite Spanish cigars, Rojo Havana. He lit it, leaned back in his chair and relaxed, trying to ignore the woman in the lace dress. The woman, clearly an aristocrat, had been following him, obviously, for the past several days. She was a most attractive woman, and he suspected her interests were professional. A lover in difficulty perhaps. He earnestly hoped so. He had not enjoyed the look of appreciation in her eyes when unexpectedly he turned to face her. It was a look he knew well. Women, countless women had given him such a look and more. And at this moment, in his fatigue, he longed only to escape from them.

He had observed Theodor Herzl at a far table behaving strangely, trying to secrete a letter he had just read, and wondered on the far edges of his mind exactly what that foretold. Herzl was deeply upset over the Dreyfus case, indeed over the entire issue of the Jews. He was a most impressive person, and not one likely to be involved in intrigue. Yet it was clear he was hiding *something*.

There were days when the Inspector thought that absolutely *everyone* was hiding something.

10

In his rooms, Herzl let the perfumed letter from Katharine drop to the floor as he felt his heart burst with envy. Envy at the passion Fullerton provoked from this woman. He was ashamed he was reading the letters, and yet they moved him strongly. He felt a part of him reach out and yearn to touch this Katharine whose honesty was so overwhelming to him.

My dearest Morton,

I must speak what is within my heart, which has been stopped up all these many years. Only now it feels free to break and rush over its limits to describe to you the ecstasy of my love, my incredible yearning. . . .

He could read no more.[1] What had happened to break this dam of inhibition? What person would dream of such honesty? He lay awake

---

[1] Whether Herzl's fierce attachment to his sister had any effect on his interest in this letter, which he must have known was from Morton's sister, who had just discovered she was adopted, and that therefore her erotic attachment was freed for expression, is simply a matter of speculation.

that night, moved by her passion, her self-knowledge, and feeling himself like some mere mote, an accident of history, who knew nothing of himself or his own heart.

He lay there suddenly informed by a sadness he found unspeakable.

He drifted into sleep, and dreamt the dreams of Dreyfus, his face red as the commandant tore the stripes from his uniform, tearing from him the last shred of patriotic faith in his countrymen, while Dreyfus stood, eyes to the front, unmoving in the midst of his humiliation. And the shouts and obscenities had risen from the courtroom—"Kill the Jew, the dirty Jew." And then Herzl stood next to him in the docket while the commandant, who was now Paul von Portheim, said to him, "Not you, Herzl, we don't mean *you*," while all around him he heard the screaming "Kill the Jew, Kill the Jew," and von Portheim, smiling, pointed his finger at Herzl, saying, "We don't mean *you*," and his finger turned into a gun and exploded in Herzl's eye.[2]

He woke up screaming.

11

The Countess was worried. The anarchists whom she had foolishly supported were in terrible trouble now in Paris, and she was certain that Félix Fénéon had set the bomb. Twenty people had been injured at the cafe, she had been shocked to read. She had understood the bomb was to be planted *after* the cafe was closed. She was still shaking at the thought. She would never support violence; this Philippe knew.

---

[2] This dream refers most probably to an earlier incident in Herzl's life. When he discovered an anti-Semitic proclamation, the Waidhofer Resolution, that had been posted in the hall of his fraternity he was shocked. One of his classmates came up and stood beside him and said to him, "We don't mean you of course," but Herzl resigned at once. It was the beginning of Herzl's recognition of the depths of anti-Semitism. He resigned from the fraternity and his classmate, Paul von Portheim, then led an action to prohibit all Jews from joining. Three months later, von Portheim, who said he was "of Jewish extraction," killed himself.

The plan, she knew, had been to make matters better, not worse. Most of the anarchists she had met were incredibly naive idealists. There were always, of course, the violent few, but she had made it clear she would oppose them. Now, there was Philippe's problem.

Word had it, at least word around Montmartre, that this Inspector was sympathetic to certain aspects of the cause. He was reputed to be something of a bohemian and an intellectual, unheard of in a policeman.

The Countess trusted none of the gossip, so she had taken it upon herself to follow him for several days, attempting wherever possible to overhear his conversation. Apparently he had been ill and had only emerged from his house over the last days. Nonetheless she had gained some idea of his habits, which ranged from drinking in dull cafes to balls and soirées. And to think he lived in the center of Montmartre with a woman from the Moulin Rouge.

The Countess smiled to herself. He was clearly a man who inspired affection from the most amazing range of women: everyone from the princess to the prostitute. Philippe had entreated her to protect the anarchists, and above all Philippe.

Yet in light of the deaths from the bombing, she did not know if she *should* fulfill her obligation. But she knew it would be almost impossible for her to resist Philippe.

12

The doctor sat back in his chair and took out a new cigar. He leaned forward, lit it, drew a long slow draught and then blew the smoke, now bluish, into the air. He was particularly struck by something in this woman, the Countess. She had come to him because she suffered from a debilitating compulsion, and occasional but deep depressions, of two to three days' duration, and because she could not bear a child. There were no organic reasons and she had sensed herself that the nightmares which had haunted her all her life might in some way be responsible for her childlessness. He was excited by this case and saw a new opportunity for his treatment. He mused at the odd conjunction of events that had sent her to him.

"The herbalist," she told him, crying, "Didi is her name, said this is too deep for herbs . . . she had heard of you. The Baroness des Champs had come for help . . . she . . ." and then the Countess had broken down.

Her reference made him immediately remember the Baroness des Champs, whom he had treated briefly in Vienna. A strange case. She had given away her illegitimate child prior to her marriage and now, eighteen years later, for reasons they were about to discover, was overwhelmed with guilt. She had taken to obsessively cleaning the glasses and dishes in her house, washing and rewashing them a hundred times a day. He sighed at the thought of it now. He had made a mistake. He had proceeded too quickly and she had broken off treatment suddenly, after three months, just as he felt they were on the edge of an important discovery. She had sent him a note and he had attempted to contact her but received no answer. He often wondered what had happened to her. The case had been frustrating and disappointing because initially he had had remarkable success despite overwhelming opposition from her husband, Dr. Eduard Loeffler, a rather notable anatomist. Loeffler seemed to believe that Freud's psychological approach was pure poppycock, and he had called *The Interpretation of Dreams* a "wildman's dream." The compulsive disorder of washing had ceased, however, upon the baroness' admission to him of the giving up of the child. Nonetheless, the symptom would recur whenever she went to her dressmaker for a fitting. He had no idea what it was at the dressmaker's that might have given stimulus to this memory. He thought of it now and was chagrined that his thoughts had taken him away from the Countess. He heard her now anew.

"And then," she said, "I have to follow them, the men, if they beckon me, and I . . ." She broke down again, awash in shame. He pondered this. The Countess' compulsion to follow strange seductive men, accompanied by the contradiction of both intense erotic desire and an absence of physical sensation, was linked in some way he had yet to discover with the idea of the birth of a child. Her pregnancy fears might be caused by her thoughts that the child would necessarily be female, and if it *were* female, would suffer the same compulsion to which the Countess fell prey. His diagnosis was hysteria, obsessive compulsive disorder, and something more.

Although filled with shame and guilt, the Countess was extremely intelligent. She resisted his suggestions with impeccable logic. It would take him some time to persuade her that logic was only of limited use here. In the meantime they would have to proceed carefully, circling the abyss of her memory, the place that delivered the incessant nightmare, until it delivered it wholly.

"Every night?" he asked. "You have this every night? It wakes you and yet you remember almost nothing?"

"Nothing," she whispered. "Every night I wake up it is as if I am choking on it, throttled by it so I cannot call out, I . . ." And then she was overwhelmed again. It was, he noted, the same pattern in the dream as in her response: intense feeling, sufficient to wake her, then nothing. He was confident nonetheless that he would have success with this treatment.

13

Sometimes in the morning I would open my eyes and see the grey light steal through the window, filtering onto the soft pink covers of Cecily's bed, and then I would look at Cecily sleeping and my heart would stop because my sister when she was sleeping was sometimes so beautiful I couldn't believe that she, in any way, belonged to me. You think of children and husbands and mothers and fathers belonging to you, but not sisters. But when I would look at Cecily like that, I thought oh . . . she does belong to me and look at her, her face so pink as if she had been running in her dreams, the fat black curls, tossed all over her face, the fine blue veins barely visible near her eye, running like faint turquoise rivers beneath her skin, and then her smile, the small, thin heart-shaped mouth would curve upward and then she would roll onto the other side, her face would snuggle further into the pillow, her fist—small, and plump—really, for an otherwise fine-boned, petite person—would grasp the pillows, and she would sigh, and toss again. She must be dreaming, I would think watching her sleep, so struck sometimes by the expression on her face that I thought I was dreaming. And then I would lie back, pull the covers up to my eyes, and fall asleep again.

Once she was up, and dressing, Cecily's face had an altogether different look. It was mischievous, the eyes were bright, but it was a harder, harsher face. When we read about King Arthur, I thought Cecily was like that, putting a visor on for the world. Sometimes I wondered if she thought about which knight she would be. I thought about these things for years and then one day Aunt Ida said, "Why do you think of Cecily as a knight rather than a queen like Guinevere, or a lady like the Lady of the Lake."

"Why? Because," I said quickly, "Cecily is the *rescuer,* she would never *wait* for the knight, don't you *see* that?" I immediately regretted my tone, because I sounded as if it were the most obvious thing in the world and that Aunt Ida had not a brain in her *head,* but I needn't have regretted it because Aunt Ida laughed and clapped her hands with pleasure and said, "Oh, what a clever girl you are." And then she hugged me![1]

14

Henry James had been reluctant to see the doctor. Now he knew why.

"I think," the doctor said, "you will remember now, that afternoon with Miss Woolson." Henry James felt the warm hand on his forehead. Could he? Oh yes, he could. He knew too painfully, much too painfully, everything she had been feeling.

MISS Woolson and Henry James strolled back and forth in front of the painting in the Palazza San Giorno. She wore a hat

---

[1] I feel my scholarly interests require that I note that current, albeit feminist, re-evaluations of Arthurian literature do not construct women, particularly Guinevere, as passive.

made of lavender lace, with a wide brim and had put, quite felicitously, Mr. James thought, a bunch of violets on one side. She cast him sidelong glances that made him think that perhaps she was shy, not a conclusion he might have come to based on her behavior toward him so far. In fact, she had been quite insistent that he accompany her this morning to the museum, not that it was in any ordinary sense a burden, as he found her company quite stimulating, and the morning was, for Venice in October, unusually bright and fine.

Miss Woolson cast a sidelong glance at Henry James and wondered at the excessive heat she felt emanating from his person. He saw her glance, and turned to her imperceptibly and smiled. Did he know? Did he know how hot a person he was? She had been startled by the rather odd fact of Mr. James' radiation, as it were, and had looked at once to his face to see if he were well. Expecting to see a ruddy complexion, she was surprised to note the usual grey, almost ashen tones remained unaffected by what was clearly an excessive body heat. He made no effort to move from her side and as she attempted to analyze the painting before her, listening as she was to the interesting contrast of volume and form here, so like the Ingres they had viewed earlier that week, she found it difficult to gather her thoughts and reply with any degree of charm, or perspicacity. Instead, she felt the vague discomfort and increasing alarm of his physical presence, brought about, she attempted to reason, by the thickness of his wool jacket, and his trousers, as well as his hat, and thought perhaps if he took the hat off—well, she dare not move abruptly away, although she noted that if she stood there too many minutes longer this strange heat, which passed most embarrassingly across the air from his body, would press against hers, and the perspiration had already begun to gather on her brow and across her upper lip. She quickly reached into her bag and pressed the handkerchief across her lips, absorbing the excess moisture hoping he would not think the lesser of her for it.

"It is warm, isn't it?" she said finally, blushing at the same time, "I mean for October," and she walked purposefully then to the window.

"I find it very pleasant," he said agreeably, and turned back to study the painting. He liked the setting for the painting as much as he liked the painting itself. As he stepped away to engage himself in a second look, his glance swept across the marbled floor, the fine, detailed fluting of the Corinthian columns, absurd and at once perfect in the seventeenth-century house, giving rise to a curving ceiling that seemed to hold the paintings on its walls in a most felicitous embrace. Miss Woolson, who had walked to the balcony and stood there, her pale dress outlined against the Grand Canal, a profile, he thought, of a well-dressed middle-aged woman of some means, and considerable purpose, as one could immediately tell from the stance she took against the rail, and then something more, some hidden aspiration, he saw in the tilt of her head and in the change so visible now, from earlier this morning, some tension, as she clasped and unclasped her pocketbook and attempted however discreetly to remove the perspiration from her brow.

Did he not feel it? she wondered. Was it possible that a man of his distinctions, his achievements was not aware of these strange temperature conjunctions that kept arising due to the proximity of their bodies? She thought, although she did not know, that she had actually looked quite fetching this morning, and his comments on her violets seemed to her, although she could not be sure, to say that he was taking additional interest in her, not only as a person, but as a woman. He had not married, Mr. James, but certainly one could not say he was not interested in the company of a charming, and she thought this morning, most particularly attractive woman.

15

The doctor was annoyed at the insistent rapping at the door. Where *was* that maid? When he needed her to be *in,* she was out. When he needed her to be *out,* she was in, interrupting his studies, his patients, his wife, his life. Irina, Irina, Irina. He would fire her if he dared.

Grumbling to himself, he rose from his chair and went to the door. And then he remembered. Of course. Irina was not *here* in Paris, she was back in Vienna. He had momentarily forgotten. Puzzling over this, he approached the door. He expected no one; perhaps it was a letter. He was most disturbed that he had received no letter from Martha. But when he opened the door, the face that met his was a singular one; the sensuous face of a large, rumpled, and handsome man whose eyes just now were full of scrutiny.

"Dr. Freud, I presume?" the Inspector said. "If you would be so kind, I'd like to ask you a few questions."

16

The report on Voll's desk the next morning was alarming. Rumors were rampant that the body taken from Dr. Freud's study had been a young girl, who was killed in a Jewish doctor's house as part of a "ritual murder."[1] Voll grew extremely uncomfortable at reading the report. This was becoming more complicated than he had ever anticipated. It would suit everyone to find a solution *quickly*.

17

Edith Wharton hurried down the rue de Varenne stuffing the pale blue writing paper into her purse. Furs flying from her brocaded coat, she looked like an extremely well-dressed aristocrat in an absolute panic. She excitedly hailed an oncoming Panhard driven by a chauf-

---

[1] The rumors were probably related to a case in Polna, in 1899, in which a shoemaker's apprentice, Leopold Hilsner, was accused of having murdered a nineteen-year-old seamstress in a ritual murder in order to get Christian blood for matzoh. After serving eighteen years Hilsner was pardoned. The case was widely publicized at the time.

feur in a pale grey uniform, who was tooting the horn incessantly. The automobile pulled up alongside her. She climbed in, gesturing to the chauffeur, who got out and allowed her to drive. She turned the car around in the middle of the street and headed east.

Henry James stood outside Freud's office. His gaze was temporarily fixed on the woman with the white parasol with magenta trim who had just entered the house. As he looked up into the light drizzle, a strange cold wind seemed to steal over him. He pulled his elegant brown frockcoat with the velvet collar more closely about him. It seemed impossible for him to forget. He was relieved when his thoughts were interrupted by the bleat of that most astonishing horn as the great metallic Panhard rolled around the corner with Mrs. Wharton driving and Cook, the chauffeur, seated amiably by her side.

"Good heavens," Henry James said, astonished.

"Get in," she said.

He saw at once it was all part of her high good spirits, so with a small, amused grin he stepped upon the running board, his hand to Cook, and leapt aboard.

Although Mrs. Wharton was making an effort to appear in high spirits, she had actually spent a rather sleepless night. She had decided after much hesitation to post another letter, a copy of which she made and kept in her handbag. She had already written William James once, but she felt the matter was becoming quite urgent. She had a sense of impending disaster; that was the only way she could put it. And that telegram didn't help. On the news that morning from the Riviera. About Nietzsche. After years of sorting out the ghosts from the ether, he was, the telegram had advised her, no longer a sane man.

It was that, she supposed, together with her observations about Henry that made the letter so imperative. She had thought up until then that she was living in a perfectly good time. Now, she was no longer sure. It was the turn of the century, and she saw traditions, rules, and lives cracking open in hopes of improvement. But she was no longer sure this was so. And with a delicate constitution like Henry's, well, after what he had said the preceding evening and what she had been able to glean from her friends, there were too many odd things going on. This doctor he intended (secretly, she realized) to see again, for example. Her mind tracked back and forth to Nietzsche, to herself, to Henry James. She sighed. All of Europe knew it, it was a dangerous time. Europe knew it, but people did not. Not even Edith Wharton really knew it. It was the kind of knowing, perhaps, that would come only in the perspective of history. But people sensed it even as they danced madly against it. Which is why she had written the letter.

"*A la droite,*" she said merrily, her scarves flying in the wind as the car tilted on three wheels, and she took the corner mercilessly. Henry James grabbed his hat, and only when they were righted did he let a smile cross his face. Cook suffered Mrs. Wharton's driving with alarm.

18

I should like then," the Inspector said, concluding, the doctor hoped, the interview, "to make a few inquiries of your wife." The doctor blanched almost imperceptibly, and the Inspector, pretending that he did not see it, noted it.

"I see no reason why that should be necessary," the doctor replied in the cold tones he so readily adopted. Ah, the Inspector thought, I have hit the nerve, or possibly, he thought as he finished shaking his match and throwing it into the ashtray, possibly an artery. The doctor was pacing now, more rapidly than usual, in front of the shuttered windows of the office. He found this Inspector odious. He wanted him out immediately. He leaned forward and gripped the edge of the chair, just to keep his temper. The Inspector noticed, but did not mention, that the blood had left the doctor's knuckles, and they were almost glowing white.

"Uhhh...huh," the Inspector said, and the doctor winced. He found this little utterance irritating, as if the Inspector were ruthlessly judging the veracity of the doctor's voice.

"Well, I fully understand you might not think it necessary, but after all, Herr Doktor, with all due respect, you are the doctor, and I am the inspector, and in matters as grave as this, I am afraid I shall have to pursue the inquiry."

"This is preposterous!" Freud exploded. "You have all the information necessary, and you have no indication as far as can be established, that there is any reason for any pursuit of *anything*. You have no body and only conflicting witnesses to an event that in all likelihood did not occur."

"You doubt your own wife's testimony?" the Inspector asked sharply.

"My wife, Inspector, is as subject as any woman to fits of hysteria. Even gentlemen," he shot him a meaningful look, "on occasion have hysteria. I am away; there was a storm. She is very frightened of storms."

"But your sister-in-law," the Inspector said. "She is only afraid of blood, and this she saw."

"She is an insomniac. In a half-alert state anything is possible."

"Your wife, too, saw the blood . . ."

"Saw the blood*stain,* Inspector," he snapped, and then felt himself withdraw. A mistake.

"Yes perhaps old blood . . . why would there be such a dramatic pool of old blood on your carpet, Doctor? You do not do surgery, am I correct? Or is it possible that on occasion you might—"

"I do not do surgery," the doctor said coldly.

"Ah . . . you do no surgery . . ." The Inspector was walking toward the windows, the long coat swinging easily behind him. The Inspector's manner was always calm, even as he drove on relentlessly after his quarry.

"But is it not possible *someone* else there *might* do surgery?" he asked.

Freud sat down. The Inspector noted his change in color. A film of perspiration covered his brow. "Inspector, I am afraid this interview is over. Neither myself nor any members of my family are available to you for this preposterous inquiry. Good morning."[1]

The Inspector looked at the doctor without a trace of rancor. "Ah," he said, "that is most unfortunate." He took his hat and walked toward the door, then paused.

"I regret to inform you, Herr Doktor, that I shall obtain the neces-

[1] Freud's tension here is understandable because it is likely that he would have realized that Fliess' faulty operation of Emma's nose could be publicized by the discovery of the blood on the floor.

sary papers and will present them to you, and you will, I fear, be obliged to answer further questions. It will also be necessary to make inquiries of both your wife and your sister-in-law in Vienna. It is my duty to inform you, Herr Doktor, that there is something amiss here. It may be, as you suggest, an event only in the minds of your wife and your sister-in-law, but in all likelihood there was a stimulus to those minds that remains unexplained. It is my obligation and my desire to make myself more familiar with those minds, in order to trace the reality of the events. You see, if the event does not describe itself, it is my task to describe it for others in order that they may see it. Good morning, Herr Doktor." The Inspector put on his hat and shut the door behind him.

Sigmund was fuming. An inquiry. An inquiry into the minds in his own house: "There may be thoughts in the minds that are not immediately expressed, clues to our understanding." This was too much. In his own house! In his own house and upon his own wife, the man proposed nothing other than a psychoanalysis! This was the final, final outrage! He went out and walked. He walked to the Champs Elysées, through the Jardin des Tuileries, about the park, about the fountains. He walked and walked, fuming still, and those who saw him saw that he did not in fact *walk* but rather *stomped* and *stomped*.

19

There was no question in the Inspector's mind that Freud was hiding *something*. He had difficulty accepting the idea of murder from *this* man, yet it *was* curious how he insisted so emphatically that both his wife and the sister-in-law were hallucinating. The Inspector had just received a telegram from Captain Voll that suggested he was about to embrace this theory also. The Inspector found *that* curious as well.

20

Freud opened the window shutters and stared out at the Seine. Ignominious nonsense, the entire investigation. Still, he must take precautions. There had been enough damage already. How had he uncovered the blood spot? He stared out at the river. It was a strange river, full of garbage and filth. This must be kept out of the paper. There were his other patients to think of. But as he walked back and forth from the window to the hearth, bending occasionally to stoke the fire, he knew it was not just his other patients he was worried about. His chest seemed to cave in on itself at the thought and he stood up quickly, trying to ease the pain there. Indigestion perhaps. Too much breakfast. Upset. He absolutely did not want the entire business with Emma and Fliess coming out now. He must speak to Emma at once. And Fliess. At this, he felt his blood turn cold, a momentary sensation that alarmed him as if his entire physical being had changed in a moment's thought, and the blood racing through his veins now were not blood at all, but as grey and cold and repellent as the effluvia of the Seine. He felt the enormous pressure that he must at all costs contain this exposure. It came back to him now, those endless visits before his discovery.

21

EMMA'S NOSE

THE doctor paced nervously up and down the study. He had told her many times the operation had been a success. He glanced at her then, filled with such rage that it bordered on hatred. He had determined long ago not to shrink from any thought regarding a patient, he allowed it only for a fleeting moment and then it was immediately replaced by his passionate concern as he saw the blood run from her nose, spilling over her lips and chin and pooling in the space between her thin white neck and lemon colored silk blouse. He lunged forward, scooped up a handkerchief and stemmed it with pressure on the right side. He looked down at her eyes, those grey blue eyes wild now with fright. She was holding her breath.

"Breathe," he said calmly, "it's all right to breathe. It's nothing. It is stopping now." He pulled the soaked, white linen handkerchief away, wondering briefly that it took so long to clot, and then, relieved, saw the flow had stopped.

She stood, mopping up her neck, and turned to him. How he loathed the look she would get, that stricken look, as if he were at fault, as if he were attempting to hurt her, "I thought I was cured," she said finally, "I thought that that operation . . ."

"The operation was a total success," he said quickly cutting her off. "These symptoms continue due to the hysteria, as I have explained to you." He was furious that she should doubt, for a minute, that Dr. Fliess had not been successful.[1]

The woman shrank from his words. That is to say, inwardly she shrank. Outwardly she nodded, grateful for his consideration. She knew he had been exceptional, he had been kind, he was very concerned for her welfare. She herself had secret doubts about the operation. If it were better, why did it seem so much worse? She only allowed these thoughts a moment's presence, then quickly put her hand to her head and lay back down.

"I can continue now," she said bravely.

"Good," he said, sitting back in his chair.

He rose then, on impulse, seeing the shaft of light had fallen on her eyes, and pulled the drapery across the window. Then he sighed and returned to his chair.

---

[1] As I said earlier, Freud's close friendship, bordering on adoration of Fliess, prevented Freud himself for some time from recognizing that Fliess had botched it. Freud had allowed Fliess to operate on Freud's own nose some years earlier.

22

Timothy was studying hysteria. He now wanted to know who Anna O. was. He thought he knew who Anna O. was. He read her tale by Breuer and Freud. Still he wondered, and each night he walked by the river, through the park, looking for the girl in the long white dress. Sometimes he sat on the bench, and saw her. Sometimes she ran through his dreams. He had heard the father was very ill.

THAT morning when she dressed she braided her hair in a different way. On impulse she found some narrow pink satin ribbons, a very pale shade of pink, and wound them into the braid that hung down her back. She turned, momentarily in the glass to see herself, surprised to find herself pretty, to find herself interested that she was pretty, surprised by it all.

The dreams . . . the dreams were so vivid, she wished nothing more than to put them out of her mind. She tiptoed then past the servants' door down the stairs and into the cupboard. She made herself some blackberry tea, and with the small tray steaming, took it back up the wooden stairs and sat by her father's bed. He was still sleeping. Feeling like a small child she crept into his room, her face close to his and said, "Papa, do you sleep?" She stared at his face for hours this way, seated on the floor, legs crossed, her dress puffed up about her, with her long braid, sipping her blackberry tea, studying his face. And once in a while she said, "Papa . . . are you awake?" When he woke up, always with a startled look, she got up at once, flooded with relief, and began to straighten the bedclothes in a flurry activity.

"Oh Papa, it is a lovely day today, and you are looking much, much better," she felt compelled to say. She did not for a minute know if he looked much much better or even much worse, her fatigue at this crisis of her father, fallen and bereft, was so great she could only plunge on, thinking this temporary, attempting to give to him in her optimism, her enthusiasm, the strength his body lacked. But her lack of conviction circled about them both. About the knowledge that his troubles were very deep, that they were engaged in a long dance of parting, and although the music of this dance could barely be discerned, although its beat was harsh, and new, and both of them could barely hear it, they determined to dance in the old way, to old tunes, om bah bah, one two three, the waltz, whose measured rhythms were known, whose patterns were familiar, whose ending could be anticipated, and with it could come the comfort that there was no real ending. Simply a pause, until a new one started up again.

But this other sound which they both heard did not fall into neat rhythms of ready anticipation. It sang through the house in cold, unmelodic arrangements whose ending could not be anticipated nor even tolerated, whose irritations insisted that it should end, must end, but there was no relief, they thought, even when it did. Like a siren sent to curse, its haunting cry filled the house. Only Bertha's ready energy held it at bay, fixing, smoothing, making tea, shopping, until one day she too was held by the music. She went to move and could not. She went to turn her head away this time from the music and could not. She was held. Her entire right side was fixed to her, unmoving, as if pinned under a train. She was paralyzed.[1]

23

The next morning just as the Inspector was boarding the train to Vienna, Lieutenant Cuvée rushed up to him and handed him a paper. "The page from the appointment book, sir," he said rather breathlessly, "in Paris. I copied it."

"Very good," the Inspector said, putting it into his pocket, "thank

[1] "Bertha" was Bertha Pappenheim, the real name of "Anna O.," Freud and Breuer's famous case history of hysteria.

you," and he turned to mount the steps to the train. As he did so, a beautifully attired woman in a starting green silk dress and huge veiled hat with green and magenta feathers swept in front of him to climb the stairs. She moved down the aisle ahead of him and then suddenly she dropped her bag.

"Oh," she said, as she turned, feeling it fall from her hand.

He bent to retrieve the purse and when she raised her veil and those yellow eyes fell upon him, recognition tore through him, something so surprisingly deep that he reared back from it. The fine-chiseled face, the soft, amber-like skin, struck him like a thunderbolt. A Russian to be sure. She asked him questions, and then said, "Excuse me," suddenly aware of her impact and touched by the expression in his face. His eyes were so transparent; she was surprised that she had moved him so

He turned his back to her. He did not wish to be affected. Certainly not now. It occurred to him she was traveling heavily veiled almost as in disguise, that perhaps the disguise had been constructed for someone's benefit, namely his. This was the woman who had been following him for days, but he did not know why. It was unusual, to say the least, for a lady of her obvious position and wealth to be traveling alone.

He turned away from her and took his seat. He gazed out the window of the train, hoping for sleep, for some darkness that would disguise for him what he knew, somewhere in his heart, she set him dreaming of. He sighed and tilted his head back, permitting one last thought. He hoped to God she would prove to be stupid. If she was intelligent, he must evade her. Or else, he knew, he was lost.

It was absurd for such a woman to disguise herself with veiling and a heavily plumed hat. It was always, the Inspector thought, women with beautiful faces who thought they might escape notice by subterfuge. Her fur-trimmed cloak and that elegant hat declared an aristocrat, but she was bold, much too bold in manner, for a woman traveling the Paris–Vienna Express alone, putting her foot up on a footstool so that her entire shoe was revealed and even, the Inspector observed with shock—and there was little in the world that could shock the Inspector—even her stockings. He noticed now that she was studying him, and as he was not attired in his most elegant frock coat, he thought it interesting that she seemed to be observing him in a way that could only be described as interested and even amused.

The Countess adjusted her gloves as she looked at him. This Inspector was a very attractive man, although not attractive in the ordinary sense. He had a rather full face, almost a rumpled face, but one would not expect, at least Bettina did not, such intense blue eyes in such a dark face: such sensitive, melancholy yet beautiful eyes in the face of a renowned Inspector. But it was even more the quality of his demeanor—his unusual laugh, the way he held his cigar, the élan with which he conducted his rather large self down the aisle of the train. When she had dropped her purse, and he had gallantly retrieved it, and with the most attractive little bow begged her to precede him down the corridor of the car, she had, for an instant, thought he might have been suspicious, but immediately put aside that thought. She'd been clever at following him. He could suspect nothing.

When he awakened, he saw she had moved and now sat almost in front of him. He was watching her when a strand of her hair escaped from the pin.

He saw the nape of her neck where the tendril had escaped, and her pale fingers replacing it. The hair had been pulled back and gathered into a soft roll. The gold hair gleaming against the almond-colored skin held his attention for a dramatic second, and then he thought of her voice, her face, and as he fell asleep these images whirled across his mind like a soft wind against an ancient monument, blowing the dust from an old inscription, engraved, long ago, in the interstices of his mind.

24

It was some time before the Inspector awoke with a start as the train lurched to a halt. He got up to see what had caused the train to stop. As he walked down the aisle he thought of the lady in front of him. As he had retrieved her bag, she had spoken quickly—was he going to Vienna? Did he know their arrival time? Had he traveled this track before? He had developed a face that strongly suggested you *not* ask him questions, so he had been surprised at this display of her boldness. A vague sense of some impending threat in those questions made him answer in a way that was more elusive than he might ordinarily have thought necessary. And then, of course, she had no idea he knew full well that she had been following him for days. Why, he did not know. But he knew that soon he would find out.

He passed the man in the hat sitting in the back with his note pad. Some journalist covering the eternal and infernal Dreyfus trial. He thought the trial would go on forever, that it had been struck from something deep and crooked in the French soul and, like all crooked things, it would be difficult to see to the end of it.

The Countess enjoyed watching the Inspector. He was clearly one of those men, much too rare in her view, who enjoyed women and had most certainly enjoyed looking at her, shocking as it may have seemed for a woman in her position to have raised her skirts so far above her shoe.

Of course he was wondering what she was doing on this train alone.

Bettina loved taking the train. Here no one knew her, even though on one occasion she had run into that dreadful mayor and his wife. Her husband, she felt certain, no longer cared what she did, as long as she appeared at public functions with him and did not interfere with his hunting. And now Philippe was in trouble, insisting Bettina assist him. She had hoped that, if she could engage him, the Inspector might be of help and Philippe would leave her alone. But she would have to be careful. Very careful. If the Inspector found out too much, it might be more dangerous in the end.

She looked out the windows; the train was starting again.

As she lifted her veil to gaze out into the fields, a man in a hat, a reporter for the *Neue Freie Presse,* exclaimed "Countess!" and she drew back so quickly it was almost a jump. "I never expected to see you here," he said with a smirk upon his face, "and all by yourself. . . . Now, however do you explain this? My editors will be terribly interested, as will my readers, in your travels."

The Countess loathed this man, Wilhelm Auerbach. He was a gossip, a sniper, a petty, mean, vain little man whose sole interest was in destroying lives. Had he seen her with Philippe? The Countess stood up and looked about desperately. Spotting the Inspector, who was just returning to his seat, she said, "I am here with my uncle," as she ran down the aisle, grabbing the surprised Inspector by the arm and turning to smile at the villainous Wilhelm Auerbach.

"Now you must leave us." the Countess said, "We have many affairs to settle, due to the recent death of my dear aunt. I must ask you not to trouble my uncle further." And with that the reporter retreated to the next car, and she turned her bright eyes to the Inspector and whispered a barely discernible, "Thank you."

"My dear lady," the Inspector said, "I am not ordinarily in a position of confounding the truth. Perhaps you would explain to me the need for this deception?" His eyes were full of light when he spoke to her. He seemed beneath that gruff manner to be kind, although he had brought a blush to her cheeks.

"Here is my card," she said, pressing it into his hand. "I am in urgent need of your services. I dare not explain here. I beg you to come and see me in Vienna, and I will explain everything." She looked swiftly about the train. "One more favor, I beg you; when we arrive, if you would be good enough simply to stand near me, at the station, that would be sufficient."

"You think the reporter remains unconvinced?" the Inspector said.

"The disgusting toad is convinced," she said softly. "I am an excellent liar."

"A dangerous skill," the Inspector said to her, pocketing the card. He saw her hesitate, caught by his remark. "The experienced liar is the last to know himself."

The Inspector sighed as he sat down. He had seen the blush rise to her cheeks. In even so bold a woman as this, he thought, I cause the blood to rise.

The Inspector sighed again, looking desperately into the landscape as if he might find there a temporary solace from the sudden vision before him of the myriad female hearts which flew after him no matter what he said, did, or did not do. Had ever a man received so many letters, billets-doux, and secret notes requesting assignations, assurances, a word, a glance, some indication that he returned, in whatever small measure, the vast uprisings in their all-too-human hearts?

He knew that he was a man who was fond of women, liked having them about, liked looking at them and talking with some of them. He took pleasure in them, regardless of their ages. He took vast delight watching the washerwomen in Le Havre carrying their huge loads up the stairs; he enjoyed, yes, he would have to say, was swept with pleasure at seeing their swaying rumps ascending the stoops with their huge loads on their heads, and, yes, he enjoyed the ample bosoms of the barmaids in Berlin, and also the tiny, bare breasts he had seen on occasion in those undernourished young women of the French upper classes.

Did he take advantage? At this his expression grew rueful. No, he did not take advantage. He availed himself of opportunities which seemed, he thought, to be unusually numerous. The Inspector never disclosed this side of his nature to anyone, although it seemed to him that somehow the women always knew this. He had been fortunate in the area of diseases. A doctor, some years ago, upon hearing the history of the past few years of his life, had stared at him with total incredulity and then said, "A man of your experience should have been dead of syphilis years ago."

The Inspector, although he loved making love to women, was not a man to take this lightly. He had never, he thought, had the misfortune to go to bed with a woman whom he did not, at that moment, desire mightily with heart and soul. He knew the prevailing convention that married men on occasion had to perform this act as a duty, in order that their wives bear children, and this struck him at once as so ridiculous, and so tragic, that he could do little more than shake his head at the horrors the Catholic Church, like any church, in the Inspector's opinion, had wrought on civilization.

The Inspector spent a considerable amount of time wondering about what various institutions had done to civilization, and because of his profession, he occasionally wondered at the future of it. He supposed that his overexposure to man at his worst had given him too dark a view, and it was against this darkness that he sought solace. It seemed to him that he was a man of unending hungers—for food, music, poetry, women. He found his solace in the voluptuous folds of the female body, its warmth, its darkness, its odor. He could not live without it. It balanced out the black and terrifying specters of his days, his workings, and his wanderings through the streets of Europe on the trail of man the murderer, the ravager, the rapist, the thief of life. So it was that almost daily, and frequently twice and occasionally thrice daily, the Inspector restored to himself, and the women he held, the sweet, brief promise of love.

Seated in the back of the train Theodor Herzl saw the Inspector talking with Countess von Gerzl. And that reporter Auerbach as well. How curious. He was about to go up to them when he caught a glance from the Inspector that suggested he stay in his seat. This, of course, only further provoked his curiosity. He leaned back against the seat and stared out at the landscape. The Dreyfus trial was much on his mind. He had agreed originally to cover it not realizing, at first, that it would become so central to the issue of the Jews. And now he wondered if the feelings he had were those of a frightened man or a seer.

He had met the girl the Inspector grieved for. In that cafe. He thought of it now because it was there he had told the Inspector of his plan. The girl, Elise was her name, had brought them coffee.

''I' V E been thinking," Herzl said, leaning across the coffee table, "and I think I have solved the problem of the Jews." The Inspector's eyebrows shot up. "I think, I have spoken with Pastor Clement, there is the possibility of a mass conversion . . . a great public meeting in which we convert all the Jews. That way, you see, this uncomfortable issue of their being so different, so . . . will be solved." The Inspector had looked at him aghast.

"You can't be serious," the Inspector said, ordering another coffee.

Herzl was incensed. "I am perfectly serious. I admit it's . . . but," he took the Inspector's wandering gaze for lack of interest; it was in fact despair. "Don't you see," Herzl said, "that something must be done? There are too many things. The beatings . . . and Dreyfus . . . don't you sense it? Don't you?!" In his zeal he had pounded the table and the coffee washed over the sides of the cup, drowning his notes and papers.

"I sense it," the Inspector said, "but we don't need the sensitivity of a blind man to solve it. You are a fool!"

"I am not a fool. Even the Pope has agreed to meet with me. He endorses this!"

"He does?" said the Inspector, laughing suddenly, viciously,

"Are you so deceived you now turn to the *Pope* to save the *Jews?*"

"It is the only way the Jews will be safe!" Herzl replied.

"There is no such thing as a safe Jew!" the Inspector hissed, intense and sorrowful. There was a terrible, silent moment. "The trial upsets you," the Inspector said, suddenly weary. "Go home. Clear your mind." He turned to Elise, and when the girl came up, he seemed to soften. She brought more coffee and smiled and, laughing, told him she would paint his portrait yet.

There had been an awkward silence while they had paid for coffee and walked outside. There the Inspector bid him adieu and said they would talk again. "It needs more thinking," the Inspector said, patting him on the shoulder, which had incensed Herzl more. Did he think that Herzl had not thought a great deal about this already? There were many who said it was ridiculous. A Jew, as long as he was rich, was in no danger at all. Certainly not in Vienna. And the Jews *loved* Vienna, in a way the Jews in Paris never loved Paris. The Jews were passionate Germans. In France there was a little local trouble because of the Dreyfus business. Just a little local trouble. That was how they saw it.

Herzl had been unhappy about that meeting with the Inspector. Now, he realized how naive his plan had been. He had been too desperate then, he now thought, to think it through.

25

With some irritation, Sigmund Freud finally opened the letter from Sabina Spielrein. He was having enough difficulties this morning, and he had already written the tiresome girl that she was suffering from a very common fantasy on the part of women patients regarding their doctors. He had assured her in no uncertain terms that Dr. Jung was a man who was most happy in his marriage and that furthermore he was a colleague for whom he had nothing but the highest admiration.

It was preposterous to suggest that he had made advances toward her in any way that could be interpreted as unprofessional.

Nonetheless, he read the letter on his way to the study. After he sat down, he read it again. The girl's tone impressed him. Either she was *very* clever, or there was more to this than he imagined. The letter was extremely sympathetic towards Jung; imploring Freud to intervene in what the girl clearly felt was a matter that bore ill for Jung's entire character development. The girl was an astute observer, and the charges, if true, were very serious for Jung. The odd thing was she didn't want him punished; she felt no rage. She wanted him reformed because she knew that continuing this behavior would also be extremely damaging to his position.

Freud got up and began to pace back and forth. It was unlikely, he told himself, that there was any merit to her charges. He had with extreme discomfort finally written to Dr. Jung, who had explicitly denied them, and then he had written this to Sabina. Sabina Spielrein. A young Russian woman as he recalled, whom Jung had treated for schizophrenia at the Burgholzi, in Switzerland.

He got his coat and hat and cane and walked toward the Les Quatres Vents bookstore. Perhaps, he thought, he should take up the matter with Jung once again. He had felt in Jung's denial, he realized now, some vague inauthenticity and he had repressed it. There would be no harm in raising it again. But it irritated him that he could not shrug it off. He had *carefully* prepared Jung to take over as head of the psychoanalytic establishment. In addition to Jung's interest and abilities, Freud knew it would be far easier to get psychoanalysis accepted if the head of the organization were not a Jew. This was his plan, and he did not like having it disrupted by this Spielrein girl.

26

The worst part of her feeling for Morton Fullerton, Edith Wharton thought, was that she was like a character out of a poor novel, a pathetic middle-aged woman who was learning about love for the first time. Then she chastised herself for thinking such ungenerous thoughts. She was deeply moved by Fullerton. She knew, too, that Fullerton was passionately attached to her, whatever his complexities. And his complexities were many. She knew that, too. There had been *many* women in his life. Now, who was this woman, Katharine, and why did she keep sending him letters? She had been fiercely jealous at first until Morton in his smooth, soothing way had calmed her.

She got up and walked to the dining room. The table was adorned with her favorite flowers—pink rhododendron—and Henry would be coming in for dinner soon.

She walked energetically back and forth the length of the parlor, filled with the pleasure of remembering her most recent afternoon with Fullerton. When she heard the bird, a nightingale she occasionally heard later in the night, trilling, making the most beautiful sound, it seemed to her a perfect echo of the soaring, swelling emotion that possessed her whenever she saw Fullerton. She walked at once into the far parlor and saw Henry sitting quietly reading his paper. Should she tell him? Now? How could she tell him? Just blurt it out? I've fallen madly in love with Morton Fullerton. It was really quite all right. Henry knew that she had no real marriage with Teddy. He wouldn't be shocked. And he was fond of Morton.

But she didn't want anyone but herself and Morton to know about it. The secrecy of it, that it was theirs *alone* brought a kind of dizzying pleasure to her.

The bird sang again. She looked at Henry. Her heart was pounding, with a feeling so deep and moving her throat caught.

"Henry." Her voice was a crack.

"What is it?" He looked up from his paper.

"The bird," she said, "do you hear that?"

As if on cue the creature trilled forth its fullest-bodied song.

"Oh," she said joyfully, "oh, listen, oh!" as the sound of this bird filled her with such emotion she thought she would burst from her skin; her eyes spilled tears. She grabbed her handkerchief.

"Ummm," said Henry, who mercifully had glanced toward the door, listening for the bird. He was actually annoyed at being interrupted, but something signaled him, some vague discomfort at the dimension of emotion Mrs. Wharton projected that could not be supported by this reference to trilling song. This disproportion in her character he attributed to the presence of Morton Fullerton. Some sentiment, long held back, had been unleashed, and although it was beneficial, he felt, to her, it irritated him. He lived and breathed the interior lives of women, but as he imagined them to be. In his writing, the finest response was under his control. In the presence of her intellect, he felt soothed and at home. But not in the presence of this feeling. Something was changing now, in the landscape, and threatened an avalanche. He felt he should remove himself, soon, lest he place his own being at risk.

"Oh," Edith said, "it's stopped singing." But Henry was reading and seemed not to hear her. Looking up, drying her tears, she thought that lately Henry seemed more remote than ever. She gazed for a while out the window and then went to dress for dinner. She resolved she would speak to Henry at dinner. Whenever she thought of Morton she grew happy. And it was a new feeling—happy. She smiled a lot. For no reason. And she felt buoyant, as if the air around her had turned to water, and its only purpose was to float her, like a duck, on its surface. You never knew, she thought, what life was going to bring you. Henry would not disapprove; that was not what she feared. But he seemed so delicate of late, and she was a trifle disappointed that he appeared, in some way, to shrink from her happiness, as if he did not want to know its source. Thus she had been reticent, but she was joyous now as her feet bounced up the stair, thinking again she must share it with someone, she simply, simply *must!*

27

At the train station in Vienna the Inspector bowed to the Countess and agreed to visit her at two o'clock the following Tuesday. "The house will be full of my American cousins," the Countess said. "They have just arrived, and I have yet to meet them, but the father is a renowned banker, and I know he would be honored to meet you." This told him that she had, as he suspected, deliberately provoked his attention on the train. She had intended something else, which the miserable little journalist had thwarted.

It seemed to the Inspector that he had taken an extremely passive role in allowing the Countess' deception to involve him, and this was so contrary to his nature, that he had observed it in himself from a distance, even as it happened. He knew that human nature was such that anything totally out of character was frequently in character, if one looked hard and long enough at the life of the individual. The quiet accountant who murdered his family in a rage, the dutiful daughter who poisoned her parents, the Inspector had seen this and more. These events were not "wildly unpredictable," as the press and the clergy made them out to be. These were not the acts of one "possessed by the devil." The seeds of violence were sown inside the containers of too enclosed a life. The provinces, with their secrecy, their enforced intimacies, the small villages of restraint—it was here that some of the most heinous crimes occurred. But he was a man who indulged his appetites, so it was with some mystification that he found himself so "out of character" in his compliance with this lady. He thought of Flaubert and *Madame Bovary*—the book had moved him deeply—a perfect unfolding of the inevitable.

28

As the carriage horse clopped its solitary way through the gaslit streets, the Inspector noted with approval that a new system of electric lighting had been installed. This alone, he thought, would help to ward off the barbarians who preyed on the innocent at night, but even as he thought this, a strange discomfort welled up in his chest. It came from the barely perceptible awareness in himself, which seemed to increase with his age, or that of his century, that it would take more than the wonders of electricity to keep the roving beast at bay. Perhaps he would go to the opera tomorrow evening. At that moment a carriage passed and he looked up briefly to see the back of a large hat adorned with pinkish feathers. He knew it must be the Countess. He leaned back against the carriage seat and made his plans. He would go to the opera, to a cafe, drink his favorite Viennese coffee, indulge in his favorite pastry, listen to the artists argue at the Cafe Central, perhaps steal a moment with Lena or Katarina or Eva; he would encase himself in the pleasures this wondrous city offered in order to keep the impending melancholia that he felt here, in this city alone, at bay.

His father had died here among the best physicians in Europe, his every symptom beyond the cure of the best. His father died slowly, ebbing a little each day, his heroic countenance and noble manner making it even more difficult for his son to bear.

Perhaps it was his father's death that was the impenetrable mystery that drove him to penetrate the deaths of others. But fear seized him here in this magnificent capital, a fear of the future. His father had left him a title, money, and the privileges of the rich. His mother, an exotic dark beauty, had disappeared on a journey when he was nine. She had promised to return for him in a month, explained it was best now for him to stay with his governess and his father's family, and a tear gathered now in the Inspector's eye as the thought of that beautiful face pressed against the window of the carriage—the small gloved hand, a magenta glove, waving from the carriage, blowing kisses to him as she drove off into the night.

In a month, she was dead. Her ship went down crossing the Strait of Messina, a deadly crossing in the winter but seemingly safe in the bright bliss of summer. A sudden gale rose up, and all were drowned. It was the site of Scylla and Charybdis, or so people said, and he thought from what little he knew of his mother's life that she had run between them many times before. She had written him, "My dear son, I have gone away to gain a little time. I am crossing tonight to the most beautiful island I know, where I will be safe with my sister, and these simple people and green hills. When I have recovered my strength, I will come for you. With all my loving heart. Mother."

He still remembered word for word his mother's last letter. He had no way of knowing the tears that welled inside had been growing for hours, at the first sight of the lady in the coach. He was left now, wondering, if it was love, or the lack of it, that left such a long, desperate trail in the human heart.

It was some time before the fiacre drew up in front of the boarding house. He had been told it was a clean, reliable place. He paid his driver and climbed wearily out of the carriage. He was pleased to see he was so close to the Prater, he could enjoy long walks in the park. Perhaps he thought, hopefully, he might even go to the trotting races.

And then he remembered; it was a while until spring. Still, the park with its long alleys and reserves of marshland was a place he could get lost in. This relieved him.

29

Henry couldn't stop:

At the hour of midnight they dragged the miserable victim from her bed, and deep in the horrific dungeons of the prison plunged the distracted nun!—Groans, sighs, and shrieks, alternately rung echoing round the rugged walls: the torturing horrors of famine awaited the unfortunate nun; no pity alleviated her misery; and in the centre of the place stood the coffin destined for her; whilst round the walls and floor, in all directions, were strewed the ghastly ensigns of woe and torment. A faint glimmering lamp, suspended from the massy bars of the roof (as if with a refinement of cruelty unequalled, to blast the sight of the victim, and shut out every contemplation but her immediate fate) served to shew her the horrors that overwhelmed her, and the terrific engines of her tortures.

"Really, Henry," Edith walked in and Henry James dropped the book with a startled look. She saw it hit the floor and asked curiously, "Whatever are you reading?"

"Nothing," he said to her and scooped it up.

"Well, Henry you obviously are reading something, you can't very well be reading and be reading nothing, can you? If you don't want me to know what you're reading that's perfectly acceptable to me, of course." She said this with an expression that suggested it was not perfectly acceptable at all, and Henry looked sheepishly at his feet.

"I thought you were working," he said quietly.

"Of course I wasn't working, it's after 1:00 P.M. Whyever would I be working?" She bent over to change the flowers, "I'm not at that point. You know I finish at noon." Indeed he did know this. He could imagine her sitting here every morning, pages drifting to the floor, like petals from a flower dropping, littering the floor.

"Henry," she said suddenly, "I must speak to you once and for all. This I promise you will be my final warning. I believe Dr. Freud is dangerous to you. I have seen him myself in Les Quatres Vents bookstore and he was buying a book on witchcraft. There," she said, "I've said it."

"He isn't a witch," Henry said, "and he has relieved my dyspepsia. Even if he were a witch and he relieved it I would still go to him," he said. "Dyspepsia is a terrible thing."

"If he isn't, well, strange, then why would he be buying a book such as the *Malleus Maleficarum?*"[1]

"I can't imagine," Henry said, feeling irritated by the conversation, "perhaps he's just curious. Or perhaps he's training to be a witch. He's rather impoverished, I believe. I've heard he doesn't have many patients. Perhaps he's insuring his economic future. It may be the coming thing." Edith smiled despite herself. Henry, when he didn't want to discuss something, often became jocular.

"I think you're upset," Henry said quietly after a moment "because you must have read of his theories, or heard of them, and they frighten you."

"Frighten me? Yes, of course. Witchcraft—demonology—frightens me when my close friend is involved in it."

"No, I mean the business about memory."

He saw her face pale ever so slightly, and she stood up then, suddenly interested in the flowers, sweeping the petals off the table into her hand, something she usually asked the maid to do. She would pick the fresh flowers, but the old ones she would ask others to take away.

"It's true I don't particularly like to think about the past," she said. "I don't like it at all, but it isn't that, really. I mean, I've heard something that—" suddenly her face turned bright red, to his astonishment, "that there are things he's said, or written, about children that seem totally shocking to me. I hear he gives absolutely scandalous lectures in Vienna."

---

[1] Freud was interested in the similarities between medieval theories of possession and a "theory of a foreign body and a splitting of consciousness." The *Malleus,* which is also called "Witches' Hammer," was an immensely popular fifteenth-century misogynist treatise written by Dominican monks who suggested that all women are potentially witches.

"He doesn't strike me in the least as scandalous," Henry said, suddenly very uncomfortable at her introduction of the term. "But if you'll excuse me I have errands to do."

"Henry," she said, her back to him and her voice trembling, "tell me, what exactly does he do to you?"

30

I was lying in bed, remembering the first morning in the Countess' house when I had arisen very early, and when I looked out the window I saw the man with the gun looking up at me. It was barely daylight and for some reason, a reason which to this day I cannot fathom, I felt very drawn to the window. I was not yet dressed, and as I stood by my bed in the beautiful blue room with the dark blue velvet draperies, I saw the man, and somehow he saw me, for at that moment as he was wrapping the gun in its package, surreptitiously, glancing to right and left, he looked up, directly at my window, and that is when I discovered that no matter who you may think you really are, you do not know. I so surprised myself by my next action that I still cannot believe that I did what I did. I can only say in my defense, which is admittedly a weak one, that I became a victim, a victim of an as-yet-unknown passion, one that totally overwhelmed my conscience and my reason.

I was so ashamed that even now I can barely admit these thoughts to myself. I only know that that morning, as my eyes met those of the man with the gun, I found myself opening my night dress, untying my chemise and letting it fall open so my breasts spilled out. And as I touched them, the man who had been watching, just then, as if secretly knowing, raised his head and looked directly at my window, and I, hypnotized, stepped fully into the light, my gown open, and he stopped and stared, and I stared down, and then as he held the gun and I saw it glinting in the morning light, he put his finger to his lips as if to say *shhh,* and I, I confess, I did the same. Although I was some distance from him, his face was nonetheless clear to me and most unforgettable, and in that moment, not knowing what it was that the two of us had, by sheer fate, coconspired to reveal and to conceal, not knowing what it was that impelled me, for that is the only proper description, to step into his full view, I knew then, at that moment, we were joined.

It seemed, as I reflected upon it, which I did with some frequency, for it was one of those occasions that present themselves in life when one finds oneself moving so fully out of character that if one has the luck not to be awash in shame, one can discover that one has aspects that society has made difficult to claim, and that such aspects, un-claimed, can play havoc with the arc of one's life. I was young at the time, that is to say, I was in my seventeenth year, and as yet unmarried, nor did I find myself interested in that pursuit, at least not in the gentlemen who had presented themselves to me, who were, in every-one else's estimation, quite suitable. I thought I had, within myself, some special destiny, which either fairy tales or fancy had given to me and if I did not meet it, I would come to wrack and ruin, for that has been and still is my opinion of what happens to women who believe too well that if they but sleep strongly the prince will deliver them to their full promise. But I hoped that it was not illusion or fancy but some knowledge cast deep within me that told me if I could separate myself from other women of my class and character, if I could find for myself who it was that I *was,* if I could, in effect, separate myself into some hitherto unimagined but still *known* self, as Alexandra Kollantai[1] had said, then I might finally be who I was really *destined* to be.

Until then I felt terribly trapped. I believed that I, if I permitted myself, could live as if I were some bewitched creature—the King of Lions condemned to live in the mouse's body, or worse, the Prince who, until the spell was broken, had to live his life as a frog. I did feel as if someone, whom I did not know, but someone early on had snapped the noose of enchantment round my neck and in a flurry of witches' words had consigned me to my inauthentic fate.

I eventually began to think that perhaps I was not a lion, but, like Cecily, I had the heart of one, only its size and capacity were unfed and underexercised in the daily routine of curtsies and corsets and

---

[1] This woman was a Russian revolutionary who was a friend of Ida's. In an excerpt omitted from this manuscript it appears she visited their home on several occasions.

carefully controlled reading that was my lot. I felt the cage shaking that morning as I looked out at this man looking at me and knowing I was embarked on a perilous journey upon which this secret knowledge would impel me.

I hesitated to record it, but I had found recently that when I was very upset it was profitable to me to start sketching. At such times, I made drawings on a small pad I kept with me at all times. I wondered now, what I had done with it.

31

Sigmund Freud was worried. He had given Martha explicit instructions. This Inspector was a problem. He did not want anyone taking samples from the carpet. He did not want the issue of blood aired *at all*. He did not want the matter of Fliess and the operation on Eckstein's nose to become public. He had given specific directions to Martha, yet still he felt uneasy. The Inspector was too clever a man. He decided on that reflection that he had no choice. He must return to Vienna at once.

32

Edith Wharton had ascertained that that dreadful Dr. Freud, the one she called the little weasel, had returned to Vienna "very unexpectedly" because the authorities in Paris were after him. There had been some kind of incident which excited the police—which hardly surprised her. She had already persuaded Henry that she should accompany him to Vienna where he would be overseeing a production of his play, as that wretched little man had already nearly destroyed him.

The only way to get over the way he was carrying on about that cat was to confront the doctor head on.

She failed to understand how the doctor had somehow convinced Henry that the death of the animal was a murder. It was, to be sure, most uncharacteristic of Henry to engage in such an act, but as she understood it, the cat apparently had been disturbing him in the night, and he had simply thrown a shoe at it, or *something,* in a fit of rage, and well—it was surely an accident—the animal expired. At this unde-fined idea she felt her attention wander. She didn't spend too much time worrying about this because she had concerns about Mr. Fuller-ton and an appointment at Worth for a fitting of a new gown, which she hoped to have ready in time to take to Vienna.

She had arranged to meet Mr. Fullerton there, and at this thought she reached out suddenly and grasped the yellow irises he had brought her. They were so old they were dried and fading, and she had pressed two of them into the pages of her diary, where she had written thoughts she never knew she would have. She, a writer, had written things in the diary she had never dreamed of, had placed feelings on pages she never thought could possess her. She was not a woman who was used to being moved in such a deep and passionate way, and never by a man. She looked carefully into the mirror at her face. The hard chin she had never liked looked softer to her now. Her face, which she knew had never been pretty, had displayed a certain formidable character she had found reassuring; now she believed she saw it changing. It made her a trifle uneasy, this new softness, and she turned quickly and gathered her parasol for her morning errands.

33

The doctor had had quite enough of that odious police inspector. And then he had the misfortune that morning to be confronted by the offensive Mrs. Wharton, who had rung his bell impetuously and demanded to see him. He told the maid to inform her that he'd already left for Vienna. In response she had left him an insulting note, but he was in no mood to explain the basic assumptions of psychoanalysis to a woman who was clearly beyond their grasp.

Freud paced his study. Although he was worried about the Inspector he could not stop thinking about the James man. An important case. He had come, he said, about his sister. But his symptoms were severe. Insomnia, dyspepsia, and now an obsessive compulsion stemming from the strangulation of a cat and everything, Freud mused, it represented. His identification with the woman, Constance Fenimore Woolson, for example, was most extraordinary.

Freud walked to the west end of the room and thought. He needed to talk to someone about this patient, and he could no longer talk so freely to Fliess. They were arguing frequently. James, the poor man, was convinced that he was responsible for the death of Constance Fenimore Woolson when clearly it was a suicide. He recalled James' torrent of confession, "I know her, I know her, I knew all along, I knew she *longed* for me, and I loathed it. I, I—" and he collapsed.

And then the business about the cat. He had taken to washing his hands. They smelled of cat, he said. Dead cat.

What an extraordinary example of displacement. Marvelous in a way; perfectly suited to his purposes. Freud looked up then, cheered suddenly by the prospects of a solution.

34

All of London was talking about it. The distinguished American writer Henry James, a seemingly mild-mannered, elegant bachelor of great distinction, had gotten up in the middle of the night and stalked outside, and there in the light of a silvery moon—a January moon so huge and bright its luminescence left no question that they saw what they saw—on his lawn in his green pajamas, in the light of that particular moon and in full view of an audience of his neighbors, Henry James had strangled his cat.[1] It was just as well, said the lady next door;

[1] It is one of those unusual biographical incidents that have nonetheless been substantiated. For the inquisitive reader Stephen Donadio's book, *Nietzsche, James and the Artistic Will* (New York: Oxford University Press, 1972), explores the incident.

it was *such* a dreadful cat. But when the lady from the animal society came to investigate the circumstances surrounding the discovery of the body, she was told he'd gone quite *suddenly* to the Continent. Which she found strange. He had not even unpacked his bags (his maid told her), from America.

35

The Inspector, totally uncharacteristically, had put the paper from Lieutenant Cuvée into his pocket upon boarding the train and had been so distracted by the Countess that he had forgotten all about it.

The next morning when he awoke, he suddenly recalled it and leaping from his bed, reached into his coat pocket. He scanned the list of Freud's visitors in Paris the day after the murder—and then he saw it, gleaming like a pearl:

22 February, 7:30 P.M. Henry James

and in Freud's fine handwriting, an additional note, "spoke of murder."

He would have Cuvée interview James immediately.

He dressed quickly and made his way to the station house to introduce himself to Captain Voll, the man on the other end of the telegrams. It was so odd, that he felt no curiosity about him.

36

The Inspector was surprised when he met Captain Voll to find him in such an agitated state. Voll explained to him that matters had taken a most unfortunate turn in the last few days. The wife of the chemist who had taken the sample from Freud's rug was a gossip, and she had loudly proclaimed all over town that there had been a murder in Berggasse 19, and worse yet, she said it was another perverse Jewish murder. This time she said they had engineered the ritual killing of a poor and innocent girl.

The populace was in an uproar.

The Jews were in an uproar.

Rumors were flying that it wasn't safe to go out at night now because Jews were looking for victims to sacrifice. Voll had said nothing of this rumor until the Inspector arrived. For rumor it was, the captain now was convinced no murder had taken place at 19 Berggasse at all. It was simply the fantasies of hysterical women. Voll was not in the mood to start policing riots. He wanted to wind this matter up, declare it closed. It put him in ill-humor. And tonight, to make matters worse, he had to have dinner with the man who described himself as "your less fortunate brother, Wilhelm, the poor tram conductor." The self-pity that overwhelmed this brother made Voll wonder if there was anything to this blood relationship business at all. How such a pitiful wretch as Wilhelm had sprung from the same source as himself was a mystery that disturbed him beyond all comprehension.

"I think clearly the Freud case is a case of hallucination," Voll said firmly to the Inspector. "We should make the announcement at once that there was no body, and no murder, and clear the air of this ritual murder business. It has come down from the emperor that we cannot afford to have this rumor about, as the anti-Semites are already causing considerable agitation." Voll looked at the Inspector as if expecting his immediate acquiescence.

"I have yet to make my own investigations," the Inspector said. "But *I* have done it all," Voll said quickly. "There is nothing from the chemists at all, nothing strange in the hairs or fibers, absolutely nothing. It was a stormy night. Women see things all the time."

The Inspector looked at him. "I will make my own investigation. Tell the emperor I will have word for him shortly. Now, as to these other murders in which there *were* bodies, perhaps you will review for me the details of their execution."

Voll's mood changed, the Inspector noticed, almost at once. "I will have my associate go over them with you. It is quite hopeless. I've been at it for some time." He shrugged and left the room. The Inspector sat there thinking. A strange man, Voll. Perhaps frustrated.

There was something in this Freud murder that did not fit at all. He knew this at once. It would require an analysis that was different from his usual approach. He wished fervently and uselessly that it had occurred some place other than Vienna, for it was here he felt he was at his weakest. Some vague, threatening mood hung over him from the moment he stepped from the train. As he had walked to the station house that morning, across the Schwedenplatz, he thought ironically what a magnificent city it was. He had always been struck by the large number of monuments and caryatids in the city; looking up he would see stone eyes staring at him, and unexpected conjunctions—human faces, mermaids' tails, wings of dragons, and an angel's smile. The architecture, particularly the historical sweep of the Ringstrasse, awed him. Beauty and ambition seemed to touch every corner of the city, and yet instead of inspiring him, as Rome or Venice did, it brought on a sense of doom. He must do his best to shake it away, but even as he thought this, he felt that light quivering that began along the back of his neck and descended along his spine, circling finally around his waist and coming to rest in his solar plexus. Perhaps it was his very breath, he thought occasionally, that began to quiver with fear as he walked the streets of his childhood home.

37

Ah, such a day, such a life," said Wilhelm, the police captain's unfortunate brother, as the tram pulled up along the stop on the Kärntnerstrasse. Two gentlemen in homburgs came aboard. He took their tickets, nodding sadly. Ah, he moaned to himself, such a weary day, such a dreary day, and I, I have nothing to do. He hoped such days for rain. Eagerly he hoped for rain, for when there was rain at least he could reach forward and move the stick that held the wiper back and forth across the front of the tram car. He liked doing this. It gave him a sense of purpose.

Otherwise what else was there to do? Around and around and around the ring. The Schubert Ring, the Kärntner Ring, the Ringstrasse, around and around. Some days, when he was lucky, they assigned him to take the car in the reverse direction.

Wilhelm never spoke to anyone. What was there to say? What was there to do? No one ever *did anything* on a tram. His brother Johann had thefts, his brother Johann had murder, his brother Johann had prostitutes, his brother Johann had death and mysteries, blood and propaganda, guns and knives and terror, and he? He had nothing.

He rang the bell. Albert Einstein, dusting his hat, wearied from his conference, came aboard and handed Wilhelm the ticket. The tram stole off silently into the night. At the next stop, the Akademiestrasse, there was one lone figure standing in the station. He was a young man with an angry glance. He snarled as he handed the tram conductor his ticket, struggled with a painting he carried. He had signed it on the corner A. H.[1] Two rings later Gustav Mahler, who had planned to walk to the opera house, boarded the tram with his Symphony no. 5 under his arm. He was pleased to see at the next stop Gustav Klimt and Margarete Wittgenstein, whose father was underwriting Klimt's museum. They greeted Mahler and explained their coach had broken down. Wilhelm noted the strange clothes of the man coming aboard with the woman, with no idea that this was the artist who was causing so much commotion in Vienna.[2]

The other passengers noticed Wittgenstein's dress. This was clearly a lady. Wilhelm noticed with a small stab of resentment that such an aristocrat would ride his tram only if the coach broke down. With that nose, and that money, there was no question in his mind that she was a Jew. It was the Jews, he thought, who were taking the best jobs, making all the money. The dirty bastards. And he'd heard they killed and drank the blood of Christian children.

At this he felt better. The priest, his priest, had told him of the gore and greed of the Jews until it made his blood run cold. In a strange way, if he were to think of it, he actually *enjoyed* thinking about the horrors of the Jews. It excited him. Tonight he would go to a meeting. He had been invited by a follower of Schoenerer. The emperor did

[1] I doubt very much that this was Adolf Hitler, as has been suggested. He was not in Vienna until around 1909.

[2] This is probably a reference to the Seccessionist movement in Vienna which was an avant-garde movement inspired by Gustav Klimt. Margarete Wittgenstein is Ludwig Wittgenstein's sister.

not like Schoenerer, he knew. Damn the emperor. He had a right to *some* revenge for his miserable lot. Why should the Christ killers have everything and he, *nothing?* At this thought he pressed the pedal and the tram moved on, Wilhelm cursing his luck, his life, his destiny, his fatigue, his miserableness—this pathetic existence that touched on nothing, offered nothing, got him nothing, the puny pilfered existence called life.

38

Martha had been alarmed when Sigmund had telephoned her to announce he was returning early, in a day's time. It was an expensive and cumbersome device, but they had decided finally to have one installed, for emergencies. Sigmund *hated* the telephone but lost no time in communicating to her the urgency of his message. He had surprised her with the vehemence with which he spoke about the police inspector and forbade her to speak to him. So she was very surprised when the charming, amiable man at the door introduced himself as precisely that and told her he wouldn't dream of interrogating her, he just wanted to have a look around, smiling as he showed her a document that he said gave him full legal right to do so. Sigmund had forbidden her to give the Inspector *any* cooperation, but since he had such an agreeable manner that she wondered if in fact he were the one, she saw no harm in letting him in.

Smiling easily at her, he said, "It won't take long." She saw Irina, the maid, lurking in the background in that desultory way she had, with the feather duster poised, as if arrested in flight. Martha found herself maddeningly irritated by this girl. She was always lurking and listening and rarely *doing* anything. Sigi had hired her from an agency in the hope it would facilitate the children's command of English. And then it turned out she spoke *dreadful* English and was a very troublesome maid to boot.

"Irina," she said sharply, "the Inspector wishes to look around the premises."

The Inspector glanced at the girl. "Who is this?" he said, smiling. Irina pouted and smirked. Then she looked him over. "Oi'm the maid," she said, "fresh from London if you don't mind. Irina's the name."

"I see," the Inspector said, barely disguising his amusement.

"Irina has been with us for six months," Martha explained quickly. "She had left already the evening of the, the—" The Inspector turned to her. It was curious that she seemed at a loss for the word for it. "The storm," Martha said finally. "Sigmund reminded me how impressed I am by storms; they leave me very upset."

"Of course," the Inspector said. He was scanning the premises. "And your sister-in-law, was she upset during the storm also?"

"Why, uh, yes," Martha said. "She was upset about something clearly. I mean, of course, she was upset." Martha was dimly aware she should not be talking to him, yet he had, in an instant, made her feel very comfortable.

"Do you mind if I sit down?" the Inspector asked. Then, to her astonishment, he walked straight into the kitchen and sat down on one of the chairs.

"Why, you can sit in the living room," Martha protested. "Please." She indicated the parlor. She thought to herself, these French are impertinent!

"No, this is just fine. This is where you first spied the body, is it not?"

"Oh yes, no, no, I mean there probably, there wasn't any body. Sigmund has explained to me how this could be, *was* a hallucination."

"Look," the Inspector said, jumping to his feet and holding her by the arms in a forceful manner, "this is very important. Either you believe you saw it, or you didn't. Now did you?" His intense blue eyes stared into hers with a ferocity that surprised her.

"Yes, yes, of course," she stammered. "I mean I . . . *believe* I saw it, but Minna says . . ."

"Never mind," the Inspector said, "*what* Minna says. You tell me what *you* saw. Leave it to me to get it sorted out." He released his hold on her arms, and Martha looked at him wildly. Sigmund had been so firm, so explicit, and yet he seemed so . . . so, so *official*.

"Now, tell me if I'm wrong," he said, grabbing one of the wooden kitchen chairs, "but is it not true that you," he pointed to the stair, "having been awakened by the storm, proceeded down the stairs and found your sister-in-law seated there?" He pointed to the chair across the table. "Is that correct, madame?"

Martha nodded, "Yes, she was there, slightly to the left." To her surprise, the Inspector moved the chair the small distance she indicated. "There," he said, "would that be right?"

"Yes."

"Good, and now tell me exactly, retrace precisely the steps you took that evening, everything that occurred, as best you remember it."

"Well, I, I," Martha said, "I came in here, and Minna was there, and she was drinking tea, and then there was a sound, like a shot, a shot or a door slamming, I couldn't be sure, and then Minna screamed and pointed, pointed there, and I looked, and I saw a body."

"Did you see blood?"

"Yes, no, well, I think so, a man, lying there, and I ran upstairs to see about the children, and then I came down and Minna looked pale, very pale, then there was more banging and . . ."

"Before or after you came down the stairs?"

"Oh before. As I came down, there was another sound of another door, and Minna looked pale and said, call the police and—no, before that I made some tea, I thought we needed tea, Minna can't take the sight of blood, so I made some tea."

"What tea?" the Inspector said, noting that there *must* have been blood.

"What tea?" Martha seemed startled.

"Yes. Would you be so kind as to show me?"

Martha hesitated.

"Well," Martha said, "I went and got some tea, a strong black tea, and I, I made it." He suspected something in the hesitation. "You made it . . . you prepared it because you were in an excited state. Did you do anything else to it? Did you add anything you might add for a person in an excited state, any brandy, anything at all?"

Martha looked at him, chagrined. "I did add a bit of brandy."

"Go on," the Inspector said. She was relieved that this did not seem to disturb him at all.

"And she drank it, and I drank some also, and . . ."

"Did you leave the room at any time after you made the tea?"

"Did I what?"

"Did you leave the room at any time after you made the tea?"

"Why, no," Martha said. "Why would I . . . oh, oh, yes. Actually I went to the telephone before I drank the tea, and then I went for the gun."

"The gun?" the Inspector said, his look quizzical. This was the first he had heard of a gun.

"The gun we keep over there." She pointed in the cupboard to what looked to the Inspector like an impossibly old-fashioned blunderbuss.

"Do you know how to shoot it?" he said softly.

"No, not really, but I grabbed it, and when I went into the living room, the body was gone. There was nothing there."

"And Minna?" the Inspector said, "Your sister-in-law?"

"She fainted," Martha said.

Aha, he said to himself. So there was blood. This was not in the captain's report either.

He was congratulating himself on his interrogation technique when he saw a shadow shift at the far end of the kitchen. It was the maid he was certain, eavesdropping. He pushed back his chair and pretended to walk toward the stove, whirled suddenly, and lunged behind the cupboard to grab the guilty Irina.

"Are you in the habit of hiding in cupboards to listen to talk?" he said, holding her by the wrist and speaking rather harshly.

"No, sir, I, I just been hearing bits 'n pieces of the story for days now, sir, and I wanted to hear the whole thing once through just to see, sir, just to see if I could be of any help to the authorities," and she looked at him with such totally undisguised hypocrisy that for a moment he was genuinely amused.

"I see," he said. "And now that you know everything, how can you help the authorities?"

"I don't rightly know yet, sir, but I'll be putting my mind to it at once, sir."

The Inspector was disarmed at her brazenness despite himself. Surely she had little else to recommend her. Her face had a pinched, sallow quality, and her hair lay on her head like dried grass. The eyes, which he thought capable of no expression save suspicion, were a watery, lifeless grey with thick overhanging lids that gave them a hooded look. He estimated she was no more than nineteen, but she had such an ashen quality one could have taken her for forty.

The Inspector looked in her face. He decided she was too stupid to be a good liar.

"Well, from now on announce yourself. I will speak to you later. For now, please go on with your duties."

Irina skipped out of the kitchen while Martha stood there with her mouth open.

"I must apologize. Really, that girl . . ."

The Inspector held up his head. "The only maids who are not curious, madame, are dead ones."

He was disturbed not by the foolish girl's indiscretion but by the fact that she had interrupted an extremely important moment. Interrogations were always delicate affairs. He felt something was about to emerge, something was about to be *given* to him. He attempted to recreate the mood.

"Now once again, if you will forgive me, I would like to retrace your movements." He moved in such a courtly way that Martha found herself quite relaxed again. "Please, madame, have a seat." He indicated the chair, and she sat and watched him pantomime precisely the movements she had just described to him.

"And so," he said, deftly moving to the stove, "if you were here and your sister-in-law was there when you came down the stairs, then you went over here," he retraced her steps to the cupboard, "to get some tea, is that correct?" Martha nodded. He looked over the tea tins in the shelf. He saw there were only three. "Would you be good enough to show me which tea it was?"

Martha looked at him and smiled in a hesitating way. What a strange fellow he was! Whatever difference did it make which tea it was?

"Why, I'm not sure, we always drink coffee, oh yes, that one," she said, pointing to the yellow tin at the far end, and then added, to her own surprise, "Well, I think so."

"Are you certain?" he said inquisitively.

Martha blanched. She hadn't wanted him to know, actually, for some reason which tea it was. In fact she knew perfectly well it hadn't been that one. It had been the herbal one Minna had bought; she was certain because it was so strong she knew she could pour the brandy into it almost undetected.

"Why, actually, no, no, I don't think so," she said. "It was the other. In the green tin." He had made her feel ashamed about this very insignificant business. She did wish he would get on with it.

The Inspector lifted the top of the tea tin and inhaled it. "A very strong tea, indeed," he said. "Would you be good enough, I wonder, to make me a cup? And if you don't mind, exactly the way you did that very evening." Martha seemed startled. "As well as you can remember," he assured her. "It does not matter if it is not precise. We will find out eventually what happened, but at first our efforts may be a bit clumsy."

"It was such a terrible storm," Martha said, as she attempted to move about the kitchen in just the way she had described, making the tea.

To her surprise, the Inspector sniffed the tea heartily and then proceeded to drink it.

"A very strong brew," he said to her and smiled at her again. "It's quite pleasing to me." He sipped some more, "Actually I'd like to buy some for myself. Where did you purchase it?"

Martha found him *most* appealing. She was surprised at the violence of Sigi's reaction to him.

"Oh, I didn't buy it—it's, it's something Minna bought, to help her sleep."

"I see," the Inspector said. He leaned back in the chair and took a long puff on his cigar. "Would I be wrong in thinking that I had read, somewhere in the police reports, that your sister-in-law actually was in the habit of drinking camomile tea as an aid to her insomnia?"

"Oh yes, she did, she does have camomile, but this tea was something she purchased recently. I made myself a cup once, when Minna was out, and it was so strong, and I thought that evening she needed something strong, and it was right on top," she shrugged, "so I used it."

"It's not making me drowsy yet," the Inspector said.

"Well, it's not nearly so strong as Minna drinks it," Martha said quickly. "She drinks it so strong I would never give it to you that way."

"I see," the Inspector said. "And that night, did you drink the *strong* tea as well?"

"Why, why, yes," Martha said. "I did."

"How much?" he said.

"Why, why I don't know," she said turning to him. "Whyever should it matter?"

Before he left, the Inspector announced he would reappear at one o'clock tomorrow afternoon to speak to Minna.

Martha found herself apologizing, with downcast eyes, that Minna was not available and he would be forced to return.

"Quite all right," he said. "You were assuredly not expecting me."

Of course they *had* been expecting him, he knew. They had been forewarned. With Martha this had been easy to undo. With Minna, from the captain's reports, he suspected otherwise.

39

As we hurried down to breakfast that morning we heard arguing downstairs, and the banging of doors, and just around the second landing in the staircase we saw a group of men in black coats and hats, filing out the door, followed by a very large gruff man, whom I knew at once was the Countess' husband Leopold, who was shouting, "No, I said no! My wife is not turning my house into a synagogue!"

By the time we reached the dining room the last man had disappeared out the door. The cook arrived and explained that Leopold, the Countess' husband, had been "upset," and had left hurriedly. Father was looking very strange and Mother said to him, "Well what is going on, Frederick?"

Father said, "I don't know . . . he seems extremely upset. Something about Bettina converting to Judaism." Mother looked extremely puzzled. "Why would she do that?" Father shrugged. "I really don't know."

"I know he was very upset, he showed the rabbis out."

"Well," Mother said, looking about, "it did seem there were a lot of them . . . what strange-looking men," she said.

"Look at all the animal heads!" Cecily screamed suddenly from down the hall and I ran to look through the open door into a room which had been closed since our arrival. It was full of the most awful dead animal heads I had ever seen.

"Those are Leopold's," Cecily said. "The cook told me he goes to places and hunts them."

Slowly, we walked through the room looking at the elaborate carvings on the ceiling and the animal skins on the floor. There were endless little statues and rosettes absolutely everywhere, and every inch of silk wallpaper positively covered with paintings and photographs. It was very crowded.

As Cecily and I had taken some time dressing, Mother and Father were ready to leave by the time we arrived at the table. We were about to sit down when the cook advised us we should wait for another guest, a young woman named Sabina. I had not seen Timothy all morning and was told that he had gone straight off to the medical school. "He is so *nervous*," Cecily said, "I am glad he is learning about nerves. Why he seems so *very* excited. I am beginning to think he has Aunt Ida's 'fan-da-sea-clay' disease." And then she turned and continued her conversation with the cook, Berta, with whom she had made friends quickly. Berta was a large woman with a pink face and she smelled of cookies. She ushered us out of the kitchen finally and told us to sit down to breakfast at the huge dining room table and wait for the young guest of the Countess' who would arrive shortly. There was a newspaper lying on the table and I opened it. The front page was very strange. Here and there were *huge* blank spaces, as if the ink had not worked. I was showing these to Cecily when Sabina suddenly appeared.

She was a tall, rather pale young woman. Although she greeted us somewhat shyly, she spoke almost perfect English, and when I asked her how long she had studied, she told me, blushing, that she thought she did not speak at all well. She was favorably impressed that Cecily and I both spoke some German. Cecily had surprised everyone with her ability in languages. I realized she could hear the language, and then she had discovered some French and German novels she loved to read because Mother did not know what was in them.

Mother had a Latin tutor as a girl but knew no modern language save English.

Cecily lost no time asking Sabina why she was there, where she lived, and I thought that Cecily was being almost *rude,* but Sabina was most gracious about the questions, although she seemed quite frail to me. Her large brown eyes seemed almost too big for her delicate face and I noticed that under her eyes the skin was very dark and had been covered over with powder.

I decided to interrupt and divert Cecily's attentions to the blanks in the newspapers and I asked Sabina about them. Sabina told us, to our amazement, that if there were stories certain people didn't want in the Vienna papers, they were eliminated, and so the large blanks would appear instead.

"How curious," Cecily said. "I would so like to know what *isn't* there, wouldn't you?"

Sabina smiled and said in Vienna many times what wasn't there was the most interesting story of all.

A maid brought in several other newspapers, including the *Paris Herald,* remarking it amused the Countess no end. She apparently liked to read the "Salons" column, in which everyone told what fabulous necklaces and rings they gave to everyone else. Cecily turned to it immediately and read from it: "The King of Italy, Umberto, had given his nephew, who was to be married, a villa near Turin and four magnificent saddle horses; the Pope sent a sacred relic studded with diamonds; and the Duchess of Mouchy, a collection of jewels, including two black pearls, a diamond crescent, a carriage rug, and an English pony cart with two ponies." And it also said that Prince Edward of England is running about Paris with baguettes on his gloves and driving all the glovemakers mad trying to keep up. "In addition," Cecily read, "he has purchased ten homburgs, and they are all the thing in Paris." She put the paper down thoughtfully. "It sounds ever so lively," she said. "I would so like to go there."

"I'm sure you will," Sabina said. "The Countess is away in Paris often, I understand."

Cecily turned to Sabina. "Do you go often to Paris?"

"No," Sabina said, "I am going to medical school."

"Here?" Cecily asked in astonishment. "A woman? They let you in?" And again I saw that most peculiar expression on Cecily's face. She positively scowled and bit her lip at the same time.

Sabina said, "I had influence. Some are hoping, of course, I will fail."

"Oh," Cecily said, to my astonishment very much affected and voicing both our fears, "you *mustn't.* You cannot," and with that Cecily stood up, her face turning pink.

"I shan't," Sabina said firmly. "I can do it if my spirits remain good. That is the only problem."

Cecily looked at her and said, "Oh you *must not* get discouraged. I am *certain* you are a good student."

Sabina looked at us then with quite the saddest expression.

"It is not my studies," she said softly. "I am frequently in the grip of emotions beyond my control."

There was a shocked silence. Cecily and I said nothing. We were uncertain what this meant, and I think even Cecily was afraid to know any more.

I changed the subject at once and we discovered that Sabina was only a very recent friend of the Countess. Cecily was about to inquire further when the doorbell rang, for about the fifth time that morning, and I saw Sabina stand up as the butler admitted a girl about our age, perhaps a little younger, who looked nearly frozen to death. Cecily got up immediately and followed Sabina. I, of course, could not contain my curiosity and went into the hall as well.

The girl, frail and very cold, was wearing several sweaters and a strange pair of very old boots. They were tied on with rags. Sabina was speaking to the girl who, to my surprise, spoke English rather well. "I'm pleased meet you," she said, curtsying in her dreadful torn clothes. "I read about America in my book the Countess gave me," and she curtsied again. Sabina was looking at her boots, which were tattered and enormous.

"Why are you here?" Sabina asked.

"I have a letter for the Countess," the girl said and handed it to Sabina. "The Countess gives me money and clothes, and sometimes books. I need this very much now. I have only my brother's shoes, and I must go to work. I must walk home by tonight and begin work tomorrow morning."

"Do you go to school?" Sabina asked gently.

"I work. At night I read," the girl said and went into a lot of German talk that only Cecily could understand. Cecily's reaction to the girl was altogether unexpected. She had turned pale, I noticed, yet she seemed utterly fascinated. Usually Cecily asked so many questions, but she stood there for once quite stunned. Sabina spoke to the girl in German again for some minutes and then disappeared into another room. While she was gone, Cecily spoke.

"What factory do you go to?" she said.

"Bronze," said the girl.

"What time do you do it?" Cecily said.

"At five o'clock in the morning."

"Is it fun?" Cecily asked.

The girl looked at her incredulously, as if she hadn't heard the question. "What?" she said again.

"Well," Cecily said, "is it any fun, you know, working in a factory. Do you like it?"

The girl's face was grim. I think that she thought Cecily was jesting with her, but she was persuaded otherwise when Cecily said, "Well, I'd like to do it once or twice just to see . . . now tell me what do you do there?"

"I solder with a pair of bellows driven by gas," the girl said. "It is very hot and very hard, but I save enough money to buy my own shoes." She spoke with pride. I felt something in me draw back at this confession. "I made money in the spring to save for the winter because I would not need shoes in the summer," she said, "but then mother got sick, and there was no money, and then I fell ill, so I could not get shoes." I could see that shoes were central to her. At the same time I could not really believe her. It seemed to me that she had wandered into the Countess's home out of Mr. Dickens' novel we had just been reading.

Suddenly the girl's attention was drawn to a book of Cecily's. The book was blue, and the girl stared at it.

"You are reading Schiller?" she said, her eyes alight.

"Why, Aunt Ida gave it to me," Cecily said, turning to pick up the book. "Have you read it?"

The girl shook her head. "Not that one," she said quietly, and Cecily, as I knew she would, picked the book up and gave it to her, insisting she take it. The girl seemed quite overwhelmed.

"I do not always have time to read," she said. "At night I help my mother sew. If I finish, I can read. But we are all in one room, so it is difficult."

"All in one room? You only have one room in your house?" Cecily asked.

The girl nodded.

"Who is there, you and your mother and your father?"

The girl shook her head. "My brothers, my sister, and my mother, and sometimes my mother's friend."

Cecily stared. "How many beds do you have?"

The girl looked at Cecily and then at me. She was trying to decide whether to tell us.

"We have two," she said, looking at the floor.

"What's your name?" Cecily asked. The girl looked up proudly. "Adelheid."

Sabina had returned, followed by Berta, who was carrying a new pair of boots and several articles of clothing.

"Come with me," she said. "We will see that you are clothed, and I will give you some money, but you will have to return for the Countess. She is not here now. Do you have very far to go?"

The girl looked crestfallen. "I cannot come back. It is a day's walk for me," she said, "and I must be in the factory. On Sunday I must help my mother sew." She seemed about to burst into tears.

"We'll bring it to you," Cecily said suddenly. "Whatever you need, Adelheid, we'll bring you. I have extra shoes and sweaters." Sabina looked at Cecily. "I'm not sure your parents will allow you to go so far," she said gently.

"Well, I will come, nonetheless," Cecily said. I stood there in amazement at her sudden generosity. She had never offered to give me anything, or our cousins, or anyone else I knew. And then I thought, perhaps uncharitably, that Cecily wanted to go because we would so definitely be forbidden if anyone ever found out.

The girl looked at Cecily, not quite trusting her. Then she looked at Sabina. "Thank you," she said and followed Sabina up the staircase. When Adelheid returned some time later she looked transformed. She was wearing shoes, a coat, and hat, she seemed to be extremely happy. She thanked Sabina and wrote her address down on a piece of paper which Cecily had gotten for her. She gave it to Cecily with a look that I would best describe as the look of someone who never expects the other person to arrive.

"Good-bye," Adelheid said, and then like a ghost she was out the door.

Cecily was full of questions the minute she had left: who was she, why did she work at a factory, how many girls worked in factories, what was it like, why was she so poor, didn't her father have any money, why didn't she have a father, why didn't she go to school, how many children were there like that? and on and on in such a torrent of inquiry that after a while Sabina was exhausted.

"I think that's enough for now," she said finally. "We can talk tomorrow about it if you like," and she told us the cook said we were to go upstairs to change because Mother was returning and we were going visiting in the afternoon. She told us the Countess had gone out early in the morning, but she would meet us at a cafe for lunch.

"Will you be coming?" I asked her. Sabina smiled and said no, her mother would be arriving shortly.

Cecily told me she really didn't understand at *all* about Sabina, because the cook told her she'd been found nearly frozen to death in the snow. Cecily was very impressed that she was going to medical school, as was I.

Cecily and I spent the rest of the morning exploring the neighborhood around the Countess' house on the Strudelhofgasse. It sounded like the pastry, so I would remember it, and it was near a magnificently sculpted staircase which I knew I would always be able to find. There were beautiful houses and parks in the neighborhood and many statues and monuments. We hoped we could stay in the Countess' house forever, as it was very large and inviting. After our walk, when we had returned to get dressed for lunch, we heard a commotion at the door. We expected that it was Mother and Father returning. But to our surprise in the salon there was a rather tall man with a beard in a black coat and a tall hat, walking back and forth with some agitation and speaking to the Countess' husband Leopold, who had greeted us with something less than enthusiasm.

He and the man in the black coat were having a very animated conversation, which got louder and louder as we descended the stairs. The man in the black coat seemed very angry at the count, and Cecily, who stops at nothing, was about to intervene when Father and Mother suddenly opened the door. This caused the man in the black suit to stop talking, and Leopold turned around, looking, as he always seemed to do, highly annoyed. Mother ushered us up the landing to the next floor, but as they were talking quite loudly we could hear and see almost everything when we looked over the balcony.

Father immediately rushed over to greet Leopold, and I heard Leopold speaking English then and introducing father to the tall man, whose name was Rabbi Bloch. I couldn't hear exactly what they were saying but after more quarreling they all began to walk toward the door, Father looking very worried. Leopold finally said, "Well, if this ritual murder business is in the Torah after all, Rabbi, what are we to do?"

The man in the black coat seemed to get even taller and angrier. His eyes rolled around in his head and he pounded his fist on the table in the hallway. "Of course it is not in the Torah! How could you for a moment think such a thing!"

I did not know what the Torah was, but it was clear that the rabbi was extremely offended. After some further discussion Leopold walked out, and then the rabbi also left. Cecily immediately wanted to know what the business about the ritual murder was and what the Torah was. Mother, of course, didn't know, but Father said the Torah was the Jewish Bible and that some terrible crime had been committed, and that we shouldn't ask any more questions.

40

Cecily and I were very excited. We were to meet the Countess at a cafe called Demel's. Vienna, we discovered, was absolutely full of wonderful places where people spent the entire day drinking coffee, reading newspapers in German, French, and Italian, having intense conversations and eating the most marvelous sweets. Aunt Ida said it would be impossible not to fall in love with Vienna because so much of Vienna was devoted to both the pleasures of the mind and of the stomach! We had arrived early in our eagerness to meet the Countess and no one asked "How will we know her when she arrives," because we were all sure we would just know. We hadn't long to wait before Cecily, who could hardly eat her cakes for constantly staring out the window, began to squeal, "There she is! There she is!" and Aunt Ida, who up until that moment had been very thoughtful, jumped up as well and looked out the window at the most magnificent woman I had ever seen.

Her hat was made of lace, a white frilly, frothy confection of billowing sweeps and flounces, and her dress! The dress was shocking and wonderful and exactly like the hat, white lace pouring down her body in the most suggestive way, and she was twirling a white lace parasol and stepping from her carriage onto the street where a gentleman in a blue fedora awaited her.

"The Countess, the Countess!" Cecily whispered, and we all stood up, Mother looking extremely alarmed as this extraordinary woman entered the cafe flashing her dazzling smile and proceeded immediately to our table.

Father stood up to greet her, and as she bent to kiss him the smell of roses wafted through the air. Diamonds sparkled on her neck. Father said, "Bettina, this is my wife, Emily,"—and Mother nodded— "and you remember Ida,"—Aunt Ida nodded also—"and the children." Father stood behind each of the chairs as he introduced Cecily and me. Timothy stood up and attempted to kiss her hand, which he wasn't very good at, and his lips landed smack on her lace-covered wrists, but she didn't seem to mind as she rather breathlessly introduced her companion, Monsieur someone, and amid stares from everyone in the cafe two chairs were brought and Monsieur someone and the Countess sat down to have their cakes with us.

The Countess slid silkily into her seat beside me, her white lace rustling like taffeta. Her eyes were the most beautiful I had ever seen, gold and brown but rather more gold, and the whites around her pupils were dazzling. One did not ordinarily go to great lengths to comment upon the whites of people's eyes, but these were a startling white perhaps, I thought, the more noticeable because of the very dark lashes which framed them, and they were not exactly slanted, but very almond shaped and her cheekbones, which were rather high and prominent, seemed to accent this so that one's impression was of a very exceptional and strong face.

The Countess talked very warmly and quickly, speaking English, French, and German, often in one sentence. Mother said barely anything, which the Countess, to her credit, pretended not to notice and simply went on in that lilting voice she had, commenting on us, her pleasure, the lovely things they had to offer in the cafe, and then launching into a description of her trip, the train, and where we must go to buy dresses. We had been told that the dress shop immediately adjacent to the Countess' house was one she operated herself, but that as it was considered inappropriate for an aristocrat, and her husband did not approve, no one knew of this. Aunt Ida had told us that some of the Countess' designs had even been seen in Paris, but that she did her work secretly at night so no one would know.

The Countess was very amusing describing to us the way a M. Worth in Paris had designed a gown for her. Mother began to laugh despite herself as the Countess pretended to be M. Worth before his sketch-board, "pretending," the Countess said, "that he is Rembrandt," as she made these motions with her hands, weaving back and forth and then collapsed onto the table, imitating his spiritual exhaustion from his effort. It was very funny, and Cecily and I could not stop giggling.

The Countess had encouraged Cecily and me in our choice of pastries, and we were about to order our third when Mother intervened. I was so fascinated by the Countess that I could scarcely speak, but Cecily lost no time in telling her about the young girl who had come to the house with no shoes, and that the maid didn't seem to know what to do, but as Sabina insisted something be done, the maid gave her some clothes and told her to come back. There was a pause as Cecily told the story and then the Countess' face changed. She began to look very sad and then very angry.

"Of course she shall come back, and I shall clothe her properly," she said. "I clothe many of them, but charity is no solution. I know the girl. She is intelligent, and I am seeing to it that she receives an education." She paused. "But she is only one, and even if I saved five hundred, which I cannot do, it is nothing." She looked at Father. "It is absurd, and it must end. Don't you agree, Frederick?"

Father's face was grave. Cecily was silent. It was very awkward to bring up something so unpleasant so soon, but the Countess said, "You needn't be embarrassed at bringing up such a painful subject. It is always there. It doesn't go away, and it is my hope that with proper thinking some solution will eventually make its way clear, although," she paused, "I confess I am no longer certain what that solution is."

Father said, "Well, there is a housing measure before your Parliament. That is promising. People here sleep in the trees I'm told."

The Countess shrugged. "Yes, they are without homes, and they sleep in the trees, and it is before Parliament, which is all we have at the moment, this Parliament, which is pathetic," her face looked sad, then suddenly brightened, "and often amusing," she said. She turned to us. "Would you like to be entertained? Then we must go tomorrow to Parliament." Her eyes lit up again, "We will sit in the gallery and watch them argue the resolution tomorrow. It promises to be a most enlightening day, but first I have an appointment with a tailor in the morning, so we shall meet at ten."[1]

41

Where oh where is Gertrude Van De Vere?
Her head is in the bedroom
And her arms are over there.

Captain Voll pushed the piece of paper across his desk "How long have you been getting these notes?" the Inspector asked.

The captain shrugged. "Perhaps two months. I have reason to think it is the same murderer at work in several of these cases. Originally when I believed there had been a murder at the Freud residence, I believed it was the work of this man. But now I am certain it was hysteria. After all," he said to the Inspector, "there is no evidence of a body."

The Inspector looked at him keenly. Was the police captain pronouncing this information as if he were proud of it? The Inspector shook his head as if to wake himself. He suddenly felt a terrible sense of fatigue. Last evening at the opera he had felt quite splendid. A new conductor, Gustav Mahler, had been appointed despite a uproar over his Jewishness, and he had been brilliant, the Inspector thought. And then he had seen that woman. The Countess. She had entered her box

---

[1] This was probably one of those unbelievably rowdy sessions of Parliament which Mark Twain, who was living in Vienna at the time, reported on for *Harper's*. Count Badeni, a reformer, had proposed a series of language ordinances which included making Czech the official language of Bohemia. Conservatives and German Nationals united to filibuster and create unprecedented obstruction until Badeni would fall. Every time someone attempted to speak, the group brought out whistles, sleigh bells, harmonicas, trombones, hunting horns, and snare drums, until the speaker was drowned out. Badeni fell a few days after he had summoned over sixty policemen into the Reichsrat to clear it. The Reichsrat was nearly paralyzed by conflict during this time, and the emperor, on occasion, had to resort to emergency rule.

late, during the middle of the second act. It annoyed him. It was, he thought, the habit of women who had lovers to attend only the opera's last act.

He read the note before him again.

"May I see the others?"

Voll nodded, and produced three more notes. The Inspector scanned them. "Have you found any body parts?"

Voll nodded again. "A hand. Some boys found it on a playground."

The Inspector looked carefully at the other notes. "The one about the hand," he said, "says her *leg* is over there, it doesn't mention her head."

"No," Voll said.

"Keep searching," the Inspector said. "When we find the second body part it may become easier."

"Why would that be?" Voll asked quickly. The Inspector did not answer. "Where is the appointment book?" he asked, intent on his thought. Voll fidgeted in a drawer. "It was necessary to return the original," Voll said, "so as not to arouse suspicion."

"But you have already told me you are *not* suspicious," the Inspector said, "you are convinced it is hysteria."

"*Now,* Inspector, I am convinced. Originally, however, I did not wish to give my suspicions away. You understand."

The Inspector nodded. He didn't understand, the man was inconsistent. He reviewed the results of interrogations, with the grudging acknowledgment that Voll was, however, a rather good interrogator, but pleased also to know that he, himself was better.

He left the station house and walked over toward the Prater. Disturbing cases. Amputation, murder, and then this confusing business in Freud's house. He crossed the street and got lost amid the beautiful overhanging trees in the park. He loved this park, that he could say. It was a very beautiful place. He continued to walk, musing, thinking of nothing, but every once in a while, thoughts of the Countess would rise up in him. She was not beautiful in the ordinary sense. Her face was strong, and somewhat tense. She was easily startled, he noticed. He was drawn to her. As for Voll, he disliked him. He didn't know the reason for this either, but Voll's entire person repelled him. He'd felt himself step back abruptly upon being introduced. The Inspector shrugged. He would make the best of it.

He sat on the park bench for some hours, thinking of absolutely nothing. He resolved when he got up that he would go and see Lisette. He thought this should lift his spirits.

42

Timothy watched Bertha Pappenheim[1] running in her thin linen white petticoats, her camisole top, white socks, and shoes, running along the Danube, flickering in and out of the light and darkness as the moon moved behind the clouds, the trees. The young man watched from the trees, turning his kite in his hands as the white specter of a young woman, with blonde hair flying, ran, ran as if she were mad. He saw her now stop and pause at the water's edge. As if in a trance she weaved back and forth, back and forth as if caught in some primitive religious ceremony, caught in some harmonic keening with the water, at the same time, eyes wide open as if searching the skies for the proper goddess to instruct her.

[1] This is the kind of reference throughout the manuscript that I personally find quite irritating. It is simply not possible of course according to any chronological order, that this is Bertha Pappenheim, Breuer's first hysterical patient, the one that Freud and Breuer wrote about together in the famous case history "The Story of Anna O." It is possible that it was a dream figure for Timothy suggested by the case, which he read. He had already been dreaming about her in America. Of course it could have been a real woman upon whom he projected his own knowledge. In addition Anna O.'s remarkable symptoms, not the least of which were extraordinary powers of imagination, that caused her to imagine herself pregnant with Breuer's child, and indeed she even began to "show" and develop psychosomatic symptoms to such a degree that poor Breuer found it was more than he could handle and took off with his wife, leaving the poor girl still adrift in her hysteria, although, of course, that is not how the *official* report of it went. In any event, the time frame of this document does not permit the woman perceived by Timothy to be Bertha Pappenheim. The best guess I can make is that it was probably some kind of fantasy figure for Timothy, who, after all, was a medical student in Vienna at the time and must assuredly have known of the case. It is interesting to note that although "Anna O." was never "cured," she went on to a most commendable life in public service. I have always found the case most remarkable myself. Particularly the aspect which caused her to "speak in foreign tongues" in moments of emotional crisis. It is also Anna O., of course, who was responsible for the technique of free-associating, so popular today. It was her idea to pursue this course, although it was Freud, of course, who theorized it. She called it "chimney sweeping," by which I suppose she meant, getting the dirt out.

The young man took a puff on his cigarette and then put the kite down, looping it carefully around a tree and tying a knot. No one would find it, but he didn't want to take a chance on the wind.

He walked stealthily down along the border of the trees to where the girl was standing. There remained about another hundred feet to where she stood on the edge. He looked about, certain of his success, and plunged forward. He took her firmly by the hands, which were extended now across the water as if reaching for someone, and pulled them sharply to her sides.

"Oh!" she said, startled and then as he held her arms to her sides, the eyes, still open, seemed to change.

"It is quite all right," he said to her softly. "You are dreaming. I must take you home." He was struck with the beauty of her face, and the warmth of her neck. She was strong and attempted to break his grasp, but he held her firmly and as he did so he felt the warmth of her breasts against his skin. The shock broke his grip, he released it slightly, she pulled her hands away and turned to run. She had only got several yards when he reached her again, and she struggled, screaming now, as he pressed his hand across her mouth, and, forcing her down upon the ground, kept insisting in his growing excitement, his fear now, and his concern, "It is all right, I will not hurt you, it is all right." Wild her eyes, and wilder her body, which heaved so voluptuously under him, but he held her firm, and eventually she quieted and then, her head turned in resentment, said coldly, "What do you intend to do."

"I," the young man, shocked, suspecting her intentions, "am to do nothing, but to help you ... you cannot go about at this hour in this condition."

"I am not dreaming," she said, "I am in the park ... am I not?"

"Yes," he said, although his head was getting tired from the position of holding it up, across her as he was. Yet he was afraid if he stood she would escape again.

And she asked another question. And another.

And he answered. And they went on this way some time. With the moon moving in and out behind the trees, and a cloud in a constant rhythm to her questions, and the young man's head sank lower with each effort until his face alongside her was so close she could feel the warm clouds of breath from his mouth. And he then, lying in this way upon her could feel the softness of her breast, and she could feel the sharp crinkled hairs of his chest and his shirt and the magnificent weight and hardness of his body, and her breath, which was coming in gasps she knew not from fear, from something else, and the cloud of his breath coming closer now to her neck, his bearded face against hers now, and then soft moist lips speaking to her in kisses as he answered her questions into her neck. And she felt then this astonishing sweet trembling throughout her body as if the earth was shaking, and the young man too had lost all senses except the sweet odor of the moist place of her neck, the perfume of her dress, and the wet darkness of her hair curling across her neck. He had no idea how long they lay there or what spell entrapped them but when they got up her dress was wet from the dew and clung close to her hips and her buttocks and his shoes were wet.

He led her to the back door of her house and she unlatched the servants' entrance and let herself in. She did not turn to him or say anything at all, he just saw her back in the white camisole, the white petticoats still clinging to the rounded shapes of her thighs, her stockings and shoes soiled with grass and wet. He saw her enter the house and close the door, heard the latch turn, and stood there, stricken for some moments, not knowing what procedures could have brought him here or how he should leave. He desperately wanted to follow her into the house and held himself accountable for days for lacking the courage or the spirit or the imagination to have found in this encounter the way to achieve some perfect end. To end it, or climax it, or continue it, but not to have it drop off in secrecy, all the feelings that had surrounded them, as if he had been thrown into the kettle of first cold, then boiling water, and then plucked out blind, to have suffered the most extreme bodily sensations he had ever encountered to be left with nothing but a white linen handkerchief.

He stood on the doorstep until it was daybreak and when he heard the servants moving about inside, he seemed to awaken then, as if his desire had put him in some kind of spell. He got up then and took the white linen handkerchief from his pocket and wrapped it around his wrist.

He waited for her every day and every night, and at the end of his kite people saw something that was not at all a kite's proper tail, but almost a sail, a square sail that went forth causing the kite to skitter and sway, as if to keep it off balance, and a man passing said to him, "You should remove that cloth, it gets in the way of your kite's flight." But the young man didn't say anything. He would let the kite sail, fall, up and out over the Danube while he sat under a tree, sometimes without moving, for hours.

43

It was early the next morning in Paris when the servant announced to Edith Wharton that there was a policeman downstairs asking for Mr. James. Feeling alarm, she told him to wait, and quickly dressed. She ordinarily did not dress until late morning, when it was time for lunch, but this morning she would put even her writing aside to find out what this was all about. Surely, she thought, hurrying toward the staircase, Henry could not have gone to the police voluntarily over this matter of the cat, although her maid, Bridget, had told her that Henry would cry out in his sleep, "murder, murder, murder," several times a night. She sighed as she entered the drawing room, and advised the policeman that she did not have much time but she wished to know the nature of his business as succinctly as possible. Lieutenant Cuvée surveyed her.

"Actually," he said, "I've come to see Mr. James."

"I understand that, but he is not in, and when he is in he isn't well. I don't wish to have him unduly upset, so you can tell me what this is about."

"Are you his wife?" Lieutenant Cuvée asked, although she was sure he must have known.

"Certainly not," she said. "I am Edith Wharton. I am his friend, and I am also an acquaintance of the prefect," she said haughtily. Cuvée seemed unimpressed. Actually she was floundering for the prefect's name, although she had met him at some awful dinner for someone, somewhere.

"I am afraid," Lieutenant Cuvée said, "I must speak with him personally. What time is he expected?"

She looked at the clock. She had noticed that Henry went out every day at eleven. "I imagine he'll be back around four. He usually is," she said. "Can I tell him what it's about?" she asked, feeling annoyed.

"It's an investigation," he said, bringing forth a small black leather book and patting it on the cover, "It's just a few questions." Something in Edith Wharton's spirit fell like a rock from the sky. She recognized that book... She had seen another just like it. It must be a coincidence. He saw her staring at the book. "That's a doctor's appointment book, I believe," she said nervously.

"Yes," he said.

"Does this business concern a doctor?" He was struck by her sudden nervousness and became suspicious that perhaps Henry James was somewhere in the house.

"What makes you think that?" he said.

"Well obviously, you have a doctor's appointment book in your hands, so I think it must."

"Is Mr. James seeing a doctor?" he asked.

She felt guarded. "I have no idea, actually," she said.

"Have you ever heard him mention Dr. Sigmund Freud?" he said suddenly, taking her off guard.

"Why no, I mean yes ... er, no, that is, I haven't heard him speak of him exactly, but I have heard of the doctor. A total charlatan, of course, don't you agree?"

Lieutenant Cuvée said nothing. Then he said, "He is quite respected in Vienna. But I understand he is seeing patients here as well. For a short time. The incident occurred in Vienna, but I have been instructed to interview his Paris patients as well to see if they can throw any light on the subject. Tell Mr. James I shall return, unless, of course," he said, glancing around, "it is all right for me to wait?"

"I'd rather you return," Edith said quickly. She was feeling very nervous, but had to ask the next question. "What incident?"

"There has been an incident, in Vienna," Lieutenant Cuvée said. "I have obtained the list of his Paris patients and we are hoping to close the inquiry—perhaps it is nothing—before the newspapers get hold of it, and I must warn him the names in the book may get into the hands of reporters and—" He tapped the book but he got no further. He saw the sudden change in her color at the mention of the word newspapers and in seconds, the indomitable woman before him was in a dead faint on the floor.

44

Edith Wharton had never been so driven. As soon as that police lieutenant left her house, she called her maid to pack her small bag immediately and cancel her lunch plans, as she must make the Vienna train. She was not thinking, she later reflected, she was just desperate, determined. She knew she had to get to Vienna and get rid of the evidence, at once, at once, at once.

Bridget had rarely seen Mrs. Wharton in such a state of total agitation, so as she finished packing the car, which Cook was driving to the station, she pressed the small vial of laudanum into her hand. "Only a little, remember, just a little. You should sleep on the train. You don't look at all well," she said nervously, and Edith Wharton took it, glad for anything that would calm her. She felt suddenly as if she were losing her mind.

It was night when the train arrived in Vienna, and Edith Wharton was awakened by the conductor. Still dazed by the laudanum, she nonetheless gathered herself together and got off the train. Clutching her purse and small bag, she hailed a carriage. She had no idea *how* she was going to do it, but she knew she would do it. *She must not fail.* And at this thought she quickly tore off her gloves and replaced them with another pair from her purse. This was her second change of gloves. Each time they had been soaking wet.

45

In Berlin Dr. Fliess tore open the envelope from Sigmund. "How irritating," he thought, shaking his head. Sigmund was always worried about something. First about dying young, then about powerlessness, and now about some police investigator regarding Emma Eckstein's blood. He shrugged and didn't finish reading the letter. His wife was calling him to dinner.

46

Edith Wharton waited in her hotel until after midnight when she was certain they were asleep before ordering a carriage. She bid the coachman wait a distance from the house, and made her way down the darkened street. She was too determined to be afraid, despite the warning of the hotel clerk that she must not take the carriage alone, as there was a murderer stalking Vienna.

She found 19 Berggasse and made her way around the alley to the back. Without moonlight she realized suddenly she could not have seen anything at all.

She groped her way along the ledges, and then just about shoulder height she felt the draft and looked. The window was open. She pushed it further with her hand and allowed her eyes to get used to the dark. Sticking her head through the window she realized suddenly how absurd it was to have worn a hat. She took it off and lay it on the ground. Then she pulled herself up by both arms and managed to get most of her weight nearly through the window. She raised one leg in a most ungainly way to the ledge and leaning forward, let out a cry as she felt her hips roll and her balance give way, landing with a thump through the window smack in the middle of Dr. Freud's carpet.

She blinked a moment, brushing off her clothes before she tried to rise. Her cheeks were red, she knew. She was mortified that someone might discover her. She waited a moment to allow her eyes to adjust, and then taking out a small candle she had brought for just this purpose, she lit it and proceeded to look about her.

She was relieved to find herself in the right room and saw in a moment that the desk with the visitors book lay right in the hall outside the door. She tiptoed to it, moving slowly lest there be something on the floor on the way, and finally she reached the book. As she thumbed through it looking for the fateful day, she heard a sudden noise. Her heart raced and then she saw her name and, snatching the paper, tore it from the book, blew out the candle, and made her way across the carpet to the window.

The sound was sharper now. It was someone walking, and she felt the sudden sweep of perspiration and a slight trembling through her entire body as her hands reached up for the ledge. She pushed forward and in a daring leap plunged through the window and landed on her side, painfully, and rolled through the bushes until she straightened herself up and fled to the corner where she had kept the carriage waiting.

The coachman noted that his customer was returning sooner than expected. She had forgotten her hat and her hair was quite disheveled. She refused to look at him, leaped in the coach, and cried out to him through the window to return to her hotel.

In the coach she was frantic. She had the paper in her hand and it revealed that *rton* had been left behind.

Edith Wha was all she had.

47

Henry began to think that perhaps his concerns about the events of the last weeks were producing some serious alteration in his mind. He had given up all of his normal literary concerns and seemed to have fallen into a kind of lurid fascination with "the engines," as he liked to think of the narrative that pumped through these tales. Nonetheless, he did maintain his old curiosity about murder trials and it was with some relief that he began to read that evening about Madeleine Smith:

> Gentlemen of the jury, the charge against the prisoner is murder and the punishment of murder is death, and that simple statement is suffi-

cient to suggest to us the awful solemnity of the occasion which brings you and me face to face . . .[1]

48

After waking up to a loud knocking, Carl Jung opened the door to receive a phone message. It was from Freud. What sort of emergency could it be that Sigmund was rushing to his hotel to meet with him at eight in the morning?

49

Minna sat fidgeting in the chair opposite the Inspector. She wished Sigi were here. He had arrived late last night, and hurried out early this morning to meet Dr. Jung. Martha had said the Inspector wasn't coming until one o'clock and Sigi had said he would be back well before that. And now the Inspector had arrived four hours early! She was quite uncomfortable. It was cold; the stove had not been properly heated. The Inspector had chosen to keep on his large macintosh, and as he paced and turned, puffing on his cigar, it swung out like a cape, the rubber edging scraping against the wooden chair with a rhythm to it. She remembered later the cadence of his voice, so soft, so inquiring, and then the sharp slash of the coat against the chair as he turned and puffed and talked and then, pausing, knocked his ashes into the large ashtray he'd brought into the kitchen.

He noticed she was highly agitated. He wondered about this and decided to proceed with questions about Martha.

[1] This is the dean of faculty, John Inglis, Madeleine Smith's brilliant defender, in the Madeleine Smith trial, in July 1857, in which the educated and quite comely Miss Smith was charged with poisoning her lover Émile, having returned, according to testimony, from seeing *Lucrezia Borgia*.

"Tell me," he said, "from the beginning, how things happened that night. Move about, if you don't mind, and show me precisely what you remember, and exactly where you were sitting and where you were standing—the best that you can recall, of course."

"I don't remember much," Minna said. "As you know, Dr. Freud has said it is my overactive imagination, the night, the storm..." She shrugged.

The Inspector held in his ire at the mention of the doctor. It was almost like a conditioned reflex, he noted to himself.

"I know the storm, but you are not ordinarily disturbed by storms, are you?" He looked at her intently. Minna dropped her eyes. "No, I'm not, normally."

"And that night, that night you were more disturbed than usual. Disturbed about something? Finding it difficult to sleep?"

"Why... yes," she said, her eyes cast down. He saw her press her lips together primly. So, he thought, there is something she doesn't want to talk about.

"I... I often find it difficult to sleep," she said.

"But there was something special about that night, was there not?"

She looked up at him now, her eyes wide. "No... no, just the usual thing."

"Aha," the Inspector said, "so there was nothing," he paused dramatically, *"special* about your inability to sleep that night, nothing that kept you anxiously pacing the floor, is that correct?" He looked at her with such innocence and so directly, she was taken aback. He had the most startling blue eyes.

"Why yes, that's correct," she said. She pressed her lips together again. He smiled and relaxed. A woman who was not a habitual liar was so *bad* at it.

"All right, then, let us proceed with the events of the evening. Now Martha, I would guess, is also a light sleeper, and you often meet in the kitchen for your camomile tea together, is that right?" The Inspector knew full well this was not the case, but he was waiting for information.

"Oh, no, not really," Minna said.

"Oh? Is Martha then not kept awake as well?" he asked.

"No," she said and began to laugh. "Quite the opposite. Normally Martha sleeps the sleep of the dead. I am quite surprised she awoke."

"Aha," the Inspector said. "So it is not true she is afraid of storms, then?"

"Oh, she doesn't like storms," Minna said, "but there have been worse storms than this that failed to wake her. I don't know why she woke. Perhaps because Sigmund was away, although," she couldn't resist saying, "he is called away frequently in the night by distressed women."

"Aha," the Inspector said, his eyes lighting up. "Frequently in the night, by women?"

Minna resented the implication at once. "Most of his practice concerns women, as surely, Inspector, you must know by now. They suffer from nervous disorders which can become aggravated at any time of day, most particularly, it appears, with some of them, in the evening."

"I see," the Inspector said. "I know so little about this. Is it that most of his patients call him away at strange hours of the night?"

"No, not most," Minna said. "You can ask him. I know of only one, the Baroness von Frisen. She has been a patient for many years."

"I see," the Inspector said, taking out his notebook and making a little note.

"But as Dr. Freud must have told you, it is highly confidential, and she is an extremely nervous woman. I do not think he would approve at all if you attempted to interview her. I believe, in fact, he would employ all means at his disposal to stop you. He arrived here last evening. He had no idea you were coming to interview us. He has forbidden me to speak to you at all, but I see I have no choice. However, I will not speak further about his patients."

"Regardless, Fräulein, of the good doctor's wishes," the Inspector said, "it is fully within my right, not to mention my responsibility, to proceed with this inquiry. There has been a murder here, and it is my obligation to find the culprit."

"Indeed," Minna said wryly. "And what of your obligation to find the body, to find proof that there was indeed a murder? Is that not primary also, Inspector?"

"Perhaps, if you will forgive me, they are one and the same inquiry. Do you deny you saw a body lying on the floor?"

"I am no longer certain of what I saw," Minna said smugly.

"Fräulein, may I remind you, that if a murder has been committed here, and the culprit is abroad, you or one close to you are as likely victims as anyone else, and should I fail, on the basis of an appeal to your sense of justice and your concern for humankind, I appeal to your sense of self-protection as a woman not to make light of this matter. It is of grave consequence, particularly for females of an independent nature who choose to go abroad alone at night."

Minna sat straight up. "Why . . . I . . . I do not go abroad alone at night, and indeed only occasionally in the day. It is not my habit."

The Inspector disliked her, but he would make do with what she offered him. "And in the day, when you go alone, where do you go?" Those intense blue eyes once again focused relentlessly on her.

"Why anywhere . . . for a walk, just out, to stroll, perhaps to the market, why it depends," she said in such an offhand manner, with such studied casualness, that he immediately suspected he had something, and with the sure instincts of his profession he took the moment to turn to her. Holding the tea box he had taken and hidden under his overcoat, he produced it dramatically and said in the most accusatory tone he could muster, "To buy *tea,* Fräulein?"

He was delighted with the calculated effect. Her face turned crimson. Her teeth bit into her lower lip. Clearly she was caught. At what, he didn't yet know. But it would come.

"Why, I might buy tea," she said, quickly regaining her composure. "Is it a crime, Inspector, purchasing tea?"

"Not at all," he said, impressed with her composure. "In fact, I quite like this tea you bought, tea that your sister prepared that evening, and I would like to have some for myself. Would you be so kind as to tell me where you obtained it?"

Minna's face was now pale. Her head tilted back in a strange angle and her chin jerked toward the ceiling. In a moment she composed herself again. As she turned to him, the expression in her eyes was glacial. "Possibly at Schönlichler, . . . I . . . no longer recall," she said quietly.

"And why is that, Fräulein?" he asked. "Was it so long ago?"

"Quite, quite long ago," she said, almost stammering.

"How remarkable a tin it is then to keep the smell, the flavor so pungent. Can there be so many purveyors of herbal teas in Vienna that you no longer recall which?"

"I no longer recall," Minna said.

"Is it not strange, that in this household, which had at last count only three teas, one of which is herbal, that you cannot recall *where* or when you purchased it?"

"I have a poor memory," Minna said, by now quite shaken.

"Very well, that will be all then, Fräulein, for today." The Inspector rose with a nod and a bow, placed his notebook in his pocket, gathered his great macintosh around him, and swept out through the parlor.

When from the upstairs window Martha saw the Inspector's great-coat swinging down the walk, she hastened downstairs. As she entered the kitchen she was startled by the sight of Minna sitting in a chair, her head tilted back and her hand on her throat. It was as if she were in a state of total panic, or perhaps, Martha thought, later, a kind of pantomime of panic.

"Minna," she said softly, "what is it?"

Minna immediately sat up, her hand moved from her throat, but her eyes were sad. "It is nothing," she said softly.

"Has he done something to upset you? Was he rude to you?"

Minna closed her eyes. "I, it's nothing," she said. "I am tired, that is all. Please excuse me." She got up and without ever looking directly at Martha went up the stairs to her room.

The Inspector had known but had not raised the question that it was necessary for Minna to go through Sigmund and Martha's room in order to reach her own. There was no other access.

50

The Countess was swinging along one of Vienna's most fashionable streets, the Kärntnerstrasse. She turned down the block and swept into Hr. Moser's to have the buttons fixed on her dark green velvet gloves. With her brocade coat and her coppery hair spilling out from under her brown felt hat adrift with white ostrich feathers, the Countess was a sight to stop both men and women who crossed her path. As she swept into Hr. Moser's the attendants came rushing out of the back room all aflutter. "It's the Countess, it's the Countess, it's the

Countess." Of course, at this time, Vienna had its share of countesses and duchesses, but when the workers and shop girls came running out from the back to have a look, Hr. Moser knew that it meant only one: Bettina von Gerzl, who had captured the heart of everyone, save two, in Vienna.

"Betttttttttttttttina," he said, holding his arms wide as she rushed forward to embrace him. As he went to kiss her cheeks with his cheek, he smelled the rosewater she always wore. He felt the pleasure he knew so well in her presence.

"Oh," she said, her hands pressing down on the green-gold velvet bolt he had lying on a counter. "It is beautiful," she said, fondling the fabric. "I must have some. Wouldn't it make wonderful gloves, Hr. Moser? You know how I *love* extravagant gloves."

Hr. Moser smiled. "Of course, if you like. It is a new design, from Jouy of course. Nonetheless no one anticipates this for gloves; it is for an elegant coat."

"I shall have it in gloves," the Countess said.

"Bettina," he said, "we must speak," lowering his voice. "There are dangerous rumors."

"I know," Bettina said, smiling. He looked at her. She could not know. She could not know the infamy and be so casual. He bent low and whispered in her ear, "The Countess de Pougy was here this morning from Paris. She . . ." he looked about the room worriedly, "she is telling everyone that . . . that your grandmother, in Russia, that," he paused again, puzzled by the imperturbability in her amazing yellow eyes, "that you are Jewish. You must stop this rumor."

"There is no need to stop it," she said. "It is a rumor to be sure, but one I started myself." The blood began to rise in his face, "to show that all this talk of anti-Semitism is untrue," she said, stroking his collar. "Why you yourself see me no differently now that you know, do you, my friend?" She looked at him, and he saw the cutting edge, like the side of a diamond, which he had seen in those eyes before, those yellow eyes once topaz, had turned into diamonds for him now —harder, more challenging, riskier.

"Bettina, this is a most dangerous game. You cannot do this." He held her arm firmly now.

"I must do this," she said and slowly released her arm.

51

Timothy stalked the river at night, looking for his beautiful somnambulist.

That night, tonight, he had taken some special precautions and had lodged his camera near a tree. He would catch his ghost on film, then he could have her evermore.

It was near morning, and he decided it would be best to hide the camera in a small copse, not far from the river. There was a bench there, and he had plans. He took pains with his secret and then left it and strolled by the river. It was well hidden. He walked up and down the Danube and it was now very light and he saw no sign of her, so he turned dejected. So disappointed was he, that he at first forgot his camera hidden in the brush. He soon turned and saw that the bench he had chosen to take her to was already occupied. There was a woman sitting there. Her eyes cast down, her hands folded, seeming, he thought, deep in thought. She seemed not to notice him. He looked around, plagued by a certain desire. He wanted to take a picture, now. The camera was all set. There would only be the disconcerting flash. He knew if he asked she would refuse.

He decided to make a bold move and simply filled his tray with powder and set off his light and shutter. The woman never moved, no glance, no cry, nothing, which left him even more distressed. But he shrugged from fatigue and the morning damp, hoisted his equipment to his shoulder and strode off.

When Cecily encountered him on the stair she glowered and said, "Now I see you with your camera! Whatever are you up to?"

52

He hurried toward the latest body. At least this time it was not a woman.

"There is a tendency," the Inspector said, bending over the body, "to hold the victim responsible for everything, even his own murder. It is not enough to be a victim, he must be the aggressor as well," and then he folded the sheet back over the dead body and told Captain Voll to take it to the morgue.

Captain Voll looked at the Inspector strangely. "But we have a note. He has written a suicide note."

"Yes, Hr. Voll," the Inspector said, "but the gun was fired from this angle," he placed the gun against Voll's neck. "There is advanced arthritis in the right arm, as you can see. The body is still warm, yet it is impossible to raise the right arm, and certainly not to the back of his head. Therefore, he was shot and the gun was placed in his hand afterward. There is no evidence of robbery, you say, so we must inquire slowly and carefully of his family and associates to discover the motive and find a murderer who plots enough to leave a suicide note, but not enough to fool us." And gathering his macintosh about him, the Inspector left.

53

The Inspector had his fill of deaths and bodies. It was now time, he believed, to take advantage of Vienna's more agreeable attractions, so he decided to go again and visit Lisette, the *very* best strudel maker in Vienna. He found her full of baker's charm: she smelled of raw dough and had a yeasty polished look to her skin like the shiny surface of bread that has been worked just right. Her arms were covered with flour, and her bright pink cheeks were blazing from the heat in the ovens. The tablecloth was hung over the edges of the table so that it spilled out onto the floor.

The last time, seeing her stretch and pull and push the strudel dough thinner and thinner until it spilled over the edges of the table had thrilled him. Never had he seen such a strudel maker! And the taste! The baked strudel, its feathered flutes lying on his tongue for just an instant before they melted around the nuts and raisins and tang of the apples, sour with a sharp sweet taste in his mouth. He had, of course, made love to her, it had been impossible not to. Although he wondered at his inspiration. If it were strictly in the baking, why, he could be compelled to fall upon the wife of every baker and chocolatier in the city. Such was not the case, he assured himself. Although, he sighed, if he gave in to the full range of his appetite, with sufficient time this possibility, too, might manifest itself.

"I am glad to see you again," she said, her pink face dimpling with delight. She had nice eyes, he thought. He liked the expression in them, and he found a reminiscent longing stirring at the sight of her short plump arms buried deep in the mixing dough, her apron and her face flecked with tiny spots of flour. A white cap covered her hair from which some blond ringlets had escaped and flour seemed to drift everywhere in the kitchen. On the windowsill he saw small pots of lemon thyme and smelled their snappy essence filtered through the air. The warmth of the oven, her breathy laugh, the sweetness— yes, that was the word—the sweetness of her person made him quite content, and he drew up a chair, happy simply to be in the warmth of the kitchen and to watch her arms dive again and again into the vast bowls of dough.

"Ja," Lisette said, "I make the strudel now. First I make the rye breads, then two pumpernickel, ja, then the strudel."

The Inspector sighed and looked out the window. He would be here for several hours. He imagined that Voll and the rest of them were running about after heads and feet and bodies, and he felt a bit of a cheat to be here. But only a bit. After all what was the point of wisdom if a man didn't know when to use it?

He smiled at Lisette as she flirted gaily with him. Lisette had put the rye bread into the oven, and just removed a pumpernickel. Its fragrance assailed the air.

It was with special relaxed pleasure that he stood by the stove stirring the thick yellow custard while he watched Lisette roll out the pastry crusts.

When the pastry was safely inside the oven, he turned his mind to his next project, sugared angels. He had agreed to help Lisette in the laborious task of making spun-sugar angels and harps and saints for a feast in honor of just which Austrian Catholic saint he no longer recalled. The process was tedious and the sugar had to be spun to precisely the right length. He had agreed to help her on the condition that she would reveal to him the source of her chocolate for the chocolate macaroons. There was a flavor he could not quite duplicate. When he had offered his assistance as part of the bargain, she eyed him coldly and said, "They are *my* macaroons."

"But I would make them only in Paris," he protested.

She refused, but conceded this: "If you help you can take half the harps."

He considered this and agreed. The sugared harps were quite marvelous. Perhaps if he had not been so eager, perhaps if he acted more casual, more leisurely, more nonchalant she might give up her source for the chocolate. He would try that approach, but for the afternoon he contented himself with the harps, and he began mixing the sugar on top of the stove, stirring with the rhythm that pleased him so, that made him know his mind was working on all the ingredients at hand, and if he were lucky and resolute a solution might be forthcoming by the time the harps emerged from their spinning.

"If you are warm," Lisette said shyly, but not too shyly, "you can leave your jacket in my room." She pointed to a small door at the end of the kitchen.

The Inspector nodded agreeably.

Lisette stood suddenly before him now. "No one comes now," she said, "until six."

She locked the back door and the door from the main house to the kitchen. She disappeared into her bedroom, and when she came out she was wearing a long, thin, white smock and her feet were bare. He was amazed how light she was on her feet as she moved from oven to bread bowl, humming to herself. There was something hypnotic in watching her large breasts rising and falling as she moved, sometimes from table to stove to bowl to oven to icebox, cracking eggs and crushing poppy seeds, releasing some exotic fragrance of nutmeg or clove or honey from each stop in these whirling stations through the kitchen. And then she was in his arms, the mixed fragrance of sugar and almonds and dough rising in the air about her pink, floured face. His lips sank against her breasts, and he inhaled the smell of vanilla. He tasted crushed almonds near her ear, and then his head bent into the sweet dough of her belly, and there they were, the two of them, on the straw mats, rolling. Occasionally he felt his leg or back against the cool tile floor and rolled again onto the mat where he became lost in the sweet bulk of her body and the fragrant wafting smells of baking bread.

When he was dressed, he knew he had to say something to her. About next time. For as pleasurable as it was, it had stung him to know his heart was not in it, his heart was elsewhere.

He sat there at the long wooden table and held both her hands in his own. "I will not see you for a while," he said softly.

"How long?" she said.

He did not like it. "I will be a long time. I have to go away." He saw the tears begin to gather, and he was glad for the lie.

That night before he went to sleep he took out the volume of Nietzsche he had been reading. It was a most exceptional mind, and there was rarely a time when the intoxication of the man's prose did not speak to him. Then he sighed. Not tonight. He did not have the nerve tonight to look so hard into the darkness. Nietzsche's words were printed in starlight; they shone through the dark; they burned in his mind. They were too profound, too disturbing, and too compassionate; underneath the lines that seemed cruel he sensed a compassionate being. He saw the man he had heard stories about, throwing himself onto the cart horse that had collapsed from a beating to prevent the creature any further pain. Tonight, smelling of Lisette and vanilla and dough, he could not read Nietzsche. Feeling his lids close on a sated body, he wondered why he was not happy. It had something to do with that woman, the Countess, and being in Vienna once again.

54

Whenever Rabbi Bloch had a conversation with the Countess it left him wondering. Mostly today he wondered if perhaps she was right. He had charged her with being outrageous and superficial. Now he did not know. Was it possible that she was right and what stood between him and his people was a *suit?* He wondered about this as he walked the streets. It was ridiculous, he thought, on the one hand; on the other hand he didn't know. Who were his people anyway? The world was full of Jews who didn't read the Torah. Jews who converted to Christianity, in order, they said, to win university professorships. Jews who resented the *Ostjuden.* Jews who hated Jews because of their *payeses* and their black coats. He should give a sermon. He should tell the world that the despised black coat was the coat of the burgher in the Middle Ages, unchanged since that time.

The rabbi was weary. He thought no one knew who was a Jew, who was a German. There were, he thought, no Austrians at all: there were Croats, Magyars, Bohemians, Germans, Poles, Serbs, Slovaks, and Italians, and maybe, he sighed to himself, maybe a handful of Austrians. His Jews didn't read the Torah; they read Goethe and Schiller with passion; they were more German than the Germans and he wondered, sometimes, if it was this that made for all the trouble.

He walked past the Danube Canal, watching its swiftly moving water, and looked out across to the thick ice-encrusted banks on the other side. The wind was blowing bitterly and he stood there for just a few minutes, before he turned away. Perhaps he should not accept any further invitations from the Countess for her dinner parties. He was fond of her, personally, and thought it amazing that she wished to convert. But those dinners were unnerving. He was a man who was proud of his faith and his ideas. To hear Herzl talk now of sending the Jews to a promised land, the man was a fantasist. He turned away from the river with a sinking feeling.

And he heard that fanatic Kraus' voice echoing in his ear: "Tell me,

Dr. Freud," Kraus had said, "the meaning of *this* dream, for I have it every night. There stands Jesus, among the dead, and they are very, very forsaken and he says to them, 'God is dead. I lied. You have been resurrected for just long enough to get this news,'" and then Kraus had cackled in the most ominous way. It had been theatrical and shocking, and the rabbi had resented it. All of life to Kraus had become a bitter joke, the rabbi thought. He walked faster now along the Franz Joseph Kai. Kraus' dream, or whatever he called it, infuriated him. Kraus was a brilliant man, but couldn't he see that people were floundering? They needed something inside themselves, some confidence, some guidance, and talk of this sort didn't help. Kraus was floundering himself, the rabbi knew. The kind of man who would probably convert to Catholicism.

The rabbi walked faster, feeling sadder and sadder, his steps suddenly slowing even as he tried to will his pace to quicken. He didn't know. He didn't know. The dream had stung him, he didn't need Jesus to give him this news. There were times when he felt a terrible heaviness pervade his being, times he doubted. There were times even he, the most dedicated of rabbis, had doubts. God was difficult. There were times one was convinced He had completely deserted mankind. He hadn't gone much further when the rabbi felt a terrible tightening in his chest and despite himself, felt himself fall forward.

55

I am *compelled,*" the Countess told Freud, angry and enraged. "I have no choice—do you know what it means, to have no choice? These men can do what they want with me . . . and I follow. They beckon, and I follow!" She was screaming now, and it would end in tears, tears of rage and sorrow. "I follow them . . ." she said, her voice breaking, "like a dog, a desperate, fearful dog." She broke down completely. These were some of the hardest moments for the doctor. They must try to recover the original trauma. He would not help her if he merely comforted her. But he felt her humiliation. It was especially difficult, he thought, for a woman of her temperament and her character to bear up under a submission compulsion. He shifted uncomfortably in his chair and suggested that they continue tomorrow.

56

As he walked the streets, the Inspector pondered the interviews. They confirmed his hunch that something was definitely going on in that house that the doctor had no interest in disclosing. Whether it was specifically related to the murder or murderers or hallucinations, he had no way of determining at the moment.

He walked down the winding medieval streets running off to the east of the Rotenturmstrasse and the Kärntnerstrasse through the alleyways and courts that linked the narrow streets to each other. He then turned into one of his favorites, the Sonnenfelgasse, with its perfect examples of sixteenth- and seventeenth-century burghers' houses, remembering, as he strolled, the beautiful Schönlaterngasse, the Street of the Beautiful Lantern. He soon found it and perused it carefully, remembering that his father had taken him there, as a child, to visit the "Basilisk House." This was a place where, legend had it, the dreaded beast had lived, terrifying and poisoning the inhabitants of Vienna with its murderous fumes. He had stood there, a frightened boy, his hand in his father's, as he heard how the brave young apprentice had descended into the well with a mirror, felling the beast with its image; when it saw its horrible countenance, it died. He stopped now, looking for the house and the small sandstone replica of the event that he remembered tracing, with his child's hand, across the rough-hewn wall.

He could not find it. Disappointed, he walked on and turned down a narrow lane off the Bäckerstrasse. He let the rhythm of his steps direct his thoughts while his mind wove through them, searching for the pattern he knew would emerge.

Vienna confounded him, he supposed. He felt, as he walked its wandering streets, the presence of some animal nature that had striven mightily against the magnificent edifices the city so valiantly displayed.

Its myriad church steeples, Gothic victories, Renaissance facades, baroque theaters and small medieval buildings, surrounded by woodland, gave off a spirit he could not capture. As he looked up now, along the parapets he saw before him endless mythological figures—fauns and chimera poised in the moonlight, and on the rooftops, gargoyles temporarily held at bay, and here and there mermaids pouring water for pagan gods of stone. And over there a set of doorways embraced by satyrs. The grinning gutters, the beasts of steeples and stone, the arrested spirits poised on every corner quickened his thoughts as he moved through the winding streets.

And often, in the night he found himself looking up, when they were silhouetted in the moonlight, when their strange staring presences took on another quality altogether. Some nights, when he was weary, he imagined he saw movement there along the rooftops, as if they had begun to dance, and then quite suddenly it stopped and a weird stillness prevailed. It was the stillness of a cat, ready to spring. It made him shudder. He felt that if these mythological primeval forces were ever to break their cast of stone, it would be here in Vienna, the city they called the City of Dreams. It was not something he wished to witness.

57

This morning he had other disturbing news. Captain Voll had told him that since the new chemist, Igor Slotkin, had turned up nothing and there was no evidence of a corpse, there was no question there had been no murder at all, and this must be announced at once. This would relieve the rumors and the tension. There had been only an hallucination, or rather two hallucinations. As for the blood, it was too old, at least as far as the chemists were concerned, to be related to a murder that night.

But the Inspector did not hold this view. He walked and thought. When walking he did his best thinking. And what he thought was that blood was blood. And it would tell.

Just as he rounded the corner of the Schulerstrasse some instinct made him turn and wait, his back pressed against the wall. In minutes a man, his head down, came walking quickly on the far side of the street, and as he looked up, his face swathed in scarves, was clearly startled to see the Inspector, waiting for him, and then he ran, leaping over a wall before the Inspector stood a chance of catching him.

58

Sigmund Freud was *very* upset. He held his head in his hands. When he raised it he looked at Jung.

"Why did you deny your involvement with the Spielrein girl so emphatically at first?" he said.

"It is nothing," Jung said, "there will be no scandal. I will fix it. I realize it was an . . . error."

By the time Freud was ready to leave the hotel Jung had reassured him to the point where he was feeling almost cheerful. However, he was pleased Jung would be returning, soon, to Zurich. He regarded him as an unpredictable element.

"I suppose," Freud said to Jung with an amiable sigh, "in any experiment it is necessary to break a few bottles."

"Quite," Jung said, smiling. "After all, I cured her."

Freud then hurried home in order to be in time for his appointment with the Countess. He was concerned, as she had sent him a note urgently requesting to see him and then not shown up for the appointment. He knew she had been feeling overwhelmed by what they had discussed. "I will not, will not . . . be a slave," she railed, and then she had collapsed. He worried now that he may have been proceeding too quickly and resolved that if she did not appear today he would have to visit her.

It amazed him the energy she had for the endless disguises, both physical and emotional, that were required for this compulsive life with these men. But he was also encouraged, convinced there were changes in her behavior already. The compulsions were lessening, if only now she could avoid the despair, what she called "the abyss." Of her ability to avoid this he was less confident. The origins for it he guessed lay in a very early trauma that she could not call to mind. But perhaps—and again he felt the fervor of his ambition and his hope— perhaps this too, was in his power to change. His rising confidence was followed immediately by his own anxiety. He *must* be careful. She was delicate and the work was difficult. He had pushed her too far, once, he now realized, and nearly lost her.

59

We were surprised the next morning to learn that the Countess, who had promised to show us some dresses in the atelier next door including, Cecily said, some of her *own* designs, would not make any appearance at all. This perhaps would not have seemed too unusual, had it not been for the extraordinary vitality we had witnessed the preceding day. Cecily had found out from the cook that the Countess frequently had "spells," during which she would lie in her room for days without eating, staring straight ahead almost as if she were dead.

This affected me deeply, and although Mother and Aunt Ida took us shopping, I kept worrying about the Countess and wondering why such things happened to her.

Sometime late in the afternoon when we had returned to the house I told Cecily that I didn't believe it. I suppose it was because I had been reading *The Castle of Udolfo* that my mind turned to this. Perhaps, I thought, something awful had happened. Perhaps Leopold had locked her up and we ought to go see. Cecily was surprised at this suggestion coming from me, but she finally agreed and we went up to the third floor and peered through the keyhole. Cecily looked first, and her head drew back immediately and she said to me, in a loud whisper, "She's dead."

I immediately bent down to the keyhole myself and saw the Countess lying on the bed, her eyes open and her arms draped over one side, her hair uncombed, her face pale and without animation. As I stared, I saw her hand move and fall the other way. Cecily kept tugging on my arm and saying that we had better tell Mother when I whispered, "She isn't dead at all," for as I stared, I saw on the Countess' face, which was no longer beautiful, no, not beautiful at all, but quite an ordinary and very tired face, I saw tears.

"She's crying," I said to Cecily, who immediately pushed me aside to confirm this for herself. For reasons I could not immediately ascertain this had a totally chilling effect on both of us, and we proceeded up the stairs to our rooms with leaden feet and hearts. And we never, not even Cecily, told anyone about it.

60

Something else for you," Voll said. "Another woman. In the park. A suicide, fortunately. A widow." He shoved some papers across the desk.

"Are you sure it's suicide?" the Inspector's tone was testy.

"*I* am certain. She was alone. The gun was found behind the bench. Clearly she shot herself in the head. But feel free to make your own investigation," he sighed with some impatience, "as I'm sure you will."

61

Timothy was in the developing room pulling the film through the brine. When it hung to dry he looked at it closely and something caught his eye. There was a dramatic dark outline on the bench, in the dew, of someone who had been sitting next to the woman. The figure was clearly wearing trousers. The camera had caught what his eye had missed and the day itself had evaporated. He held it up. It was not, after all, a very remarkable piece of photography, he thought. He might not frame it after all.

62

When the Countess did not appear on the third day, Cecily told me that the cook had gone upstairs. It was only Berta, she explained, who, after days of this, might be able to rouse her and give her some soup and wash her hair. "Berta says," Cecily whispered, "the Countess is two people, one is dead and one alive. And then she clucks under her breath and shakes her head and says, 'A pity, a pity.' "

"My goodness," I said, not knowing what to think. I heard Mother say that a doctor had come early that morning, she had seen him in his tall hat and his black bag climbing up the stairs, and when she asked anyone in the house what was wrong with the Countess they all shook their heads and said, "Nothing."

63

Timothy had spent many mornings following the girl in the white dress who ran, sleepwalking, through the park. He stood enchanted now outside her window, watching her naked in the mirror. He saw the breast, her breast hovering there, fading in and out of the drunken twilight, its pink brilliance glimmering through the moon-beamed glass. Pink rose, amber, gold, and blooming, the nipple floated now out of the soft dense mass of blurred white flesh, the waves in the old mirror billowing it forth into a soft pale balloon, the skin, her skin, all perfumed musk, roses, he later said. The smell of roses, where he stared outside the window in the night, the vines climbing the window wall making him drunk with pleasure, the petals falling in the rain from the vines, on his hair, in his mouth.

His head grew dizzy as he watched. He was dizzy with the spectacle, with the glowing wonder of that gold and rose and white white breast blooming now in the drunken twilight in the ancient silvered glass, and then her hand, three fingertips, reached up, brushed against it and scissoring went closed, then open, then closing again against the pale pink bud, and then the palm, reaching to cradle the breast, smooth, soft, full, heavy, it must be heavy, he gasped, the silver fruit gleaming on the palm, all perfumed, fallen, falling, the weight swaying in her soft gold hand, the ancient glass breaking, the rising moon falling, a thousand silver pieces all at once slivered, shivering, flying in the light. Then she lifted her head and stared into the mirror, straight at him.

Timothy backed away. He was out of breath with the sweat pouring down his face under his straw boater, his white suit all mussed up and his face red as if he'd been running, and he was holding his heart and kept saying to himself out of breath, "It's all right, it's all right."

The girl stepped away from the glass, her face an unread smile. Had she seen him seeing her? Had it been him watching her through the glass that she had eyed and not the amber budded fruit she held so well?

Timothy tore himself from the window only with the greatest effort.

His head was buried in the roses, the petals in his mouth and a thorn unfelt, clinging to his brow. Had she known? His heart was pounding. He had saved her, saved her from her own despair, pulled her back into the night, onto the grass and the glistening dew when she had been about to hurl herself into the river. Yes, it had been he, Timothy Johnson Main, who had been in the park at dusk and seen this girl in a white dress with her blond hair streaming running across the grass, but running like an automaton, her eyes seeing nothing, and he had followed her then to the river and pulled her back from its edge where she had wanted to plunge in, frightening her, and he fought her as she tried to run from him, and then he grabbed her and she fell, her soft breasts pressing against him as his hips locked across hers, and they rolled over and over on the wet grass as she struggled, fists pounding, trying to flee from him, to throw herself again into the river, crying, moaning, tears bursting until he had suddenly slapped her, slapped her as a medical man might do, slapping a hysteric back onto the surface of this world, this place, this ground. And she had seen him then, terror flooding her face, terror in her eyes as the moon high on a rise had turned her face to a pale fevered disc and she had twisted free and run from him, and he had taken after her, slipping twice on the grass, muddied now with the oncoming rain, the moon clouded over and the rain came. And he ran after her, reaching her as she ran up the steps into her house and closed the door, and in pursuit, an indefinable, desperate pursuit, he had hidden himself then, by the side of the house and seen the light and gone to the window and raised himself up on tiptoe to see her undressing, playing with her hair, showing him her breast. And he knew somewhere that she knew he was watching her out there that night, pinned in the dark behind the glass.

His breath had stopped when he saw her nipple there, and her smile and her leaning into the mirror, her back to him, her reflected face to him, and he had been so stung with beauty and desire, so enraptured by her fight, by his noble effort to save her, so swept away by the depth of feeling she had provoked on that bright moonlit night that he had no recourse but to stand trembling on his toes and continue to gaze into the window, staring into the mirror where her image had been long after she had put the light out, long after she had gone to bed, long after his muscles, trembling, had finally given way and insisted he lower himself to the ground in the raining rose-strewn night.

64

The Inspector lay back on his bed, smoking. He found himself thinking often of the Countess. Why was she seeing Freud? These thoughts had emerged that evening as he was reading Freud. What went on in the mind of this man? He had put down *Studies in Hysteria* and decided it was the work of a genius. Whose genius? He couldn't be precisely sure. Breuer or Freud? He made a note to interview Breuer

PART IV
MEMORY
AND DESIRE

1

It being a bright and sunny day, perfect for a walk along the Prater, the Inspector turned that way. It was not long before he found himself strolling toward the rolling park and woodland. He remembered suddenly that the Countess had mentioned that she often rode there on Sunday afternoons.

He had not been in the park fifteen minutes when he saw her. Of course. He smiled to himself. He should have known. She was riding a beautiful white horse, a horse so graceful in its carriage he was sure the animal had lineage in the Lippizaner line. It was characteristic of the breed almost to dance, so springy was its step, and the long graceful tail swept almost to the ground. There was no mistaking it was she as she cantered along with great ease, in her bright copper-colored riding habit, her gold hair piled up beneath her brown velvet riding hat. He was walking directly toward her when she saw him and turned the horse toward him.

"How lovely to see you," she said. Her waist was smaller than he had imagined, and her hands were small in the gloves that held the reins. He wondered if she were strong enough for what seemed to him a rather spirited horse.

The horse, he imagined, had had little exercise during the winter and was prancing and backing away from him, but the Countess seemed unperturbed as she clucked to it.

"Would you like to ride with me?" she asked him.

"Now?" he said, surprised.

"Yes," she said, "it's such an unexpectedly pleasant day," and then she turned to the rider behind her. She called, "Darling Oskar, I know you never wanted to ride this morning, so here is your perfect excuse. My friend the Inspector would like to take your horse."

"But I am not dressed," the Inspector protested mildly.

"All you need are boots," she said. "The stable is full of boots. Come for an hour. Oskar," she turned to the young man, who had dismounted and was leading an extremely lean black horse his way, "perhaps you will loan him your boots, they may fit."

"But what shall I walk home with?" Oskar asked in a tone that suggested he would do whatever the Countess told him to do.

"We'll drop you back at the stable. Your mount can carry two for a half mile."

"She looks frail," the Inspector said, studying the black horse.

"She looks frail, but she is very fast, and it would be good to exhaust her before you ride too far, unless," she said, "you are very expert."

"I am reasonably expert," the Inspector said.

Oskar, under the Countess' orders, had sat on a bench and was struggling to pull off his boots. He threw one to the Inspector, who, to his surprise, slipped into it easily, and then the other. The Inspector noted gratefully that the horse was standing near the bench, which made his mounting easier. He had little confidence he could mount from the ground without practice. He swung onto the horse, amid much laughter and gaiety, and Oskar jumped up behind him. The animal to his surprise bounded off at once.

"Pull her in," Oskar gasped, his arms tight around the Inspector's belly. The Inspector was trying, but the horse had the bit in her teeth. The stable loomed up suddenly, and somehow the Inspector engineered the excited animal into the proper gate, and Oskar, with relief, quickly slid off as the Countess rode up with a great stamping of hooves. "You see, she *is* a strong animal."

"Indeed," the Inspector said, having rather enjoyed it. "Are you leading the ride?"

"Of course," she said, smiling, and tapped her horse. They were off into the park at a brisk canter. The Inspector quickly brought his horse under control just a pace or two behind her. "This way," she called to him, and jumped over a small stone fence into an open meadow. The Inspector's horse turned quickly and jumped it well, but it nearly unseated him, a possibility he thought she might have been planning.

As they turned into the field, the Inspector saw at once that the ground was still almost frozen and the turf was dug up, as if a herd of horses had only recently run by. He was grateful, for his mount was ready to run, and he let it have its head and was thrilled and astonished at the fast pace the animal achieved, galloping past the Countess and clearing two fences before he brought it around and cantered halfway back down the field. The Countess did not stop for him but turned her horse once again, and he was after her as they entered a long straight stretch of path, covered with a canopy of huge oaks.

They rode through at a gallop, then suddenly as they rounded the bend, his horse's head shot up. By a trick of balance, he caught himself and his weight went forward as the animal reared. His hand shot up to warn the Countess behind him as he smelled smoke, and they came upon a small woodfire someone had left unattended.

The Inspector dismounted, tied his horse to a tree and walked back to douse the fire. When he returned, the Countess was sitting on her horse, the light coming through the trees and the smoke forming a kind of halo around her, and he thought he had, like a child in a fairytale, come upon a piece of magic that was his and his alone to see, and a fierce, explosive happiness rose to his heart with a force that brought tears to his eyes.

When in a few paces she saw that his eyes were moist, she turned away. It was normal for a person who'd been near smoke to have tears in his eyes, and that, at that moment, was all she could allow herself to think, although the intensity of silence between them as he looked into her eyes told her it was more.

The Countess had turned in her saddle and was instructing the groom when out of the corner of her eye she caught a motion from the Inspector and stopped talking to watch him. He was stroking the neck of the black horse, and seeing the animal's ear bent toward him, she could tell he was speaking softly to it. The groom, she saw, was more than eager to take the horse from him, but the Inspector waved him off, and the two of them sauntered away together, the Inspector's large shoulder bumping occasionally against the shoulder of the horse. The Countess had known more than a few animal lovers who talked to horses, but the way the Inspector's face lit with pleasure as his hand passed down the neck revealed more.

She dismounted and walked over to the Inspector, who was just coming back from several large circles with the horse.

"You are affectionate with a horse that most people find difficult to ride," the Countess said. There was admiration in her voice. And curiosity.

"She is difficult," he said, patting her again, "because she appears ugly, and people misjudge her."

The Countess laughed. "Do you think she knows people find her ugly?"

"No," he smiled, "but she knows they do not stand in awe of her. They expect her to submit."

"And did you make the same mistake yourself?"

"Of course," he said. "I am not really an exceptional man, although my ambitions are grand."

"I have ridden her," the Countess said as they walked back to the stable, "but not as successfully as you did. Nor, I might add, as fast."

"I didn't ride her," he said with a sigh. "I got on and stayed on, prayed to a God I don't believe in, and had good training in balance as a child."

The Countess laughed. "You are too modest."

She had been surprised with the ease with which the big man rode. When Oskar dismounted, the Inspector had undone the curb chain, to Oskar's horror. "She'll kill you, she'll run smack into a tree," Oskar had warned. But the Inspector had not had that problem. The way the horse had cleared fences was astonishing. When Oskar rode, the mare balked at every fence. The Countess wondered if the animal sensed Oskar's lack of confidence.

The Inspector, after handing the mare over to the groom, ran his hands down her legs and carefully instructed the groom to put special ointment on a hock.

"She nicked it here on the stone wall," he explained, "and it was my fault. I had no idea there was a ditch on the other side."

The Inspector walked with the Countess to her waiting carriage and they climbed inside. When the carriage stopped at his hotel, he turned to her. "It was a marvelous ride," he said. There was an excitement deep within him that he had not felt for twenty years or more, an intense sliver of joy at being at the side of this particular woman, a feeling of such intensity that he was grateful there was only a sliver of it, for more would have undone him—and he saw in her eyes the same. He would have been relieved to cast it aside as lust. Lust was easily spent, and as easily forgotten, but this like moss that had an unexpected tenacity, grew around stones. The entire afternoon had been converted into an exquisite pleasure, a bursting forth of the joy of life. They were being discovered and seduced by their daring, their desire, their pleasure, and at the same time they were alarmed. There was a prickling sprinkle of sharpness, a sudden spurt of woodsmoke in the otherwise clear and dazzling air. The Inspector was a sensual and sensitive man, and experienced enough to know that this time he was not in control. It was an effort to hold his hand steady as he descended from the carriage.

2

It is my habit since I was a child to make sketches, especially when something excites me. Cecily finds them surprisingly accurate. She says that I am very good at rendering with some detail the expression on people's faces. Aunt Ida insists that I go to art school, but I have told her and everyone that I have no interest in pursuing this further. It is perhaps odd, this habit of mine, but I rather like to keep it to myself. So I have drawers full of sketches I have made, sometimes on very small pieces of paper indeed. There is a pleasure in working in this almost miniature form that intrigues me. Perhaps because of this interest I found myself drawn to the Countess' sketches for her dresses.

The next day it was raining and I asked the Countess if I might go into the dress shop with her. I knew that Leopold was away for several days. She smiled and said of course, so I followed her into her room, through which there was a secret passageway directly into the shop.

"Don't tell anyone," she said. "Sometimes late at night I like to come here and do some sewing. It makes me remember my childhood and I like that."

There were quite a few women in the outer room of the shop, sewing sequins and tassels and feathers and pearls onto the most glorious fabrics. The Countess moved among them clucking and measuring and showing how the dresses should fit. I soon sat, quite content to look through the sketches while I listened to the women sing and tell stories.

Several Russian women in the shop were telling me a wonderful Russian tale about Baba Yaga, a magical witch seated in a mortar who rowed with a pestle through the sky. Then the Countess brought me a very beautiful shawl that she was embroidering. It was white silk with small blue flowers and sheaves of golden wheat on it. The Countess told me her mother told her that the peasant women in Russia believed that whatever you sewed into the shawl you would receive. So in the spring the women sewed wheat and bountiful harvests. Then she showed me a figure at the end of one shawl, in blue, called the Great Goddess, and she said it was a fertility sign that was also sewn on the napkins for brides. She began to sing a Russian folk song, which of course I could not understand, but she said it was about a girl who embroiders a napkin with the moon and the stars and the sun, and then she embroiders herself a husband, who will come to her in a ship, and she told me that once you have embroidered it, of course that is what happens.

I asked the Countess what she was embroidering for *herself* and she looked at me for a long moment and then said, "There is no picture for it," and looked away. I wasn't sure what she meant. I wasn't going to ask anything further, but something prompted me. I surprised myself when I said, "Why what is it?"

She looked at me again and said, a little sadly, "I want to be free. I don't know what it looks like yet," and then there was quiet. It suddenly seemed the shop was very still and then she said, "Come," and she took my hand and said it had stopped raining and now we would go to visit her friend, Emilie Floge,[1] who was making a dress that a great painter was going to put into a painting.

3

As Sabina's mother settled into her hotel room, her hand clutched the letter that she knew, now, she must bring to the attention of the police. She had come to Vienna out of concern for Sabina, who did not, however, want her to get involved. She got up then, nervously, and walked into the sitting room. It seemed there was nowhere she could be comfortable reading that letter. Her hands dutifully unfolded it as she tried to calm herself, to read it again. She remembered now, the morning she had received it.

When she had seen whom it was from, her heart froze: Dr. Jung. She had been prepared to hear the worst: that he was in love with Sabina. She disliked him intensely and had begun to feel that his interest in her daughter was truly unprofessional and damaging. However, that Sabina was much better, there could be no question. She had told her mother just the other evening that she planned to continue her medical studies in the fall. But Mme. Spielrein suspected Jung had led Sabina on. She was furious that Sabina was suffering so from a broken heart.

By the time she finished reading the letter again she was once more white with shock. The nerve! The outrageous justification that the man had offered was beyond the pale!

> . . . a doctor and his patient, on the other hand, can talk about the most intimate matters for as long as they like, and the patient may expect her doctor to give her all the love and concern she requires. But the doctor knows his limits and will never cross them for he is paid for his trouble. That imposes the necessary restraints on him.

---

[1] Floge was the name of Gustav Klimt's girlfriend. She ran a dress atelier in Vienna, and it was her dress that was painted in Klimt's work *The Kiss*.

Therefore, I would suggest that if you wish me to adhere strictly to my role as doctor, you should pay me a fee as suitable recompense for my trouble. In that way you may be absolutely certain that I will respect my duty as a doctor under all circumstances.

As a friend of your daughter, on the other hand, one would have to leave matters to fate. For no one can prevent two friends from doing as they wish . . . My fee is ten francs per consultation . . .

With friendly good wishes, etc.,
Dr. Carl Jung[1]

Words sprang to her mind. Foul words she had heard on the street and in the assemblies. Words she didn't know she knew. An admission he had taken Sabina, in exchange for money! Her head was reeling. To think that he, a doctor, had written such a letter to her about her daughter! She was shaking with rage but she knew that if she did not want Jung murdered by her husband, she had best tend to this matter immediately herself. Spinning quickly on her heels, she took her feathered hat from the armoire and, buttoning up her coat, left the hotel room.

4

Shortly after the girls and the Countess left, Sabina threw on her emerald-green and ermine cape and adjusted her hair in the mirror. She would see Carl one last time. Although she was going with certain final intentions, something in her still wanted to look her best. As she glanced in the mirror at her face, a kind of bizarre thrill traveled through her. She always thought she looked extremely beautiful just before and after making love with him. Surely she could not even be

[1] Editor's note: This is historically verifiable. It is the exact wording of the letter that Dr. Jung wrote to Mrs. Spielrein, copies of which are in *The Collected Letters of C. J Jung,* 2 vol., exec. ed., William McGuire (New York: Pantheon Books and Bollingen Foundation, 1967–1979) vol. 2., p. 3 as quoted in Aldo Carotenuto, *A Secret Symmetry,* New York: Random House, 1982. There is really no defense for this outrageous letter. Clearly Jung had fallen passionately in love with Sabina and, in some misguided way, believed the issue of not receiving a fee excused his inappropriate behavior.

contemplating such an act? Not in the midst of this other intention? Surely she could not! Her cheeks flamed at the thought, and she turned and lifted the small brown purse she was carrying and tucked the knife inside it.

Freud, thinking no one was watching, turned the corner at a quick pace. He checked his watch. He knew Minna would be waiting for him at the hotel.

5

The doctor moved across her in the bed. She had come, he thought, to break it off, but now the thin white sheet lay coiled against her thigh, the stark whiteness against her sweating tawny skin. He saw the rise and fall of her abdomen and mused, "She breathes with her guts." He liked that. The damp black hairs of his chest lay across her breasts and her thighs. His marks, he thought, those small black curls of hair, lying like brands, his own, across her body. He liked watching her now, she was always so exhausted, so fragrant, so wary. She never looked at him. In the beginning, she was so fierce, so desperate, so driven, it had overwhelmed him, and in the heat of it he thought her in a kind of madness—some women, he had been told, got like that. She did not, he thought, at that moment know who she was and when it was over, she retreated totally, never looking at him, overcome with shame. Then, only then, did he feel the least pity. He reached for her long hair braided against her neck. But she stiffened and got up and went into the toilet.

He lay back on the bed, smoking, staring at the ceiling. No one would ever know. No one would, if they did, ever believe it. He looked at his watch. It was four o'clock. He had a patient at five. He would leave soon. The patients looked to him for answers, and he? He would spend his life, the rest of it, looking for an answer to this. She stood there now, in the doorway to the toilet, wearing her hat and her coat. She kept all of her clothing in there. She entered this room naked and left it the same way. When she was dressed, she was ready to leave.

He felt that sudden twisting inside. So many times.

"I think we should stop," he said.

"No," she said after a while. "It keeps me alive."

"There are other solutions," he said.

"No," she said. "There are none."

"I think we should stop," he said.

"Do you still want me?"

"You know that is so."

"Then we can't stop, so we won't stop. So," she said, and then, "Until it is never, don't talk to me of stopping again," she said.

"Let me kiss you," he said, feeling wretched when she left.

"Yes," she said, softly, bending down, she had never done that, kissed him with the veil of her hat over him, kissed him gently on his eyes, his hair, his ear, the neck, the lobe, the shoulder, the arm, the armpit, the chest, the veil askew, her tongue against his navel, in his groin, there, her mouth firm and hard. His hands beneath her skirt now, feeling the garters, unsnapping the stockings, rolling them down, his hand raising, tearing the pantaloons, a tear they heard as she sucked him hard and raised her head, and his fingers were into her, two, then three, then four, one behind, flickering, pulling while their tongues met, the tips flickering, pulling his hand on her nipple, flickering, pulling hard, their mouths, tongues folding, the skirts up, through the ripped pantaloons, over her thrusting hard, "Please," she said, and it made him wild again the way she said "please" as if begging, begging him to stop when she was begging him to enter, and he thrust in hard then.

It was dry now, she had washed too well, and dry and hard he pushed, and it hurt her, and then the steady long thrusting, and she grew smooth and deep, and then he could feel her wet and he went on then, his head swinging around his shoulders like a stone on the end of a rope, like a child throwing a stone around and around and around and then letting it go, the stone went over and over and over and over and her teeth were into his hand, hard, as the harsh gagging came into her throat. And she cried that cry; she had the sound of someone strangling, aghh, aghh.

His hand was bleeding badly. He would explain it as a cut.

6

Sabina's mother hurried along the street, clutching the letter from Dr. Jung in her coat pocket. She thought she had made up her mind: Mme. Spielrein was going to the police.

But then as she rounded the corner, she realized she might bring on a great and public scandal. She froze, unsure as to what to do.

When Sigmund Freud returned to his house he discovered Irina had given Jung's address to the Inspector. He went immediately to the telephone to warn the two people the Inspector might surprise—Dr. Fliess and Dr. Jung. Fliess agreed to come from Berlin in a week, and Jung did not answer. Freud then insisted the clerk deliver the message immediately to his room. The clerk had gone upstairs and pounded on the door but heard nothing. As he turned, he saw a young woman running down the stair.

Mrs. Spielrein was entering the police station just as the Inspector was leaving it that morning in order to surprise Dr. Jung, who was staying, he had learned, at the Hotel Sacher. She swept past him as he walked down the stairs and turned his steps in the direction of the hotel. For reasons not entirely clear to him he felt he must hurry to the hotel before Jung escaped. Something told him that Jung would attempt to avoid this interview. Mrs. Spielrein proceeded down the corridor of the police station, worried that perhaps she should not have allowed Sabina to see the letter after all. Sabina was, of course, upset, but there was a look in her eyes that positively terrified Mrs. Spielrein. She had never seen anything like it. She stood in front of the police sergeant's desk, uncertain, once again, that she could speak at all.

7

That evening when Martha returned early, she was relieved to see that Sigmund was already home. He embraced her, as they discussed the dreadful events of the last week. "What have you done to your hand?" she said.

"I know . . . I know," he said waving his hand. She grabbed it. "A cut," he said, "it is nothing."

"Are you certain?" she said, concerned.

"Absolutely nothing."

"It is not like your hysterics, I hope," Minna said, suddenly entering the room, "some psychic shock that has caused you the loss of your hand? Let us see," she said, reaching for it, "perhaps it is only your thoughts that interfere with your hand." She smiled then, that slow insidious smile she had. It made Sigmund sad. He relied on Minna, terribly. Intellectually, there were moments he felt she was his main supporter. He knew the difficulties of her household situation of course, and it was this, he concluded, that drove her to alienate him in this way. It was only the impossibility of her situation, he concluded, that drove her to it.

8

At the Hotel Sacher the Inspector pounded on the door, and when no one answered he obtained a key from the manager and opened the door to find a very surprised Dr. Jung lying in bed, ignoring the commotion at the door and nursing what clearly was a fresh and very bad wound in his hand.

The Inspector introduced himself, and inquired about the hand.

"I was distraught," the doctor said, "over a personal matter. But I am calmer now. It was self-inflicted. I just have to bandage it," he said, turning away quickly.

"Let me help you," the Inspector insisted. He doubted it was self-inflicted.

"Let us talk," the Inspector said, pulling out his chair and settling back with his cigar, which alarmed Jung. The Inspector seemed ready to spend the entire day if necessary. "Let us talk about this wound, and other things. To begin with, where were you, Doctor Jung, and who were you with, on the night of February 22nd?"

9

Freud was in his study, grappling with the irritating Irina, who was insisting on dusting his artifacts, when there was a commotion at the door. Martha was out marketing, and he didn't know where Minna was, but the housekeeper had answered the door. He heard arguing and crying, and then to his astonishment Sabina Spielrein burst into his study.

"I must see you," she said sobbing, "I cannot go on . . . " and she fainted on the chair.

He moved quickly to revive her with ammonia, attempting as he did so to soothe her and get from her the cause of her immediate problem, although he feared that he already knew.

When she regained consciousness, he allowed the housekeeper to bring tea, and when she left, he locked the door. As he turned around, Sabina handed him the letter from Jung to her mother. She said nothing as she watched him read its contents, and she saw his face turn white and his hands grasp the edge of the desk. His knuckles had turned white as well. But his voice when he spoke was full of composure: "I will speak to Dr. Jung about this immediately," he said. "I am certain this has been a very troubling business for you."

"This is not only about me," she said, making, he could see, a real effort to compose herself. "We have had, tried to have, a very free, pure, unconditional love for each other." Her eyes fell to the floor. "I have not behaved well . . . I have failed to *understand,* in the way enlightened love must understand. . . . And we have failed each other. He told me his love for me was sacred, that no one had ever understood him as I had," she got up now, more intense than ever, "and this was true." She paused. "But he suffers now from a character flaw, and if he is to help any more women, or be the great man he is destined to be, you must help him." She said this last to him firmly, but quietly.

Freud sat there, rather stunned. Of course, he knew about the character flaw. About several of them. She was quite forgiving of him. He remembered with chagrin his last meeting with Sabina. Now again, he was impressed with her compassion and understanding. It exceeded his own. If that Inspector or the papers ever got hold of this, the future of psychoanalysis was in jeopardy.

After the doctor had steered the interview with Sabina to a conclusion he collapsed on a chair. Sigmund Freud was in a state. My God, my God, he said to himself, imploring a God he no longer believed in. Here was scandal. Sabina Spielrein. He had to concede the girl's brilliance, an intellectual force that took some dealing with. Light-years beyond Jung. It annoyed him to concede it, but he had to concede only to himself. The man had clearly taken her. Jung, the bastard. And the letter to her mother! Oh God! Outrageous behavior. Unforgivable, and yet he'd have to forgive him for his own purposes. Yet he had to admit he had never expected such magnanimity from a woman. It went against all his assumptions. But he must do something. He went to the phone and demanded again that the hotel clerk order Dr. Jung to come to his house at once, regardless of the hour, it was a *great* emergency. God, oh God, he must never let that prying Inspector ever get wind of this. Not ever.

He leaned back against the door, aware suddenly that perspiration had broken out over his entire face and neck and that he had pressed his body against the door as if, at any moment, that imaginary invader, the Inspector, might hurl his bulk against it.

When he relaxed in this position it happened that Irina took it upon herself to crash into the door from the other side. Moving at high speed and with such thrust, she sent him spinning across the waiting room to land smack into the far wall.

"What are you doing over there? I wonder," she said, moving right in and beginning to dust the very air with her impossibly overactive duster. He straightened himself up, contemplating her with a scornful gaze. She was always surprising him, and yet she was ubiquitous.

"Is it necessary," he said between gritted teeth, "to proceed with that dusting just now? You just did it yesterday, it seems to me."

"Oi believes in doin moi job just right, yewwww knoow-ow," she said, "even though half these things on your desk is broken already. Oi can't break 'im any more," waving the wand over the statuettes with a mixture of revenge and glee.

He found her character, what he knew of it, totally reprehensible. Sadistic, shiftless, and heaven only knew what else, she filled his house like a toxin.

He would have had her out in minutes if Martha hadn't protested so loudly about the difficulties of finding help. He paced off for the inevitable duel.

"Very well. You can proceed here. But you are not to come into my consulting room for the next three hours. Is that *quite* clear?"

She looked at him under her rheumy lids.

"You'll choke on the dust, sir," she said, giving a little curtsy. He thought he heard her add, "I hope."

"So be it," he said. "I do not want to be interrupted. If I am interrupted, you will have to find work elsewhere."

He closed the door. Irina sulked.

He must think she was stupid, very stupid, not to get an idea of what a fakir he was. Why, people came from all over the world to see him too, that's what a good fakir he was. Him and his kind. She'd had quite enough of 'im, that was for sure. What a strange group. They came from Paris, London, even the United States. And most of 'im most of the time talking nonsense as far as she could tell. Like the good-looking one, Jung, here all the time, and what nonsense they talked. And then those crazy women crying and their eyes looking terrible. The pretty young one, she'd just left all in a snit, heaven knows what that was all about. And the one that came with the bleeding nose; that was a terrible thing.

She dusted the top of the bookshelf. She'd like to get her duster on them statues he had in the other room, disgusting little naked statues with everything hanging out of some of 'im. African he said, or some other foreign thing. Antiques he said, very old. Something to do with foreigners and funerals. Well, that made sense. He was always talking about death, 'ee was.

Well, the man was scared. She knew that. Him and that Jung the other day, the tall good-looking one with the mustache, talking death all afternoon. She was removing the ashtrays, and when she went in there, they were talking about death. The first time the doctor was talking about houses, and houses meant graves, he said, some dream he had about a house and put it in his book. A crazy dream she'd heard about before, where he drives a cab through the house. And then the younger one with the blue eyes he had dreams about death too. Death and caskets. She'd heard Dr. Freud say to him, "You dream of replacing me," and they both laughed. Replacing him? Who was he to be replaced? The nerve of him, like he was the king or something.

She couldn't figure out for the life of her why everybody came to see this man. All he did was *talk,* and when he stopped talking these patients would start. Talk and talk and talk. Ha. And he had the nerve, the nerve to call it something like a *cure.* She'd heard him call it the talking *cure.* Some nerve. She could cure people by talking too, if they'd pay her for it. He and that sister-in-law of 'is were up to all hours of the night talking and drinking their tea, talking and talking and talking some more. And then she didn't know what they did. She had always gone to bed, but she knew for sure she (the sister-in-law) climbed the stairs late, sometimes as late as four. Maybe she should mention some of this to that Inspector. She hadn't said nothing to him yet, nothing she'd really *wanted* to say, but he was *quite* good looking, a very attractive gentleman, she'd say.

10

I *must* see him," Carl Jung said to Martha. As she opened the door, and he swept past her to the waiting room, she saw his hand was bandaged.

In minutes, Freud stormed into the waiting room, his face rigid with anger. Jung barely noticed it, only nodded, and followed Freud rather jauntily into the treatment room. Freud firmly closed the door.

Jung held up his cut hand. "We've fixed it all up," he said, his blue eyes sparkling. "Sabina and I. A bit of a row to be sure." His eyes fell to the ground. "It was wrong of me, of course, ever to have written to her mother."

"Wrong! It was the height of obdurate insensitivity!" Freud roared. "It was totally unprofessional and unethical. I believed it only after I was presented with irrefutable evidence. That girl is a model of generosity and intelligence. Superior to you in every way." He had not intended to say this last. It had slipped out. It seemed to him that lots of things of late were slipping out.

Jung, for his part, rather enjoyed seeing Sigmund so agitated. He didn't know what it was, possibly his height, for he realized at such moments that he was at least two heads taller than Freud, but when the good Dr. Sigmund got fearfully angry, intimidating all the rest of the Vienna circle, Jung felt mercifully calm, weirdly untouchable in the face of the tiny man's wrath. It amused him. Now he turned Sigmund's anger aside by pointing to his hand. "I see you have a cut as well." Sigmund, started suddenly, held up his bandaged hand which Jung, in a spontaneous gesture, placed against his own, much the way children do in patty-cake, and the two of them stared into each other's eyes.

Sigmund immediately pulled away. "You have settled it with the young woman and her mother, then?" he said, his voice still cold.

Jung nodded. "Oh yes. She has forgiven me." He smiled, preening like a peacock. "She quite loves me again."

Freud suddenly felt totally revolted by this man. "And her mother?" he said. "She may go to the authorities."

"Sabina has fixed it," Jung said, smiling again. "I have seen to it. After all, I have cured her." Freud looked at him shrewdly. The bastard was capable of lying. This he now knew. It filled him with a terrible regret. Too late, too late now to find another.

Irina, had of course been eavesdropping, one of the few daily activities in the household other than the laundry that gave her any pleasure. Irina's inspirational experiences were usually of a mundane sort, which nonetheless, as mundane things sometimes do, had powerful consequences. Her thought now was to rap sharply on the bookcase from the other wall, causing the vase to topple and both Jung and Freud to jump.

"Good God!" she heard Dr. Freud say, and repressed a giggle.

"You see," Jung said with composure, "it is a perfect example of the paranormal I have been talking about. The supernatural."

"Oh, do not be idiotic, at least in my presence!" Freud said with irritation. He thought to himself, it was he who had chosen this man to take over the profession of psychoanalysis. He alone was responsible. A wave of emotion swept over him then so completely that he did not know what had hit him, and the normally implacable Dr. Sigmund Freud suddenly passed out cold.

Irina, on the other side of the wall, heard the thud. It didn't sound like a vase even to her mind. It sounded like a body.

Carl bent over Sigmund, fanning his face and slapping his hands. Then he rushed to the door. As he opened it, he found a startled maid standing against it.

"Get some cold water," he snapped, "at once," and Irina scurried off. All she could think of was that she didn't want to be accused of murder. To her relief, when she returned, the doctor was sitting up on the floor and attempting to struggle to his feet. He seemed vastly annoyed that Irina should witness him in such condition and ordered her coldly from the room.

"Oi was just trying to help," she said, somewhat miffed, and flounced out.

Freud sat there, contemplating Jung.

"What's the matter now?" Jung asked.

Freud looked up. Dare he tell him? Dare he tell his protégé, the man upon whom the future of psychoanalysis rested, that he, the esteemed Dr. Freud, thought that possibly the esteemed, or rather, formerly esteemed Dr. Jung was not only morally deficient but mad as a hatter?

Freud held his head in his hands and moaned.

"You're not well?" Jung asked. Jung thought he knew what was going on. Freud had never sufficiently dealt with his own competitive feelings toward Jung.

Jung knew that Freud had fainted cold on two previous occasions. Once on that boat trip with Ferenczi, when Jung had quite generously offered to interpret Freud's dream, the meaning of which Jung had already guessed. But Freud refused to tell Jung the rest of the dream. "I dare not risk my authority," he'd said and then fainted dead away on the decks. Jung had felt personally cheated. He was *dying* to know what was in the dream.

Then there was the time in the hotel room in Berlin, where Jung recalled they were discussing the issue of Jung's chairing a meeting. Jung knew the old boy didn't like his authority interfered with. No wonder he fainted. Too much oedipal conflict. At least, according to *his* terms.[1]

Freud continued to hold his head. He could not stop moaning to himself. Did Jung really believe in spirits? Oh God, he did. The old bookcase had crashed, and Jung went into ecstasy. Freud realized now what he had repressed about Jung and his fascination with his cousin, Helene Preiswerk, a *medium* for God's sake, who went on about communication with the dead.

The dead . . . the dead . . . the dead. He rocked back and forth, holding his head. He was sick to death of the dead. It was as if his entire house were haunted.

Jung watched Freud bent over as if in grief. He assumed that Freud was upset about the murder in his house. That Inspector was being extremely difficult. He hadn't yet told Freud about his encounters with him and was contemplating the best way to approach it when suddenly it came to him.

"You know," said Jung, his blue eyes crinkling with pleasure at the thought, "a wonderful idea has just occurred to me. What a pity I didn't think of it sooner." He decided he would tell Sigmund about the Inspector's actual questions at a later time, but just now he felt inspired.

"My cousin, Helene, you know, Helene Preiswerk, is taken quite seriously as a medium . . . I know, I know," Jung put up his hand in protest, "I know how you feel about such things, but I have seen this girl, and I know her to be very authentic. She is able to contact the dead, and it is she, I believe, who can clear up this mystery regarding the unfortunate incident in your house. What do you think of that?" Freud looked up. His expression was peculiar. Later, upon reflection, Jung could only call it incredulity.

---

[1] This is another example of chronological incongruity.

11

The Countess was not in the mood for a dinner party that night. She had spent the afternoon with the Inspector, walking through the park. He had spoken to her of the philosopher Nietzsche and given her his book.

As the Inspector had read sections of Nietzsche's book to her, she had been bewitched, troubled, and amused. The Countess in her conversations with Kraus had heard his name many times. He had no use for churchmen, Catholics, Protestants, or Jews, this philosopher. He seemed to believe that God was dead and that it was man through his art that created value, if indeed there was any value or meaning in the world. He railed against the hypocrisy of "truth." As the Inspector walked beside her, reading and speaking of Nietzsche, for reasons that were not clear to her, images came up behind her eyes, almost like dreams.

These were the same images that came up as she was lying on the doctor's couch. The images were of a man, some man she had known as a child, who had in some way stolen her will.

She had shuddered suddenly and the Inspector had turned and asked if she was cold.

The same thoughts now sailed through her as she entered the elegant house and greeted her hostess. As her head bent to kiss the soft powdered cheek of Baroness von Rittenheimer, her high soft voice greeting her with genuine pleasure, she felt a sense of relief. She couldn't help noticing that there was something new happening, with this Inspector. Ever since she began her appointments with Dr. Freud she had felt an increasing sense of withdrawal in the presence of men. With the exception of this man. He made her feel safe. She found herself thinking of him now, even as she tried to turn her thoughts elsewhere.

She was uncomfortable, and this was not the first time. She had been almost ashamed of her wealth and that of her friends. It disturbed her that they sat, all of them, in the Baron's and Baroness' magnificent dining room eating and drinking the finest food and wine while they discussed poverty, hunger, and saving the masses. Moreover, at least half the guests she knew, had spent many an evening squirming in their seats over the Dreyfus affair. She sighed. Thus, she suspected, it ever had been, and thus it always would be. The grandiloquent capitalists were all there, making their fortunes while their thoughts turned occasionally to the plight of the poor. She supposed it would take Socrates to argue whether this was virtue or not; as they were, of course, free to ignore the poor entirely. There was a part of her that might have felt more comfortable with that.

As she smiled at the latest witticism, she longed to return home and read more of this Nietzsche, who would, she felt sure, have overturned the entire table and accused them of lying. The Inspector had sent her into quite a whirl, had made her feel deeply the uncommittedness of her position. She wanted to have the sinew Nietzsche spoke of. She had been inspired by what she read. She felt her own very personal freedom hovering behind his words. If she could not know the truth, at least she wanted to act wisely and with justice. But she wanted more than this, too.

She felt especially that night, that whatever had assaulted her personally, had assaulted the world as well. She felt it through the warmth of the wine, the kisses, the laughter of a very privileged society; she felt it behind the smell of the cacianda blossoms in the air, as she bent her head to kiss the finely powdered and perfumed cheeks of Mme. de Pouvignon, the most famous courtesan of her day, as she reveled in the light glancing from the diamond and ruby and amethyst on her own necklace, preening in what she knew was the envied beauty of her golden hair, and the enthusiasm of her spirit; she felt it and a great sadness consumed her. She wished that somewhere far back in her heart, like a hallway with a forgotten dream, there did not lurk this shadow, the sound of the steps of a lone man walking, not as a stranger and thief but as one who had every right to be there, a proprietor so brilliantly disguised that the children, running from the light into the darkened parlor mistook him for their father, and he emerged, cutting them down, slashing them to the floor with a blade hewn sharp, honed to a fine edge on the wheel of calamity and sorrow.

12

I think," the doctor said to the Countess, "as a child you were sexually compelled by someone, but not by a stranger. If the original seduction in your case had been with a stranger, you would continue to feel anxiety in the presence of strangers. Based on what you tell me, I believe it was a familiar figure, someone who was not a stranger to you, someone who had access to your house, your room, someone you trusted in the household. You were clearly a self-possessed child and would not have felt so compelled to submit if it were not someone who had a legitimate claim to authority."

It had taken him some time to say this in the proper way. He struggled as to how much to tell her; he had the intuition that sometimes he said too many things. With his patient Ida Bauer,[1] he knew he had gone too fast.

"The feeling," he began, "the belief, that you have no choice is a repetition of your original experience. You were correct as a child, of course. You had no choice."

"But now," he heard her anguish, "now it feels the same. I am not a child but why do I behave as if I *must?* . . ."

He interrupted her. "It is the way the mind works, I have found. It is the nature of neurosis. The mind drives you to repeat this, hoping," he said, "that you will be the compeller, and that the end of the story will turn out differently this time." He paused, "It is also in the nature of neurosis, that it never turns out differently. It simply repeats."

"I don't understand," she said. "If it was someone . . . in my house . . . why then with strangers? It is not with my husband that I suffer this."

He interrupted her. "It is precisely in public places, with strangers you feel compelled because originally it was private and someone familiar. The mind will reverse things. That allows it to express the original seduction at the same time as it still conceals it."

---

[1] As earlier noted, this was the young girl Freud wrote up as his "Dora" case.

"This is ... too much," she said. "Why is it so terrifying, and ...?" and then she stopped.

And it was here, he reflected later, at precisely this moment he made his error.

"And you must realize too," he offered gently but firmly, "that there was enormous pleasure in this for you as a child.... You have," he hesitated, "an unusually sensual nature, and in a child this is easily stimulated. The pleasure in a sensual child can be, shall I say, overwhelming. The pleasure, I believe, can feel like it annihilated you. Do you understand that?"

She said nothing. Then a small whisper. "Oh, God, you mean I *liked* it?" she said. He could hear her struggling to ask him, "But why," the voice had gone thin, now, like a wire, as if it might break from the tension, "do I feel such excitement at the seduction, self-contempt, yes, but excitement, and then *nothing, nothing,* as if I am ice? There is no pleasure, only defeat."

"It is difficult to understand," he said. "In order to survive you only allow yourself part of the feeling."

"Odd twist of fate. I might have remembered only the pleasure," she remarked.

He did not expect her to be humorous at this point so he was surprised, and misled. He allowed himself a smile.

"Unfortunately, human beings and society are not organized in such a way."

"*Unfortunately...*" She repeated the word and it hung in the air as she examined it, "such a small word but it means that a lack of fortune, a lack of luck, and that is precisely it, isn't it? a lack of luck is sufficient to ruin a life."

What could he say? He could assure her, as he already had, that there was a way to ameliorate the "luck" of a child's circumstances. He could ameliorate it. But he could not undo it. No. He found himself getting up quite suddenly from the chair and crossing to the window. He felt possessed quite suddenly, not only of his ideas, which were each day reinforced, but of an overwhelming sadness about the limits of his power, and at the same time, he realized later, an undaunted towering ambition, a blazing need to go on against all odds, like a blind and desperate surgeon who must grope his way, trusting only his hands to pluck the diseased fates from the soul's core. And something more than ambition. Revenge, perhaps. He would later call it revenge, revenge that he felt now, causing this anger in his body, this trembling in his hands, revenge against an unknown figure in a long black coat, proper and "good," a teacher, a preacher, a father, a lawyer, but a man. He felt it deep in the palms of his hands as he stood there, attempting to think, but engulfed in feeling that he himself, Sigmund, must go forward now, like David against Goliath. He *must* slay it; the twisted malice that could ruin, in one swoop, the force of trust in the life of a child.

13

The Inspector was having his third cup of coffee as he reviewed the appointment book when he saw the torn page, with the letters *rton.* On impulse he checked it against the copy Cuvée had given him. It was not there at all. Either it was an error, and Cuvée omitted it accidentally, or it had been entered and removed *after* the murder. He would pursue this, he thought, tucking it back into his pocket, pursue both lines of explanation at once.

14

The Inspector found himself the next morning awaiting his afternoon ride with the Countess with an almost feverish anticipation. He had been unable to concentrate all morning, and when he arrived at the stable and saw the black horse had already been saddled for him he felt a supreme happiness swell through his breast. They had been riding almost every afternoon for two weeks. He saw Bettina now making a small series of jumps at the end of the show ring. The joy he felt at simply seeing her there almost undid him.

15

The Countess and the Inspector finished their afternoon ride and were walking their horses slowly back to the stable. The tails of the horses were swishing easily, almost in unison, flicking the flies from their flanks. They had spent a languid afternoon, cantering easily through the meadows, stopping for lunch by a splendid stream, but the Inspector felt he was like a spring too tightly wound; if he moved a fraction closer to her he would explode. He had never been so restrained in the presence of a woman he desired. He had never spent so much time *talking* to a woman he longed to touch. Yet he had a powerful sense that he *must* hold back. He felt almost as if he could touch with his fingertips the tremendous turbulence within her. Sometimes, at night, in a quiet moment he would caution himself that he must not get involved with a woman of such complex temperament. But it was already too late. He did not know the full extent of the Countess' complexity but he felt the power of its contradictions. He could feel through the accidental touches, her hand against his leg, once, as she dismounted, his arm against her waist, the instantaneous rising heat, and he knew if he ever held her, it would be like holding a firestorm in a glass.

Their horses were joined at the flank. He felt his boot against her skirt as they pressed through a small trail in the brush and his heart started to beat so rapidly and loudly he thought she must hear it. Then he saw where they were, the stable looming only yards ahead and the thought of parting from her swept through him powerfully.

"What is it?" she said, caught by his dramatic change of expression, "Are you all right?"

He turned and looked at her, and the words flew from his mouth before he realized their import. "I can't bear the thought of parting from you." At first she looked almost alarmed. Her eyes held his for a moment and then she looked away. He immediately felt foolish and he could say nothing. Nothing at all. He had been too bold. It seemed to him then humiliating as the horses continued their walk, the silence so intense between them that the flicking tails now sounded like cymbals in the air.

"Come with me," she said, suddenly leading her horse away from the trail and into the field where he had first ridden with her. She had pointed out a hunting lodge that day at the far end of the field, almost hidden in a copse. She had pointed to it and said it was never used. They had mounted now and their horses were heading straight for it.

They entered the lodge, which clearly had not been used in some time. Dust was thick on the windows, which were curtained and draped, and the sun was spilling in in great, gold streaks. It had a cold, woodsy smell.

She turned to him, her eyes, he thought, uncertain, dancing.

"I'll—we should make a fire," she said nervously, proceeding to the fireplace without taking off her coat. She bent over, throwing some small firewood into the fireplace, the dust and ashes rising in small swirls with each throw.

"It's cold, isn't it?" she said nervously, turning her face up to him.

He stood next to her, her face, when it turned, just above his knee.

She kept her face turned to him, her other arm extended with the firewood, speaking quickly, hurriedly, "I think it's cold and we should build a fire, don't you, I mean?"

He leaned down then and pulled her up to her feet, put his arms around her and said, "No need, Bettina," and drew her softly to him.

16

The Countess told us she had invited some people to tea that afternoon who were very interested in meeting Americans, especially some young people. Of course we also knew that everyone was interested in meeting Aunt Ida, who had already had several visitors. This upset Father no end. Father had been embarrassed by Aunt Ida on more than one occasion and had hoped, I think, that by accepting this venture in Vienna he might leave Aunt Ida safely in the States. And now it seemed there was some sort of burgeoning feminist movement in Austria. I had seen Aunt Ida "going for walks," often enough with the Countess to know they must be meeting people that Father would find objectionable. That Aunt Ida was a suffragette, among other things, was very disturbing to Father, although she was careful, especially around Father, not to attempt to "sway us." "I only wish to speak my point of view, Frederick," she would say. "The girls have minds of their own, let them form their own opinions."

The Countess, who was very interested in politics and knew people in Parliament, was sympathetic to Aunt Ida's view, although they clearly had their disagreements. When we came into the room and they were arguing, they would stop. Although once Aunt Ida said to me, when Mother and Father weren't there, "Oh do come in. What is the use of all this pretending? You may as well know what you're being forced to guess at." I never told Mother or Father this, of course. The argument between them as best I could understand it apparently was this: Aunt Ida believed that women had to gain control of politics, and the Countess believed that women could gain their rights "only when there will be no government and people can govern them- selves." Aunt Ida had a horrified look on her face when she said to the Countess, "Surely you cannot be so stupid, an intelligent woman like you, as to be an anarchist, can you?" The Countess had replied, "I am sympathetic, as long as there are no civilian casualties," she said, and then Aunt Ida said very angrily, "We must discuss this later," and that was that.

Nonetheless Father felt that Aunt Ida was a dangerous influence, most particularly on me, as no one thought Cecily, who was beautiful, capable of thought of any sort, that is, until recently, but I was fast approaching the conclusion myself that Cecily's thoughts were becom- ing dangerous. For I had noticed that Cecily, formerly rose-cheeked and rambunctious, had grown increasingly pale. This did not happen at once, but in strange and unexpected increments.

Mother had noticed it, too, and ascribed it to reading too many novels. Aunt Ida had found Cecily's involvement with Mr. James' nov- els most amazing. One morning at breakfast Cecily suddenly ex- claimed, "Oh I am so *upset* that Isabel Archer should ever have gone back to Mr. Osmond. It isn't right at all, do you think?" She said this to, of all people, our mother.

"Whoever is Isabel Archer?" Mother asked wonderingly.

"She's a character in a novel," Aunt Ida said quickly, as she gave a worried glance in Cecily's direction.

Cecily, seemingly not hearing this, went on, "She's someone I know rather well, and if you knew her as well as I do, you would find it intolerable, really a disappointment of a very grand order to learn that she had gone back to him."

That afternoon as we were preparing for tea, Aunt Ida remarked to me again that she was rather concerned with Cecily, as she seemed to be extremely involved with Mr. James' heroines. Although Cecily had also read Mrs. Wharton's books, they did not send her into the kind of tizzy the characters in Mr. James' novel did. We were both aware that we had several breakfasts in which Miss Archer was unduly present, and then a lady from *The Golden Bowl* took over the conversation for several days; this was most exciting to Cecily as she was someone new, and Cecily spoke about her as if she had just arrived in town. Then there was the Princess Casamassima in whom Cecily also seemed to have an extreme interest.

Of course this meant that I read these novels as well, and I have to say that when all was said and done there was no question but that it was Isabel Archer and her fate that seemed most disturbing to Cecily. This seemed to become such a serious matter that I saw Mother one evening speak to Aunt Ida, and a few minutes later, Aunt Ida pressed *Portrait of a Lady* into her hands. This was just before she went to the German woman's suffragette meeting, to which Cecily, after attending the first one, had been forbidden to go.[1]

Cecily had spent the entire morning after the first suffragette meeting crying. A most uncharacteristic activity, yet at the same time not exactly surprising. For it was becoming clear to me that something in Cecily had been disturbed, like a tree torn up by the roots and re-planted; its formerly secure mass had entered the new ground incorrectly. So there were Cecily's roots, flailing in the air, freezing in the wind, desperate to find new soil, whereas half the mass lay buried, split from its former self, incomplete and dying, longing for the half

[1] There were few Austrian feminist associations, since women in Austria were not legally allowed to form political associations, although Rosa Mayreder founded a General Women's Association in 1893, before which, incidentally, Mark Twain made a sympathetic appearance.

that were helplessly exposed above the surface. How would it survive? Would it survive?

I found myself wishing, to my surprise, that Cecily were more like she *used* to be, instead of the way she was *becoming*. It made me feel safer when she was more superficial, more amusing. But something profound had happened at the suffragette meeting. Cecily had gone ready to be amused, to take it lightly, and she had returned quite a different person. Aunt Ida told me that Cecily had been persuaded that it was not all "nonsense." She had told Aunt Ida in an emotional breakdown that she desperately wanted to go to medical school and had "pretended to be a flittery girl" because that was what everyone wanted her to be, and that *she* ought to go, and not Timothy.

Whereas Timothy, whom I originally thought was the serious one, seemed lately to be of an altogether different sort. Timothy had gotten very interested in taking photographs and was at it with his camera, day and night. He had even joined the Vienna photographers' club and told Father that he would keep up his medical studies, although he felt he had the soul of an artist, and must find expression some- where. Timothy had been "smitten," I believe is the word. He walked about with a dazed expression, and, according to Cecily, came in at odd hours of the morning, which made Cecily think he was involved with a chorus girl or some creature of the night instead of his medical studies, which he claimed were keeping him late at the university.

But there were times, Cecily said, when she heard him coming in just as the sun came up.

17

Upon leaving the Countess the Inspector felt like an infant learning to walk. He felt himself sway and begin to lose his balance, as if his entire body and mind were not used to the creature they now housed. And it was on these long nightly strolls that he would begin to hear the sounds, softly like water lapping against stone, and then louder, sounds of a memory tapping to be let out. He would feel them surface briefly and then be muffled again. He felt these sounds, whatever they were, were the cries holding him back, causing him to walk around and around the city where, if only he had a keener sense of them, he could divine their direction and head straight for them.

18

The Countess, although a dressmaker and always surrounded by her reflection, had little sense of her own body. Now as she dressed for dinner that evening, her hand would strike casually against her breast or thigh, and she would shiver with delight at how lovely it was. Her whole being seemed to her quite suddenly remarkable, as if she had never really experienced it before.

19

Although the Countess was giving a dinner party that evening, for some reason Father and Mother decided that we should not attend. So we were all going to the Hotel Bristol for dinner. I was very sorry to miss the Countess as I had seen very little of her that week. Everyone noticed that she seemed immensely happy. I realized I had never seen her smile so much. She had been riding almost *every* afternoon and had not, much to Cecily's chagrin, invited us along. Aunt Ida made quite a fuss about missing the dinner as she said she would have been very interested in meeting some people attending. Aunt Ida was mad for the Viennese. "These Viennese," she said, "are the gayest, smartest, most charming people in the world." I really felt we were quite missing something exciting and even Aunt Ida, who appeared most disappointed, said, "Before we left, I met the Rabbi Bloch," she said, "and we had quite a good conversation regarding Otto Weininger, of course, who was going to be *late.*"

"Who is Weininger?" Mother wanted to know.

"Oh he's written this dreadful book," Aunt Ida, said, "that they are selling quite a lot of, it's all about how women and Jews are inferior to the rest of mankind, it's quite a vicious terrible book."

"And he's coming to dinner?" I said. "Why would the Countess have anyone so awful to dinner?"

"He is brilliant and awful," Aunt Ida said, "and she said that Karl Kraus will demolish him in a minute. Kraus is supposedly extremely sympathetic to women," Aunt Ida said. "I have met him."

"And you found him sympathetic?" Father asked, sounding I thought surprised.

"No, not a bit sympathetic," Aunt Ida said. "He may like women, but he doesn't like individuals; this city is so strange in that way," she mused.

"What do you mean?" Cecily said.

"Well," Aunt Ida said, "all this talk of anti-Semitism, you know it's ferocious. Yet individually, meeting Mr. Kraus, or Mr. Mahler, or Mr. Szeps, why at dinner the other evening people were positively hanging on their every word. They elect Karl Lueger mayor on an anti-Semite platform, and then Lueger says, 'I decide who is a Jew and who isn't'! It's as if individually, Jew to Jew, there is no anti-Semitism. Almost as if the anti-Semitism is an idea."

"It's not an idea when a group of university students bash in the heads of the Jewish fraternity members," Father said. There was a moment's quiet. Cecily and I had heard about this from Sabina. I was surprised, as I thought that university students were supposed to be open-minded, as that was, I thought, the entire idea of an education.

"It is difficult," Father said, "apparently for anyone who is Jewish to gain a university appointment, unless they are in the medical school."

"The medical school is one-half Jewish," Timothy said, "the faculty as well. But I have seen this anti-Semitism, it is very real," he said soberly.

We were all surprised that Timothy had agreed to join us. Ever since our arrival in Vienna he seemed to have been consumed with his medical studies and photography.

20

Henry James was feeling very hungry. He had begged off from dinner because he simply couldn't take any further inquiries from Edith. He told her he was sick and he was. Sick with guilt about Constance Fenimore Woolson. Sick, too, with guilt about that cat. He hadn't told Edith he'd actually strangled it. Of course, it was a dreadful cat, but he had been so impulsive. He told Edith he'd hit it with a rock. But the shame was over Fenimore. He had known what she was feeling, and he had burned her letters. He rang for Bridget, the maid.

"Biscuits please," he said.

"Are you feeling better, sir?"

"Oh quite."

"Would you like some jam, sir?"

"Oh quite. Jam would be lovely."

The maid brought three biscuits. When she returned in an hour and saw that there were none left, she thought Mr. James must be feeling some improvement. But she was startled when he said, "Do you have more?"

"Oh yes, sir," she said, "I'll bring you another."

"Bring several," he said.

She brought him the additional three, with jam, and when she returned at seven to fetch the tray, she saw they were all gone.

When Bridget went into the kitchen she was startled to see Mrs. Wharton there. When she saw Bridget with the tray, she said, "Where is that from?"

"From Mr. James, ma'am."

"Henry? Oh, he's feeling better?"

"I believe so, ma'am."

"What did you bring him?"

"Biscuits, ma'am," the maid hesitated.

"Biscuits . . . well, those biscuits are heavy. They are not at all the thing to have brought. I should have thought soup. He can't eat the biscuits."

"Oh, he did eat them, ma'am," she said.

"Indeed," Mrs. Wharton said, feeling suddenly suspicious. "Well, he may have ordered them, but unless he recovered he couldn't have eaten more than *one.*"

"Six," she said.

"Six," Mrs. Wharton said after a moment's pause. "Are you sure?"

"Yes ma'am. Three at first, and three on the second run."

"Well, they are lovely biscuits, indeed," she said, and wandered out the door toward the veranda to ponder this. What in the name of God had got into Henry? Excusing himself from dinner and eating six biscuits in his rooms? It was all because of that dreadful doctor.

21

Feeling somewhat better, henry continued to read:

In the spring of 1856 the corrupting influence of the seducer was successful, and his victim fell. . . . And how corrupting that influence must have been!—how vile the arts to which he resorted for accomplishing his nefarious purpose, can never be proved so well as by the altered tone and language of the unhappy prisoner's letters. She had not lost her virtue merely, but, as the Lord Advocate said, her sense of decency. Gentlemen, whose fault was that—whose doing was that? Think you that, without temptation, without evil teaching, a poor girl falls into such depths of degradation? No. Influence from without— most corrupting influence—can alone account for such a fall.[1]

---

[1] This is the same defender in the Madeleine Smith trial that I mentioned earlier.

22

The Inspector could not help but think of Freud as "the little man." He realized his own tendency to disregard authority in this matter, but there was little he could do about it. He did not like this doctor. He was not, in fact, a likable man. Although he had a reputation for charm and wit, the Inspector found him arrogant, stubborn, and driven. And yet, the Inspector saw there was something in the broad intelligence that was unique.

The wife—the wife was another matter. The wife was a dutiful creature whom, the Inspector suspected, was mortified by the persistent subject of the doctor's investigations. This was a bourgeois woman, a passionate sort who had, nonetheless, buried the passion under a mound of duties and responsibilities, a hausfrau supreme who put up with this husband about whom, the Inspector was certain, she had mixed regard.

The sister-in-law had a wild underpinning that interested the Inspector. He saw that she was in love with the doctor. The wife was a jealous woman, and this had cast a certain tension in the household. The doctor, however, for all his brilliance, and of this the Inspector was convinced, brilliance somehow skewed, was quite unaware of the nature of this tension.

That a man so devoted to emotional truths could be so blind under his own roof fascinated the Inspector, who, of course, also understood it. He had understood little or nothing of Violette, finally, he had concluded. Nor she him. Strangers when they met, then intimate, he had divulged more of his hopes and fears to Violette than to any woman he knew. They had lived together, after a fashion, for over two years, and yet now they were strangers again. Perhaps, he thought, sometimes we cannot bear that someone else should, by knowing us, reflect back to us who we are. And so the Countess, who perhaps did not understand him, really, but desired him, gave him more consolation, more intrigue, more excitement, more feeling than Violette even had, or could.

He felt a wry twist in his heart, that this should be so. The Countess held him, because she expected nothing: no past, no future, just the power of the moment and because of that, she received the past, he held her in his arms and dreamt dreams he never could. In this way, she received his future as well. This she knew, he felt it in her movements, her swaying hips, her head hung back, swinging as he held her, legs wrapped around his waist as he waltzed, naked, around the deserted hunting lodge with her, the sun dappling the dark floors, blazing off the green tiles around the fireplace, the two small windows on either side lighting up with the morning sun, and the Countess, her long thick blond hair swinging behind her, would attempt to hold on to his neck in this impassioned dance, but she would grow weak, her arms would fall down, he could even feel her legs give, but he could not stop, he carried her then, with some enormous strength, even as he loved her, again and again, in some unstoppable current, pulling her down on him and then again, this rag doll flinging about him, moaning in some exhausted ecstasy until finally his energy gave way and he would explode hurling her back up against the wall in a loud cry, and then still holding her, fall to his knees to the floor, where still joined, they rolled over and over.

The Inspector had made love to many women, but he had never felt what he felt for Bettina. It was as if every regret, every fury, every aspiration, every passion that had lain in his body, like a kite waiting for the wind, had risen now, curling into the sky in boundless dips and sweeps, taking with it a full train of unfettered joy and leaving in its wake his fury, his despair, his meanness; every constrained pocket of feeling had fallen now, giving wing to his flight. Freed then, to a new state of vulnerability, he felt this newness with a kind of ecstasy and terror. He was in the middle of his life; he did not think this was the time for such astonishing news.

23

After Edith had gone out that morning, Henry James attempted to deal with his mail. His finger opened the first letter, folding back the thick tissue paper he recognized as coming from Hals. His hands were trembling as he read in the fine, unwieldy scrawl—strange that a painter could have such poor handwriting—that he had seen Miss Woolson in Venice before the incident, and she had spoken so warmly of James, was so full of regret at his departure; had sensed, he said, a great sadness about her. "She fussed so with her gloves," he read, "on and off, quite outside her knowing she did so. It was most distracting." His heart stopped for a moment at that. Tiny beads of perspiration broke out along his upper lip. He felt ill. He rang the bell, and the maid appeared.

"Yes?" she said, "what is it, sir?"

"Bring me some water, please, quickly, and a splash of scotch."

He was pacing the study when she returned with it. He took it swiftly off the tray and turned his back to her at once, staring out the window.

"I think," the letter continued, "that it must be extremely painful to you to know of Miss Woolson's fate. I have guessed what you have not told me, because of what she had told me. And until now I thought it not proper or fitting to write to you. But now that this awful event has transpired, and I am perhaps the only one besides the two of you to know what may have contributed to it, I feel I must write and tell you that *you are not to blame,* that you are not to take undue responsibility in this tragic matter. *There is no single precipitating event."* He read it again and again, the perspiration moving from his lip up along his cheek and over his brow as he attempted to soothe himself and felt instead sick, with a nausea the scotch could not quell.

He saw again and again that hand crossing the table in perhaps the boldest move she had made in her entire life, the hand without its glove crossing the table to rest on his, the urgency of her expression, saying to him, "Oh Henry, I feel we share so much I would like you to stay," and his recoiling from the sensation of her flesh against his hand, not meaning to at all, his nerves jumping before he could control them, the shock and horror on his face as he realized, indeed felt, the depth of her attachment, and how utterly it revolted him, imperiled him to see that need, so naked upon her face. He heard his own sharp contemptuous voice, "Oh I couldn't possibly, really. Let us go," standing up before she even got her glove on, standing up and pushing back his chair in order to recover from such a desperate moment.

He saw her, flushing with humiliation, getting up too, hastening to put her glove on, all aflutter, fighting tears, running out to recover and then coming back to see him, never once raising her eyes. And then the two of them in the gondola, and he could not bring himself to say, "I had no intention of offending you, I truly regret . . ." Instead there was a sea of silence, an unbearable weight, until the gondolier pulling to the side of the canal enabled him to say, although she would not take his hand, only the gondolier's, "I should like to stay on, but I fear it is a figment of my character that it chills me to change plans."

"Of course," she said, smiling too hard, too pale and too shaking, "thank you so much for such a lovely day."

"I'll see you tomorrow at one," he said, "for the churches."

"Yes," she said biting her lip, "of course."

The next day was grey. She sent a note. The weather was inclement. She wished him a good journey.

He berated himself. He might have allowed her hand to stay a moment. He might have allowed that.

The maid came in and found him asleep in front of the fire and thought he looked quite ill. The fire was blazing, and he was shaking like a wet dog in from the cold, shaking and shaking, as if to rid himself of some damp, dreadful climate before it made its way into his very bones.

24

Freud was feeling weary. He had not expected to be seeing patients this morning but she had told him she had something to tell him; it was urgent.

"How often have you had this dream?" he asked the Countess.

"For years," she said.

"But you felt you must tell me this *today.* You have never mentioned it before."

A very quiet "no."

"And why is that, do you suppose?" he asked gently. Minutes passed. He heard the clock tick.

"I was too ashamed."

"And why, then, today?"

She twisted her handkerchief. "There is a man, a new man I like very much . . . not like the others. Very special, to me. I want to get well . . . quickly. So I thought I must tell you what I could not before . . . I do not feel ashamed with this man. It is so different." Her head however turned away.

"Your dream, this dream that haunts you, is it every night?"

"Almost every night," she sighed. "I wake up screaming," she said.

"You have come to me today because you think it important you tell me this dream. And yet you do not tell me about it."

"I forget," she said. "I forget I have it until I have it again. . . . I can't remember after I awake what it is."

"Try," he said, "to remember something."

There was silence. Then she said. "I see a shape . . . it is a letter."

"Describe it," he said.

"I can't. . . . I cannot read it," she said.

He was alarmed by the expression in her face when she left. Her eyes had a hollow look. But when he asked her, she said she was fine.

25

The Inspector was disappointed. Worse, morose. He had been sent a note from the Countess announcing she was ill and had to cancel her riding engagement with him. He looked at the note mournfully, hurt to the quick that it was not even in her own hand but had been written by someone else, probably a maid. Had he misjudged her? Had she done with him? He wondered in torment and then tried to put his mind to his work.

26

Sigmund Freud looked at his watch. This was the third day the Countess did not come for her appointment. He had perhaps misjudged her fortitude. Perhaps he had gone too far. He ought not to go to her, of course, unless she asked. Unless someone called. Yet. He paced his study nervously, hoping that tomorrow would bring her arrival. If not, he determined there was too much at stake, and he would have to make a visit to her house.

27

Where oh where is Gertrude Van De Vere?
Her feet are in my pocket
And her head is over there.

Captain Voll unfolded another one of the notes. Gertrude Van De Vere was indeed among the missing. But so far, no one had been able to find the torso, or anything else. There were days when he thought all the crimes of the century were crimes of absence. Missing persons. Slipped identities. Missing bodies. Fortunately Detective Bertillon in Paris had devised a system of identification. A laborious system of classification. But even Bertillon could make a mistake. So they charged in the Dreyfus case.[1] The Captain preferred not to think about it.

---

[1] In Dreyfus' first trial an important piece of evidence was the note he allegedly wrote, the *"bouderau,"* that was found in the wastebasket. It was Bertillon who identified, incorrectly it later turned out, the handwriting as belonging to Captain Dreyfus.

What was happening in Vienna now they claimed went beyond even the amazing Bertillon. So they had sent for the Inspector. You called the Inspector, they said, when all conventional methods failed. But even he would not solve *this!* Suddenly Captain Voll let out a loud strangulated laugh and banged on the desk like a hammer. Everyone in the police station looked up in total surprise.

28

Life, Edith Wharton thought, was increasingly absurd. Now here was a policeman seated in her living room, asking her questions, all because that dreadful Baroness von Tulow had given her a book on automobile etiquette!

"Yes, of course I have a gun, and I had a gun, or whatever. It's quite lovely, you see, and you are advised if you are a woman, and driving, to carry one. And so I did."

"And you happened to be carrying the gun the night you visited Dr. Freud's residence in Vienna?" Lieutenant Cuvée coolly asked.

"Yes, it so happened I did. I had put it in my bag."

"And what was the purpose of your visit may I ask?" Cuvée inquired.

"I'm afraid that is quite confidential."

"Is it possible, Mme. Wharton, that you carried the gun," Cuvée asked suspiciously and intensely, "with a nefarious motive, perhaps to shoot someone in the house?"

Edith Wharton looked at him, stupefied.

"This is absolutely ludicrous!"

"Nonetheless, Mme. Wharton, is it not true, that on the night of February 25th, at approximately midnight you hired a coach from the Hotel Regina to take you to Dr. Freud? And is it not true that you entered the premises that night and removed, or attempted to remove, your name from his appointment book, and that, in fact, you were interrupted as you meant to do harm to the person in that house? And did you not leave evidence, indeed one of your own hats," he sprang forth with it and Edith nearly tottered from her chair, "already claimed by your maid as your very own, and found the morning of the nine-teenth by one of the Freud maids? And is it not true that you attempted to expunge your name from his appointment book, leaving a trace, however, of *rton,* of your visit, and how, madame, I should like to know, do you explain all of these very suspicious circumstances?"

To Cuvée's total surprise Edith Wharton did not seem at all upset and instead proceeded to lecture him on literature.

"Oh this is absurd. Really now, do you think a murderer is going to be so clumsy, as to wear a hat, first of all, and to return and get only half the note? I must say, Lieutenant Cuvée, you are not at all well-read in the genre or you would see at once the utter preposterousness of your logic, not to mention your assumptions.

"Now, come over here," she continued, patting the settee near a brighter lamp, "and I will help you get to the bottom of this unsavory business. I have read quite a lot in the crime genre and there are rules, you know, and motives, and you are not paying proper attention at all."

"It is not, madame, a question of reading," he said, almost curtly. "We require not interpretation but an explanation as to your circum-stances. There is, madame, such a thing as a fact, and we require explanations for it. I must advise you, you are under suspicion."

He left after a rather mystifying hour, having no clue as to whether she comprehended her situation as a suspect. She seemed to under-stand it only as a literary situation. All she wanted to know, as far as he could tell, was if Cuvée would swear, absolutely swear, not to mention her activities to M. James and to keep her name at all costs, out of the papers, or in any way from being connected to that of Dr. Freud.

He noted on his report her deep antipathy to Dr. Freud, which was all the more remarkable because he had studied his suspect well. He had followed her for days, making inquiries as to her purchases, and she had bought within a few days' time, several volumes at the book-store on subjects befitting a woman of intellectual interests. Her activi-ties were extensive: in addition to an array of visits to museums, fashion houses, and salons, she spent considerable time purchasing books and seemed to read a great deal. She was reading not only books on Renaissance art, which did not surprise him, but the latest volumes on the social and natural sciences as well. Therefore, the antipathy to Freud had to be personal.

29

Sigmund Freud had a headache. He was surrounded by fantasy, fantasy on the left, fantasy on the right, and now in his very own house the biggest fantasy of all: an imaginary murder, witnessed by his wife and his sister-in-law, who swore they had heard the shots and seen the body. Proof of the fantasy was that they couldn't agree on who had been killed, or whether anyone even had. He had no doubts on the matter himself. Martha, he knew, particularly during thunderstorms, had a tendency toward hysteria. But Minna. Insomnia, yes, uncertainty no. And then this odious Inspector with his arrogance and his prying. He had barely saved his notebooks, which the dreadful maid had been about to put into the Inspector's hands that very afternoon.

"Well, 'ee asked for 'im 'ee did," she said.

Oh God, oh God, he implored that deity he never believed in; he remembered Schemuel's explanation: "God directs plays, but he forgets the heroine, he forgets the plot, he does what he wants; that is the only explanation—forgetful, specious, impetuous."

Perhaps Schemuel was right. The entire foundation of his beloved theory was not sufficient to explain the miserable quandary in which he found himself. Strangers milling about in his living room, interrogating his servants, holding his wife hostage to destructive conversations for hours, putting mischief into the minds of his children, and fear and suspicion into his patients. It was a dreadful hour. And that loathed Inspector was at the heart of it. And Minna! Minna, on whom he had always counted. Caught in the rhapsody of the Inspector's insidious charm, she had actually said, "Well, he is quite intelligent and most persuasive!" Intelligent! This utter bull of a man with the disposition of an ox and the perspicacity of a chicken. Minna the astute! Oh woe!

It was that night that he concluded: Schemuel was wrong. The Deity was not a fool. There was no deity. It was a need, a profound neurotic need to ascribe powers of the Father to an impersonal universe. He had found the need himself. That night, had he allowed it, bitter tears would have stained his pillow. But he would not allow it. He felt his resolve harden. He would defeat this Inspector. He would annihilate him. He, and not God, would put an end to this at once.

30

The Inspector was weary. Had she done with him then? Ill, she had said. She would contact him. It had been three days. Surely it had been longer than that.

31

We were a bit surprised when the Countess, who had been feeling ill all week, quite suddenly recovered and announced that the Inspector, who had come to the Countess' house several times, would be joining us at the Baron Todesco's Ball. The requirements for the masked ball were that everyone dress as a historical or literary character. Cecily wanted a dreadful dress that was almost orange. The Countess had designed it, and since there was nothing orange she had made it from red and yellow swatches, which come together in the most marvelous way. Cecily was going in this orange dress as Lady Macbeth and I was going as Marie Antoinette, which upset Aunt Ida no end, but I liked the wig.

The Countess was going as Queen Guinevere and the Inspector went as Emperor Frederick I who, he proudly said, was some kind of barbarian. Mother and Father were not going, and the Inspector, who was to escort Aunt Ida but really accompany the Countess, was looking extremely impressive, and we were all very excited.

The ball was quite the most marvelous ball I had ever attended. The

Countess told me that there were 90,000 yards of red carpet that had been installed all the way up the front lawn, and 120,000 lights which were, it seemed to me, everywhere. Cecily and I were both quite excited when we saw Mrs. Astor arrive and a girl who was a friend of the Countess' whispered that three French maids had died and that was why Mrs. Astor was so late, because the French maids were frail and had died from lifting up all the diamonds and rubies onto Mrs. Astor's head! This was the first time we had actually ever attended a *ball* in Vienna—although of course there were parties in Vienna almost every evening, so I was secretly hoping that we would see Mr. Strauss himself conduct the orchestra and we would get to see all of the people dancing the Blue Danube waltz. Cecily didn't know if it was the Blue Danube waltz or another one but she said that she'd heard that in the waltz you went round and round and got very dizzy and you went so fast for so long that people actually died right on the spot from it, and it was considered dangerous.

Aunt Ida said that was some ridiculous rumor that the Viennese must have started because they were always making such a great fuss over dying, giving actual *parades* when people died and carrying on so, and we shouldn't make so much of it.

Things were going along quite merrily until the moment we were all lined up along the dance floor and Aunt Ida, responding to a question from a Baron von Aehrenthal,[1] suddenly quoted some Russian writer (Aunt Ida was becoming quite fond of things Russian) and then Baron von Aehrenthal said, yes, as the great Russians have told us, "Life is a tale told by an idiot, full of sound and fury, signifying nothing."

There was a gasp from everyone as Aunt Ida explained it was actually from Shakespeare.

"Well," I said, uncomfortably, "it's quite an awful thing to think . . . isn't it?"

"It's a brave thing to think," the Inspector said quietly. "If you believe it, it is difficult to continue."

"You don't believe it?" the Countess asked. The Inspector seemed surprised.

[1] This Baron must be Lexa von Aehrenthal, who became responsible for annexing Bosnia-Herzegovina in 1908.

"No," he said with a slow, reluctant, smile, "at least not the last two words."

"Ah you think then that a tale told by an idiot could be meaningful?" the Countess said, her eyes bright. Sometimes I thought she was teasing him.

The Inspector sighed. "It is all a question of what meaning is. Everything means, the chirp of the bird, the ravings of the mad. It is our inadequacy only, or at least my inadequacy, that the meaning, at times, lies beyond my understanding."

"But aren't there some things," Cecily said, "that mean nothing? They don't go anywhere or do anything, like those dreadful music concerts we have to attend where the music is beautiful and so are the people, but they only care how they look and talk of money."

"Meaningless, yes, for you. Painful, I think, for you, but the observer, when his eye is clear, sees it as part of a pattern in a way that is meaningful."

"Who is this observer?" I asked.

"Time and history, and the man who lives a hundred years hence." I looked at the Inspector, but I could not tell if he was smiling.

"Do you think they offer clarity," the Countess interrupted, "these things we call time and history, whatever they are?" The light caught the diamonds at her throat and the small tiny beads of perspiration gathering between her breasts. The Countess' body, I came to believe, converted heat to light.

The Inspector shrugged. "It is all we have," he said, taking her arm. "We will dance," and they moved out onto the floor. I stood there mesmerized by the Inspector's manner, and the fact that he had not said, "May we dance?" but simply took her arm, until Cecily interrupted me with that jealous glance and said, "I understand from Timothy you are reading about electricity!" My face turned red. "Only a little," I said.

"Father had better not find out," Cecily warned. "But, of course, there's no reason to worry. You'll never understand it," and tossing her mane of black curls she made straight across the dance floor toward Carl Lobmeyr, leaving me there alone, caught and strangling on her last words, the challenge converting my until-then timid quest into a savage determination. I swore at that moment that I would indeed conquer electricity, but would keep it secret, never letting them know, owing to them, then, in my moment of increasing pain, the wretched pleasure of their illusions about me, their unjust evaluations, believing as I did at that intense, transcendent moment that this act, somehow, was revenge, and in some way, they would die.

I turned on my heel like a gladiator and made for the terrace door.

"I'm cold," she said, turning to the Inspector, and he reached back and pulled her wrap up on her shoulders, then stayed a moment too long. She was not used to a man like this, a man capable of anything. She felt within the Inspector a steely resolve now. He was a man who would not be deterred, and something in this alarmed her. The Countess was not used to being alarmed by him. Fear was reserved for those oppressive, suspended hours when the strange men beckoned to her, and she followed them. As if he had read her thoughts, he shocked her now by laying his hands against her hair for a moment, saying softly, "Do not worry," and then turned back to the other guests. That gesture, the way he laid his hand on her head there in front of the guests, claiming her but not compromising her, claiming her with care and affection and concern, caused her to blush.

It was quite late in the evening when I noticed that Cecily had been dancing almost exclusively with a young and very handsome Russian cavalry officer. He had a white jacket and red trousers and was wearing a lot of goldbraid and a sword! I saw her get a look that she occasionally got, of over-excitement, as if she were almost bursting through her skin. She began to speak very fast when she got like this, and to jump up and down in a most excited way. She had been drinking a great deal of punch, and I saw the Inspector go over to her once and remove the glass from her lips. She smiled at him and didn't seem to mind and threw herself into a polka again. I could see that the Inspector did not like the handsome calvary officer whose name was Nikolai. I overheard them, because I had become quite good at overhearing things. The officer was saying to the Inspector, "But you have a dossier on Kollontai, and I would like to examine it." The Inspector told him in no uncertain terms, "I do not share dossiers. She is no threat, I can assure you, to your privilege."

"How can you say that?" Nikolai asked, astonished.

"She would like to be," the Inspector said, "but you have more to fear from other anarchists."

"I should like to have it," the young man said decisively. "I shall order you to give it to me. I shall get authority from the czar." The Inspector had shrugged. "The French," he said, "are terrible about losing things," and he walked away.

I lost sight of Cecily and Nikolai, and it was not until much later when I heard Aunt Ida whisper to the Inspector that I became concerned about Cecily. She whispered to him that Cecily and Nikolai had been gone for some time. She had been looking everywhere, and would he please assist her in locating them. I had never seen Aunt Ida so agitated. When I asked her what the problem was, she said, "Oh, Cecily looked unwell, I thought she had eaten too much of the fish," which I knew was not at all true. What she was worried about was Cecily's temperament and the punch.

The Inspector disappeared, and I continued to dance with an extremely boring young baron, who insisted I join him for a bicycle ride the next afternoon. Since this would be less boring than visiting his mother with the Countess, I agreed to go. He was, fortunately, an expert at the waltz, and as there were several waltzes next, I soon forgot the agitation about Cecily.

It was only later that I realized something serious must have occurred. When we were about to leave and I asked where Cecily was Aunt Ida said, her lips tight, "She's already in the carriage." I saw the Inspector speaking with Nikolai in the corner. They both looked extremely upset. I imagined Cecily had had a cigarette with him or something, and I hastened to the carriage. Cecily had a dreamy expression and seemed very happy.

"What has happened to you?" I asked, but she only rolled her eyes and said, "You understand nothing of life," and then she fell instantly, completely asleep. I sat back irritated while Aunt Ida got in, quite furious, then the Inspector and the Countess. Aunt Ida was saying, "She should not have been allowed to drink it; it was much too strong, the punch," and then she said she felt she was to blame, she should not have encouraged a girl of such high spirits.

In the morning Cecily announced to me that she was madly in love with Nikolai and had arranged to meet him secretly by the museum. I told her if it was a secret I certainly didn't need to know about it, but that everyone was very upset about her behavior last night. Her face became bright red at that, and she tore through the bureau drawers and her trunks, looking for something. She looked at me haughtily and said she was a woman and not a child, and she expected to be treated like one. I felt challenged by this and said, "If you are a woman, so am I. You are only a year older." She looked at me directly then and said with a pitiful gaze, "But you have not known love," and flounced out of the room.

But I know, because I followed her, that when she went to the museum, Nikolai never came. That was why she cried all through dinner, *not* because she had a terrible headache.

32

Freud had been feeling heady with success over the change in the Countess. She would not reveal the name of her new lover, but it did not surprise him that now she felt safe enough that her nightmares were about to emerge.

As the Countess lay on the couch, she remembered her dream.

"It is about a child," she said. "The child is my child . . . she has a mark on her forehead, an *S*. That is the letter I could not recall." Her voice was slow, almost mechanical. "The nurses who bring her to me say, 'She is born to you, but she will belong always to someone else and never, never to herself,' and they nod their heads and sigh and chant the most horrible sounds."

He saw she had paled now as her fists pulled at the handkerchief in her hands.

"But no one else can see the nurses, no one can hear them, and no one can see the mark but me." She collapsed then, sobbing, "So I cannot do this. I will not have a child, who is born a slave," and she became so agitated she rolled from the couch with fists pounding onto the floor in a fury and crying "no, no, no."

He intervened at once to help her.

33

Cecily's morose mood continued for days. And then, one morning when I came to breakfast, there was a new concern. Apparently Mr. James was on his way to Vienna, and Mother was now worried about the effect *this* would have on Cecily. Only this morning Mother had heard from the Countess that Mr. James was to be here for a play of his that was to open, and the Countess had invited Mr. James to have dinner with us the following week. The Countess, it appears, was acquainted with his friend Mrs. Wharton and was always invited to her salons on the rue de Varenne in Paris.

"We Viennese," the Countess said, "are much in demand in Paris. They treat me like an exotic."

"You *are* rather exotic, actually," Cecily said, appearing at once at the door. "I mean you're not like anyone I've ever known."

"Uniqueness is insufficient to constitute exoticism, but I will not object if you see me that way," the Countess said. "So you know of Mr. James?"

"Oh yes," Cecily said, "we are quite good friends, actually. He is a most remarkable novelist."

"I have not read his work," the Countess said. "I wonder if I should like it."

"What is so very different about Mr. James," Aunt Ida said, "is the scientific quality of his mind, his psychological analysis. I must say, especially in relationship to women. Most people do not like it, but I like it quite a lot. Of course," she said "it is always reflecting a rather exclusive and privileged group of people. You would never know from reading his work that dreadful things went on in the world, things like the retention of a peasantry or slavery."

"Really, Ida," Mother said, "I cannot have you disturbing everyone's digestion with these endless ruminations about dreadful things. I think you should concentrate instead on Christian things."

Aunt Ida looked a bit miffed and said that it was unfortunately extremely "Christian" in the worst possible sense of the word to have slaves; that the meanest and cruelest slaveholders had all whipped their slaves, sometimes to death, because "they did not obey God."

By now Aunt Ida had made herself very angry and said, "In the name of this Christian God, more evil has been committed on the face of the earth than in the name of anything else, except perhaps another god," she declared.

I had never seen Aunt Ida so vehement, and I concluded that she was probably *right,* but perhaps she should not be spending so much time with Alexandra Kollontai[1] or I did not see how she was going to continue to live in our house. Something was taking shape in our house that no one was prepared for. I felt very bad for Mother, who did not understand any of this and thought a Christian was always a kind person who did the proper thing and who couldn't even imagine slavery. I don't really think she believed it ever happened, and that's what Aunt Ida said made some good people positively dangerous.

34

Leopold wondered what had gotten into Bettina now. She was unapproachable to him, and on top of that there seemed always to be rabbis in the house. First there was Bloch, then he saw Güdemann, and he didn't know the one who was now gathering up his long black coat and black fur hat as he entered the living room.

"Rebbe," Bettina said, "this is my husband." Leopold strode back and cried, "Rebbe!" in shock. Good God, Leopold thought, now there were Hassids in the house as well. He looked at the man strangely. There were no Hassids in Vienna—he must be from Minsk.

As soon as the rabbi left, the doorbell rang, and Leopold saw Rabbi Güdemann coming in. The rabbi bowed to Leopold and greeted the

---

[1] As earlier noted, she was a Russian revolutionary who knew Ida, clearly, from sections I have chosen to omit. She was not, however, a feminist.

Countess. "I cannot stay long," he said, "I just wanted to give you this letter personally." He handed her a note, and then nodding his head toward the Hassidic rabbi receding down the walk he said, "I see the Prince of the Torah has been here," which forced even Leopold to smile.

It was later in the evening when Leopold remarked to her, "You may wish to convert to Judaism, Bettina, although you will be the only person converting to Judaism in a world where all the Jews are converting to Catholicism, but be that as it may, I am not going to have religious services going on in my home."

"They did not come about services," Bettina said.

"Then why were they here?" he said.

She sighed. She was impatient with Leopold's irrational jealousy, which was provoked by anything he did not control. "It is all about Herzl and that pamphlet he has published," she said finally. " 'The Jewish State.' Everyone is in an uproar."

"I heard," Leopold said, "that the rabbis do not like it."

"Güdemann changes his mind, all the time," the Countess said. "First he thinks it is a good thing, then he thinks that being a Jew has nothing to do with being a nation, that it is reactionary to be nationalistic; then he thinks if the Jews are anything they are Germans first, more German than the Austrians, and Jewish second; then he thinks the Jews will always be regarded as outsiders and—" she sighed, "I don't know. It seems to have upset everyone. No one knows what to do."

"It's in all the papers, every day," Leopold said, snapping the front of the *Tageblatt,* "I see that Morris Szeps has called out for an Austrian Zola,[1] but there is none."

"There is Karl Kraus, of course," the Countess said.

"Kraus will never come to the defense of Jews who want to go to Palestine. Kraus is the most passionate about Vienna of all and perhaps the last Viennese."

"Yes," the Countess said, "the liberals have turned against the Jews now, only the emperor defends them . . . for some issues there do not seem to be solutions, and this is one of them." Leopold watched her

---

[1] Zola was the French writer who bravely published *"J'accuse"* on the front pages of the Paris papers. It was an accusation of anti-Semitic conspiracy in the Dreyfus case.

as she said that, and then she moved, quite suddenly, without so much as excusing herself, from the room. It left Leopold furious. He felt more and more superfluous.

35

The Inspector was walking, trying to sort it out. He walked through the Belvedere Gardens. He liked, these days, to stand on the upper Belvedere and gaze down at the city below. The large sphinx mounted there intrigued him; it had a petulant expression. He had noted that Dr. Freud, too, in his walks, seemed drawn to the Belvedere. The Inspector, upon following him, had found Freud, on more than one occasion, standing for some time in front of this very monument.

36

After they had settled themselves on the train to Vienna, the steady beat of the wheels stimulated in Edith a certain reflective calm. She found herself thinking rather insistently about Dr. Freud. She had learned that Henry was not quite so displeased with the doctor as he had originally indicated to her. In fact, at times he seemed to display real respect.

After some time had passed, almost to her surprise, she found herself saying, "Well, what *do* you talk about when you go there?"

Henry was quick to catch the irritation in her voice. "Oh," he said, "he keeps asking about one's childhood."

There was a strange weighted pause.

"Do you tell him?" she said finally.

It struck him that what she meant but didn't say was, "Do you tell him the truth?"

It would not have occurred to him to tell him anything other than the truth, as best he could recall it. Still the doctor pressed in strange directions.

"It is," Henry paused, "informative."

"In what way?" she asked.

"In the way that you might have had thoughts that occurred to you, but that didn't occur as well, that is, once they've been pointed out to you, why you rather recognize them, especially about your mother and father."

Edith found herself reclining farther and farther in her seat in the compartment until, to her surprise, she had reared so far her head hit the lamp hanging behind the seat.

"Oh," she said. She found it odious, disgusting, that this doctor talked about the *sexuality* of children. Morton, of all people, had told her he'd heard Freud lecture on the subject and she had been *furious* with him. "It is hateful," she had glowered, and Morton, she remembered, had seemed surprised and then cautiously dropped the subject.

"I mean," he said, "one doesn't often sit around thinking of feelings about one's mother and father, actually recalling events from one's childhood, now does one?"

Edith felt quite strange as he said this, a combination of nausea and a peculiar kind of jealousy invaded her. And yet she didn't know why.

"Does he *do* anything to you?" she asked.

"He tells you to lie down on the couch. And then," he said, "he puts his hand on your forehead and asks you to think of your mother and your father, and then you have memories."

"Show me," she said, getting up and moving to the other couch in the compartment. Henry was quite startled.

Edith felt a bit awkward. She didn't like thinking of memories. She didn't mind *writing* them sometimes. She imagined she could write about it more easily than *think* it for some reason.

To Henry's astonishment, she asked him to place his hand on her forehead, which he did for only a moment. Edith seemed to fall asleep almost at once. He took his hand away, relieved actually. He had found it awkward, touching her.

E D I T H Wharton was coming down the stairs, watching the bright shaft of sunlight on the dark living room floor when Lucretia, her mother, rose suddenly, flew from the couch, and pulled the red velvet draperies savagely across the window.

"Mrs. William Overson is coming at two," she said, surveying her daughter with a disdain that bordered on contempt. "Whatever will she *think*, look at *you*."

Edith paused on the stair for a moment and looked sharply from one end of the living room to the other. She felt a release in her breath. The dining room door was open. The doors to the living room had been tightly shut, but she still could escape. She stepped down the last step and ran to her mother, holding her breath as she kissed her lightly on the forehead and then mercifully backed into the dining room. She went toward the pantry looking for the cook, and as she went she heard her mother's high-pitched voice, "Where do you think you're going? Why I want you here beside me," she said, emphatically patting the green velvet tufted sofa.

Edith turned timidly, her head tilting toward the kitchen. "I shall return immediately, I am just getting a bit of muffin," and daringly she pushed open the kitchen door.

"A bit of muffin," Lucretia said, angrily slapping her fan against her palm as she paced nervously in the living room, not realizing that her nervousness was the result of having sensed in this daughter, for only a moment and on a level so deep she could not discern it, an assertiveness, an independence, a decision actually against Lucretia's wishes to go into the kitchen. Lucretia knew none of this, continued to pace and snap her fan, and pretended to go through the mail before her on a silver tray.

Edith confronted the cook and found a muffin. She could feel her mother pacing, one-two, one-two, across the hardwood floors along the edge of the carpet in the same beat, she realized suddenly, as her fearful heart. She could feel the long line, like a lounge line on a horse, controlling her circle. She had no appetite. She pushed the muffin away, got up, and walked obediently out the kitchen door.

When she returned to the living room her mother snapped at her sullen glance. "It is important that you become much better company. Mr. Stevens is coming at four to take you for a walk, and I don't want you tired."

Lucretia's voice cracked like a whip against Edith's delicate and increasingly nervous disposition. They were at war, this mother and this daughter, and both were unaware of how desperate the battle was. Lucretia found herself furious at Edith, furious for her, well, her differentness, for her seeming disinterest in everything that was important for a young woman to be interested in. And then she was too intellectual. Still she had ordered the dress. The dress might help. It was a surprise. Lucretia did want to please her, make her happy, if only because if this daughter were happy, Lucretia might feel better about things.

Edith sat there saying nothing. Thinking. She was thinking, am I this quiet, am I really this quiet, or does she make me numb; does she make me not want to say anything at all because she is always so angry? She was afraid of her mother at times. And then there were the times when she would awaken early in the morning, seized by a panic so profound she could not name it. She would run down the hallway into her mother's bedroom and fling herself onto the thick heap of white down on the bed, feeling for a moment safe at last until her mother would awaken, open her eyes, and then immediately become angry, as if she could never get used to Edith's awkwardness. That is what Lucretia thought it was—the child's awkwardness, and her hair, un-plaited, looking so dreadful when what she wanted was a lovely daughter, a creature with blond hair and pink cheeks, simple not contrary. She wanted to open her eyes and see some simple creature there instead of this . . . she did not know what to call it.

Perhaps the dress would make things better.

"I have a new box from Paris," Lucretia said as Edith walked into the room.

"Oh," Edith said, her face lighting up for a moment. She did love the boxes from Paris, with their elegant dresses and the soft rustle of the tissue paper.

The maid brought in the huge box and laid it on the sofa. She took off the enormous top and began to shake out the first dress. It was mauve with handmade lace on the collar and the cuffs, a beautiful black velvet bow on the back.

Lucretia, consumed with her appearance, was having a wonderful time with the box. She held up the mauve dress and walked around the room.

"Mrs. Henry Fitch will simply die of jealousy when I wear this to the Appleton Ball on Saturday." Edith thought her mother was beautiful. When her mother was beautiful like this and almost happy, she felt warm inside, warm and good and almost safe again. Her mother took out dress after dress.

And this, her mother said, pulling something from the tissue paper, something pink and green, "is for you." Her mother shook the dress from its tissue, and Edith stared. The dress was covered with grapes! Bunches of beautiful grapes swirled around the bodice, the sleeves were of bright green silk, fashioned in leaves which rose and fell in a vast array of greenery. The dress—a deluge of color, silk and shaped not right. . . . not for her. She saw her mother's face.

"You don't like it," she said, indignant.

"Oh . . . yes," Edith said, "but it, it's so fancy . . . so purply." She knew she looked wretched in purple. It turned her skin yellow and made the red in her hair turn orange.

"Of course it's fancy, you need something fancy you're so . . ." her mother didn't finish. But Edith winced under the judgment. Whatever her mother bought for her, always struck her this way. *I don't like you the way you are,* and yet it wasn't at all clear. Because her mother in other ways . . .

"You will wear this dress when you come out in the fall." There. The announcement without a moment's consultation. In the fall.

"Coming out . . . the fall?," Edith protested, "But I couldn't . . . this fall I'm only seventeen."

"I know how old you are, you needn't remind me," Lucretia said, "and you're coming out in the fall. We can't have you publishing poetry and not coming out."

Edith looked up, startled. So that was it. Still her mother had been nice. So unusual for her mother. She had been nice about the poetry. Her mother had actually arranged to have her poems published privately, although in fact, Edith did not want them in a book at all, she really didn't think they were quite good enough, but it seemed to have set off some kind of alarm. Her mother had dashed around, as had her father, for months, setting up social arrangements that she had no interest in whatsoever.

"Go right now and try it on," Lucretia said, shaking the last tissue from the dress. She would have so much have preferred a *blue* one!

"Well, well," her father said, entering the room, "what is going on here?" Edith turned to him.

Lucretia re-entered the room just in time to see her husband encircle their daughter in a rush of tissue paper, spinning her around, bloom rising to the girl's cheeks in a thrill of delight as her face pressed against her father's beard, scattering the boxes and the gloves, a scene of flying debris to Lucretia, who cried out, "Really, stop it! *Stop this!*" They stopped and turned, startled. "Really, George," she said grasping at her composure. "Mrs. Overson is coming, and you just created the worst mess!" She was annoyed too at this impossible husband she had, and as she bent to retrieve the tissue, Edith inexplicably blushed.

Lucretia did not know why she was so angry at them, just that she was. It seemed that they were always messing things. Lucretia felt terrible—sad, ugly, angry. She had just glanced at herself in the hallway glass, and the fine lines crinkling up her neck had displeased her, the thickness of her waist had displeased her, as had the thinness of her daughter's, and yet her daughter's inability to carry out any image she might have had, any fantasy of her own, distressed her, and if she had, what then? Lucretia did not think of any of this, simply felt these thoughts, half-formed, press momentarily against her consciousness and then fall away, like the tissue paper which would be quickly scooped up and destroyed and never thought of again.

Henry James found the train ride most pleasant. Mrs. Wharton as usual had been stimulating company, although he noted this morning that she was rather testy. He had made mention of Constance Fenimore Woolson's short stories, which he had been reading. He was never far from thoughts of Fenimore, tortured though they were, so it gave him some comfort to read the stories in which, he noted wryly, she attempted to mimic some of his own style, but failed miserably. But now, he wondered what he had said exactly to upset Edith.

Her entire mood seemed to have changed ever since her question about Dr. Freud's technique. When Henry had placed his hand upon her forehead, he thought she had fallen asleep, but he saw that if she was sleeping she must have been dreaming, because her body began to shiver suddenly and then she cried out and woke up. He asked her if she had had a dream, and she replied in that tense voice, that had not left her since, that no, absolutely not, she had not had a dream at all, but a memory, and an unpleasant one at that. Then she sat up, seeming, he thought, quite embarrassed by the entire incident, and said no more but stoically took up a book and read.

37

The Inspector returned to the Freud house at unexpected moments. He politely, but firmly, demanded entry. Today Minna stood in the doorway as he walked about through the rooms.

"None of these rooms have anything to do with this, if there was any *this*," she said disdainfully. Then she added, "If there was anything here at all, it occurred between the back door and the other side of the house, so I would like to ask you to leave us our privacy and contain your investigation to the *other* side."

She pointed, expecting him to comply. He didn't. He smiled indulgently. "This is the Freud bedroom?" he asked, walking to one of the rooms.

"You know that it is," she said.

"And Fr. Freud was asleep, here—" he pointed to one side of the bed, "is that correct—until awakened by the storm?"

He saw her hesitate. Then she pointed to the opposite side of the bed.

"She sleeps there," she answered.

"Aha!" the Inspector said, as he had discovered something. He caught her frown.

"And you, Frl. Bernays, you sleep right here in the adjoining room, an extension as it were, of the Freud bedroom, isn't that so?"

"It's a separate room," she said, "not an extension."

"Indeed," he said, "but there is no separate entrance."

"You've already established that," she said.

"So," he said, ignoring her, "as you are not a sound sleeper, must you not disturb the Freuds as you walk in and out of their bedroom in order to get to your room?"

"Martha is a sound sleeper," she said.

"And Sigmund?" He turned suddenly. She looked coolly at him.

"He is not disturbed," she said.

"Aha!" he said again, taking time to light a cigar and then begin pacing again.

"And you, Frl. Bernay, as you are, shall we say, a 'restless' temperament, a light sleeper, subject to insomnia, is it not, shall we say, inconvenient, to have your room so close to the Freuds'? Are you never disturbed," he paused elaborately, "by noises?" There was no pause as she said, "There are no noises." Then she turned away.[1]

38

I was not surprised when the Countess informed Aunt Ida that she would like to attend the meeting at the university with the Paris ladies who were coming to Vienna to talk about women's suffrage. Cecily, upon hearing this, cornered me in the hallway and said she would love to go also, as one of the Paris ladies, she had heard, dressed exactly like a man, and it would be ever so amusing! Cecily said this in the rather tense, childish voice she acquired on occasion, and I cannot say how but, I knew in the tenseness and her giggling that something was hidden.

The Inspector was very concerned when we told him the next morning that the Countess and Aunt Ida had gone off to a meeting at the university.

"The students there are always causing problems ... there is some

---

[1] All the written evidence currently available suggests Freud had no sexual activity after his fortieth year so the conversation, in this regard, is probably accurate. What the Inspector hoped to elicit from Minna here is not altogether clear.

incident with the Jewish fraternity this afternoon," he said, "something about a duel." He frowned when he said this and immediately went down the steps.

I turned to Cecily and said, "You see, there was a good reason you did not go." But Cecily had disappeared. I confess I thought no more about this myself until late in the afternoon when I heard a loud banging at the door.

"Quickly," a young woman whom I had never seen before said. "The Countess and Ida are at the hospital . . . they were hurt," she said.

39

Mother was hurrying from Aunt Ida's room with tears in her eyes. I thought this was because she was so upset at seeing Aunt Ida in this condition, but I found out it wasn't. This was later in the afternoon, when Cecily and I said we wanted to go back to Aunt Ida's room again and Mother absolutely forbade us to go in unless Aunt Ida was awake.

Cecily became quite agitated and just marched right in and there was Aunt Ida, asleep and *speaking,* speaking actually quite loudly and eloquently, and I saw Mother stand near the door, not knowing what to do, and Father was trying to comfort her, and Cecily and I stood there utterly amazed at Aunt Ida in her white sheets and bedding, her hair soft around her face like a halo, and the sun streaming in. There was Aunt Ida in a daze but looking like an angel and saying the most unangel-like things. This is what we heard:

> Let him kiss me with the kisses of his mouth
> For your love making is sweeter than wine
> Delicate in the fragrance of your perfume.

Then there was some moaning and she repeated it again. Cecily was staring at her amazed.

"Frederick, please," I heard Mother imploring Father to make us leave the room, which I had no intention of doing. Cecily was looking at Aunt Ida and listening to what she had to say with the most extraordinary fascination. I thought it was odd and of course shocking that Aunt Ida should be saying such things as this, but I was certain that Cecily in the course of her perusal of the anatomy books had seen many things more shocking than this and I could not understand what the look on her face meant.

Just then the rabbi came in with Leopold, of all people, I think they had been visiting the Countess. Mother rushed to them and insisted that Aunt Ida not be disturbed. I knew she did not want them to hear what Aunt Ida had to say but just at that moment Aunt Ida sat up and said in a very clear voice:

> My love is fresh and ruddy
> To be known among ten thousand
> His head is gold, purest gold
> His locks are palm fronds
> And black as the raven.

Mother was imploring the group to leave and Leopold did, but the rabbi told Mother to be quiet, he was listening, and she suddenly did become quiet and then Aunt Ida's voice rose loud and clear.

> Let my love come into his garden
> Let him taste its most exquisite fruits.

And the rabbi too, now, had an amazed expression on his face and he approached Aunt Ida's bed and said something in some strange language, and he turned to Mother who said immediately, "She is ill, Rabbi. You must remember that. She has no idea what she is saying." Mother's face was very pink, and her lips were held in a straight line.

The rabbi was smiling. "It's the Song of Songs," he said to Mother. "She is in excellent company."

"What?" Mother said, looking confused.

"You mean," Father said, "from the Old Testament?"

"Yes," the rabbi said. "She told me she had been studying it, and she's learned some of it quite well."

"What?" Mother said again.

"Aunt Ida is quoting the Bible," Cecily said to Mother, proudly, as if she'd thought it up herself. Then, "I must read this part," she whispered to me. "I don't understand why I never saw this part before."

Mother was arguing with Father and Aunt Ida was continuing the chanting, and there was a fuss all around until the doctor came in and made everyone leave the room. We spent the next two hours walking back and forth and back and forth in the hospital until a nurse came and said Aunt Ida was awake.

We rushed down the hall to see her and I think Cecily was a little disappointed that she had stopped quoting from the Bible, although I personally don't believe Mother believed the rabbi, that what Aunt Ida was quoting was from the Bible, but Mother said we were forbidden to speak to Aunt Ida about it. Cecily said later that maybe Aunt Ida had been in love with Mr. Biddington Jones and that when she got hit on the head, all of the love just came out when no one, not even Aunt Ida, was looking, because otherwise, Cecily said, she could have quoted the Twenty-Third Psalm or something dreary.

Aunt Ida was sitting up looking quite cheerful but with an enormous bruise over her right eye. "Well," she said, "I never thought they'd attack us, I must say. The Viennese have fine manners, normally." Mother ran out to speak to the doctor while we continued to talk to Aunt Ida. Cecily thought it was all quite marvelous in a fearful way.

"Thank God one of them, a real gentleman, saved us."

"What happened?" I asked.

"Well I don't really know . . . we were picketing at a meeting and then all of a sudden this group of rather rowdy students came by, and then another bunch of men and they were all shouting and yelling, and Bettina said to me, 'We're in the middle of an anti-Semitic riot,' and we were suddenly surrounded and some of the young men were terribly polite, and they were trying to protect us, and Bettina was so brave she just stared them down and said, 'Let us pass,' in the most marvelous way." Aunt Ida began to get very excited, "It was really quite something, quite courageous, and we were suddenly in a sea of angry young men, chanting something I do not know what, and then Bettina started yelling, I am Jewish, I am Jewish, very loud, and I got behind her and she was cutting a swath through this mob, who just didn't dare lay a hand on her. She was so brave and so fine; they knew she was an aristocrat, and then I don't know something started in the back, and then we were sort of run over. There were just too many of them and two of the men grabbed us and one of them started slapping her telling her to shut up—and and—" Aunt Ida was breathless at this next, and Mother and Father came in and told her to calm herself but she said, "The Countess hit him back," she said, "raised her hand with tremendous force, and knocked his jaw so hard he fell over," she said, marveling. "And then the other rescued us—they took us over to the side, but by then the Countess was badly hurt and almost couldn't stand, there was blood everywhere, and then I saw blood on myself and one of the young men was yelling that it was terrible, he never meant to involve us, it was only the Jews they were trying to fight, and Bettina kept saying, 'I am Jewish,' and he kept saying, 'Not you, madame, not you,' and he was very upset and started to cry, and—I don't know—these young men were beside themselves when they saw what had happened to us, and then there was the doctor." She looked around the room. "It was so . . . odd, I shall never forget it."[1]

"Are you afraid now," Cecily asked, "to demonstrate?"

"No," Aunt Ida said, and then she burst into tears, which Cecily said she thought meant she was afraid but I didn't think so. I thought she was sad, very, very sad.

40

I don't understand why there are so many problems," Cecily said, "for women and Jews. It isn't as if they've done anything. It's as if people attack them simply because of what they are and not for what they've *done*."

Mother didn't say anything. She knew it was on Cecily's mind because of what had happened to the Countess and Ida.

"Perhaps you'll go hiking today," Mother said, her voice thinner than usual. "You can go out toward the Wienerwald and take the path

---

[1] This was an unusual incident. Another aspect of anti-Semitism in both Austria and Germany was that, unlike Russia and Poland, where there were pogroms, actual physical violence in either Austria or Germany was a rare occurrence.

you told me about—that you liked, remember?" she said, trying to be cheerful.

I looked at Cecily. Cecily looked at me. "I don't want to go," she said.

"Why not?" Mother asked. "It's a perfectly lovely day to take a walk. Why there is nothing so beautiful in Vienna as the woods on a fine day—there is so much here that is so beautiful. Why, there are days I think this must be the most beautiful city in the world."

"That's what Aunt Ida said, before she was attacked," Cecily said.

"I don't want to hear any more about it. We'll pack a lunch and go hiking today."

"You *never* hike," Cecily said to Mother, with surprise.

"Well I can start today," she said. "We need to think some cheerful thoughts in this house." There was a pause and no one said anything for some time and I thought Cecily was going to let the matter drop, but I should have known better.

Timothy was looking at Cecily as if he knew what she was going to say.

"The other day," she said, "Timothy and I were walking on this trail behind the Prater and we were stopped."

"Stopped? What do you mean stopped?"

"We weren't stopped, Mother, we were just questioned," Timothy said quickly. "It was nothing." He was glaring at Cecily.

"Whatever about?" Mother asked.

"They asked us if we were Jewish," Cecily said, "and I decided to say yes, and Timothy got angry, and said no, and then they chased us off the trail. They said there were separate hiking trails for the Jews."

Mother's face had gone white. I suppose she had had quite enough excitement with Ida and the Countess and she suddenly put her head in her hands and burst into tears.

Timothy said to Cecily, "Now look what you've done."

"It isn't me," she said and got up from the table. We decided not to go hiking but to go calling instead.

41

Because Cecily had been so depressed about hiking, we were planning something special that morning. We were going to the famous Spanish Riding School, where the beautiful white Lippizaner stallions perform. They jump and dance like ballerinas—in levades, courbettes, and caprioles. I had been wanting to see this spectacle for some time.

We were just on our way out the door when the Inspector unexpectedly arrived. He apologized for interrupting our plans but explained he had some questions to ask about the evening of our arrival.

I decided, for reasons I only partly understood, to say nothing. The Inspector did not stay very long. Just as he was leaving Timothy told him that everyone in the medical school had heard about the murders.

42

The Countess and Aunt Ida had only been out of the hospital a few days when Sabina returned to the Countess' house and inquired if the Countess had found her walking stick the night she had found her in the snow. It was beautiful, she said, with a smooth silver head. The Countess said how very odd, for she did remember a walking stick with a silver head, only it wasn't smooth, she was certain. She remembered now quite distinctly, that she had in fact picked a cane up and she had noticed, but quite forgotten, that it had quite a remarkable carving on it. It was not smooth at all, it was the head of Pan.

"Well, that couldn't be," Sabina insisted. The Countess went to look for it, but the servants couldn't find it anywhere.

43

Irina had told the Inspector that Fliess was due to arrive on the four o'clock train from Berlin. He waited unobtrusively inside the busy station and watched Freud on the platform pacing anxiously. In his black homburg, black coat with velvet collar and grey pants, the doctor looked most imposing and almost, the Inspector thought, fashionable. There was a look of intense concentration on his face as he watched a woman with a child in one of the carriages. It was a sunny day, and the child played an endless game in which he threw something out of the carriage and then with a string wheeled it back in. The woman had been in the station earlier with the child, and the Inspector had graciously retrieved the toy, much to the child's displeasure. The infant wanted to retrieve it himself.

Freud was now greeted with a similar series of observations but was drawing different conclusions. He saw in the infant's game the symbolic relief of leaving and return that the child experienced with the mother. As he heard "fort" and "da" he knew it was the child's conquest of the mother's loss that was being re-enacted in this game.

He felt alone this morning on the platform, and he did not know if this loneliness was the effect of knowing the hopelessness of the child's act, which in another mood he would have seen as a miracle of achievement, or of the fact that he must soon confront Fliess over this very unsavory matter. He heard a whistle and looked up to see the train steaming into the station. Fliess suddenly appeared through the smoke at the opposite end of the platform, and waving, rushed towards Freud, who embraced him warmly.

"He runs to him like one runs to a lover," the Inspector mused from behind the window. "How uncharacteristic," he thought. He had seen none of this display with anyone else, save Freud's children; he was a most attentive father, the Inspector was happy to recall, but this attachment to Fliess gave him pause. For reasons not entirely clear to him at the time, it seemed utterly consistent with Freud's genius that he should esteem too highly a colleague who was not his equal, who had something of the crackpot about him. Freud was somewhat blind to this sort, he suspected.

Freud and Fliess hailed a carriage and already had heads bent together in intense debate when the Inspector took a coach and followed. To his surprise they did not go directly to Freud's house but to a small cafe on the Passauerplatz. There Minna and Martha were waiting. Fliess and Freud greeted the ladies quietly. The men seemed to ignore the women as they continued their conversation. The Inspector, curious, inched into the booth behind them. The cafe was very crowded, and he was sure he would not be seen. He was in time to hear talk of a "new patient." His ears perked up.

"Of course he is an exceptional and quite public person, but he is suffering from a severe problem with his mother," Dr. Freud was saying. "It is a most unusual circumstance. He is deathly afraid of her power, although he hides this under a convincing veneer, seeming to be a totally happy-go-lucky sort of chap. He is sexually compulsive, although I have as yet fully to understand it. And he has come to me for treatment."

"Will you treat him?" Fliess sounded anxious.

"I don't know," said Freud.

"It is far too common, this fear of the mother, and I see it as the root of what you call your 'male hysteria,' " Fliess said.

"In this case, it is not hysteria," Dr. Freud said. The Inspector could see him stirring his coffee and adding an extra lump of sugar.

"Are you sure?"

"In this case there is some justification for the fear of the mother. It is a fantasy, yes, but it is also not a fantasy, a most complicated kind of case to analyze."

"And who is this mother? Is she really so powerful? You know, of course, you can confide in me," Fliess said.

The Inspector waited expectantly and half turned in the booth so he might hear. He saw Dr. Freud looking steadily at Fliess.

"Queen Victoria," said Freud, and Fliess dropped his cup.

After some time the four of them rose and went for a walk. Martha was frowning. Fliess with his endless discussions of the nose struck

Martha as odd. She remembered the afternoon that Fliess operated on Freud's nose. Sigi was bleeding badly when Fliess entered the kitchen and asked for towels. Regardless of what Sigi thought, she thought Fliess was a butcher. And stupid. She didn't like him, or his obsession, and felt sorry for his patient, Frl. Eckstein.

As he followed them, the Inspector recalled Martha's words from an earlier interview: "Well, they talk a great deal, yes. Always about the nose. They are very good colleagues. They talk and talk about death and noses. They meet in Berlin, they meet in Vienna, they go to the mountains for weeks at a time. They talk about numbers. Sigmund comes back disturbed. He is convinced he will die at fifty-nine."[1]

44

The Inspector left off following them after some blocks. Something was preying on his mind. Why could he not get closer to the cause here? He was beginning to feel like a poor version of that chap in the Strand, Sherlock Holmes. He had the uncomfortable feeling he would come up with deductions that yielded nothing—a left-handed man who was used to a scalpel, with three nails in his left shoe, and the killer would strike again. He decided then, to go into the sewers. There were many vagrants and poor people camped out in the sewers of Vienna who were only too willing to share information for money. They vigilantly guarded their inhospitable space; intruders were rejected. He had made contact with a man who waited for him now, by the fountain, off the square. He had told them there were people underground who had information about a murdered coachman.

The information had been incomplete; he was disappointed and decided to return once again to the park.

[1] This has been noted in almost every biography of Freud. On frequent occasions Freud expressed this fear.

As he walked he saw high up along the roof lines two figures that he thought at first were stone. Then he saw them move, rolling over and over, and then one threw the other to the edge and, with hands and rope around his neck, began to throttle him. The large figure on the bottom rose and wrested the snare from the other. In the mist, through the cold night, the Inspector sat and watched this match. He knew it was none other than Nietzsche and the Angel of Darkness up there on the roof now, rolling one over the other, over and over and over.

The Inspector sat there until morning, staring at the trees, sitting in the fine rain like a man who is not quite here but sits staring straight ahead, enchanted by shadows no one else can see.

45

The Countess announced unexpectedly that Inspector M. LeBlanc was coming this evening for dinner. Cecily was quite excited, as the rumors were becoming increasingly bizarre about dreadful murders taking place, especially the one where some woman's head had been separated from her torso and they'd found the torso miles away but never the head. The Countess had said that was all very well, but she was forbidding us to speak of murder tonight as the Inspector was a cultivated man and wanted to talk to Father about music and philosophy.

At dinner the Inspector did indeed speak to Father at great length about Mozart and Brahms and Beethoven and Cecily was bored until the Inspector looked kindly at her and told her of the American Buffalo Bill, who was all the rage in Paris, and promised to send her American moccasins when he returned home. Both Cecily and I noticed that the Inspector kept trying to inquire of the servant the secret of the asparagus soup. She apparently made several trips to the kitchen in an effort to find out, but each time told him that Berta, the cook, had told her that she would not reveal what was in it. I saw the Inspector frowning, and a determined look appeared on his face.

. . .

The Countess was feeling very unhappy. Her husband had ordered her to sleep in his boudoir that night. She thought that she would rather die than do this. She hated Leopold at the moment. She was also feeling remote from the dear Inspector, a man she felt had affected her in such a serious way. She had been seized with longing for him the minute he entered the room.

That evening as she looked at him, the turbulence began again. She would feign illness with Leopold, again.

The Inspector dipped into the soup. Asparagus was one of his favorite soups. He tasted it again. It was an elegant, smooth soup, but not *too* smooth. He had had asparagus soups in Germany that had been beaten so smooth there was no texture left to them. So lost was he for a moment in the rhapsodies and mysteries of the soup that he failed to hear the remark the Countess had made to her husband.

"Why, it's quite true, Leopold," the Countess was saying, "I've had my lineage researched."

"You are Russian. From aristocracy!" Leopold said, his face red and his hand pounding the table. "I heard this from the tailor and I will not tolerate such talk. Desist at once."

"But really, Leopold," the Countess said, "you have always remarked that Jews are running everything in Vienna, the music, the art, the architecture, the newspapers, the banks, so I cannot imagine that you think it a bad thing that I have discovered I am *Jewish* and have no need to convert."

"I am telling you, Bettina," Leopold said, "we will take this matter up privately. I wish to hear no more about it."

The Inspector marveled at the Countess's daring, yet he wished she would not pursue this at dinner. The Countess' eyes went from gold to a greenish color and her dark pupils seemed to expand. The Inspector saw that her lower lip was trembling, and he knew she was about to unleash her fury. He also knew, from a brief conversation with the ill-tempered Leopold, how dangerous it was for her. All of a sudden the Inspector stood up, grabbing his neck, as if he were strangling, making the most awful sounds, and then he pitched backward in his chair and it fell over. The Countess was immediately at his side.

"Oh heavens," Mother exclaimed, and Father rushed over as two of the servants came running. Leopold sat transfixed. He seemed to have no impulse to help.

"Quick, smelling salts," the Countess urged as the two servants attempted to lift the enormous form from the floor. With Father's help they succeeded, and with the smelling salts he soon came to his senses. The Countess urged them to take him into the living room and lay him on the sofa. She followed quickly.

The Inspector, whose eyes were open, insisted he was quite all right, and the Countess insisted Father return to the table. He entered the dining room and said the Countess would be with us shortly and we should all continue with our dinner. Which we did, but we all wanted to know what was going on in the other room.

46

The Countess held the Inspector's hand and pressed a cold compress to his forehead as she sat by his side. His hand caught hers in a firm grasp, and as she returned his glance, a smile came to her lips.

"I can't believe this is a ruse," she said with some delight.

"In order to hold your hand, madame, I would stoop even to dissimulation, but my reasons were more urgent than that."

"What is it?" she asked.

"You endanger yourself," he said quietly.

"I cannot bear that fool," she said harshly.

"You accomplish nothing," he said to her, his tone fierce.

"He can divorce me. I no longer care."

"You cannot risk it," he said, grasping her hand. "You will be reduced to nothing."

"I do not care," she said.

"I care," he said, "and you will care. The Princess of Albrecht," he said, "is a pitiful example."

The Countess paled before him. "Oh, God," she said, and her head fell onto his chest. He stopped himself from putting a comforting hand on her back. Too many servants. But he whispered to her fiercely,

"She is in an insane asylum, and he intends to leave her there forever, which he has the power to do. He has forced her there for disobedience, and you know it. It is not right, but it is so."[1]

The Countess rose then and walked to the far end of the living room. He heard the doors to the terrace open and close and knew she was walking in the garden. In time she would compose herself. Leopold was capable of destroying her and she knew it. The Inspector closed his eyes.

"I must apologize for my wife," Leopold was saying. "You know Bettina is a wonderful woman, but she is very imaginative."

"Surely the business about being Jewish is a jest," Father said.

"Oh, she imagines all sort of things," Leopold said, and he and Father had a hearty laugh, although I thought I saw a frown appear on Father's face at the same time as the laugh.

The Countess returned just moments later, followed shortly by the recovered Inspector. Her servant announced the cook had saved them plates, but the Countess waved her away and settled down to coffee and dessert. The Inspector seemed quite calm, and the discussion never came up again. Yet I knew that we had not heard the last about it. It wasn't like the Countess to bring up something that seemed so important and let it end there. I knew Cecily would ask Father about it later. Leopold had turned to the Inspector and inquired about the afternoon's ride.

"It was splendid," the Inspector said.

"Do you find riding another man's horse a pleasure, Inspector," Leopold asked, "or do you find it a pleasure only at first, and then after a time, find yourself wishing you had your own horse, as a borrowed one is never really fresh?" He had a strange expression on his face as he asked this.

"Quite the contrary," the Inspector said. "In the same way that each rider prefers a different mount, so the horse too, has preferences

[1] This reference to the Princess of Albrecht was a story that had a great deal of coverage around the turn of the century. Her husband had her declared insane and imprisoned her in an asylum because he believed she had committed adultery. He stripped her of all her property, a rather sizable income, and she became destitute. Women who contemplated divorce faced this risk.

about the rider. I believe Oskar is not really interested in riding her, or in pleasing her." With that he took a sip of water and I saw the Countess relax.

"How is it," Leopold said, annoyed, "that I have never seen Oskar with this animal?"

"Oh, she is just newly acquired," the Countess said. "She has an excellent trainer who has brought her around."

"Brought her around?" the Inspector said.

"Yes," replied the Countess. "The trainer says he found her running wild along the Ringstrasse in a broken harness. He believes she had been purchased for coaching, but as no one has claimed her, he trained her to the saddle. She is most intelligent and trained easily. Oskar says she was never meant for the traces at all. She is too light and headstrong."

The Inspector stopped with his coffee halfway to his lips. "The body is missing," he heard Voll's voice in his memory loud and strong, "and the second lead horse as well."

47

Shortly after sun-up the Inspector was at the stable, and took the black horse out and turned her toward the Second District, where he knew a crooked man who kept horses and coaches for hire. Hidden.

He was relying on his supposition that the horse knew precisely where she was going, and he let her have her head.

There was a brisk trade in Vienna, the Inspector noted, in the hiring of funeral carriages. The black horse, he saw, had been used in this way, for she led him directly to an area where he knew they were engaged in illegal activities. There was a small group playing cards near the stable. He tied the horse and approached the one who was watching him. He seemed perfectly eager for *any* assignment.

"Ya," the man said, "we'll do a job for you, *anything at all* that needs carting, you know what I mean." The Inspector conquered his distaste.

"This location," he said producing a map.

The man, who was toothless said, "there's a big hill there—you're going to need a big team—especially if there's ice."

"I want," the Inspector said, "six."

"Six?" The man squinted.

"It's heavy . . . ," the Inspector said. "Six."

"Oswald then, Oswald's the one you'd be looking for."

"Is he here?"

"No," the man said, "haven't seen him for weeks. Disappeared."

"Well," the Inspector said, "this is quite important. Do you know where I might find him?"

"Never came back from his last job." The man pointed to a small shed. "Clothes is still here, never found the horses either. Just disappeared. That's what happens with messy business." He turned then, spitting, and went back to the stable.

The Inspector went over to the small shed and the door was open. There was a fireplace and some bedding on the floor. It was stunningly neat for such a shabby environment. The few clothes were folded neatly on the chair, which had been mended with twine. Over the back of one chair was a uniform of some official sort, with gold tassels and epaulettes. Perhaps a military uniform, he thought, tailored to a new purpose. He did not hear the man come in behind him.

"What are you looking for?" a voice asked.

48

The next day, the Inspector traveled to Berlin. He spent some hours observing the comings and goings of the Fliess residence, and then that night, shortly after midnight, when the Fliess household was fast asleep, he pried open the window and leapt in. He had no trouble justifying that burglary was on such occasions justified.

The Inspector sat through the night, reading the letters, notes, and journals on Wilhelm Fliess' desk. The man was obsessed with the nose. And timetables. Periodicity, he called it. A schedule for everything. It seemed to the Inspector wild and improbable, a kind of scientifically presumptuous numerology.

With his notes, there were letters. He found one he was looking for. It was from Freud: "I find it necessary to move my residence at once. I am perfectly serious about a change of occupation and residence, in spite of all the improvement in my work and income." And what might have brought this sudden urge to move? The Inspector's eyes filled with light. That was significant. The Inspector got up and walked around the desk. He sat down. He read on.

Upstairs Wilhelm Fliess, his wife and child slept while below the Inspector ransacked their lives, and Fliess' relationship with Freud. So much talk of death! My God, the man Freud was obsessed with it. And then he found it. The business about Emma Eckstein. The missing nose, the missing blow. So. Was this at the heart of it? Freud's protection of Fliess. Death and noses, letter after letter. Humph, he thought, Freud was a hypochondriac, too. And Fliess was nuts, with his talk of tables and periodicity. But the *letters!* Rather astonishing; the man Freud positively *adored* Fliess.

As the hours wore on, he realized the letters were not as conclusive as he'd hoped. Still Freud, despite his fierce attachment, was obviously outraged over Fliess' treatment of Eckstein. He had to give him that. But then he saw a change in the tone of the correspondence. One week before the murder: he read these letters carefully. Fliess was furious; charging that Freud had "leaked" Fliess' theory of bi-sexuality to his patient, who told someone named Weininger, who had stolen his ideas and was writing all of it in the book called *Sex and Character*. The Inspector sighed. "Everyone is male and female," he read. "This is *my* discovery. We are all bi-sexuals . . ." The Inspector read on. Then a reluctant reconciliation letter from Freud. Would anger over a theory be enough, he wondered, to make Fliess want to discredit Freud? Not that he suspected Fliess of murder, but perhaps of wanting it to look like there was one and discredit Freud. At 3:00 A.M. he gathered the papers he needed, lifted the sash, and left. There was a freight train passing through at 4:00 A.M. He needed to be back in Vienna the next day.

49

The Inspector was only a block away from the police station when he came upon Captain Voll having an altercation with a tram conductor in the street.

The odd little fellow was agitated, as Voll, red faced and almost hissing, said, "I told you never to come here, you idiot." There were more words, which the Inspector could not make out and then the little one, having received money, the Inspector noted, hurried away.

The Inspector went up to Voll, who was astonished to see him. "I couldn't help overhearing . . . may I ask who that was?" Voll had failed to compose himself in time to lie completely. "That . . . that is my unfortunate brother," Voll said, turning to smile. "You know the kind. Always needs money for the rent. That sort of thing."

"Where does he live?" the Inspector said.

"A bad area," Voll shrugged, "near the Ottakring." He turned to the Inspector. "I am sorry if he disturbed you. I told him never to come to the station." The Inspector nodded and walked away. He did not ask a most important question: he was certain he heard the man address Heinrich Voll as Johann. It made the Inspector extremely uncomfortable, set something off in him that he couldn't quite fathom, while at the same time he wondered what possible difference it made who called Heinrich Voll what. The case was getting to him. The strange layers of coincidence built into it, the complete failure of any theory to begin to explain it. That and the gruesome body parts, each announced by a poem, which kept appearing over the city.

50

The Inspector desired a very good Viennese coffee and some cakes. By sheer coincidence, a factor that had come to his assistance on more than one previous occasion, he saw Edith Wharton leaning on the arm of a quite smartly dressed gentleman, making her way out of the *Konditorei* on the corner. He saw immediately in their walk that they were lovers, which surprised him. He had talked at some length to Mrs. Wharton, and he thought her a type who did not take readily to pleasure. A formal, stuffy woman, clearly of great intellectual accomplishment. Intrigued, he kept his distance but decided to follow them.

When they entered the Hotel Europa, he waited a few discreet moments and then crossed the street and motioned to the desk clerk, who established the gentleman as Mr. Morton Fullerton in room 22.

He was about to turn and leave when he noticed Mr. Henry James making his way up the stair of the very same hotel. Intrigued, and somewhat surprised, he stepped quickly into the stairwell so as to escape notice and saw Mr. James hurry into the hotel dining room. Curiosity made him decide to boldly push on through the French door leading to the cafe, and, spotting the table of three, he sat down not far from them and ordered a coffee, cognac, and pastry.

It was as he was about to lift his fork for the third time into his sacher torte covered with *schlag* that the laughter and conversation suddenly died and Mrs. Wharton stared at him and straightened up in a military way while her face went quite white. She leaned forward to whisper to the two men, and they turned together to look in his direction. Mr. James had the expression he frequently had of puzzled astonishment, whereas Mr. Fullerton sat back without the slightest bit of self-consciousness and surveyed him with a faint trace of amusement.

The Inspector nodded graciously at the three of them, and after some hesitation, Mr. James and Mr. Fullerton returned the nod. The Inspector raised the *schlag* in a merry salute and continued to lean forward and spoon it into his mouth. He wondered as he did this at the three. Surely this was no ménage. Although he had been surprised before, he simply could not imagine such a tryst. And yet, watching them he had the distinct impression that all three of them were involved in the same romance.

51

Dr. Freud was feeling quite elated. He cautioned himself against too much optimism, but he felt his treatment of the Countess was a great success. Her compulsive submission to strange men had been almost entirely eliminated. She seemed now to be very much in love with this other man, a man she would not name. But the real issue was, for him, her infertility. There was no question in his mind that this, too, was a result of hysteria.

He finished his morning ablutions and went down to breakfast. The children were chattering and he was trying to concentrate, so he was annoyed with them. But when Anna looked up at him with that surprised hurt expression, he felt immediate remorse and took her by the hand and helped her on with her hat and coat for school.

Later, when he went into his study to go over his notes on his several cases, he found himself thinking again about the Countess. He had, at some cost, just revised his theory. He now believed that all of the hysterics he had been treating were suffering from fantasies, rather than real seductions by their parents or other members of the households. This was a major turning point in his theory. And yet, here was the Countess. In this case the evidence was nothing short of overwhelming. He did not want it to be so; he wanted it to fit his theory. But there was no denying it. She could not recall who, but the reality was there, every day, in one way or another. It was when she was very young, he thought grimly, and she was so loyal to the needs of her seducer, who eventually became, as all seducers of children did, her tyrannical molester, that she had buried years of rage and shame and self, along with his or her name.

He got up and went for his daily walk around the Ringstrasse. "A slave . . . a slave, I will not have a child who is born a slave." With those words she had collapsed upon his couch.

He had delicately and gently pointed out to her that she was imagining her own slavery would be re-experienced. "You do not think, or imagine," he had said softly, "that it might be otherwise for your child?

It might be a male child and then there would be no possibility," he said, hesitating. He felt immediately he had made a mistake. She had simply cried out a furious, "No!" Screamed it, really. Her terrors were suddenly with them in the room and he felt he was inadequate to the task. He had proceeded too quickly. Once again, too quickly. Too eager, in his arrogance, to let her discover for herself. He went on then, thinking about this, and walked more slowly in a state of self-castigation he had not felt for a long time.

He did not want to lose her now. He did not want to fail. He must listen now for the next few days. Or her rage, which was volcanic, would destroy his efforts totally.

52

The Inspector paced the living room, jealous of a husband's privileges. He thought of Leopold upstairs now, and knew that although the Countess had her own boudoir, her husband could be there, watching her emerge from her bath, watching her powder.

When she appeared she announced that Leopold would be joining them later. She came immediately to him, the warm spontaneity she expressed so readily, except in Leopold's presence, seeming to flood the room. Although several people had gathered in the parlor, she was quick to make introductions and project an air that promised a marvelous evening.

Unfortunately that is not what transpired. There were a variety of stops and starts and arrested conversations. There seemed to be tension between Mrs. Wharton, Mr. James, and the writer Karl Kraus, who had just started his own newspaper. When he heard that Mr. James was to have one of his plays put on at the theater he quipped, "I hope it will be in English as the German spoken in Vienna is so corrupt all your words will be reduced to babble."

Mr. James said that it was not being produced in English, at which point Mrs. Wharton asked Kraus why he felt it necessary to condemn the German language instead of the individuals corrupting it.

"I do not bother myself with destroying something as petty as individuals," Kraus said to her, glancing at Mrs. Wharton with that strange smile he had.

"Ah, after legions of philosophers have declared otherwise, you have suddenly decided the individual is a petty affair?" the Countess interrupted. "What then is sufficient subject for your destruction, nothing less, I suppose, than the state?"

"The state, at least this one, is a perfect example of the insane capacity of the worst aspects of the human mind to survive."

"Why I thought," said Mrs. Wharton, "that Dr. Darwin has shown us we are capable of surviving quite beautifully; you miss the point, there is no insanity in survival."

"The survival of this overblown, pompous, destructive, *lying* society is a mockery, and it marks the end of civilization. When the society rots, the rot starts in the tongue and then spreads to the rest of the body," Kraus said in a characteristically dramatic flourish and stood up at the table.

"I believe," Henry James said, "you are in agreement then with the philosophy of the Talmud. Is it not in the Talmud that it says, that 'the omission or inclusion of just one letter could mean the destruction of the entire world'? I'm rather admiring of that myself."

Edith Wharton shot him a look. Vienna certainly had strange effects on people. Imagine Henry, of all people, quoting the Talmud.

"You are quite right," the man sitting next to Mr. James said. "Mr. Kraus is often in agreement with the Talmud, more times than he may wish to know."

"What I *do* know," Mr. Kraus said, "is that nothing means anything here, language here is simply sounds pretending to be words, aimless parries to fill up the void. When language has lost the meaning, so has life." Kraus turned and raised both hands in a startling gesture.

"Very dramatic," said Mrs. Wharton, "but not entirely accurate. Which means you should just sit down." To everyone's astonishment Karl Kraus did just that.

"Tell me, dear lady writer," Karl Kraus said with a sneer, "how am I wrong?"

"You have brilliant writers here. I have just been reading this young man, Hugo von Hofmannsthal. He seems to be depressed about the same subject, I might add," she said, speaking in a way that made me think she was not depressed about it at all. "But his *Letter to Lord Chandos* is anything but corrupt."

"He is young," Kraus said, weaving around his glass like someone who has had a lot to drink. "He too will turn into another Heine," he said. "A Moses who strikes the rock of the German language with his rod, and all that spurts forth is eau de cologne."

Kraus laughed theatrically, but no one else did.

"Really, Karl," the Countess said, "you are convinced you are the *only* person who uses German with the care and beauty it deserves, but I don't believe it's solely the misuse of the German language you're complaining about, you're complaining about something you can't have here—it is something the Russians do have." She paused. "The Russians have a soul. Not so the Austrians."

"Oh, come my dear," said a man with a monocle and a long white beard. "Half the Russians I have met have German blood in their veins, those who aren't like yourself, partly *Italian,* that is, so I don't believe you know what you're talking about."

"Of course they have German blood," she said, "but it is not the blood that makes us Russians," the Countess said, her gold eyes turning green now with anger. "It is Russia that makes you Russian."

Leopold, who entered as she spoke, countered, hoping to trap her, "Why, then, isn't it Austria that makes you Austrian, my dear?"

"Because there is no Austria. There are just competing ethnic groups, barely held together by an aging emperor and an outmoded idea," she said.

"Oh I quite disagree," Kraus said. "Austria has a soul, its soul is Vienna, warped, confused, demented though it might be."

"Please," a woman whose name was Wittgenstein and who had been painted by a famous painter was speaking. "Of course Vienna has a soul, you cannot have this much beauty, this much music and artistic expression without a soul. The language is German I grant you, but the soul is Viennese."

"Vienna has its muses, but Russia has a soul. There is a difference," the Countess insisted.

"In my opinion," Mrs. Wharton said to the Countess, "if you're going to discuss soul, you have to begin and end in Italy."

And before we knew it this started quite the most awful row over what a soul was and wasn't, and whether anyone had one, and then, I don't know how except the way things do at dinner parties, the Countess' talk went quickly from the soul of Russia to the American president and what he was going to do about the poor Russian people who were starving. And then Father got very upset about it because he was involved in these policies and said that America was attempting to do what it could but that Russia had become so—"disorderly" was, I believe, his word—that it was very difficult to know what to do about the anarchists who had gone completely crazy there and the constant upheaval of czars, and the people who were suffering from all of this.

The Countess had turned pale during this. "It is true," she said, with great agitation, "the situation in Russia is very difficult. I no longer know the solution myself," and that surprised me—the passion with which she'd said this—to think that the Countess had ever thought she had a solution. I mean, Aunt Ida often had solutions, but I was not used to thinking of the Countess as a person who performed social missions in that particular way. But perhaps I was mistaken. I also began to wonder what nationality the Countess really was, and of course my own as well. I mean, I knew I was American, of course. But I never did understand how we were cousins, and no one ever seemed willing to explain it.

It was later that I began to get some notion of Mr. Kraus' temper when the conversation turned to the subject of the Jews. I saw Mrs. Wharton blanch at this.

Edith Wharton had heard that Kraus was brilliant but impossible and given to radical causes, like trying to legitimize prostitution. He had a reputation for being sympathetic to women, but his remarks were outrageous. And now this Jewish business, she was sick of it. Everyone in Paris and now in Vienna talking about the Jews.

Kraus was going on about Theodor Herzl now, his voice rising to an absolute harangue and pounding his fist against the table. Henry James was stunned by Kraus' command of words. Kraus spoke brilliantly, a savage magician whose words seemed to tear into the air like so many crystal bullets, dazzling, rich, clear, and dangerous. Kraus was an odd fellow, James had come to feel, because if one were to judge him strictly from the point of view of sensibility, one could conclude that he was not a man interested in justice in the least, but a bitter misanthrope. Kraus, it seemed, hated *everyone* except, James saw, the Countess, who had gotten up from her chair, and had gone over to whisper to him. He seemed to quiet down as the Countess suggested that the discussion be held until dessert, which at the time I thought she was doing simply to prevent discomfort in her guests, although as

I thought about it, I should have known that was not her motive at all. She was simply biding her time, postponing the discussion for the most dramatic moment of the evening.

The Inspector said suddenly to Theodor Herzl, "My dear Theodor, before we continue to contemplate your range of solutions on the difficult matter of the Jews, perhaps you would be willing to turn your conversation to the theater, as Mr. James' new play is opening soon in the Burgtheater, where I believe your own play was produced last year."[1]

Herzl took the bait, and the conversation turned to the state of the theater and the plight of the playwright, a subject on which Mrs. Wharton had strong opinions. The Inspector had been interested in forestalling any further political conversation, as he sensed that the group of distinguished and powerful newspaper editors and publishers present were prepared to be against anything that Herzl proposed. Debates about the Dreyfus affair and Herzl's ideas were heating up every salon in Vienna and Paris.

Eventually the Inspector lost track of the conversation and glanced at the Countess, who was so involved in the discussion she did not notice his observation of her. She had, he thought, the most beautiful neck he had ever seen on a woman. He could not stop himself from looking at it, and with her hair swept off her face tonight and the amethyst necklace glittering against her collarbone, it was all the more dramatic. Just now a shadow was making a deep etching along the left side. He was so desperate to reach out and trace its outline along her soft white throat that he grabbed the edges of his dish with both hands to stop himself. Cecily, noticing him grasping his dish in this way, looked up at him in surprise, but he evaded her eyes.

I thought the conversation had settled down to some peaceful or at

---

[1] It is important to note Herzl's ideas were considered, for the most part, by the Jewish community as preposterous, as was initially his proposal for the creation of the state of Israel. It is probably impossible for us to judge now what the state of mind was for assimilated Jews in Vienna at this time, as they were clearly some of the most successful people in the society, and many were fiercely patriotic about anything German. Assimilation seemed, to many of them, a necessary and positive solution to the social conflicts of the time. To others, it meant a profound loss of identity and heritage. The complex and tortuous path, both personal and political, that Herzl was required to navigate during this period is carefully explored in Ernst Pawel's biography, *The Labyrinth of Exile* (New York: Farrar, Straus, & Giroux, 1989).

least civilized level of exchange, with no further agitated talk about the Jews, until the servants arrived with dessert. Mr. Kraus then leaped on Mr. Schnitzler, who was also a playwright, and a doctor as well, at the other end of the table.

"You are quiet, Schnitzler. It cannot be because you fear to show yourself. Perhaps you have an observation for our American friends, in whose honor this dinner is given." He nodded formally to us. "Perhaps you have an observation that they can take back to their country, something not too," Kraus paused for emphasis, waving his wine glass in the air, "too offensive."

Arthur Schnitzler eyed Kraus with disdain and amusement. He did not like being put in this position, it was clear, but he managed to slouch gracefully in his seat, and turning to Kraus and then to Father, he said, "I am not master of the statement that sums up all life, at least at that particular moment, as my brilliant friend Karl Kraus is." He nodded to him. "I am merely a physician and a playwright. Vienna lies like a dream, singing songs to us of our daylight selves. All masks and deception. Beautiful masks, but masks. And it seems to me that the state of mankind in Paris and in Vienna is actually quite similar." He took a sip of his wine and paused dramatically. "No one believes either in himself or in anything else, and in my opinion, they are quite right not to do so."

This comment startled the entire company, and there was one of those awkward silences that seemed to last an eternity. It was only the Inspector, eyeing Schnitzler keenly, who seemed to feel no awkwardness.

Henry James responded suddenly, "I quite understand your point about self-deception. Oddly enough it is one of your German writers, Nietzsche, that Mrs. Wharton and I have been discussing, who is so eloquent on this very same subject."

"Oh quite," said Mrs. Wharton, who began to speak most forcefully, and soon had the entire dinner party at full attention. The Inspector was listening to Edith Wharton with interest. The woman seemed to him to be a mass of contradictions—sneaking into Freud's study in order not to be implicated in his theories, and yet here so articulate, so erudite, so confident as to suggest she feared *nothing*.

"So it is rather, you see," she said with great animation, "that Nietzsche is suggesting we can go into the void, joyfully, forcefully, with all the power of our beings, that indeed we must go into it joyfully." Then she stopped, quite suddenly as if she had said more than she intended.

"But isn't it rather," Henry James said slowly, "an oxymoron, a verbal sleight of hand, those things he presumably was so opposed to, to think you can go into a *void*, into meaninglessness, with joy? I mean, how could you possibly?" He had turned to Mrs. Wharton now and there was an awkward pause as she leaned forward quite spontaneously and placed her hand on his arm, "Oh, but Henry, you must," and said, "and you *do*. Don't you realize you *do?*"

He replied then, softly, and I couldn't hear it but I thought, and I couldn't be sure because the lights in the chandelier were very bright and perhaps it was a reflection, but I thought I saw Mr. James' eyes become very shiny, as if he were holding back tears.

"Oh God," Kraus said, "here comes the mystical rubbish. The last thing this country needs is mystical nihilism, which is what *most* people, who misread Nietzsche, read. No one reads the *real* Nietzsche."

"I find it quite difficult," Aunt Ida interjected, "to know who the real Nietzsche is." Aunt Ida was surprised I think to find herself agreeing with Karl Kraus. "I've read the man and I find him most irresponsible. All that talk about herds and beasts, all that 'will to power,' why he'd have us charging out of the swamps waving our clubs."

"I don't think you have fully understood him," Mrs. Wharton interrupted. "He is suggesting I believe we wield our pens, not our clubs. It is art that will constantly re-create us; it is art that will save us from, the, er," she hesitated, "swamp, as you put it."

"How can art save us from the beast in us," the Countess objected, "if God couldn't do it, and Nietzsche says God is dead?"

"That's the point," Mrs. Wharton said. "Without God, especially, you must have art," and then she added surprisingly, "and love."

"Oh this is absurd," Leopold interrupted, "look at you, all of you, in your fine clothes and drinking your fine wine. You know nothing of beasts and clubs. I have been to Africa where all the people are beasts."

"Really!" Aunt Ida said. "I have a friend, who is an anthropologist, who has instructed me that what we think of as primitive societies are more intelligent than our own. Their attitude toward women for one thing."

"You're mad," Leopold said, as if it were a fact. "They are savages. They wear no clothes, they sleep in huts, they speak primitive languages."

"And you're a fool," shouted Peter Altenberg, a writer who the Countess had introduced me to just before dinner, "you know no African languages!"[2]

"Some black-skinned people from Africa know English very well," Aunt Ida said to Leopold, "and you all could profit from reading them. I think you should put away your Nietzsche and read a very important American writer, W. E. B. Du Bois, who wrote *The Souls of Black Folk*."[3]

It was the name of this book that started the next upset, because we were all speaking English, and a baron misunderstood and thought she said it was *The Souls of Black Volk,* as he suddenly turned bright red, stood up, and started screaming about how there were no black Germans, they were all white Aryans, and a great commotion occurred that finished with the baron yelling, "We are pure, pure, pure Germans!"

The Inspector said, as the baron left the room, "This purity business is always on people's minds—purity of both their bodies and their souls. It is a fatal concern. Cleanliness is not next to godliness—it's going to kill us all."

That really did it. I must say never had I been to a dinner party in the United States or even in Vienna that had the intensity of this one. The business about purity seemed to touch off quite the most awful row of the evening.

"This is not a trivial matter," Kraus exploded, pounding the table. Wine glasses spilled, the red wine making rivers on the white tablecloth, the veins making rivers in Karl Kraus' forehead, Herzl's red face furious with the attack. "Do you think I think it is trivial!" Herzl too was yelling now, "This is only a matter of life and death!"

"You are a Zionist; the Zionists, the anti-Semites, they are the same. *You* purify; *you* separate!" Kraus roared.

---

[2] Difficult as it may be to comprehend, certain historians believe the phrase "black is beautiful" originated with Peter Altenberg, a Viennese writer. He was in love with an African woman who was part of an Ashanti village which had been set up in the Prater sometime during the end of the nineteenth century.

[3] This was published in 1903.

"You are a fool!" Herzl cried. "You understand nothing."

"I understand you are ruining everything!" Kraus was vehement.[4]

"Gentlemen, gentlemen," Leopold intervened, but the battle was fierce.

"Why must you separate the Jews! Why must you stand apart. I am a Jew! I am as Viennese as the most Viennese Viennese!" Kraus screamed.

"You see," Leopold snarled to the Countess, "what you have started now?"

"I wish it were so simple that I had started it," the Countess quipped, "because then I would end it."

Kraus and Herzl had leapt from the table now and, followed by the Inspector and Mr. Mahler, the composer, were heading for the drawing room. The Countess was pale and held her head at an odd angle. Mother looked into her lap and said, "I hate all this dissension, Frederick." What she meant, I knew, was, do not bring this subject up again. I wondered if the Countess was indeed Jewish, then perhaps Father and I were also. I whispered this to Cecily that night, and she said she didn't care. Aunt Ida took me aside and told me it was a grave matter, and I listened to her, but I did not fully understand how grave it was, that matters of identity were matters of life and death. Aunt Ida had told me that in the Jewish religion, if your mother was Jewish, you were counted Jewish, and if your father was, you could choose, which seemed very odd to me. But I did wonder which it was in the Countess' case.

It was sometime later, when it seemed that everyone had relaxed, that Cecily, who had been very quiet, suddenly said, "I wonder," and she looked first at Mrs. Wharton and then at Mr. James, "*which* one of you

---

[4] Herzl's pamphlet *Der Judenstadt,* published in 1896, caused enormous dissension in the Jewish community all over Europe. The Russian Zionists, who claimed the idea originated with them, were angry. Many Viennese, like Moritz Benedikt, publisher of the *Neue Freie Presse,* were very upset with this separatist idea as they believed it played into the hands of the anti-Semites. Indeed, many anti-Semites did enthusiastically embrace the idea of a Zionist state as they wanted to separate and exile the Jewish community. The already complex nationalist feelings in Austria were also fed by this conflict, as was expressed in Moritz Benedikt's angry outburst to Herzl, who insisted on publishing the pamphlet despite Benedikt's objections. Benedikt said, "But you're not even an Austrian. You're Hungarian!"

will be considered to have written the more important books, a hundred years from now. Which characters will still be alive?"

There was a collective intake of breath and then absolute silence.

"Well I can tell you right now," Aunt Ida said, "it will be Mr. James. And that," she said turning to Mrs. Wharton, who seemed quite aghast at the entire conversation, "has nothing to do with a literary evaluation of your work, which, as I told you, I hold in the highest esteem."

Mr. James was looking extremely perplexed. "Mrs. Wharton is a most distinguished writer," he said, "and I have no idea how you so confidently predict the future of what can only be a very speculative matter." He felt his defense was weak, because indeed he couldn't help but think she was right.

"But I, and none of my kind," Aunt Ida said, "will write the history of the next one hundred years. And whoever writes the history, which will be men I can assure you," she said, "will decide."

"It is ludicrous," Edith Wharton said, "to maintain that because men write history they will judge women novelists to be less important than men, absolutely ludicrous. A novelist is a novelist and a critic is a critic, male or female makes no difference."

"Oh but it does make a difference," Aunt Ida said, and at this point, everyone was feeling so uncomfortable that no one quite knew what to do. Mother retreated into the kitchen. The Countess however was listening intently.

"You must have heard, Mrs. Wharton," Aunt Ida said, "that many men do not believe that women know how to think, and if writing is about thinking, and men don't esteem anything women think, well, then, they certainly can't believe that women who can't think know how to write. And that is what I mean."

"Indeed," Mrs. Wharton said, "many women do not seem disciplined enough in intellectual matters to convince anyone, men or women, that they know how to think."

"But thinking," Aunt Ida said, "consists of more than talking about wars and revolutions and politics and (this I thought was a bit unfair) Italian architecture (this was one of Mrs. Wharton's favorite subjects), and when it comes to thinking that is not necessarily intellectual," Aunt Ida said, "but is thinking nonetheless, that is where all the trouble is."

Mrs. Wharton was staring at Aunt Ida with an indescribably hard expression on her face. I thought she was perfectly furious.

Mr. James spoke again, "I don't believe there is that much difference in the thinking. A novelist is, I quite agree, a novelist first and a man or a woman second. Writing supersedes this issue."

"Perhaps in exceptional cases, or certain cases," Aunt Ida said. "Perhaps indeed in your case, and even Mrs. Wharton's, but the matter I am attempting to describe can be subtle, and I have not the means at the moment to convince you."

"Indeed you could never convince me," Mrs. Wharton said, "I find your argument pernicious, and it does injustice to everyone."

Henry James' head was reeling. Of course one did want one's works to last, and when he looked at Edith he just couldn't imagine that hers would. Oh, he loved her, of course. He thought she had the finest mind, the most entertaining, the most wide ranging and incisive mind he had ever encountered in a woman. He had always wished she had been rather more attractive, but she was so magnificent and had such sweep it almost made up for it. But her sentences. They were perfectly serviceable of course, but what was between the writer and the world were the writer's sentences. When he desperately wanted to reach out and touch the world, or bring it into himself, the only thing he had were sentences, his very *own* sentences, winding and unwinding down the dusty tracks of his thought until the vision was revealed, so precise, so exactly rendered, it brought him happiness, and relief. And Edith—he didn't know, but he imagined it was all rather different for her. She seemed to dash off the books, and he couldn't imagine she was really as attached to her sentences as he to his.

My eyes went from Mr. James' face to Cecily's. She looked suddenly as if she were about to explode with grief.

"I am *not* talking about *that!*" she said suddenly. "I am talking about who will *live!* Look at *me!*" she cried. "What of me!" Cecily said, her face contorted. Her voice was strained and she was breathing hard. "What of me, of me?" Her fist pounded her chest and we were all stunned speechless at this paroxysm of emotion as Cecily stood. "You, you," she seemed at once to be without words and then turning her face to Mrs. Wharton, "you will have made them, and you," she turned to Mr. James, whose shock was total, "you will have put them in plays, and everyone," she said hissing, "everyone will know of them, of Isabel Archer and Lily Bart, but what of *me, me, me? What of me?!*" Her face was red with rage, and tears. I had never seen Cecily so wrathful. "What of me? What will anyone know of me? I will end, simply end, and no one will ever know or care—*I hate you, I hate you, I hate you!*" She screamed this last in uncontrolled rage at Mr. James, whose face had turned the color of the tablecloth. Cecily then ran from the table. Mother had hurried in from the kitchen and now ran after her mumbling, "Cecily, Cecily, oh dear, oh dear, oh dear," in a terrible fright, as Father announced to Mr. James, "I am so sorry . . . I am terribly sorry, I don't understand, this is not like her at all . . . I, I have never seen—"

Father was quite humiliated. Mr. James was utterly stupefied. He had put down his fork and was constantly moving his tongue along his lips, turning first to me and then to Aunt Ida, and then to Mrs. Wharton. Mrs. Wharton did not seem upset, but simply perplexed. "How extraordinary, how perfectly extraordinary," Mrs. Wharton said, "to have such an idea." Mrs. Wharton seemed to be turning the thoughts over and over in her mind, rolling her eyes, most unwittingly as she did so, and indeed I was suffering the very same myself. For I thought that Cecily thought that somehow she would not be real, that no one would *know* her, unless she appeared in the pages of a book, I thought quite possibly Mr. James' book, or much the second preference for her I am sure, in one of Mrs. Wharton's.

All of this struck me as very strange and yet I understood it also. For there were moments when I did understand, at least I thought I understood what was going on in Cecily, and at such times I would feel a jump in my heart and I would think I knew exactly what she meant, for I, too, yearned to be re-created inside Mr. James' sentences, to feel myself come alive through those long, sinuous, labyrinthine exposures of the heart. I longed to be defined, sustained, and released within those closures. Perhaps it struck me as most strange that I felt that Cecily, in that second at the table, had turned to me with that brief and savage plea in her eyes. That *I* must do it, somehow was her message, and as I thought this, I felt my fists clench and unclench, fiercely engaging the tablecloth. I could not stop this and thought for a moment I would pull the entire table awry. Perhaps it was because of my concern for Cecily, I do not know, but I failed to pay proper attention to the next subject of discussion, and before I knew it, I found myself revealing the very thing I had determined to conceal from everyone. We had retired to another room when I heard someone bring up the question of the murders. The Inspector replied that he was confident that the matter would be resolved soon. He then remarked on the date of the murder, which we realized had occurred on the very night on which we arrived!

When the Inspector mentioned reports of five black horses, we immediately chimed in that we had seen such horses the very morning of our arrival in Vienna. There was considerable excitement over this, and then, the Inspector, who possibly has some sixth sense, turned to me, and said, "And did you see anything else that morning that was peculiarly remarkable?"

"Oh, well, the man with the gun, of course," I said. I felt all eyes turn to me.

The color drained from my face as I looked at the startled company. It was true, of course, that I *had* seen a man with a gun, and it was also true that I did not want anyone to know I had. I was astonished at what I had just said.

"What man, what gun?" Aunt Ida asked.

"Oh, well, I, I don't know," I said, my cheeks were aflame.

"My dear," the Inspector said softly, "where did you see this? In the house, or in the street?"

"The street, I think," I said.

"I see," the Inspector said. "And about what time did you see this gun on the street? Were you still in the coach?"

"Why, why, yes," I stammered, lying.

"You never mentioned it!" Father said.

"No, I, I never did, I, I wasn't sure at all," I said. Aunt Ida and Father were leaning over the table at the far end, bent forward at a very curious angle as if they could not quite understand what they were hearing.

"I'm sure it was of no importance. None," I said quickly.

"Well, perhaps and perhaps not," the Inspector said. "There is no point going on about it now, let us have more wine," and he raised his glass and proceeded to tell a very funny story, for which I was immensely grateful. I could not believe my luck at having gotten off so easily.

I should have known, of course, that the Inspector was much too clever a man simply to let the matter rest.

It was later in the evening when he approached me again, and in that slow, easy voice asked me about the gun. But I knew I could not tell him, yet. I clearly remembered my dreadful feelings of excitement and shame during my encounter with the man with the gun. I remembered his unwrapping it, and something else as well, something shining in the snow near the package, shining silver on the ground.

That night I went up to bed feeling that the topics of the evening's conversation, women, words, and Jews, had depressed us all. I looked out the window to see Mr. James and Mrs. Wharton maneuvering their way down the icy walk to their carriage. They were helping each other, as first one slipped and then the other. They had their heads low and were talking very solemnly, but as far out as I leaned, as much as I tried, I could not hear what they were saying.

53

Henry awoke in the night. He was thinking about Cecily. She so desperately wanted to be a character in his book and yet at the same time she was furious at him for not giving his characters, especially Isabel, the destiny she, Cecily, would have liked. She wanted, perhaps, to be Isabel Archer, but she wanted to do something else, she didn't want to go back to Osmond. And it bothered him. Had he, in fact, been irresponsible to life? To his character? Had it been a mistake, a terrible mistake as Cecily put it, to send Isabel back? It stunned him, amazed him, when she said, "Don't you have an obligation," she had said, "to your readers to *imagine something better?*" This had wrenched him. To think he had failed, in whatever way, to expand their possibilities. Should he have omitted the kiss? In a few minutes the damp clamminess on his brow made him cold. It was dark. There was no moon. He had been sitting up and the sound of his heartbeat was loud in his ear. He had had enough of this, of himself. The fear now, as if he were still writing it, as if he hadn't finished. As if he were an amateur. There were other questions—there were issues of credibility. There was art. He wasn't writing a teaching manual, he thought suddenly with great irritation.

54

I couldn't get the dinner party out of my mind. "Who is this Ernst Mach I heard the Countess going on about?" I asked Aunt Ida the next day.

"Oh," she said, waving her hand, "another one of those so-called brilliant philosophers, you know like the mad Weininger. He probably has terrible attitudes toward women also, although I don't know, I haven't read him."

"Well," Cecily said, "what is so important then? Why was everyone in such a dither, about all that 'self' business."

Timothy unusually had joined us for dessert, and he said knowingly, "Well, Mach says there is no such thing as a self—we aren't really persons." Timothy was quickly devouring the Salzburger Nockerl, which prompted me to ask, "Well who then is eating the Nockerl?"

"There is no one," Timothy said, his mouth bulging, "I am and you are just a bundle of sensations, and every moment you are changing."

"Every moment?" I asked, incredulous.

"Oh absolutely," Timothy said finishing his breakfast. "Absolutely" was a word Timothy used a lot.

"Oh honestly, I hate philosophers," Cecily said, "I just hate them. Always asking the same questions, 'What is life?' 'Is there a God?' 'Who are we?' 'What do we know?' And they never seem happy with the answer."

Aunt Ida smiled at this, I noticed, but I was not smiling. I was worried because I was listening to Timothy. "I personally don't believe that the self is an illusion," he said. "Well, actually I do believe the self is an illusion, but I don't believe the idea that there is a self is an illusion," Timothy said very grandly. Rather like a philosopher himself, I thought. But I did not like hearing that the self was an illusion. I knew perfectly well what an illusion was, and I didn't want myself to be one.

"What do you mean the self is an illusion?" I asked him. Everyone looked at me. I could see they were startled, as in fact I was, by the intensity of my tone. "Well what do you mean by that?" I said again, very angry now.

"Well," Timothy said, tilting back his chair. "Well," Timothy said again, "I've learned a lot from the theories of Freud and others. We are learning about the mind. People forget who they really are, they repress their memories," Timothy said, "and Dr. Freud says it will come back and get to them anyway. The lies," Timothy said leaning over the table and terrifying us, "will all pile up and come back and hit you, like a boomerang!" Then he sprang back from his chair and I was so startled I gasped. "We are not who we pretend to be!" Timothy said. "We are full of feelings we do not know we have! We are all actors! We are full of secret selves." I began to feel ill. I remembered the words of Schnitzler, "Theater is central to Vienna, she loves her theater, and that is both her joy and her sorrow. She is most beautiful at night, Vienna, when she lies, like a dream, singing songs to us of our daylight selves. Her masks are real. Our deceptions are as central to us as our revelations. It is this you learn about Vienna."

I excused myself and asked to leave the table.

"You look upset," Aunt Ida said. "You need some tea." I shook my head, but Aunt Ida made me stay while she poured me tea. Apparently the conversation didn't upset her at all. She was full of energy.

"I do find these Germans the most aggravating people," she said.

"Really, Ida," the Countess interrupted her, smiling at her indignation, "they are Viennese. They are German-speaking, but there *is* a difference."

"These German-speaking people," Aunt Ida said pointedly, "are ridiculous. Arrogant. Can you imagine! Did you hear that man say last night saying in a perfectly serious way that Shakespeare would be *better* if he had written in German?"

The Countess smiled. "A lot of them think that. Have you ever heard Shakespeare in German?"

Aunt Ida covered her ears and shrieked. "What an idea!" Soon she and the Countess were laughing and I was excused.

But I was not laughing. I was wondering. What frightened me most were the other selves. How many and where were they and what, I wondered, were they capable of doing?

55

THE INSPECTOR'S
FIRST DREAM

That night, the Inspector could not sleep. He had a dream.

He saw Karl Kraus, not Jacob, climbing a ladder, and the ladder was made of words—but the words were ice crystals. As he seized one and lurched forward, the one on which he had been leaning disappeared beneath his feet. In this way it appeared he was climbing upward but as he watched, his feeling was that it was a mirage of some sort, and that instead of climbing upward the sky was simply rolling downward behind these fixed crystals, pretending to be stars of light, giving the illusion of upward climbing.

He saw a face now behind the rolling mirage. It was Nietzsche. He was trying to tell him something.

"Can you change anything?" the Inspector heard his voice beseeching Nietzsche. A voiceless voice, like the sound of leaves, replied. He heard his own voice now, booming through the universe like a thunderclap. "Can you remove hatred and despair?" he cried out.

"Yes, yes I can, I can mitigate it." It was Freud who replied.

"The heart has reasons," he heard the Countess whisper.

"It is my task to know the reasons, and, where productive, to change them," said Freud.

"It is arrogant," an old woman said, "to prove the existence of God."

"And I think it is equally arrogant to assume it," Sabina said, appearing suddenly at the old woman's side.

"Yes," the Inspector said. "To claim it is God streaming through us only to find an excuse for our unfettered selves. . . . Be done with God, God is only a word, an excuse for murder," he fumbled, surprised to find himself crying.

"But there *is* evil, real evil," the Countess said to him, "and it *must* be combated."

And then he saw Pascal, sitting on a cloud, his face puzzled at the Inspector's predicament.

"I am in a dream," he said and woke up.

The dinner party had unsettled him. Not the talk. He had heard a lot of talk in Paris, but something else . . .

Perhaps the Countess, sitting next to him at the table, with her hand gently on his arm, her eyes seeming to implore him, whispering, "But this Mach, and Nietzsche, and the rest. If there is no God, and there is no self but only language, what then is there? It cannot be, we ourselves cannot all be so fragile, can we?"

"So fragile . . . can we?" seemed no longer a voice with words but a long dangerous hand, a magician's hand that had reached out from the void itself and, cutting through his body, had wrung the blood from his heart.

56

Henry James slept like a haunted man. He awoke fitfully and then drifted off again. It was Arthur Schnitzler who appeared to him in the half light: "Vienna sings songs to us of her daylight selves. All masks and disguise." Except he thought he heard Schnitzler say "Venice" instead of "Vienna," and he awoke then, his heart loud in his chest.

Perspiring and shaken, he got up, and put on his robe, and he began to pace the floor. He opened the window and looked out. The moon was full and bright. But it was silent. Eerily silent. He leaned forward, intent and straining. He wanted to hear the song, Nietzsche's song; skylark, nightingale, any marker of the day, but he heard instead a screech, a caterwauling cry, an anguished, indistinguishable growl. Perspiring and fevered, his hand moved quickly to reach for pen and paper, and sitting down, calmer then, he began evenly, and quietly, like a conductor with his baton, to strike the sweet uneven notes from the beating, not-yet song.

57

Morton hadn't meant to pry. But Edith was out. While he was waiting in her hotel suite, he went to her desk, looking for something. He had never thought much about privacy. He was looking for one of his letters, actually, which he wanted back.

His fingers had trailed through her large stacks of correspondence when his eye was caught by the blue velvet ribbon. He pulled the folder out, on impulse, and undid the tie. He had to sit there for a few moments after he had read it. It quite unsettled him. He had not expected it of her. Not at all. At first he was almost shocked. And then he thought, it must be a draft, for a story, to be sure. But he wasn't sure. All he could think of as he read it was her rage at him when he told her about having heard Freud lecture.

``THERE'S nothing so unusual you know, my dear Edith," he had said to her, "about children being taken advantage of. You're making such a fuss about this Freud."

"I think it is *disgusting,*" she had snapped at him fiercely. I had no idea that is what he was up to, until I heard about that lecture. "These Viennese are disgusting. I pity their children."

"Unfortunately," he had replied smartly, "it is not confined to the Viennese, my dear."

He had dropped the subject then, faintly amused at her rancor. What he thought was her prudery. And now this. He hardly knew what to make of it. On the other hand, he thought perhaps it was about him. Perhaps he had inspired it.

Fragment of *Beatrice Palmato* by Edith Wharton[1]
"I have been, you see," he added gently, "so perfectly patient—"

[1] This is an unpublished fragment, presumably of a novel. It was first brought to the public's attention in the biography of Edith Wharton by R. W. B. Lewis.

The room was warm, and softly lit by one or two pink-shaded lamps. A little fire sparked on the hearth, and a lustrous black bear-skin rug, on which a few purple velvet cushions had been flung, was spread out before it.

"And now, darling," Mr. Palmato said, drawing her to the deep divan, "let me show you what only you and I have the right to show each other." He caught her wrists as he spoke, and looking straight into her eyes, repeated in a penetrating whisper: "Only you and I." But his touch had never been tenderer. Already she felt every fibre vibrating under it, as of old, only now with the more passionate eagerness bred of privation, and of the dull misery of her marriage. She let herself sink backward among the pillows, and already Mr. Palmato was on his knees at her side, his face close to hers. Again her burning lips were parted by his tongue, and she felt it insinuate itself between her teeth, and plunge into the depths of her mouth in a long searching caress, while at the same moment his hands softly parted the thin folds of her wrapper.

One by one they gained her bosom, and she felt her two breasts pointing up to them, the nipples as hard as coral, but sensitive as lips to his approaching touch. And now his warm palms were holding each breast as in a cup, clasping it, modelling it, softly kneading it, as he whispered to her, "like the bread of the angels."

An instant more, and his tongue had left her fainting mouth, and was twisting like a soft pink snake about each breast in turn, passing from one to the other till his lips closed hard on the nipples, sucking them with a tender gluttony.

Then suddenly he drew back her wrapper entirely, whispered: "I want you all, so that my eyes can see all that my lips can't cover," and in a moment she was free, lying before him in her fresh young nakedness, and feeling that indeed his eyes were covering it with fiery kisses. But Mr. Palmato was never idle, and while this sensation flashed through her one of his arms had slipped under her back and wound itself around her so that his hand again enclosed her left breast. At the same moment the other hand softly separated her legs, and began to slip up the old path it had so often travelled in darkness. But now it was light, she was uncovered, and looking downward, beyond his dark silver-sprinkled head, she could see her own parted knees and outstretched ankles and feet. Suddenly she remembered Austin's rough advances, and shuddered.

The mounting hand paused, the dark head was instantly raised. "What is it, my own?"

"I was—remembering—last week—" she faltered, below her breath.

"Yes, darling. That experience is a cruel one—but it has to come once in all women's lives. Now we shall reap its fruit."

But she hardly heard him, for the old swooning sweetness was creeping over her. As his hand stole higher she felt the secret bud of her body swelling, yearning, quivering hotly to burst into bloom. Ah, here was his subtle fore-finger pressing it, forcing its tight petals softly apart, and laying on their sensitive edges a circular touch so soft and yet so fiery that already lightnings of heat shot from that palpitating centre all over her surrendered body, to the tips of her fingers, and the ends of her loosened hair.

The sensation was so exquisite that she could have asked to have it indefinitely prolonged; but suddenly his head bent lower, and with a deeper thrill she felt his lips pressed upon that quivering invisible bud, and then the delicate firm thrust of his tongue, so full and yet so infinitely subtle, pressing apart the close petals, and forcing itself in deeper and deeper through the passage that glowed and seemed to become illuminated at its approach . . .

"Ah—" she gasped, pressing her hands against her sharp nipples, and flinging her legs apart.

Instantly one of her hands was caught, and while Mr. Palmato, rising, bent over her, his lips on hers again, she felt his firm fingers pressing into her hand that strong fiery muscle that they used, in their old joke, to call his third hand.

"My little girl," he breathed, sinking down beside her, his muscular trunk bare, and the third hand quivering and thrusting upward between them, a drop of moisture pearling at its tip.

She instantly understood the reminder that his words conveyed, letting herself downward along the divan till her head was in a line with his middle she flung herself upon the swelling member, and began to caress it insinuatingly with her tongue. It was the first time she had ever seen it actually exposed to her eyes, and her heart swelled excitedly: to have her touch confirmed by sight enriched the sensation that was communicating itself through her ardent twisting tongue. With panting breath she wound her caress deeper and deeper into the thick firm folds, till at length the member, thrusting her lips open, held her gasping, as if at its mercy; then, in a trice, it was withdrawn, her knees were pressed apart, and she saw it before her, above her, like a crimson flash, and at last, sinking backward into new abyss of bliss, felt it descend on her, press open the secret gates, and plunge into the deepest depths of her thirsting body . . .

"Was it . . . like this . . . last week?" he whispered.

58

Henry James got up the next morning full of thoughts about Cecily. He had promised to take her to the museum, but he was somewhat disconcerted by the effect she was having on him. He was of course finding it impossible for someone to suggest she be a character, after all, and yet he could not quite forget it either.

He dressed and went out early, finding it agreeable to walk in the Burggarten. At one point in the party the other evening Cecily had whispered to him, "Oh, I must talk to you alone it is important," and he had said he would see her when they went to the museum, although he was aware they would not be alone. She disturbed him yet he also felt some basic sympathy towards her, so he was not totally surprised, since she was so much in his thought, to see her suddenly running towards him, arms outstretched, calling to him. Her face was ecstatic as she approached.

"Oh," she cried as she reached his astonished frame, and embraced him violently, "I am so glad to see you, so glad, only you can save me." And then he saw how upset she was, for she buried her face, lashes wet with tears, sniffling, into the front of his coat and she trembled against him. Mr. James was so distraught, outraged, and embarrassed at this female creature flinging herself against his body in such an unrefined and uninhibited manner, except his outrage was compounded, yes, compounded and composed by the mercy he felt for this sobbing girl before him.

A strange, almost inarticulate compassion flooded him and the urge to comfort her, to allay her fears, to be indeed that very bulwark that her soul so fiercely sought. This ungentlemanly, even vulgar aspiration seized him with all its foreign power, all the more powerful for its strangeness, and despite himself or for himself, he could not know, then his arms swept forward and wrapped around the frail shaking back, and the voice, stranger still, said *there, there, there,* until the shaking stopped and a huge shuddering sigh escaped and the dark curly head, its face blotched with tears, raised itself with such gratitude and beseeching that once again he felt his hand move forward and lift a stray hair from her forehead. And there and then, with that gesture, he felt himself lurch back, realizing the spectacle they presented. His arms retreated rigidly to his sides and he offered her his arm and said, "We will go to that pastry shop and you shall have tea and that will make you ever so much better," all the while aware that as they crossed the street she pressed now against his arm with some intention he could not fathom, and he felt her skip as they approached the shop and saw now, miraculously, although the face was still streaked with tears, the eyes were bright and the smile was sweet, sweeter than he had ever seen as she said, "Oh, thank you," and walked in before him ringing the little bell.

59

The Countess looked over at the Inspector. His chest, which seemed to rise in a swollen mound down to his navel, where it dropped off suddenly like a mountain ridge to a valley below, was rising and falling in a slow steady rhythm. It was early in the morning, about four A.M. as she awoke, and found herself turning, as naturally as a rose turns toward the sun, toward him. Her lips softly caressed that mountainous mound, her tongue nuzzling his flesh like a bee rolling its belly in the heart of the flower.

She wanted now only to be covered with the sense and smell of him. He was like no other man she had known. She lay back for a moment enjoying the incredible release she found in her spine and in her belly, and a kind of ease around her heart. She felt she had been delivered from the dark, cold halls of resentment that had corroded her spirit for years. Hallways full of doors where men would appear suddenly and beckon, and she would follow in that wretched, obedient excitement. But he had not beckoned her, this man. She had deliberately, willfully, joyfully called to him, and he had come.

The Inspector felt her lips on him from a long, falling place, from an afternoon long ago when he had gone ballooning with a group of friends, and in a near-fatal accident the basket had broken and tipped, and he and two others had begun to spill from its sides, hanging on precariously until they landed. He had experienced then the most delicious, terrifying sensation as they swung over the earth, of wanting to let go of the basket, and fall, and with the Countess he felt it again. When he made love to her, he did let go, tipping and luxuriating in the long slow fall of endless pleasure. His hand reached up in his half-sleep, and touched her hair.

The Countess grabbed his hand and held it, watching him, hoping he would not wake up just yet. A kind of desperation assailed her at such times, and the most extraordinary writhing hunger that was physical, as if she wanted to be flooded from every portal, to drown in the smell and touch, of him. Where once with other men, exhausted and in pain, she had pleaded, "no more," with him at the moment of her most intense pleasure, an unending stream of desire welled up from some other, primal place, an enduring cry that was, she knew, the real ache of her soul. It came, she knew, from an unreachable depth within herself that, in the presence of this love, cried out for more and more and more.

She could no longer even pretend to love Leopold. It was like rain washing a stone, covering every inch, but affecting nothing. Leopold was not a fool; he did not think she had ever loved him. But he valued highly his possession of a beautiful wife. And now she was not even remotely affectionate. So he found himself banging his fingers in his desk, yelling at the servants, and conducting his life with great irritation and distraction. He knew he would lose her if he confronted her, but when he saw the expression in her eyes, it took all the force of his self-control to keep from doing it.

PART V
PICKLOCKS

The case is opening nicely to my
collection of picklocks.
> Freud, "Dora," Or, Fragments
> of an Analysis of a Case of
> Hysteria

We have art, in order not to die of
the truth.
> Nietzsche

1

The Inspector had told Freud he would not pursue any further inquiries of his patients, and he hadn't. But when Captain Voll ushered in the tense young woman who refused to talk to anyone "but the top official," he changed his mind. She had come, she said, because of "rumors" about the murder. Voll had tried to put her off, being uninterested in such a young, curious girl, but when the Inspector heard her name, he knew this was the girl Freud's notes had referred to as "Dora."[1] She was high-spirited and extremely impressionable, he thought, but he found her unappealing: she was both stubborn and vulnerable, and this he knew would make any real inquiry difficult. He was not surprised that she and Freud had come to a parting of the ways.

It reminded the Inspector of a conversation he had with the Countess. He had once told the Countess that for all of the doctor's insight, he believed Freud had no real "feel" for women. The Countess protested but the Inspector said he thought that considering the delicacy of the matters Freud chose for his investigation, he lacked precisely what he needed. Rubbing his thumb against his forefinger, the Inspector had looked at the Countess and said, "It is here in the fingertips, a certain kind of touch, the way a tailor might tell the silk from the

---

[1] Ida Bauer is the real name of the case history known as " Dora."

shantung, the satin from the sateen." "I see," the Countess had replied icily. "Do you regard women as merchandise then?" He had been hurt at her tone and wondered at her anger. Her jealousy, on occasion, astonished him.

As Dora walked beside him now he turned his full attention to her. Being a young woman who had visited the house, he imagined she might feel threatened, but he was astonished now at what she was saying. She turned to him and said, "I thought when I heard about the murderer, that it had to be me," she said.

He looked at her. She did not seem to be joking.

"I don't understand," he said. "You believe you committed a murder?"

She shook her head. "No I, I believed it was me, that had been murdered there. That I was lying there dead, and this person now, me, the one that walks in and out of the doorways and along the streets, this is the ghost. That the real me is dead, killed and with no evidence." She looked at him with desperation in her eyes.

"Do you know what it is like to die, without evidence of a murder?" she said. She had grabbed his arm quite firmly, and he was surprised at the strength of her grip. It was so bizarre, and yet he found himself moved and asked her softly, "Who is it? Who has murdered you?" And then she was quite overcome, and leaned against him, sobbing. He could not find out if it was her father, her mother, her father's friend, Freud, or all of them, or indeed if it were the girl's own rage and futility. The girl had no sweetness. But she was so *young*. Some horrid injustice had been wreaked on her. Of this he was quite confident.

She left him finally, and as she walked off down the street, he knew he would not see her again. He had offered to escort her to a carriage but she had waved him away. She had come to him for a reason, what reason he could not be sure, and she had been satisfied. He had told her he was on the very edge of a solution and that seemed, at the moment, to quiet her.

He turned back to his desk, but her anguished whisper haunted him: "The real me is dead. They have murdered my soul and left this ghost of a body to walk the streets. They have done this, and there is no evidence, because I cannot prove the taking of my soul any more than philosophy can prove the existence of it." She had shocked him, and he remembered now the shudder that shot through him when she concluded, her fingers in a fierce grasp, pressing sharply into his arm, her eyes glistening with an opaque, trapped light, and said, "It's the perfect crime."

2

The Inspector needed more help. Precisely what kind, however, was unclear to him. Stekal was persevering, and the Inspector rather liked him. But Voll was much too contradictory for his taste. Voll was exacting, methodical, logical, and totally irresponsible. He thought now, with an ironic smile, of his visit to Voll's home. He had arrived, unexpectedly, as was his habit, on a Sunday. He had been walking the streets and some question, unbidden, had risen in his mind regarding the procedures. So he went directly to Voll's house, on the outskirts of Vienna. He arrived in a beautiful wooded area and hoped briefly that the damn mayor, Lueger, would not succeed in putting an Acropolis there, as was his proposal. It would be a pity to ruin the woods.[1]

He had found Voll and his family at dinner. Voll was clearly irritated at being interrupted, but he had been gracious enough and asked him inside. The Inspector did not decline the invitation to join their Sunday meal. It was also wise, he had found, to know one's investigators as well as possible. He declined, however, to stay for dessert, and on some excuse, left. It seemed to be a typical bourgeois household although the Inspector was startled to see a large portrait of Karl Lueger. It was set like a shrine on the sideboard. The atmosphere was oppressive. The children sat rigidly as they asked if they might have bread, and if they might speak. Voll's wife shrank in her seat and had a voice of such timidity he had to strain to hear the three words she ventured. Voll made an attempt within these constraints to be polite. But the Inspector knew he had interrupted Voll's plans, something Voll never welcomed.

---

[1] Karl Kraus objected to this Acropolis also. There was a fledgling "green movement" in Vienna at that time.

Nonetheless Voll did interrupt his meal to go to his office and produce what the Inspector was looking for. He was a tireless investigator, the Inspector had to give him that. He proudly showed the Inspector a record he kept of the investigation so far that he took home every evening and went over after dinner to be certain that all leads had been followed. The Inspector also noted a number of framed citations on the office wall; from the police, the church, some charity organization. He sighed. He knew that Voll liked praise, and would resent having to share any of the glories of solving these murders with someone else. Well, the Inspector thought, the way things were going he might not have to share it after all.

3

We decided to pursue our trip to the museum despite Cecily's objections to the "languid ladies," which is what she said they were, a point that, once made, had set Aunt Ida and Mrs. Wharton and Mr. James into intense discussions of its merit. They briefly argued about going to see the Secessionist exhibit, which Mrs. Wharton wanted to see, as she was, she said, very interested in Mr. Klimt and some painting about philosophy.[1] But finally, Aunt Ida won.

Aunt Ida, despite herself, was very impressed with Mrs. Wharton. The woman was like a tour guide. She seemed to know everything about every painter in every period in the Kunsthistoriches. In between her brief lectures, Ida noted, Mrs. Wharton mumbled about wanting to go

---

[1] Indeed, Klimt's painting *Philosophy* was considered both shocking and "ugly." Commissioned for the new University building on the Ringstrasse, the painting caused a furor, particularly in an atmosphere referred to as "a crisis in rationalism." As Carl Schorske, in *Fin de Siècle Vienna* (New York: Alfred A. Knopf, 1980) argues, in a period when philosophy thought it was becoming more "scientific," Klimt's vague and sensual forms (as opposed to rational and intellectual) were seen as "failures." Eighty-seven faculty members signed a petition asking the Ministry of Culture to reject it.

on to Italy and that she hoped the dreadful business about the murder in Dr. Freud's study was solved. And soon. Now, Mrs. Wharton was holding forth about something else. Nietzsche, whom she apparently had recently discovered. Aunt Ida hid a smile: she wondered what Nietzsche would have thought of a woman who spoke about him in one breath and about the table settings at the Last Supper in the next.

Aunt Ida had read Nietzsche thoughtfully and knew he was wrong, absolutely wrong, if she understood him, on the subject of women. But when she brought up the subject of women in any special way at all, she felt Mrs. Wharton, for all her erudition, simply stiffen at her side. She couldn't understand how a woman who had written something as sympathetic to women as the story of Lily Bart should want so little to do with the feminists. Ida decided to put it aside, and try to engage her strictly in the realm of art.

We had just turned into a new gallery of paintings when Mrs. Wharton started gesturing excitedly to Aunt Ida. I didn't know what Mrs. Wharton and Aunt Ida were discussing but I heard Mrs. Wharton say firmly, "in the sixteenth century you have to look at decorative art to see the real genius. It was a time when conventionality was prominent and in decorative art this is a strength. Devotional painting of the period is so stereotyped that I doubt a genius even greater than Correggio could free it." Mr. James then said something about this that I couldn't follow, and then they turned down another hallway and started talking again, about Diana, who was in a painting that Cecily finally conceded to look at.

"I find it amusing," Mrs. Wharton said, "that the Abbess chose Diana as the subject for which Correggio should decorate her apartments. Oh, there she is," she said, "isn't it wonderful that she chose Diana to typify monastic chastity!"

There were some paintings on view from Venice, and again Mrs. Wharton's expertise seemed to rivet everyone's attention. "Oh, this is Guardi," she said enthusiastically, pointing to a painting of a group gathered in Saint Mark's Square. "He is so much less superficial than Canaletto, don't you think?" she said to Mr. James.

Mr. James said he was making up his mind.

"But," she said, "Canaletto is only charming, here you have the *grouillement* of the crowd, the surge, the market stalls, the real life of the streets!" and I remembered being surprised that Mrs. Wharton was interested in the real life of the streets; I had always imagined her in salons. Then we went on to the Dürers, and the Rubens.

Outside on the steps of the museum Mrs. Wharton was talking again about eighteenth-century Venice. She said it was indisputably a society in which appearances were everything.

"Just like Vienna," Aunt Ida said, and Mrs. Wharton said she didn't agree with that entirely, although there was a great deal to it. She thought the Viennese were even more theatrical than the Venetians. "They play at everything," she said, "and sometimes it's a wonder, and sometimes it's a terror."

"It's always a terror, finally," Mr. James said solemnly, "when you don't know the player from the play."

"Who can ever be *sure* of that?" Aunt Ida said.

"You have to be willing," Mr. James said, "to attempt, or shall we say, express some interest, or recognize that it is important to know the difference. I'm not sure they *want* to know; they *love* the illusion."

"Perhaps," Mrs. Wharton said, "because of their musical natures. When the music is moving so quickly and the dance is so intense, you don't want to look up or see that you might be dancing on," she turned then to Mr. James and looked at him, he thought, quizzically, "dancing on a grave, do you?"

"Why did you say that?" he said, his voice suddenly tight. "Dancing on a grave?"

"Why, I thought it was rather apt," she said. "You know how these things just leap to mind."

4

As we left the museum we stopped to admire the Empress statue, as Aunt Ida called it, which was of the Empress Maria Theresa and her generals! It seemed the Empress defeated a big king, called Frederick the Great, and Aunt Ida was most impressed. Mrs. Wharton seemed decidedly unimpressed with the artistry of the monument, however.

Cecily soon began talking at a fierce clip to Mr. James while she skipped along beside him swinging the beautiful bag from Paris the Countess had given her. Under her green coat she was wearing a white dress with an enormous bow sash, and when she turned and spun around, her coat and the skirt rose just a little, and you could see the yards of petticoat underneath. Her dark hair shone under the brim of her hat, which was veiled. She and Mr. James were planning what they might do on another day as Cecily had had enough of museums. But it seemed that Cecily could hold Mr. James' attention only up to a point, and then she just as easily lost it. He would turn away and speak to Mrs. Wharton.

We turned the corner of the Bellariastrasse and were about to cross the square when a carriage with a very smart horse, its hooves flying high and its chestnut coat gleaming in the morning sun, drew alongside us and a gloved hand flew out. In seconds, the coachman was down, offering his hand to a vision of lady in pink, pink tulle dress, pink silk coat, silk veil, pink slippers. *Pink!* Aunt Ida gasped. The lady trillingly said, "Good morning, Mr. James, how lovely to see you," and tossed back her veiling as she was introduced to myself and Cecily and Aunt Ida.

Mrs. Langtry was her name, she trilled and twirled her parasol about and said she was in Vienna *briefly.* She had the smallest, *pinkest* waist of any lady I had ever seen. She had grabbed Mr. James by the arm and was twirling him down the walk, talking, as I would have said, "a blue streak," but I thought "a pink streak" and said this to Cecily, who laughed very loud. This caused Mrs. Langtry to pause and turn, and Cecily skipped up to Mr. James' *other* side, a move I found too bold. He was chortling and murmuring, and I could not hear what was said. But I saw him turning his hat, first this way, then that, as the two of them, Cecily and Mrs. Langtry, vied for his attentions.

I felt for Cecily, for it seemed to me that Mrs. Langtry was a kind of witch who had enchanted Mr. James, as she would enchant all men. She had a very pretty face and a dazzling smile, but it was her comportment, the way she leaned against him, the sway of her hips down the street that seemed to claim him in some fundamental way. Cecily, not to be outdone, was trying her best to distract him, but Mrs. Langtry had put her face *awfully* close to his and would often stop and cry, "Oh, look," tossing her arm out to the side opposite Cecily so that she turned around too late, after the sight, and was always saying, "What? What are you talking about?"

All this happened in the time it took them to cross the street. Mrs. Langtry had left her carriage with a cry over her shoulder, "Follow me," and said "she had so looked forward to the walk." When we reached the Volksgarten, she had asked Mr. James for help with her parasol. Poor Cecily was beside herself at whatever spell it was that Mrs. Langtry wove. Mrs. Langtry knew all the things, womanly things, that a man liked, and her perfume and her laughter and the way she clasped his arm all bespoke experience that Cecily did not have. I saw Cecily's face and the way her jaw set, and I knew there were things gathering in her that would be dangerous to us all.

Soon, Cecily detached herself and ran into the grass, pretending to look at something, and I could see by the tilt of her head how forlorn she was. I thought that Mr. James must see it, but he was too deeply *involved* with this pink woman—the way she picked up her skirt, pointed her foot, twirled her parasol, laughed and looked so directly into Mr. James' eyes that I, for one, was shocked. I even heard Mother say something as this woman lured Mr. James deeper and deeper into the park and Cecily moved farther and farther away until the entire frame of vision was occupied only by Mrs. Langtry and Mr. James. Cecily's dark clouded face on the return home told it all.

As we rounded the corner in the park, we saw a small crowd gathered and Aunt Ida cried, "Oh a puppet show, let us see!" Aunt Ida insisted we go to the front. In two minutes we realized something was very wrong. The show featured two puppets: Wurstel the clown, and Jude. It was supposed to be Punch and Judy, but instead of Judy was this funny-looking bearded man called Jew. Wurstel kept hitting Jude over the head with a hammer and the crowd was laughing. Just as Aunt Ida pulled us away I saw Wurstel strike him dead,[1] and the crowd cheered. This did nothing for our spirits.

Nonetheless Mrs. Langtry insisted on taking Mr. James home in *her* carriage for there were books in her house, or so she said, that he would be eager to see.

---

[1] This puppet show has been verified in other accounts of the period.

5

The Inspector was holding the Countess in his arms.

"How do you get better," he said, "by remembering?" It was difficult for him to grasp.

"Why does it strike you as so strange?" she asked. Her white shoulder gleamed in the sun.

"I think of memory, the past," he said, "as death."

"That is how most people think of the future, they fear death, which is ahead, they don't fear the past."

"I fear the past," he said. "It is dangerous. It is as I said! the whale remembers it once walked on land, and with that memory it heads for land, beaches itself, and dies. Memory produces suicide."

"For the whales," the Countess said. "But for you and me, Dr. Freud says it is only when we recall, that we will finally be free," she said. He hated hearing the sound of Freud's name in such an intimate moment, it literally made him flinch. Suddenly he felt sick, nauseous, dizzy. Perhaps it was something he ate. He did not know. He grabbed the side of the bed, holding on, while the room began to reel.

"Maurice," he heard her from a distance, alarmed, "what is it?"

6

Henry turned the page, it was late but he was straining to keep his eyelids open as he made his way through the latest book.

The man seeing a light suddenly appear rushed to the door and lay the body on the carpet in front of the doorway. He ran quickly to the kitchen for some brandy and some bandages but when he reached her she was dead.

Oh dear, Henry thought. It was awfully unexpected in the story to have the heroine die like that. Perhaps then she wasn't the heroine after all. It was really very poorly done. Yet he couldn't help himself. He got up, splashed cold water on his eyes, returned to bed, and read on.

7

Edith Wharton was reading Freud's *Studies in Hysteria* with considerable surprise. She had to say, the man was a wonderful writer with a real command of narrative. A born storyteller. There was no question that as short stories the case studies were remarkable, indeed.

She put it down and stared into the red flames of the fire. Well, that was certainly the last thing she had expected of him. A sense of poetry, after all.

8

Sabina was at her writing desk, trying to work it out in words. She had been exhausted the last months from her studies, but rather pleased that she had been able to pursue them. She had rented this small, pleasant room near the university and had found the privacy very fruitful. She was disturbed however, that the investigation of the alleged murder in Freud's study still had not been closed. She hardly knew what to make of it. She had the uncomfortable feeling that that Inspector, who had been to see her again, was actually suspicious of Carl. She admitted to the Inspector that Carl and Freud had their jealousies; but it was absurd to think Carl capable of anything as malevolent as deliberately framing an incident to discredit Freud.

She got up and went to the window. Of course she had emphasized only Carl's positive qualities. He had helped her, when no other doctor could. He was brilliant. He and Freud, if they could only manage to get along better, could eventually, she believed, reconcile their psychological and philosophical differences. She had explained all this vehemently and the Inspector had been listening, carefully.

How, she did not know, but the Inspector knew about her letter. He insinuated Carl's character was less than worthy. It angered her. "We are all flawed," she had said to him. "It is a question of degree. He didn't seduce me, Inspector, I was fully cognizant of what I was doing." But he had betrayed her, that Sabina knew. But then he had been responsible for her discovery of this strange gift, hadn't he? He had provoked, admittedly most unwittingly, this astonishing generosity she discovered in herself. An enormous ability to forgive, a level of understanding that made it easy to forgive. She had tried to explain to the Inspector how Dr. Jung had helped her, she had tried to explain that there were mysteries she believed Dr. Jung understood that eluded Dr. Freud. And also the other way around. They needed each other, even while they could not bear each other. The night of the murder, and thoughts about it, had caused her to call the Inspector one more time. But it made her uneasy, the suspicions with which he regarded Carl. Uneasy and sad. Although she had tried to distance herself emotionally from Carl, she didn't know how successful she had been. Walking back toward her bedroom she was seized suddenly with the vivid memory of one perfect afternoon that weekend months ago, which she had resisted so forcibly, at first.

S A B I N A had been reluctant to go, but Carl had finally persuaded her to spend the weekend at his country house outside of Vienna. He had spoken fondly of his grandmother, whom he wanted Sabina to meet. It was odd she thought because the old woman was not really a grandmother; she had been Carl's nurse. But he was as close to her as if she had been blood. What had made Sabina uneasy was the thought that for part of that time, Carl's wife would also be at the country house, and for this reason, she had at first refused. But Carl as usual had prevailed and she had agreed to go.

She did not know why he should find it so pressing that she meet the grandmother, but when she met her, she felt her powerful presence at once. She did not so much meet her as hear her. She had come out of the house and heard sounds coming from the orchard, and when she got closer she heard more clearly an old woman's high strong wail, as if transmitted through the centuries. Carl had said she was Russian and a great story teller, and Sabina had felt bewitched as she listened to the stories of women, powerful women, magical women capable of the most amazing transformations. She listened to tales of Baba Yaga, of witches that stood on the hill, the generation of women sent, with their tales of the future, straight to the guillotine. She shivered at the thought of prophetic women; they were always persecuted. And she knew too, because Carl had told her, that the old woman was said to have the "gift," some kind of psychic "second sight," an uncanny ability to see and hear things that others could not.

When the old woman met her, she immediately told Sabina that she knew she was Jewish, and she came and sat with her for a long time telling Jewish folk tales. Sabina in turn told the old woman some, but to Sabina it all felt so strange, the force with which the stories were coming, and suddenly she felt like they were two Scheherazades, telling and spinning and spinning and telling as a way of forestalling certain doom. But then she immediately thought she was being overly dramatic.

Of course the entire day had been impossible. Carl was her doctor, yes, but also her lover, and she, Sabina, was here, now with his family. His wife was inside the house, and she felt certain that the old woman, whom Carl said was clairvoyant, knew about their affair. "You bring a gift to my grandson," the old woman had said, and Sabina blanched. Then she continued, "but you will suffer," and then taking both of Sabina's hands in her own, she looked into her face and said, "but of course you already do suffer." Sabina had tried to smile, but there was no accommodation to social grace here, this old woman knew some startling truths, and some, Sabina thought, she would not reveal. And Sabina resented it. She should never have agreed to come. When she'd looked up, she'd seen Carl come out of the house with his wife. He waved to her.

"Sabina!" he called her. She felt her body contract. *This was impossible.* She must do something. Do *something.* But what? Sabina turned and ran down the hill.

She had walked by herself through the magnificent pasture, thinking she could not let the old woman upset her. Sabina had winced when she said, "you have the gift, also." She knew that meant clairvoyance, and indeed on occasion, she herself was convinced she had some uncanny ability to know what was in people's minds. But she didn't *want* to have it, and she thought prophecies were only for the powerless, and unenlightened.

It was a magnificent day and as she walked out by the lakes and looked out over the green turf, at the hills covered with the flowers of spring—lime and snow white blossoms, of forests full of chestnut trees, threaded with trout streams, dells, spring and glades, as she saw corn mills and sawmills, she thought what a beautiful, magnificent, and prosperous country it was. An altogether remarkable country. In many ways she thought a great country. And then she felt wistful. She loved Russia, her homeland, but she loved Vienna, too. She thought nowhere on earth could there be so many beautiful things—music and art and literature, and brilliant talk and elegant society, and new ideas— she thought it must be one of the most remarkable places in the history of the world.

"Red," the old woman's voice startled her behind her. "It is red," she said, and Sabina blushed. She had stopped by an old picnic table to rest.

"The sky?" Sabina said, again turning around to see her. She was annoyed that Carl had left her alone with the old woman. There seemed to be a cold wind, but she thought it odd that the leaves were not moving on the trees. She wondered then, did the old woman frighten her with her coal-dark eyes, smoldering now with something else, some glimpse of the future? Sabina attempted to look at the old woman more carefully, but she found she could not. She could not study her, because when she met her eyes, the black, smoldering sense in them, the sense of *fire* she realized, with a start, almost assaulted her.

"You, you," Sabina said, finding it hard to find the words, "you mean fire?"

"I see fire," the woman said and then she released Sabina's palm and looked up into the sky.

"What is burning?" Sabina said slowly. She felt suddenly some coil in her mind unwind, unwind and call forth like a siren from some dead planet, awakened and now risen, with the flames, to seize her attention, and turn her mind to unthinkable things.

"What is burning?" Sabina asked, her voice catching as she said it, and as she asked, she knew. She saw herself, and countless others disappearing into flames, she saw walls of flame before her eyes, great towers of fire and smoke, and smelled burning flesh.

Sabina reached for the edge of the table and held it firmly as the old woman whispered, "Jews. They will burn the Jews." And grabbing Sabina's wrists, pulling them from the table with astonishing strength, she looked into Sabina's eyes with that same intensity and said, "Be careful. You must be very careful," and then she dropped them and moved away with a shuffling gait across the fields like a small, determined animal, a desperate messenger. Sabina was compelled to follow her, trotting alongside the surprisingly quick pace as the old woman spoke so softly Sabina almost could not hear. Something in her caught with fear, a fear that made her knees begin to tremble.

"Burning ... thousands and thousands ... more burning," Sabina heard the hoarse whisper. "... thousands and thousands and *more,*" the fear clutched at her so now she had difficulty catching her breath.

Perhaps she was mad, and the old woman was mad, what was this?—to speak of thousands, hundreds of thousands and *more* and then to say "and no one sees them ... no one hears them ..." How could no one *see* or *hear* hundreds of thousands? It was insane ... some insane fantasy. Sabina fell back from fatigue and despair as the old woman disappeared at a quickening gait over the next hill. Sabina was annoyed at herself that it clutched her so.

Carl had come out of the house then, closing the small wooden door behind him, and stood for a moment in the sharp sunlight. The sun glared down on his tall handsome frame, and Sabina felt a start as she always did when she looked at him. He held his hands over his eyes. The sun had been so bright he could not see Sabina, who was standing not twenty feet away. He saw only his wife. He called and waved to her, and Sabina felt that sharp twist inside that she had lived with for two years now.

It was later when the old woman returned to Sabina. "Perhaps I am wrong." she said. "There is a possibility, perhaps . . . it can be prevented."

"Where, where do you see it?" Sabina asked. She reached out and grasped the old woman's arm. She shook her head.

"She doesn't know. . . . What are you asking her?" Carl said, appearing suddenly and striding over. Sabina released the arm, and turned away. For some reason, when she thought about it later, she found herself wishing to say nothing to him about this. It was between the old woman and herself.

"She likes you," Carl said, sitting down next to Sabina. "She doesn't talk to everyone. She is remarkable, isn't she?"

"Pogroms . . . , was it pogroms the old woman saw?" Sabina shivered again. Perhaps it was just an overactive imagination, on both their parts. But something else stirred in her now, looking over the green rolling hills, the clear blue skies, gazing out into the peaceful bucolic scene, the three cows on the hill, their brown and white hides startling in the bright noonday sun, the oldest one moving slowly, head bent, the large bell ringing beneath her neck, lowing with the full weight of her udder. It seemed now, against the white-painted fences and blue sky, that no pogrom could come to this clear bright country.

Perhaps she had memories, the grandmother, something awful and awful times. She had heard there were Jews in Carl's family, on the father's side. Or perhaps she was a little mad, Sabina thought. And then she sighed. The mad could see clearly on occasion; indeed it was this clarity which made them mad. She believed this. She thought of Nietzsche, his eyes wild, she heard his words, "We have art in order not to die of the truth." Was the truth horrible then? She did not wish to think so. She wanted to think the truth was beautiful, eternal, opalescent, like a thousand goddesses gathered into a cloud. But she sensed in the old woman's sighs there was something coming that even the god-desses could not witness. They would vanish. A scream that would not be heard, the old woman said.

It had been a mild spring day and the women were in summer dresses, when Carl found Sabina later he was surprised to see she was covered with goosebumps and shivering. He had told her she had the most terrible look on her face, and when he grabbed her arm to pull her to her feet, the look, he said, was of total terror.

Sabina stopped dressing and simply sat, seated before the memories of that weekend. She remembered her thoughts the next morning because it had been such a spectacular day.

S H E could feel the blood beating behind her eyes, as with a kind of ravenous rapture she scanned the heavens, entering the blueness of the blue skies as if she were the color blue itself. Those days, such days of visual intensity she knew came from a longing for love. Not so much to be loved, as to love; to enfold and capture someone, or something with such divinity, such en-compassing energy that you would restore the very thing or per-son to itself, its holy self. She felt the spiritual essence of form and color at such moments to be part of a life apart, some beating universe of being that was invisible within the sky and yet visible to some felt sense too.

She had gone out for a walk across the meadow. She remem-bered how joyous she felt in that moment as if the flowers were hurtling through her soul, a riot of blazing beauties, and she could feel their energy unfold within her. She had put on a new white dress, but had gone barefoot, so she might feel the softness beneath her feet. She had stood on the hillside, arms outstretched over her head, the wind cool against her cheek, and the high, arched poise of her body sensing the heat and the fragrance of the flowers, the wondering cosmic fruity presence of life. She felt the tingling begin in her feet and rise through her in a crescendo, moving through her body in an ecstatic union that made the world and her body one. Such union astonished her: the pleasure in being.

She remembered how enthralled she was. She remembered now how Carl had climbed to the top of the hill, and grabbed her in his arms and how both of them, drunk with the beauty and fragrance of the day, had fallen to the earth, and he lay with her right there under the full heat of the sun, both of them lost in the tenderness of their passion. Afterwards she knew he was as happy as she when he lay there rapturous, naked, and transformed in her arms.

She remembered that life seemed right then, so vigorously simple. Total freedom and satisfaction both at once. She felt joyous and open; as if every ghost had been chased from her body. Her arms, her limbs moved easily. She had wondered then, in that moment, how it was that the angels of death had danced on that same plain only a day before. It was the same hill she had climbed with the old woman. She put those thoughts aside, and turned to Carl. Then softly, from afar they heard the voices of the others, tumbling up the hill like balloons. They heard them calling. They both sat up, stood up and arranged their clothes. Only on her new white skirt there remained a brown stain. They tried to rub it off but it stuck. A nut, a berry, not grass. Grass was green, but this was a root of some sort. Some staining root had ruined an otherwise perfect afternoon.

Sabina got up then and proceeded to the mirror. She suddenly felt quite tired. She knew she must finish getting dressed or she would be very late indeed. She knew too that she had promised the old woman, Olga, that she would accompany her on her walks around Vienna one day, and that she was avoiding it. It made her feel guilty.

9

It had been a long, cold spring but this particular day the weather quite suddenly had turned warm, and the Inspector and the Countess had gone off on a picnic. It was necessary for me to become quite bold—I had to hire a horse and coach—in order to follow them. Their horses were making a slow climb up the road when in the middle of the field they stopped and got out. Their coachman had clearly been instructed to wait.

I told my coachman to proceed past them, which he did, and I alighted in a small wood down the road. He agreed to wait two hours. I had to run through the trees bordering the field in order to catch them, and that is when I heard it. A sound of twigs breaking, as if someone were following *me*. I turned and heard nothing.

Then there was a whinny. A horse, close by and hidden. I thought I must not be silly about what was surely just a country rider, and hurried on so as not to lose sight of them.

They disappeared over the hill into what looked like a clearing surrounded by cypress trees. As I got closer, I saw in the midst of the trees the ruins of what had once been an elaborate manor house. The black gate, rusted and broken, swung on one hinge. It was thick with vines and flowers. Above the gate in wrought iron letters was "L'AV-VENTURA." The Countess seemed to be pulling the Inspector toward the gate, but he resisted. The Inspector collapsed suddenly and seemed to fall ill, sitting with his head in his hands while the Countess knelt beside him, speaking soothingly. Then the Inspector got up suddenly and pulled the Countess down the hill toward the woods away from the house. I caught up with them and watched the Inspector help the Countess down the steep hillside, alternately leading her, and then catching her.

I lost them in a thick wood for a while and when I saw them again they had gone into a large meadow. Then I saw a stream and then the Countess taking off all of her clothes. She plunged suddenly into the cold running water. There must have been a strong current, for she was swimming fast against it and staying in almost the same spot. Then I saw the Inspector swimming easily toward her from the other end of the stream.

I knew I should not, but I watched them. In the sunlight the Countess was so beautiful, her skin, gold in the light, wet from the water, her hair, gold-red, streaming down her back, and then she turned in her swimming in the green stream, and I saw the Inspector, his bare arms stroking through the water, swift, easily, like a fish, a large fish. He came up near her, and I heard her laughing, the high tinkling laugh she had, and I saw her cheeks were pink like apples in the sun and the Inspector's hair was wet, his moustache was wet and dark and dripping. And then he lifted her up and the water ran down her breasts in rivulets, and I gasped, it was so shocking to me and so compelling I could not take my eyes off her nakedness, and he placed her on the grassy banks brimming with daffodils and blue leberblumen; he lifted her as if she were a sprite and placed her there, and she had her hands on his shoulders and was looking into his face with such happiness, such discovery as if she had never seen it before. He placed her there and in one swift move raised himself from the water onto the banks next to her, the hairs on his body black and straight from the water, and I did not turn away, I could not turn away, as I stood there lodged in the tree and watched as his hand, dark and heavy, passed down across her shoulder and turned her to him.

Then I watched as they kissed; he kissed her hair and her neck and her back, and I saw her white hands fluttering against his back, and then I saw his back above her, and I was not ashamed. I could not believe I was not ashamed, but I watched in a kind of fascinated terror and excitement. I was incapable of moving or breathing, and I thought it was beautiful and terrible that I was watching, and then I felt faint, I heard a singing sound in my ears, and my chest was very tight, and I knew only that I must have fallen against the branches in the tree. It is a miracle I did not fall, for I do not know how long I was there, because when I opened my eyes next, the sun was low and on the banks of the stream the grasses were flat and shiny where they had lain. But they were gone, leaving only the wind sighing and the sweet, heady scent of clover.

10

The Inspector was very surprised to see Irina appear the next morning with a message from Freud: he wished the Inspector to visit him.

11

I would like, if you don't mind," Freud felt himself wince at his deference to this Inspector, "to speak with each of those individuals you refer to as 'suspects' myself, in order to ascertain exactly what role fantasy, if any, played in their perception of events. It is important to me to conclude this matter as soon as possible. I will cooperate in any way I can."

The Inspector looked at him keenly. He was willing to accept help from whatever quarter it was offered.

"You mean you are willing to help me interrogate them?" he asked mildly.

"Certainly not!" the doctor retorted. "I cannot reveal anything told to me by a patient. I cannot. I will not."

"Then," the Inspector said, "with all due respect for your ethics, whatever use would you be to me?"

"It would be of use to everyone, I should think," the doctor said, "for me to draw my own conclusions on the role fantasy is playing in these events. I have some experience in these matters. If, as I believe, the events are largely the result of fantasy, that would be of importance to you. It might give you a new direction in which to make your inquiries. You strike me as a person who is not unsympathetic to psychological understanding; you claim to have read *The Interpretation of Dreams.*"

The Inspector ignored the implications of the word "claimed." "You might conceal material relevant to me out of your concern for disclosing compromising personal matters," the Inspector said.

"You would have to trust my character," the doctor replied, pulling himself up to his full height. "I would never betray a patient, nor would I ever withhold information I felt relevant."

"But is it not precisely in character," the Inspector said, getting up and walking to the end of the room in what he knew was a suspenseful delay, "that the effort to withhold disclosure might first occur? Have you not suggested such an idea yourself?"

When he turned, he saw the doctor's eyes dark with anger. "I am a scientist," he said, "and I am pursuing the truth."

"The truth as it appears to you is all you can pursue," the Inspector replied. "Do not misunderstand me. I do not like you, but I think you an honorable and, in your way, astonishingly brave man. However, my friend Bertillon has isolated the problem with truth-seeking of any sort. Although I disagree with his politics, it is to Bertillon we owe the observation, 'One can see only what one observes. And one observes what is already in the mind.'"

"An acute observation. But not original with Bertillon," Freud remarked.

"Let us leave it. You are free to speak to whomever you wish. You are free to tell me whatever you consider relevant. I do not have high expectations of your pursuit, but I cannot forbid it, and it may prove fruitful. Tell me about the James man. Has he spoken to you of murder?"

The Inspector timed the question to take the doctor by surprise. He saw his pupils dilate, his face flush, all in an instant.

"I cannot discuss my conversations with any of my patients. If you are asking my opinion of the characterological aspects of Mr. James, I would have to tell you that in relation to an act of aggression such as murder, I consider it so extremely unlikely as to be unworthy of your contemplation."

"But you continue to see Mr. James, concerning the question of a murder, is that not so?" the Inspector said softly.

"A symbolic murder," Freud snapped. "One which haunts many people. That is all. I have offered," he said hesitantly, "my expertise, strictly in the hope that I can prove to you the fantasy aspects of this case. I am hoping that I shall come up with such persuasive material that you will be convinced of it and withdraw. I see it as my only hope of ending this unpleasant business."

"Who has Mr. James murdered, symbolically?" the Inspector asked. "Of course I can ask *him*. I cannot continue to abstain from a direct interrogation that may prove helpful to me. Unless you can persuade me it would be useless."

"You have me trapped of course," Freud said. "In order to protect my patient, Mr. James, I must now cooperate."

"I wouldn't say 'must,'" the Inspector said coolly. Freud paced nervously up and down the floor of the study. The Inspector sat back and lit his cigar. He was willing to give him as much time as it might take.

Freud wheeled about suddenly. "He has killed a cat, his cat. In London. He has a delicate nature. It has troubled him greatly."

"A cat," the Inspector said softly, wonderingly.

"He hit it with a rock. It was making a racket in the middle of the night. An unfortunate accident," Freud said, "That is all. It is true," he said, "he has experienced this as a murder." Freud was going to explain more, but hesitated.

"Hit it with a rock," the Inspector said, slowly. "In the middle of the night. Remarkable aim for an unatheletic man, wouldn't you say?" He eyed the doctor carefully.

"Unfortunate luck," the doctor said.

"And the woman, in Venice—Woolson, I believe was her name—" the Inspector said, "what of her?"

"A suicide," the doctor said, "jumped from the third story window. He was distraught about it."

"So distraught," the Inspector said savagely, "that he raced back to Venice and burned all of his letters to her before any investigators arrived on the scene. Did he tell you that as well?" From Freud's astonished face the Inspector knew he hadn't.

"What are you saying?" Freud's voice was a whisper.

"Only that certain aspects of Mr. James' behavior are very suspicious. But he is not the only suspect, of course. The problem with this case, if indeed it is that, is that there are so many suspects. But I have said enough for today. Goodbye, and thank you doctor. We will no doubt speak again." And with that the Inspector took his leave, and Freud sat down on the chair, feeling utterly lost.

12

This man I love," the Countess said, lying on the couch, "I want to have his child."

"I notice that you do not tell me his name," the doctor said.

"No," she said.

"Have you told him of this wish?"

"No."

There was a pause.

"You are married," he said firmly, "to someone else. May I remind you that he has an uncontrollable temper by your own account, is extremely jealous, and is an excellent marksman. The situation if you become pregnant would be dangerous to you, to say the least."

He sat back uneasily. He was gratified at his success in easing the trauma and would consider her pregnancy a therapeutic success. Yet, a pregnancy now would compromise her utterly. He let out a sigh. Fortunately soon the talk turned to her latest achievement.

"I broke with Philippe . . . I did it."

"When?" He was surprised. She had told him of this intention for months now, but this seemed precipitous. "I . . . I knew I was ready. I went on Saturday." He knew she was proud; he was uneasy at the speed of the action. Something in this troubled him.

Then before she left she turned to him, her eyes brimming.

"I am so relieved, I cannot thank you enough. Thank you," she said again, pressing his arm, and, he thought, before she could embrace him, turned quickly and was out the door.

Leaving the doctor's house the Countess remembered with a shiver her final meeting with Philippe.

''S O,'' Philippe said, "you have changed. You refuse to help me with the police, with whom," he said insinuatingly, "I understand you have influence."

She did not want to give way. "I will not help you any more, Philippe. I approve neither of your politics or, I must say, your person."

"Oh, now!" he said, whirling about her like a snake and twisting his body over the chair. "You approved of me enough to sleep with me. Have you forgotten that?"

"Unfortunately, no," she said, and stood up. "I'm leaving. I've said all there is to say," and she walked toward the door.

"Well, I haven't!" he screamed at her. "Bettina, I will go to your husband and you will be locked up for the rest of your days!"

She stopped, and felt the fear go through her. Then she gathered herself and turned to him. "If you do that I will denounce you to the authorities. It is you who set the bomb in the L'Aiglon cafe. Féneon has told me."

"You can prove nothing!" he hissed at her. "It is an empty threat. Change your mind, Bettina," she heard his voice, that voice she had heard so many times, insinuating, controlling, manipulative, "before it is too late."

"Goodbye Philippe," she said.

Trembling, her face pale, barely able to compose herself, she ducked out the door. But she had *left*. She was out of it. She began to believe it now. She was breaking free. Now she worried only what he would do to her, what he could do. Perhaps it was an idle threat. She was counting on Maurice to protect her. It was this faith, all along, she felt she had wanted to find in men, and instead had settled for control.

"You are a complex temperament, Bettina," she heard Maurice's voice now, soft against her face, weary, perplexed, and true. "I have told you I would not have chosen you, not one of such high feeling, but my heart has chosen you. And so . . ." he had laughed then and lay against her, playing helpless to his own passion.

But she knew better. She knew he loved her *because* he knew her, not despite the complexity, and somewhere she trusted that he would, and could, forgive her all. She knew one thing: she must never lose him, as it was Maurice who had inspired her flourishing self-regard. She must not and she would not lose this. She heard suddenly a voice inside her head that she had not heard since she was a child. "Oh I *am* someone. I am. I *am* someone." It seemed to take up all her air as it moved into the large space within her, from which everything, even hope, had been for so long withdrawn.

13

One could not refuse a command from the emperor, the Inspector knew. But this latest summons did not bode well. Briefly he had time to review his suspect list once more before his appointment. How could he tell the emperor that although he had suspects, he did not have *the* suspect he needed. He reviewed the list:

Of the so-called suspects, he was struck by the fact that almost all were hiding something.

1. Edith Wharton was hiding her affair with Morton Fullerton and something more. Her motive for discrediting Freud was antipathy.
2. Morton Fullerton was hiding a blackmail threat from his former mistress which James had told Freud about.
3. Freud was hiding Fliess' mistake on Emma Eckstein's nose and possibly something more.
4. Eckstein was hiding the shame she felt at her father's fury.
5. Eckstein's father was hiding his guilt at what he had put his daughter through and a wish to discredit Freud.
6. Henry James was hiding guilt over the woman in Venice, Constance Fenimore Woolson, and over the cat.
7. Cecily was hiding her love for Henry James.
8. Cecily's sister was hiding real information.
9. Cecily's mother was hiding all reality. Cecily's father was hiding, he thought, from any unpleasant phenomena.
10. The Countess was hiding a trauma in her childhood of which she was ashamed.
11. Leopold was hiding his jealousy of Freud, the Inspector, and any man who spoke to the Countess.
12. Minna was hiding her passion for the doctor, her jealousy of Martha, and her secret herbal mixture to "forget." She wanted to discredit Martha.
13. Martha was hiding murderous wishes against her sister. She wanted to discredit Minna.
14. Jung was hiding his seduction of his patient Sabina and his wish to discredit Freud, who was about to unseat him as his protégé.
15. Sabina was hiding nothing.
16. Fliess was hiding his anger at Freud. He felt Freud betrayed him by telling a patient Fliess' ideas, which the patient then published as his own.
17. Ida Bauer, the young woman patient called Dora, was in a vengeful fury at Freud, although it was not hidden.

18. A mad anti-Semite might have staged it just to start rumors.
19. The dismembering murderer may have planted the body there, but why?

He went down the list. The one person who could help him was Cecily's sister. It would not be a difficult interrogation. He could tell she felt terribly guilty about something she'd seen, and was actually eager to tell him more, but something was holding her back. She was intrigued, he could see, by his passion for the Countess. He had hidden that from everyone but her. She had one unfortunate habit: she followed him when he was with the Countess, so he had taken to checking rather carefully before they set off. He was fully confident he knew how to avoid her.[1]

14

His imperial Highness, who was the Apostolic King of Hungary, the King of Bohemia, of Dalmatia, of Croatia, of Slavonia, of Galicia, and of Illyria, the Grand Prince of Transylvania, the Archduke of Austria, the King of Jerusalem, the Duke of Auschwitz, the Marquis of Istria, and the Prince Count of the Tyrol, not to mention Emperor of Austria, welcomed the Inspector to his palace. But he wasted no time with formalities.

"I want you to consider the Freud case closed at once," the emperor said. "Parliament is in an uproar. Lueger is consolidating his power with the anti-Semites and will sweep the elections if this issue is not resolved before then. The rumors of this unreported murder in the Jewish doctor's house are shaking the city. The populace believes this is a ritual murder. As there is no proof, you have no body, you have no evidence, you have nothing, I want it declared officially that it never occurred."

"Your Imperial Highness, I beg your pardon," the Inspector said, "I

---

[1] This confidence was perhaps misplaced.

have found a rug with stains on it. Bloodstains. I only need a little more time."

"We do not have time," the emperor said. The first week in May will be the Blumen Corso, an annual event. It is normally only a festive celebration of flowers. But I do not like Lueger; I do not like the suggestion that Lueger is the next 'king' of Vienna, and so I am attaching great importance to this particular Blumen Corso. It will be quite a spectacular occasion. This issue must be resolved by then."

"It is close," the Inspector said, "but I must have a few more months."

The emperor looked at him. "You are Jewish are you not?"

The Inspector nodded.

"I am trying to protect my Jews. Are you one of those Jews who is not interested in protecting his own?" The candid question upset him.

"Certainly not. But I cannot let a murderer walk free."

"Sometimes there are more important questions than a single madman," the emperor said sadly.

"It may be more than a single man," the Inspector said.

"What leads you to believe that?" the emperor demanded. "Do you mean there is a group responsible, a political group? Do you think this murder, if there was one, is connected to the other murders?"

"I think," the Inspector said, loathing the hesitation in his own voice, "that there is something here that is larger than the work of one man. As to whether they are linked, the fact that some of the women have been dismembered and some not, would suggest that there was more than one murderer at work. On the other hand, I am confident that they are somehow linked." He was embarrassed that his explanation seemed so groping.

"My informants tell me," the emperor said, "that you yourself have become a target."

"Who told you this?" He was angry.

"Lieutenant Stekal reported that on several occasions when out with you he was aware of being followed. When not accompanied by you, it did not occur. What, Inspector, if the murderer succeeds in assassinating you? Where will that leave me?"

The Inspector looked at him. "If he succeeds it leaves you with the public statement that there was never a murder in the doctor's house, and that I have met with an accident."

The emperor eyed him carefully. "So," he said, "it would be in my interests at the moment, you see, if in fact this occurred."

"I realize that," the Inspector said. "But you have shown more than once that your character is above politics."

"Integrity rules Vienna, Inspector," the emperor said, "until history proves otherwise."

"History is a mad dog," the Inspector said, looking grim.

"A mad dog froths so you can see him coming," the emperor said, "but not a mad man. In either case," the emperor said, "do not get bitten. You have five weeks. Good day."

15

In addition to the Freud case, the case of Gertrude Van de Vere was still unsolved. The rhymes kept showing up in the newspapers with annoying regularity. As he opened the morning *Neue Freie Presse* the Inspector saw a news item, "Where oh where is Gertrude Van de Vere?" The rhymes were haunting. The latest had been put on his desk by Voll:

> Where, oh where is Gertrude Van de Vere?
> Her foot is in the counting house
> Counting all the money
> Her head is in the parlor
> Eating bread and honey.

"What could this mean?" Voll asked.

"I don't know," the Inspector said and retired to his office. He had told the emperor that he thought that possibly the Freud murder and the Van de Vere murder were connected, that the murders of various women in the city that were still unsolved were also connected, but he could not really elaborate how.

At this moment of his grimmest confusion, there came a knock on the office door and he was delighted to see that the courier had arrived from his chemist with a report. He knew he had angered Voll by using his own laboratory experts, but he was sick of coddling the emotions of a bureaucrat. Voll's chemist's reports were frequently false because of contamination of materials.

Eagerly he opened the report from Slotkin on the blood from the rug and as he read, the fury rose in him. This Freud was a liar!

16

"Why," the Inspector roared, "why in heaven's name would you go to such lengths to disguise that this blood was from Emma Eckstein's nose when that very evidence would have relieved you immediately of responsibility for there having been a murder in the house? Now that you have concealed it you have forced me to continue this inquiry even further. It is maddening because it makes no sense except for one reason and one reason only, which is your passionate friendship for Dr. Fliess, which I gather is a *vigorous* attachment and I have determined, Dr. Freud, that yours is a most tenacious and jealous nature."

The Inspector felt the power of his insight like a freight train roaring through him and through Freud, a force that shook them by its power and its determination.

"You are determined to protect him, although it takes you to a risky and unprecedented length. Your effort to deny the responsibility of Dr. Fliess in this matter shows that you are also clever in deceit, sir. As deeply as I know you might protest that aspect of your nature, it is nonetheless an aspect and I am left to deal with *that* surprise." He had turned his back during this speech and was surprised now to see Freud standing behind him, his face toward the window, his head bowed. The posture was one of total defeat, which he had not expected.

"I was right about Emma Eckstein," he said wearily to the Inspector, "I cured her. I was right. She would not accept it. And Dr. Fliess *was* in error. You are quite correct. I was appalled at this discovery. I denied it to myself, for some time, that there had been a surgical error. I, who awaken demons," he said to the Inspector, "must be prepared to fight them. Should we be surprised if I should suffer damage myself, in this process?"

"I suppose," the Inspector said, "you are at a distinct disadvantage in that. The exorcist at least had God on his side."

"His advantage, if he had it," Freud quipped, "was only in believing that was the case. Surely a man of your skepticism, Inspector, would not presume to argue otherwise?

"Except this, I have noticed," Freud continued walking to the window, and shifting the focus, "I have noticed the book in your waistcoat pocket. It is always the same, these last few days. It is the same size as the little red book which you so carefully hid from me the first time you visited, but which prompted me to observe precisely which book it was, Pascal's *Pensées*. Deceit is not solely my province. Skepticism cannot survive the prose style," he said, his eyes twinkling now unexpectedly, "of one so gifted as M. Pascal. He can persuade one that skepticism is the very demon himself."

"Do you think this is a contest about prose then, and not belief?" the Inspector asked quizzically. "For if that is the issue he can be matched by the German master, Friedrich Nietzsche." Freud looked quickly at the floor. "I have not read him," he said and just as quickly, "it is necessary now that I prepare myself for my next appointment. If you will excuse me."[1]

17

Minna startled the Inspector when she walked into the station house carrying a large stuffed pillowslip.

She stood in front of his desk and said, "I emptied the wastebaskets the morning after the murder. I kept them, Dr. Freud said I should

---

[1] It may be that Freud, who denied ever having read Nietzsche but who was charged with deriving certain concepts from him, felt awkward here.

give it to you . . . although he thinks it's unlikely that the murderer, if there was one, left one of those rhymes in the house."

"Why did you hide this evidence?" His annoyance was apparent.

"I thought there might be something important from the doctor's. He had thrown away important notes on occasion."

He looked at her. He couldn't tell if she was lying.

"So you have been through these scraps yourself, then?"

She avoided his gaze. "There is nothing of importance," she said.

"If you have tampered with evidence, it will not go well for you," he said, his voice harsh.

"This is everything as I found it," she said, and then lifted the sack from the floor and dumped the shredded paper all over his desk.

"Good luck," she said, not smiling, and proceeded out the door.

18

The Freuds were attending the opera. They were to see a performance of a new opera by Strauss, *Der Rosenkavalier*. Freud looked over at Martha and Minna and felt very proud that they looked so pleased and pretty. He could not help scanning the Staatsoper for two of his patients. He was sure the Countess would be there. She loved opera, and he was hoping he might glimpse her new lover. Or possibly Leopold. Of course she had married a man as tyrannical as the molester from whom she wished to escape.

A group of six entered now and made their way down the aisle. The doctor thought he had never seen so many beautiful women. It was a sparkling night in Vienna. His interest in music was minimal, but he did not apologize for it. His ears were listening for other things, he told himself. He much preferred theater. He had hoped to go to a reading by young Hofmannsthal. But a friend had given them the seats and he had wanted to please Minna and Martha. He had been ignoring them both, of late.

As the lights went down, he saw the Countess enter her box. She was with the Americans, and Mr. James and Mrs. Wharton as well. He could not see if there was anyone in the back of the box. The Countess positively glowed. Freud was feeling almost happy, a rare experience. Just as the orchestra began to play he remembered her last words to him that afternoon.

''THERE is an old Russian folk saying," she said, "and it reminds me of how I feel."

"And how is that?" he said.

"I feel that perhaps I have the dragon by the tail, at last," she said, "and that makes me feel victorious. But I am cautious."

"It is wise to be cautious," he said. "And what is the saying?"

"It is not about a dragon, but about a bear:

'I have caught a bear,' the first man says.

'Well, good, bring him with you,' the second man from the other town says.

'He won't come,' says the first man.

'Well then, come without him!' says the second man.

'He won't let me go,' says the first man."

He smiled now thinking of the story. The bear *had* let her go, and he felt heady with excitement at the new possibilities he sensed for her. And for himself.

19

Henry wished that Edith wouldn't push him so. Of course he wanted this unfortunate murder solved. He had made some interesting acquaintances and he found it quite a wonderful city for gossip, but the winter had been awful and now that it was spring he was as eager as she to get to Florence.

He looked at the sea of scrap paper covering the table.

When he brought the scraps of paper, the Inspector had taken him aside and talked with him a very long time. Henry had rather liked him, after all. And then he'd asked to speak with Edith as well. And then he'd left.

The Inspector had left the two of them with this mass of paper particles spread out over the entire mahogany dining table. It bordered on the outrageous. Some of the pieces were torn so small there weren't even any sentences, just letters.

"I'd greatly appreciate it," the Inspector had said, "if you would see what you could do. Because you're writers, I thought you could piece some of it together." It struck him as ridiculous. There was no point to it, and besides he never was very good at puzzles.

Edith now was pouncing on a rather large piece of paper. "Look," she said, spearing it as it lay in the middle of the large dining table, "listen to this, 'You must put your hand to the paste.' Now that might be something," she said, looking up.

Henry thought he was going to faint. Those were *his* words, uttered from that very couch, which the doctor had not only written down but then thrown out!

"Unless the paste has arsenic in it," he said drily, "and you eat it, I don't quite see any relevance to this unfortunate murder." Edith, miffed, put it back in the pile and began studiously sifting for another.

"I really don't know why," Henry said slowly, "we have the idea that the murderer, if there was one, would have left anything written."

"Because one of them leaves *notes,* the one that cuts people up. And besides, there was an envelope, blue," Edith said, "found on the floor, and no one in the house has blue writing paper."

"Just because there was an envelope doesn't mean there was anything in it," Henry mumbled. He was irritated by this hopeless task.

"Keep looking," she said. "We've got to get out of here." He sighed. He knew, alas, it was true. He speared another small fragment and looked at what was spread before him. Now he had an *a,* and a *p,* and an *r,* and an *al.* He had a *pear,* a *pearl, appear, reap* and *pea.* Instinctively he went for *pearl.* This was a murder after all.

Henry was pressing now for Edith's report of her visit with the Inspector. At first she hadn't wanted to tell him.

"Well, it was the oddest thing, really," she finally said. She seemed to get flustered again as she thought about it. "He seemed very interested in my objections to Dr. Freud, although they seem extremely obvious to me, or any decent intelligent person. He found it curious for some reason that I should object to these appalling theories of his." She adjusted her dress and sat back in her seat. 'They just don't make any sense, Inspector,' I told him. And then, Henry, he told me something I didn't know, which is Dr. Freud has recently changed all of his theories."

"How?" Henry asked. "Whatever do you mean?"

"Well, the Inspector told me that he originally thought the business about the children, you know, with their parents—"

"Er, yes," Henry said. He hesitated and didn't say, "You mean that they were seduced?"

"Well, apparently he's come to his senses over *that* and his new theory, which, I could have told him myself and saved him years of wasted thinking, is that these women made it all up."

"No!" Henry said.

"Yes, just spinning tales of, I must say, the most distasteful kind."

"Hmmm, curious," Henry said.

"But, and this is the odd part," she went on, holding her head to one side in the way that she did when she thought of puzzling things, "the Inspector asked me—he leaned almost into my face and he was surprised, Henry, there was no question about it—he said, 'Do I understand that you find this theory *easier* to believe than the original?' And I said yes, of course, didn't *he?* And Henry, he just stared at me and shook his head and said 'no.'"

20

He had left the scraps of paper with Wharton and James but wasn't really hopeful that they'd come up with anything. The Inspector was feeling depressed. Never had he felt so defeated. He felt he was impeded in his search by some massive inability to see what was before his eyes. He kept walking. He walked until it was late.

Sadly, wearily, he climbed the steps to the boarding house. Nothing would console him for what he knew was a horrible failure.

21

It was late the next afternoon, when the Inspector returned to the station, that he was informed that a gentleman from Paris who refused to give his name was waiting for him.

As he approached his office he heard the sharp, agitated snap of heels against the floor, and saw the back of a well-dressed man pacing up and down outside his office. When the man turned to face him, an eerie recognition swept over him. Where had he seen this face before? The man, without giving his name, told the Inspector calmly that he had an important matter to discuss. It came to the Inspector, as he said this, that he recognized the man he had seen emerging from the bushes that morning in the Bois de Boulogne, after his tryst with some woman. He remembered being struck by the couple because their sensual fatigue was in such shocking contrast to his despair over Elise. He detested the man's manner at once.

"I suppose you must know why I am here," the man said.

"I am waiting for you to tell me."

"Come, come Inspector," Philippe said with a sneer, "you can't be as stupid as all that. I have come," he said, leaning back in his chair in a most proprietary way, "because of our mutual interest in a certain . . . lady friend."

The Inspector leaned forward. The tension was immediate.

"I am, most unfortunately, about to be arrested in Paris for," he waved his hand nonchalantly, "some anarchist bombings." He leaned forward toward the Inspector. "I do not wish to be arrested."

The Inspector said nothing. Already his pulse was racing. "You are Philippe Malville," he finally said quietly.

The man's eyebrows raised. "Very good, Inspector. But I am *not* going to be arrested, Inspector, because you are going to prevent it for the reason that our lady friend is in imminent danger from her husband should certain information," he closed his hands together, fingertips touching, in a gesture the Inspector would not forget, "become available. Letters, photographs, clothing." When he reached into a small valise he carried, the Inspector's vision blurred.

22

Sigmund Freud awoke in the middle of the night. "What is it?" Martha asked, startled awake by his cry. "Nothing," he said to her, finally. "Nothing." But it was not nothing. She could see that. It had awakened him and there was perspiration falling from his forehead into his eyes.

He tried to return to sleep. Two dreams. First about James, and then about the Countess. James had given him a fright. The blood, as far as he could tell, was all from some book he was reading! Such a suggestible mind. Astonishing! Why the man was as involved in the book as if it had happened to him. Why this particular imagery was so powerful he did not yet know. It was curious to him because by James' own admission, it was not the literary quality of the work that affected him, but something about the image of the bleeding woman. Perhaps it had religious overtones. Christlike possibly. James' father had been religious, although hardly what one would call a typical Christian.

It was not long before Freud woke again. This time he thought about the Countess. She said she would be telling her lover of her past. Tonight, this night. Sigmund Freud worried for her. He had tried to dissuade her. There were not many men who could comprehend this. Indeed, if Martha had told *him,* or Minna, *this* . . . He sighed and lay back closing his eyes, pretending to sleep. Some things had to be left to fate. Nonetheless he knew that in the fine twists fate could produce if this man really loved her, if he was as passionate as she had led him to believe, his very passion might be the thing that would make it impossible for him to forgive her.

He thought momentarily of his early wooing of Martha and the recollection stung him. If at that time he had discovered such a thing he would never have forgiven her. Never. Thinking on this he felt a strange mixture of shame that he should be so incapable of forgiveness and something more. An odd regret. A strange misgiving that he should perhaps have intervened, and cautioned the Countess to silence. He felt Martha's hand steal now across his back, seeking to comfort him. "Sigi," she said, but he pretended to sleep.

23

The Inspector sent word he would meet the Countess after the theater at midnight. She had been detained, caught in a conversation with a member of Parliament who suggested he join her. It took her some time to elude him gracefully.

She knew her lateness would annoy Maurice, and in her eagerness to tell him the story of her past, for tonight was the night for her full confession, she did not notice his mood when she entered the room. She began talking quickly as she took off her coat and hat, in a fit of nerves and anticipation.

"Oh the theater was wonderful, but I did not need to meet you to tell you that. Maurice, there is something I must tell you, and I must tell you now all at once and you must listen, so please . . ." She was relieved to see he had turned his back to her and seemed to be ready to listen, as he stood, staring out the window.

He had turned his back because he could not bear looking at her. A terrible ringing had started in his head. When he half turned, sensing her words, she appeared in a blur to him, her words coming from some middle distance. She was talking and talking. Speaking words, that confirmed the worst. *Proclaiming* it. *Telling* him. The outrage of it widened the gulf around him. She seemed far away. He lit a cigar as her words fell on him from the distance. Strange how tinny and small her voice sounded. He was making a huge effort, but it was difficult for him to hear her. After the terrible news of the afternoon, it had taken everything in him, but he had determined he would listen. But something had seized him as she spoke, a new force that surprised him, amazed him. It was hatred. He turned to her now, his face white and his eyes ablaze. She looked ugly to him, ugly and contorted, he hated her crying into her handkerchief in that miserable way, like some pathetic wretch.

"Oh, god, you hate this, I see it in your eyes." Her face was shocked, and her voice started to break. "You hate me," she said in disbelief.

Indeed, he did. He felt something descend in him like the knife blade of a guillotine, descending down his center choking off his air.

"I don't . . ." he paused, "hate you." It was his first lie. Rage was coursing through him, and then in some ironic twist, turned back and rose up behind his eyes like a fire, causing him to fight back tears of rage, betrayal. He could feel something caving in on him, and he went and sat on the bed, his back to her. He did not know when she stopped speaking.

Silence hung in the air, as if some magnificent, crystal chandelier had fallen from a great height, splintering in their midst. The Countess, he could hear in the distance, was sobbing, a kind of wracking grasp for control as she told him what she must.

Finally, he said in a voice that seemed to him like that of a total stranger, greeting him in sentences that had been translated from another tongue. "So, there were several of them, then."

"Yes."

"And you went," this was hard for him to say, "willingly."

He suddenly saw her move and felt her fingers tighten about his arm. "Maurice, look at me!" He hated it, the begging sound in her voice, and he could not bring himself to look at her. He stood staring straight ahead. She went around to the front of him and kneeled on the floor, her voice imploring him, her face distorted, desperate.

"I had to, do you understand? I had to, I could not stop myself, I could not. It has nothing to do with you and me, *nothing* . . ."

He had been aware of a certain tension in her coiled, ready to spring, and now he felt her give way, collapse on the floor. He loathed her even more for this.

"Get up," he said, his voice no longer veiling his contempt. "Get up!" He reached forward and caught her hand and snapped her to her feet, hard, and then holding that delicate hand in his, flipped her so forcefully she fell backwards, careening against the wall. His breath seemed to be coming fast, like a man who is running for his life. He heard her voice from very far off.

"Don't!" he heard her yelling. "Don't—" and then he felt something hard across his cheek and he woke up to see her anew, regaining something, and blazing. "Don't you dare touch me that way!" she screamed. "If you don't understand this," she hissed at him, now like some wild thing, "then you do not love *me,* you only love your idea of me, and I don't want it. I DON'T WANT IT," she screamed at him, and behind him he heard something crash against the wall.

He walked quickly into the other room for his coat. His heart, he thought, was going to fail him. The pounding in his ears so loud as he put on his coat, the engorgement in his throat so thick he could barely swallow, barely breathe. He turned to go.

"I suppose," he said, pausing, "you will say the same thing about me, to the next one."

Then she lunged at him; she was faster than he expected and had picked up, he knew not what, but something hard, and was heaving it against his chest, the side of his face, until he grabbed her hands as he felt the blood start down his eye.

"Oh God," she said, dropping the bronze trophy to the floor. "Oh God," she stepped back, "Maurice."

He saw her face as he held his hand over his eyes to catch the blood. "I saw, I saw you . . . in the park," he moaned.

Her eyes were wild now as she cried out, her voice curiously dead, "Maurice, I felt nothing, can you understand? Nothing. It is like being ice, sheer ice. The only thing," the dead voice went on, changing, breaking into a sob now, "I ever felt was the slapping. The slapping, the kicking, that was the only way I knew I was alive."

"I SAW YOU!" he cried out, bleeding and raw, "I SAW YOU WITH HIM."

"Who?" she said her voice a whisper, "who?"

"Philippe!" he yelled. "He gave me this," and he threw the magenta scarf onto the floor covered with the blood. "He said he would go to Leopold."

Her shocked face turned paler still. Her voice was a whisper. "How could he know of you?"

"I bought you your safety with Leopold," he said, voice trembling, the veins in his head throbbing, "at an impossible price for myself!" His voice cracked as he shouted it.

Stunned she stepped back, and grabbed for the servant's bell crying out, "I, I felt nothing, I felt nothing . . ."

The servant entered, knocking, surprised at the scene: the Inspector, standing there, hands at his sides, like a man defeated in a match; arms lying limp as blood streamed into his eyes, and the Countess, arms flailing, bloodstained and wild, yelling, "Ice, please get ice," and then laughing hysterically, "Ice, yes, Ice! Ice! Ice!" Then the servant ran to her, and casting horrible looks at the Inspector pulled her away and rang the bell again furiously until more servants descended and led the Inspector away as the Countess, laughing hysterically and crying, was led away by her maid, in what was later described as paroxysms of hysterical despair.

24

The Inspector woke from the dream in a fit. He had his arms around Bettina's neck and he was choking her. Her eyes bulged, her lips were blue, and he felt an enormous satisfaction as his strong hands grasped her thin throat and her pulse died. She was limp and still in his hands when suddenly he woke up. He was trembling and it took him some minutes to realize he was safe, or at least, in his own bed. It took him some time to calm himself. He worried he might see her on the street, and if so, he must turn the corner at once, lest, he was certain, he rush to annihilate her. *One death for her,* he moaned and mourned in the depths of his being, fathoms down below his reason, *was insufficient.* He wanted her to die daily, victim of some exquisite torture. And he wanted to watch, coldly, as she cried out for mercy.

When he recovered from these episodes, he was quite morally shaken. He had assumed, he realized quite wrongly, that he was a rather different caliber of man. A man of thought, of reason, of appetite to be sure, but not this wild circling beast, this raging pledge to destruction. He no longer assayed himself in quite his former way. His eyes dodged his image in the glass, as if by looking at himself in the mirror, his guilt at what he knew was not revealed there would be more than he could bear. This thought depressed him utterly and the landlady clucked to him often enough he was looking poorly lately and she would recommend a tonic. He didn't want a tonic. He had lost his pride, his dignity and had to do the best he could with the thin scab of commitment that was his work. He didn't care anymore who was murdering these women. He wished whoever it was would murder one more.

25

I had not seen the Countess for several days, and Mother told me she was ill, perhaps with a bad cold. I worried about this because it seemed to me the Countess never had colds or anything like that, but only those terrible nervous depressions that Timothy told me about. Cecily and I had seen her very ill that one day and I had never forgotten it. I had heard Mother and Father say something about "wiring Leopold," who was hunting boar somewhere, and I thought it might be quite serious again.

So I was very pleased and relieved to see her at breakfast the next morning, although after a few minutes I wasn't. I had walked into the room while Berta was saying she must eat and the Countess was shaking her head. I spoke to her several times before she heard me, and when she looked in my direction I felt frightened. Her eyes had always been rather gold, and bright, but now they looked totally different. They were more grey than gold and there was an expression there that I had never seen before, a kind of stillness that was alarming. Her hair was disheveled and her chin kept falling to her chest as if she could not raise it.

"Are you still ill?" I asked her, and she simply shook her head, pushed the tea and plates away, and attempted to get up out of the chair. It took her several minutes. She leaned on the table and moved like a person who is very weak, which I saw that she was. She seemed to take a long time to climb the stairs.

Aunt Ida came in shortly afterwards, and when I expressed my concern I was disappointed to see she was totally unsympathetic. "I have had enough," Aunt Ida said angrily. "Another intelligent woman

356 • CAROL DE CHELLIS HILL

sacrificed on the altar of romantic love. It is stupid." Then she looked at me. "And I know you know all about it—and why shouldn't you?—so I am not protecting you or anybody else anymore. She is a married woman. What did she expect?"

"You mean," I said, "the Inspector . . ." But I could say no more.

"Has left her," Aunt Ida said. "I don't know what happened, but she's devastated. I must say I thought she had more character than this; she's acting like a schoolgirl," and Aunt Ida then buttered her toast with a knife so savagely I was startled.

"But why?" I said finally. "Why would he love her and then not love her?"

"Because these things happen, that's why," Aunt Ida said, and I thought maybe Aunt Ida then was feeling what had happened between her and Mr. Biddington Jones, who had gone off to darkest Africa and was supposed to take Aunt Ida with him but didn't.

The subject wasn't discussed again, but a terrible gloom had settled over the entire household. There were whispers in the halls, which would stop when I came around a corner, and one night, there was a great deal of excitement in the house at a late hour and Timothy told me, although he wasn't supposed to, that a doctor had been called in on emergency. It seemed to him that she was half out of her mind.

26

The Inspector was perversely pleased to learn that Freud had come up with nothing.

"It is a testament to your powers of persuasion, Inspector," the doctor said, "that I am reluctantly agreeing that you can interview my patients, provided, of course, they should choose this. I will advise them myself of the circumstances. I have agreed to this, of course," the doctor said, brushing down the lapel of his jacket, "with one exception: you cannot interview the Countess Bettina von Gerzl."

For a moment, it struck the Inspector as a surprise. He had forgotten for the moment that she was Freud's patient. He had forgotten her entirely, in the pressure of the last few days. But his recall was instant; quick as a snakebite, he felt the bitter taste, like venom in his throat. Then quite without his asking, Freud suddenly commented, "She is in a serious crisis." He paused. "Someone she loved a great deal has betrayed her."

The Inspector's head snapped on his neck as if he'd been shot. "Someone has betrayed *her?*" he said, his voice quavering. Sigmund Freud looked up. Something in the Inspector's voice had struck him.

"Yes," he said calmly. "It is common enough. A case where a man's need to possess a woman exclusively was greater than his ability to love her, as she is."

"You speak of gods," the Inspector said. "Not of men." Freud's eyes narrowed. The bitterness in the Inspector's tone surprised him.

"Regardless," Freud said, "she is a woman who has suffered much. I took the case originally from an associate who rescued her twice from attempting to kill herself with chloral. I have spent much effort in creating for her the opportunity to find life worth living again. This man has all but destroyed it. I am confident she can find the strength to survive this blow, but only if she is treated in the most considerate and delicate of manners. These are serious matters and all I can offer you is the observation that hers is a very delicate nature. I assume you are not so foolhardy as to be responsible for one death while attempting to resolve another one. Do not see her. It can wait."

"I do not see why I should indulge a hysterical woman," the Inspector said, his voice dripping with contempt, "no matter how upset. I am certain," he said, "she will find another lover quite as good as the last. She is a woman of wealth and beauty. I am afraid," he said, "I am totally without sympathy."

Freud was walking about the study in an uncharacteristic posture, the Inspector noted. His shoulders were slumped forward and his hands joined behind his back. He seemed to be struggling with something he was about to say. "I," he started twice and then turned away swiftly. Finally he said, "I think, Inspector," his tone was clipped and professional, "that the contempt and bitterness in your tone suggest quite otherwise."

The Inspector felt a shiver run through him. "I fail to understand your meaning," he said. He noted the sound of his own voice, threatened, almost quivering, yet cold.

"Your tone suggests you are in more sympathy with her condition than you can admit. We often detest in others what we can least tolerate in ourselves. Your lack of sympathy with feelings of betrayal suggest to me that you have obviously suffered these yourself. Your contempt, I suggest to you, is most probably your own. I leave you to ponder this and insist as a medical recommendation, that you pursue no further inquiries with my patient. I leave the outcome to your conscience, and I think," he said, slowly looking directly into the Inspector's eyes, "your character. Good afternoon." Freud turned and left the Inspector standing in the consulting room by himself.

The Inspector knew that Freud would never have left him alone in the consulting room if he had not been greatly agitated. To his surprise he found himself unmoved by the doctor's remarks. He felt a kind of glacial calm, and proceeded to walk around the doctor's study examining the objects upon the desk, one at a time, making notes that he had made before, about the position of objects on the desk once again. He had turned then to leave when a sudden terrible fatigue descended on him as if he had been drugged. Yet he had had no coffee nor tea, nor had the doctor offered him anything. But it was heavy and sodden, the feeling, and it seemed to him that it took hours, rather than minutes, to find the strength to put one foot in front of the other, to navigate the door and hall and to find himself, after this great effort, standing in the street.

He began to walk. As he walked, gathering speed, he could not keep the doctor's words from his mind. "She attempted several times to kill herself with chloral . . . it is a failure of the man's character . . ." and quite suddenly the sweep of the streets, the tumult of the carriages, the shouting and bustling crowds about him seemed to take up residence *within* him. He felt jostled, crowded, pursued. In pain he began to run, words pounding inside his temples. His outrage at that doctor seemed to gather in him with a new force, joining with his fear, his memories, his hatred, his wound, his utter savage hurt; what she had done to him—the doctor had taken that and suggested he had betrayed *her,* betrayed *her* out of his love for her, his trust of her.

This doctor was a madman, mad and cruel, a messenger from hell, killing him once again with words, thoughts, and leaving him now to struggle with a tide of feeling that was engulfing him, swimming up through his arms, his pounding legs, his eyes, until, he did not know from where, a sound issued through his throat, and he hurled himself at a great pace along the streets, blind now with feeling, running, running, the wind fast in his face, his heart pounding, his throat hurting he ran as if the very furies of hell were at his heels, pulling at him, tearing the flesh from his face until quite suddenly he stopped, it all stopped and he pitched, with relief, into blackness.

Sigmund Freud stared into the night. He had been indiscreet. So unlike him, to have revealed so much about a patient. He consoled himself at first by thinking that it must have sprung from his impulse to protect her. But he didn't believe it for long. Slowly, the realization of who the Inspector was came to him.

27

It was the opening night of Mr. James' theater piece, and Cecily was being escorted by Mr. James himself! Although, of course, they were all going together, she knew that he was going as "her escort," and she had been in a dither all afternoon about exactly what she should wear. The Countess was too ill to attend, but everyone seemed convinced that she was recovering.

Aunt Ida was watching Cecily with a new eye. She had thought for years Cecily was nothing but a pouf of a girl, interested only in clothes and parties, yet she had seen in the pained expression in her face and eyes that Cecily indeed seriously wanted to go to medical school and knew how impossible, given her parents, this was. So she had, in defiance, become extremely "feminine," at least that was Ida's interpretation, and there was some struggle in her now in her love for the Russian officer, who, thankfully, had returned to Moscow, and her infatuation with Mr. James and his heroines.

Ida suspected that Cecily was in a terrible rebellion against herself, the worst sort of rebellion to be in. Her consuming desire to be one of Mr. James' heroines had too much fantasy in it to suit Ida, but she was so drawn to the struggle in Cecily that she found herself taking very seriously Cecily's effort to wear "exactly the right thing" that evening. She had gone along shopping because Cecily would never be satisfied with her mother's opinion. Ida thought she should simply try to reassure the increasingly tortured girl that whatever she liked would be perfectly appropriate.

28

As Edith Wharton got dressed that evening for the theater she was hoping for Henry's sake it would not prove to be too much of a disaster. Henry, in her opinion, had no feel for *drama*. His world was an interior one, where the drama involved an odd arrest of confrontation, a subtlety she thought totally unsuited to the requirements of the stage.

Nonetheless she was pleased to be going to the theater with Fullerton, and she had rather enjoyed her last two conversations with that Inspector, whom she expected to see there. They both shared an interest in Nietzsche, a writer whom she found so disturbing she could read him only a few pages at a time. She hoped to speak to the Inspector further this evening, although his obvious infatuation with the Countess might make this impossible. This was no deprivation; she was so easily pleased in Fullerton's presence that she knew regardless of what transpired that evening, she would be happy.

29

Henry was relieved to see Edith and Fullerton waiting for him at the door to the theater.

"You're nearly late," Edith admonished him, and he admitted it was deliberate on his part. He had made up his mind to arrive late and leave early. Cecily and her sister looked particularly lovely, and he was glad he had complimented them lavishly on their dresses. The lights went down as they were ushered to their seats.

Henry sat through the play with no idea of whether it was great or terrible. He so dreaded that he would hear booing that he at first did not recognize the polite, restrained applause. The applause brought to him once again the utter humiliation of his earlier play, *Guy Domville*.[1] How he had found the courage to try again he did not know. And then, he realized they were cheering the star, Frl. Hohenfels. At first he found himself swept up in it; he was almost giddy. And then, in the bitterly sweet excitement of the applause for Frl. Hohenfels, the actress, he found his feelings oddly compounded. For quite suddenly he *envied* her, the star. It *smote* him that he had never been adored, never been, well, *loved,* like this. He felt a great sadness well up in him as Frl. Hohenfels took her bows. Tears gathered in his eyes and his lips trembled as he fought, with years of practice, to constrain this devastation racking his body. But it was true—Frl. Hohenfels' performance made him aware of his own lost hope for the theater— to be encompassed by hundreds of clapping hands, to be embraced by bravos, cheers, and hosannas. He loved his books; each character a discovery, a precious found essence, but it was such an unreal life. It was *such* solitude. Suddenly tears spilled uncontrollably from his eyes.

Cecily, seeing Mr. James was crying, reached over in a burst of sympathy, "Oh, Mr. James, how very wonderful to see a gentleman so unafraid of his emotions. How generous, how very generous." Forgetting herself, she grasped his hand, "You are so *moved* by this reception that you have tears of joy for *her*. . . . Look, Mr. James!" she said. He looked at her and he saw her eyes lit, he thought either with a fever, for she had been flushed and bright all day, or else love. It was just possible, he thought, that Cecily was madly, passionately, consumingly head-over-heels in love with none other than his own portly person.

James, feeling Cecily's hand on his, withdrew it as if pulling it from a fire. His cheeks burned with shame that he should be so startled by a young woman's girlish enthusiasm.

"Oh," Cecily said, stammering, "I just, . . . forgive me." Although she

---

[1] This was a disaster for James. When he walked out on the stage in London amid cries of Author! Author! he was roundly booed.

had withdrawn her hand, he was relieved to see she was fundamentally undaunted. "It is so wonderful to have a spirit such as yours," she said. This last was said to him so earnestly, so endearingly, he felt something swell and burst in him. A huge sigh escaped him, and tears again welled in his eyes. There, for one bright moment in Cecily's undaunted glow, his shame was turned to glory. By virtue of this young girl's misunderstanding, her devoted love, he felt the old pain slip through his tears as she squeezed his arm again. As the house lights came up, he felt such relief that he had the merest brush of an impulse to reach out and grasp her, clasp to his bosom her loving heart, and hope that there, by virtue of its power, he might mold its fervor to his very own.

And then he was caught up in a rush of congratulations.

The next day, when he awoke, he thought about it and decided he should take measures to forestall any embarrassing situations in which Cecily might, in some schoolgirl ardor, misconstrue his intentions. He would speak to her differently and see her less and, when visiting, make a deliberate effort to speak with others more. She was a high-strung and impressionable girl. He also realized some nerve, possibly jealousy, had been struck in him when she whispered to him as she left him that night, "I am reading Tolstoy now, and he is as great as you."

30

The Inspector awoke to the annoying sight of his landlady administering ice to his head.

"You knocked yourself unconscious," she said. "Can you hold this?"

His hand went up to the ice pack and found it.

"When?" he said.

"Sometime last night, ran into a lamppost," she said. "You're supposed to rest today."

31

Although Sabina knew she had protected Carl against the Inspector's judgment, tonight she felt she could not defend herself against her own emotions so well.

It had started with that painting. She had gone to see Klimt's painting of Judith holding Holofernes' head, and it had upset her no end. It had made her think immediately of her situation with Carl. Impossible. She sat down, without thinking and wrote immediately to Freud.[1]

She went out to post the letter, and then returned, still feeling very apprehensive, to her flat. Tonight she knew, she wanted Jung out of her life, and her thoughts. Once again, she picked up her writing pad, to try to think with the pen, to try to understand, to state and thereby somehow erase the increasing burden of her thought:

> If in the life of the mind, everything takes place simultaneously or, let us say, things are telescoped and condensed and re-examined and then cast forth in new guises; if in the life of the mind the dream and the reality are often one, then what we remember, and what influences us, may be as much a dream as a reality. We are as much dream-determined as we are reality-determined. If in fact we are dream-determined as much as we are reality-determined, does that mean then that we are the products of dreams? That we have dreamt ourselves? That the dream is the verb behind our being, our actions, our concepts of ourselves?

[1] Sabina did write to Freud (see Aldo Carotenuto, *A Secret Symmetry,* New York: Pantheon Books, 1982, p. 92) that just as Judith loved Holofernes and had to murder him in order to save herself, so she, too, was in a similar position with Jung. This is interesting especially in that the story of Judith, an Apocryphal tale, did not, in its original telling, say anything about Judith's being in love with the Assyrian commander Holofernes. The story, albeit full of contradictions in various versions, was that the beautiful Jewish widow, Judith, stole into Holofernes' camp because he was besieging her people in the city of Bethulia. One night, when he was drunk, Judith cut off his head, and thus saved the Israelites. What is not at all clear is whether or not Klimt's painting was the stimulus for the letter.

Sabina Spielrein put down her pen and read her own words out loud to herself. She had barely finished the first sentence when she jumped, that is to say, lunged, out of the chair and across the room, and then back to the wall and began screaming, "Get out! Get out! Get out!" Then again, hurling herself forward through the room, she ran to the large mahogany desk covered with papers and books and charts and the good doctor's glasses—for in a tired moment, he had laid down his glasses on the desk—and swept them to the floor. With one arm and then the other swung the other way, the two arms spinning like blades through the air, she hurled the glasses, the papers, the books, to the floor.

"Get out! Get out! Get out!" she screamed.

32

The Inspector forced himself up and went directly to the area where the woman had been found. He reviewed the autopsy report. She was a widow. He interviewed her family. He interviewed her friends. He spoke to Captain Voll with annoyance. Did it not strike Voll as extremely suspicious that the woman was a dressmaker? A dressmaker who had also been in Mme. Pacquin's shop? This meant that three women had disappeared from Mme. Pacquin's shop in two years. Voll shrugged.

"A coincidence, Inspector. Many seamstresses worked for Pacquin. She was working somewhere else at the time of the suicide."

"The alleged suicide," the Inspector said.

"Mme. Pacquin may have run away, we do not know," Voll said.

"Two would be suspicious enough, but three?" the Inspector asked.

"It *is* suspicious," Voll agreed reluctantly. "But the gun is there. There are powder marks on her hands, and also her prints are on the gun."

The Inspector looked sharply at Voll. The man never ceased to surprise him.

"What?" the Inspector said.

Voll shrugged. "It is not very convincing to you I am sure, but fingerprints, hand prints were left on objects. Someone in London has told me of this technique and I am most impressed."

The Inspector looked at Voll for a moment. He had thought he was the only one on the continent to know of the English experiments with fingerprints. A personal friend of his, returning from India, had been responsible for convincing Scotland Yard of the efficacy of his method. He had shared it with the Inspector, who knew the impossibility of convincing Bertillon of its usefulness. Bertillon was wedded to his own ideas. Still, to think that a provincial sort like Voll had learned of this was impressive.

This simply didn't fit with the rest of his character, nor, on the other hand, did his sloppiness in choosing such inadequate laboratory tests. Perhaps, the Inspector thought, he had no sense of people. Voll's chief crime researcher was so poorly sighted he was nearly blind, and rumor had it too he was susceptible to bribes. Voll had earnestly denied it, but then had agreed quickly enough when the Inspector suggested someone else. Quickly, but not happily, he thought. Perhaps he had an instinct for expedience and knew the Inspector would insist on separate laboratory tests in any case. He simply didn't know.

He turned on impulse to Voll. "Did you test the Freud house for fingerprints?" he asked.

Voll's cheeks turned pink. "It is not a procedure accepted here," he said.

"I thought for your own edification, perhaps," the Inspector said.

"I am afraid it did not occur to me," Voll said. "But of course, for this reason it is not I who am known as the Great Inspector."

The Inspector ignored the sarcasm. "I do not know about the Great Inspector. I had rather thought there were other forces that might lay claim to that title. I think, sir, and I watch and I wonder who and why and when, and that is sometimes the best that we can do. A hair here and a print there, all of this is useful and necessary, but there are others who do that. In certain cases it becomes essential to enter the mind of the murderer, only there can I prevent him from striking again, only there will I find the clue that will bring him to justice."

He turned, leaving the captain thinking, for the captain had seen that he was an unusual interrogator and a scrupulous observer. He will remain a very long time at the site of a crime, Stekal had said. He had sat for *hours* in Freud's living room, as though the place might once again produce the crime, as if the events transpiring there might occur again if properly watched. Their ghosts, compelled by the passion of his inquiry, might rise before him.

"Death will dance for him, they say," his associate had said of the Inspector, and that was what he meant, that the ghosts themselves would rise and tell the story, so powerful was his concentration.

33

He decided to walk back to the Stadtpark again and stood this time opposite the bench to see from what direction she might have come, what possibilities were there. But the bench was under a tree, a very dramatic tree. There was an openness to the landscaping around the bench that in no way suggested concealment. Perhaps he was wrong after all. He knew he was getting desperate for links. He had always taken pride in his own intuitive ability to look for the unexamined clue, to obtain the unlikely confession, to get from the uncooperative witness the key detail that would lead him to the next clue. He was tireless in it, except here. Here he was all nervous fatigue. He simply wanted it over, and it seemed at times perversely as if he were being held back precisely by this desire to get it done with. The case was not opening smoothly. This woman, he was certain, did not commit suicide. She was not despondent, she was not impoverished, she was not involved in prostitution, as were so many women in the dressmaking trades. Yet her prints were on the gun.

It began to rain but the Inspector had no desire to seek shelter. He stopped walking after a time and sat on a park bench to look at the lake. He missed seeing the swans, but it was too early, yet. So he simply sat there in the rising fog, his shiny brown boots surrounded by puddles of falling rain.

He did not know how long he had been sitting there before he became aware of the drops. The red drops falling from the tree behind the bench onto his shiny brown shoe. Drip. Drip. Drip. He saw the red spots descending from the branches above his head, rolling to the edge of the green wet leaves and then falling over his left shoulder precisely onto the toe of his brown boot. The red drops rolled then to the edge of the shoe and fell down into the puddles. It had been raining for some minutes, and it was this, he later surmised, that had caused the blood to run. Later when he thought about it, he realized he had been contemplating nothing for several minutes, barely taking in the fact of what he must have known was blood, barely letting it register at first, so consumed was he with his own thoughts. And then in a flash, he knew instantly, before his eyes saw the color, and he sprang from the park bench and whirled around, his hand steady on his gun. He saw nothing but great swaying branches and trees.

As always, he would have to follow the trail of blood. Except one did not normally go up, and certainly not up a tree. He moved behind the bench and gazed upwards. Above him red water was washing over the branches and down their leaves. In the distance he heard a dog howling and then he saw it. A black dog, whimpering now as it came over the hill in the rain, alone and confused, and then turning and heading for the tree.

The Inspector looked up and saw it seconds before the animal arrived, panting and howling piteously. Then the dog stood on his hind legs, braced against the trunk and howled mournfully. The Inspector looked up aghast. Although he had never seen them before he would know those eyes anywhere. Dead eyes. Two dead blue eyes gazed down at him, vacant and unseeing. A woman's severed head was lodged in the crook of the tree.

The dog was frantic now, whining and scratching the tree. It was young, just barely full grown. The Inspector attempted to calm it, then lead it away, but all he could accomplish was to make the animal lie down, still whimpering. The Inspector looked up. He could scale the tree with some effort. He looked up at the lowest branches. He would have to jump for them, and then swing his body up, attempt to gain a foothold. After some minutes he decided this might endanger the position of the head. He wanted to photograph it. It might help them identify who had placed it there, for it took some agility to climb the tree with a bloody head in your arms, unless it had been thrown up there. He looked up again at the lifeless blue eyes and then, removing his tie, bent down and placed it around the neck of the howling dog.

The mournful sound of the animal touched him, and talking to him in a soothing voice, he coaxed him slowly toward the station.

The woman's head fit the body parts of the woman in the rhyme called Gertrude Van De Vere. That is to say, the neck that was attached to one of the arms appeared to fit the head. The Inspector sent Stekal on a search, but there was no woman of this description in any of the files of missing persons in Vienna. There was a small reddish birthmark near the hairline on the left side of the face. He was hoping it would bring him news.

In the meantime he sent out a forest of telegrams with her description to every major city and town in Austria, Germany, and France, hoping that amid the hundreds of thousands of missing persons, some match would turn up. As a courtesy, because of his alleged expertise in missing persons, he sent a description personally to Bertillon as well.

It was not until late that evening that the Inspector prepared to leave the police station. He could feel the drop in temperature, as the cold wind blew under the door. As he went to open it he felt a small tug at his pants leg, near the heel. He looked down into a pair of pathetic brown eyes, and a desperately wagging tail. The dog put its front paws up on the Inspector's legs and whimpered.

"Off," the Inspector commanded, annoyed as he pushed the dog away. "Stekal!" he ordered and the lieutenant arrived. "Hasn't anyone come to claim this animal yet?"

Stekal looked unnerved. "There is no one. No one in the neighborhood recognizes it. It could have come from anywhere. We should get rid of it." The Inspector looked down at the animal, the hope in the animal's eyes making him mad.

"Well you take it then!" he ordered Stekal. "It is not my responsibility!"

"I," Stekal said, hurriedly, "I am allergic to animals." He started wheezing. "It will have to find its own home. I will have a carriageman drive it off into the woods and leave it."

"No, don't do that," the Inspector said, looking out at the snow. He sighed. "Put it in my office until the morning. Then we will decide." Stekal, sneezing, took the animal, who left the Inspector only reluctantly, pulling it so its paws slid up the steps and its makeshift collar nearly moved over its thin neck. The Inspector saw at once in that move the animal's ribs, and the largeness of the collar. "You fed it, did you not?" he inquired angrily of Stekal.

"Yes sir," Stekal said.

"Perhaps again," the Inspector said gruffly, pulling up the collar of his coat and making his way down the steps. He realized in a dim way he was hoping the stairs would ice and he would slip, so endlessly did he want the blackness, the dark to ease his pain. He was consumed with emotion of such disorder that he no longer knew what he felt; only that it felt unbearable.

He had not gone more than two blocks when he heard the yipping and turned to see through the swirling snow, the wet, panting creature running furiously towards him, Stekal breathless quite a ways behind. The dog jumped all over him, and when he bent with a hand to chastise it, the animal's warm pink tongue sloshed over his cold hand.

Stekal came up in minutes, out of breath. "He broke away sir, sorry, sir, he seems to want to follow you. Now I have something." He held up the frayed rope. Stekal bent and made a loop of rope under the dog's collar as the wind swirled about them. The Inspector's hands were back in his pockets and he was stamping his feet in the cold. Stekal made off toward the station and the dog sat in the snow so that Stekal had to pull him, the dog's lower body now like a sled, along the street.

The Inspector watched. "Stekal!" he said, surprising himself, and Stekal turned. "Leave him to me," he called, and Stekal, relieved, let go the rope. The animal came bounding up to the Inspector, jumping on its hind legs, in an effort to lick his face. The Inspector, heaving a sigh, retrieved the leash and they went off, the two of them, one heavy, shoulders bent, the other dancing with joy and pirouetting in the snow.

The dog awakened him from his dreams. It was whimpering, and he saw it had attempted to climb up on his bed. The bed was high, and he saw that the one back leg of the animal was weakened in some way, it trembled so he could not support himself with it. He was annoyed, but after a while when it would not cease its effort, he felt pity. There was a large rocking chair in the window, and eventually to quiet the animal the Inspector got out of bed, put on his coat and

socks, and went to sit in the chair in the window. There was some
light there and he bent and saw that there was no new injury to the
leg, so he picked up the dog and took him in his arms and began to
rock in the chair, soothing himself and the animal also with the steady
creaking of the rocker. He rocked the animal for quite some time
until tears streamed from his eyes and soon they were both asleep.

"We have found more jewelry," Captain Voll announced the next
morning, "of Mme. Pacquin's on the shore. This means it was unquestionably a suicide. A thief or murderer would have taken the jewels.
They are valuable. That means all were suicides save Van de Vere."

"Hmmmm," the Inspector said.

Voll did not like the Inspector. The evidence for suicide was nothing
short of overwhelming. Yet the Inspector struck to the stubborn, un-
tenable idea that it had been murder.

34

When Freud received the letter from Sabina about Judith murdering Holofernes, and comparing that situation to her own with Jung, it
gave him more than a temporary start. He soon calmed himself, however, feeling foolish at his original alarm. It was the power of the
painting, he decided, that had stimulated her so. But it left him with a
very uneasy feeling.

35

Everyone thought the Countess must have gone off to Paris in the
middle of the night. Her maid had tried to stop her, believing she was
in no state to travel by herself. No one was sure exactly what happened

next, except a note was found in the dining room saying she'd gone. There was some concern about this, but it was later when the upstairs maid found a bottle of chloral under the Countess' bed that I heard a scream. It wasn't long before they found the Countess lying on the floor of the passageway to her atelier and doctors were called. There was a lot of frantic activity but no one would tell me anything. Eventually, Father came out of the study and when he did his face was very grave. "Sit down," he said to me. I had secretly been hoping that the Countess had run off with the Inspector or something very romantic like that, but now my heart nearly stopped as I saw the looks on their faces.

"The Countess," Father said slowly, "is very, very ill."

"What is it?" I nearly shrieked and Aunt Ida held my arm.

"She apparently has taken some chloral," Timothy said, then he added quickly, "not sufficient to be lethal but almost. She may have been trying to calm herself, or," he hesitated, "she may have realized what she had done and gone out into the cold to wake herself up. . . . We don't know."

Aunt Ida had her face in her hands. "If only I had seen her, I should have," she could not continue speaking.

"Her grandmother," Father said slowly, "is coming from Russia, immediately. We are trying to reach Leopold."

"What about . . ." I gasped, did I dare say it, "her friend, the Inspector?"

Aunt Ida shook her head.

I was speechless and said I must go to her at once. To my surprise, Mother and Father agreed finally to allow me to go up.

I ran to the Countess' bed and gasped when I saw her. The expression in her eyes was vacant, as if she could neither see nor hear, and then she closed them. I grabbed her hand, which was very warm, and spoke to her, but she never opened her eyes or said anything to me at all.

36

It seemed to Voll that the Inspector was losing his grip. He forgot things. He drank too much. He seemed to go over and over the same evidence, as if it would magically contradict itself. Dark pools appeared under his eyes. He was short with the staff. There were grumblings. Voll sighed. He had seen this happen on investigations before. It was just a matter of time before the Inspector gave up.

37

The house was full of excitement the next few days because the Countess' grandmother had arrived with several other women and there was a great deal of cooking and coming and going. The news about the Countess was good.

"It is amazing," Timothy said. "She is recovering. And they won't tell me what they are brewing in those pots, exactly. Some herbal mixture. Every day," Timothy said wonderingly, "they rub her entire body down with some oil and herbs in it, twice a day."

"You haven't seen this, have you?" Mother asked, aghast, and Timothy didn't answer.

"They want her to eat only what they cook," Timothy said, throwing up his hands. "The doctors are letting them do whatever they want."

At breakfast I asked one of them about the brides the Countess told me about who sew their wishes and dreams into cloth, and she said that the custom had changed now, with the coming of the priests. Aunt Ida translated most of this and I do not think, as Mother said later, "that she fooled with it." What the woman told me was that girls used to be urged by their mothers to go and catch the man they wanted like "a falcon bright in the open field," something that caught Cecily's fancy a lot. And then she said that it used to be that the bride's braid was cut by her mother and anointed with honey and butter and then covered with money and bread. This was to show how valuable a wife was. "Now," she said, as if she had no respect for it at all, "the bridegroom stamps on the bride's foot until it bleeds, and when they enter the bedroom she must bend down and remove his boots." She was very angry when she said this, and when Aunt Ida translated it she was very angry too.

38

The Inspector took out a piece of paper and drew up the times:

At 5:40 A.M. when the watchman made his rounds at 19 Berggasse he heard the coach, heading *toward* Freud's house.

At 5:50 A.M. Martha heard the horses outside.

At 6:00 A.M., approximately, Minna saw the body.

At 6:15 A.M. the body was gone.

At 6:30 A.M. the watchman heard the horses go up the Berggasse as he returned to his house. He saw them stop, he observed an argument, and then the horses changed direction.

At 6:30 A.M. the horses were crossing the Liechtenstein Strasse as the Mains were arriving at the Countess' house.

At 6:36 A.M. the horses were crossing the Rossauerlaende as Sabina lay in the snow. The events suggested a change of plan. Or a wrong address. It was some time later that the murderer—

What was it? Why could he get no further?

39

As the Inspector wandered through the streets of Vienna, thoughts of the Romans before him arose and he saw their thundering legions along the streets, which had set the pattern for some of the roadways of the inner city. Madmen, he muttered to himself, when it came to designing streets. The Inspector knew he was quite capable of becoming lost in Vienna and he rather enjoyed it.

His last conversation with Freud had left him plagued in a way that none had before. They had been discussing the murder and the Inspector had confessed his great difficulty solving the case. He had then said to Freud, "As Pascal has said, 'the heart has reasons of its own of which reason knows nothing,' so perhaps there is no solving this case." And Freud had looked at him then with a mixture of pity and anger.

"Surely you do not believe that, Inspector. In any case I do not. The heart has reasons of its own, but it is my task to use reason to discover them and I intend to do precisely that. 'Reason knows nothing,' is only fear. I think you will come to agree with me."

The Inspector had been taken aback by this. He had felt, when Freud said this, an odd alarm shoot through him. "Perhaps," he said, "if Pascal were here he could argue more effectively in his defense than I can."

"This is not about Pascal, Inspector," the doctor had said, "it is about you."

The Inspector turned around. He felt it again. Something. What eye was following him now through the dark streets? He turned. The thief sprinted up the steep staircase near the Rotenturmstrasse and disappeared.

He lost his breath halfway up. "Damn the Romans," he said, "and the Turks as well."

Paris did not do this to him. He did not get lost this way in Paris. But here?

His only consolation was the pastry. Topefenstrudel whispered to him in the depths of his fatigue. Palatshinken hailed him now out of the dark.

He could curse the thief, the darkness, and his stomach, or eat.

As if to reward his optimism he saw a small light beckoning around the corner and knew, as his steps drew him toward it, that at such moments he was neither a spiritual nor an intellectual man. No such man would feel the rush of joy that pulsed through him as he saw lined up rows of plums and apricots in crusts and tarts, and especially a cake, a small cake he saw as he looked closer, embedded with blueberries and currants, red and black, and its red-blue richness had melted through the sides of the cake like veins in a good blue cheese.

His mouth was wet with anticipation as he pushed open the door of the shop, too grateful for the luxuries offered there, the warmth, the light, to be aware of the footsteps retreating not far behind him.

40

Freud was surprised to see the Inspector standing at his door. "I thought you had concluded your inquiry here," he said.

"I am not here to interrogate you, Hr. Doktor," the Inspector said, "but on a matter of some urgency and of some relevance to you. May I come in?" Freud noted it was the first time the Inspector had actually requested permission to enter.

"This is a matter of some urgency," the Inspector repeated. "I myself am being followed at every turn. I believe the answer is within my grasp, but something is interfering, something I cannot get hold of." Freud was thinking he would like to assist the Inspector for one reason only: to get the entire matter over and done with. Whatever the matter was.

Freud listened. The Inspector explained: he had been driven to ask this because he realized he was suffering from a lack of vision. Some curtain had fallen on the back of his mind, where the intuitive leap took place, and he could not move past it. He thought that if he were hypnotized he would drive something or someone forth.

"It is essential to my plan to discover the murderer."

"Can you explain your reasons?" Dr. Freud asked.

"No," the Inspector said.

Freud took some time with his cigar. "I am not inclined to do this. But I will think about it," he said. He paused then and asked, "Inspector, do you really continue to believe there was a murder on these premises?"

"I *know* there was a murder on these premises," the Inspector said. "But," the Inspector said, "something in this is quite beyond my understanding. I feel—" he stopped. Freud was impressed that the Inspector had been willing to risk his authority in confessing this.

"I feel there is something here, some personal failing, something I remember and do not remember that is impeding my solving this case. I can assure you I have arrived at solutions in more perplexing cases than this. But I—" he went no further. Then he turned. "If you refuse, could you not instruct me in this technique so that I could apply it to myself? I am at a rather desperate hour and I am convinced that I am now a target of this murderer. If I do not find this criminal, I am convinced he shall find me."

Freud looked at him. "You are *not*," he said emphatically, "a good candidate for hypnosis, and, as to other techniques, well . . . I am the only person so far to be able to analyze himself, so I do not expect you will be able to do *that*," he said. "But there are a few means by which you might stimulate your memories since you feel it is something in your memory that is interfering in some specific way."

"Yes," the Inspector said.

"You might begin," he said, "by visiting your childhood home, especially as it is here, in Vienna."

The Inspector's face grew taut. "It would be quite fruitless," he objected. "It is in ruins. Overgrown. What would be the point?" Freud noticed the change in tone. It was a most uncharacteristic one. Almost a plea.

"It may help you recall," the doctor said. When Freud looked at him he saw the normally implacable Inspector's face had gone white and sweat was pouring from his brow.

"It was called *L'Avventura*," the Inspector said slowly, "built by an eighteenth-century Italian count. It is in ruins now for many years." He said this last very sadly and vaguely. "My mother loved it very much," his voice broke.

But he was angry when the doctor asked further about his mother. "Do not drag my mother into this, I beg of you," he snapped.

"But you already have," the doctor said quietly.

Later as the Inspector was leaving, the doctor turned to him and said, "I also love my mother very much. And I have always been her favorite. It is a good omen, your affection, as regards your destiny. I believe it is commonplace among distinguished men," and with that he closed the door.

PART VI
BONFIRE

Souvenir, o bûcher, dont le vent
d'or m'affronte.
Memory, o bonfire, whose golden
wind assaults me.

Baudelaire

1

It was two days later after midnight that the Inspector stole into the stable and saddled the black horse.

He fastened his gun and was quickly astride, turning her down a small side street to pass unnoticed from the stable. In minutes they were out of the city and he put her into an easy canter, as it was a long ride out and back, but she was a strong and willing animal. He was counting on the bright moonlight and became momentarily alarmed when the clouds piled up making the road quite dark. He was forced to trot her for miles as the road was rutted and he could not see, so he was relieved when the wind came up and cleared the clouds, and then he turned her off the road and across a field he knew. It thrilled him and filled him with dread to see the turrets rising just beyond the hill. He had been told it had not been rented for the last five or six years. He saw that it was in ruins.

He drew up to the gate, the old wrought iron fence collapsed on one side, but still readable: L'AVVENTURA. He had an intuition that he ought not to leave the mare in clear sight. It was absurd to think there could be horse thieves out here in the middle of the night, but he felt cautious and led her around, through the tangled brush, toward what he knew was the rear of the house. The moon moved in and out of the clouds and he could see at once, as if spotlighted, the ivy-throttled rooms, stones falling and fallen, and here and there an entryway, an exit, something he knew, standing untouched as if time had wandered through, with a cautious hand. He felt extremely nervous, as if he were treading on a holy site, and he tried to shake off his superstition. He knew he had come for a reason, but what the reason was he was not entirely sure.

One door creaked and fell off its rusted hinges as he entered. He heard the scurrying of a small animal as he picked his way across the floor, guided only by moonlight. He had brought a lamp, and realized he had left it in his saddlepack. He hesitated, but then thought better of it. There was enough light, he was certain, for there seemed to be nothing he wanted to see so much as to recall. He moved his feet slowly across the drawing room, and then through the hallway, the wind blowing through the windows with a wild, singing sound. The clouds were over the moon again, and he thought he smelled rain in the wind. He did not want to get wet. He would hurry. He crossed the hallway into the main ballroom. He had worried about coming here, and what it might reveal. As if to dislodge himself from a dream, he moved again into another room and was swept with an old familiar fatigue. He felt the brush of a memory here, but turned again and hurried on. It was amazing to him that whoever had left the house had left occasional pieces of furniture which were still decaying there. Then, quite suddenly, he felt he was foolish to have come. This would simply bring on more bad memories, and it had taken everything in him to make this Vienna trip as it was. He felt betrayed by that stupid doctor. He had simply wanted to make him more miserable, to get rid of him. Well, he had succeeded. He was ready to leave now, to leave Vienna to its crime and murders and to return to Paris. He didn't think he could bear to be in the same city with Bettina anymore.

He lit a match and saw he was near the stairwell to the basement. There might be candles there, was it possible after all these years? The match burned out, but it had lasted long enough for him to calculate the stairs. He proceeded cautiously down the steps until he felt the door directly ahead. One more match and he pushed and it fell open and he saw the wine bottles ahead of him. The second match was gone, but he felt his way and yanked and pulled at the drawer until it finally yielded. His hands moved across the darkened drawer and he found them. Candles. Still there after all these years. They were kept there for the trips to the wine cellar. He was astounded that the wine was still there, covered with cobwebs.

He had a candle now and was making his way back up the stairs when he stumbled against the shelf and a jar fell to the stone floor, releasing a rush of potpourri. In the dark he smelled the flowers, they seemed to rush up at him out of the wintered halls, like a sigh of spring. Roses, he smelled the roses his mother had everywhere in the house. And remembered her rose garden, her love. He had forgotten it entirely, and with astonishment he realized how much it had been part of his life as visions swept through his mind—holding the bucket while she cut them, helping her arrange the flowers in the vase, her sweet high voice congratulating him on his floral compositions. "Why Maurice, you are very talented, perhaps you will be a painter." He remembered at once with such stunning clarity standing at the edge of the ballroom with a vase he had arranged himself, and his mother's joyous receipt of the vase, of him. He felt an emotion rise and then took a deep breath and made his way to the ballroom.

The clouds had cleared and now the moonlight shone full down upon it, and he paused, overwhelmed by the sight of it, and the sounds of the waltzing, and his mother and father swinging about the grand ballroom, his mother in a white filmy dress, her dark hair adorned with roses, and roses wound around the dress at her waist, and everyone had said, fresh flowers, how strange, how different, how beautiful. His mother, how strange, how different, how beautiful, and he had stood watching them as they swirled around the room, dancing as if there were no others on the floor, and for his eyes there were not. He heard the chatter rise and fill the room, the sweet happy moments there, the wonderful music and dancing in the home filled with beauty which he loved. He stood there reveling in the joy of that memory and wondering suddenly why he had dreaded it so, as if by coming here he might remember only her death when he had been given this, to see her again, dancing in the moonlight, and then, opening her arms as she danced with his father and calling to him, and he ran joyously across the dance floor and she scooped him up between them and the three of them danced, and he was happy.

He did not know how long he stood there or quite what his state of mind was but he heard quite suddenly the snap of a branch and it struck him that it was close, just outside the moonlit room. He stepped out of the light an instant before a shot shattered the silence and ricocheted off the wall behind him.

He reached for his gun and realized he had left it, too, in the pack.

Thinking and moving quickly he felt his way along the old bannister and descended the steps into the basement. Who was it? A robber? Leopold? Someone protecting the property? That was laughable! The place was ruined. In the pitch black he made his way, groping the walls until he could go no further. He reached into his pockets frantically and found a match. There was a door from the basement that led up to the garden.

There were footsteps now, directly above him. His assassin was in the house. He fumbled for the match, lit the candle, and his eyes swept the basement walls for the way out, and he saw it. Something was shoved in front of it, but he could squeeze by, and with the candle directing, he saw the stairway outside. He hesitated. He was not about to emerge into the moonlight until he heard the footsteps closer to the door. A board creaked on the steps. He shoved his way through the doorway and through the dark, dank passage up into the night. The moon was bright.

Something smelled here, too, something he could not quite recall. It was a long run to where the mare was tethered. He turned immediately to his right where he saw the high hedges, and squeezed his way through them. The labyrinth! His childhood dream. Designed and kept for his childhood fancy, he had loved enticing visiting children into the labyrinth, culled and kept by his father's gardener in beautiful curving shapes, twists, and boxes of beautiful design, from whose clutches the visitors could never escape. He had been proud always to lead them out.

The maze was still there; he could see in the moonlight, although overgrown with ivies and vines. Then he heard the steps behind him. How many were there? He had been warned the anti-Semites did not want him solving this murder and were eager for his demise. Would they go this far? He could get to his gun on his saddle only by leading them through the labyrinth; he'd lose them there. He had to get them to follow him in. He made a crashing sound and then moved swiftly ahead, sliding through the hedges and running fairly freely through one of the lanes of the labyrinth. In minutes he felt his ruse had worked. He heard his pursuer behind him and then, nothing.

Quietly he stole slowly through the labyrinth, remembering the serpentine turn, now fallen over with trees and debris, but still keeping its shape and the thickness separate from the path. Whoever it was would have come up against the first labyrinth wall. By the time he figured his way out, the Inspector would have time to run to the end and get his gun. But then he heard it, only steps away. By some luck his opponent had gotten through the first wall. He moved quickly then, running down the next lane and twisting around and around feeling his way, stepping over rock and rotting wood as best he could, panicked at the thought he might lose his way as well. He heard another crash and then mercifully the clouds covered the moon again, giving him time. His eyes adjusted to the dark and he saw he had made a mistake, the brush was too thick to move to his right where the hedges were overgrown. He had thought there was an exit, maybe there, and he had pressed into the hedge, but it didn't yield, instead he dislodged a branch, which crashed, giving him away.

He heard the footsteps quicken behind him just as he found the exit and, crashing through, found himself in a new lane, and running as fast as he could in the dark, remembering almost exactly the length of the next run, he made his way almost to the end and was about to turn into the exit when he heard his mother's voice, calling to him. "Maurice—" and then it was Bettina calling, "Maurice—" and then his mother, how *alike* were their voices! And then he heard the mare whinny, all in seconds, as he was about to crash through the exit, and the moon moved in and out, and he was clear, and then it was dark and he realized with a horrible certainty that whoever was on the other side of the labyrinth could not be so overseen by luck: this was someone who knew the labyrinth as well as he and with a sudden lunge, he flung himself back and rolled over and over to the ground into the far hedges as the shots ran through the night, one, two, three, four, five.

He had not tethered the mare tightly, and upon hearing the shots she broke and ran into the trees. His assailant fled. He heard him hit the saddle, heard a yell of some sort, was there someone with him? and then the sound of horses galloping. The mare had run off.

It was later as he was stepping carefully over the area where, except for the voices, his slain body would have lain that he saw in the moonlight five shells from the gun. He picked them up and put them in his pocket, and then went and sat on the ruined steps of his house. He had heard her, he had heard Bettina, sounding so like his mother, and the emotion of terror and pity, for himself, for the world had overwhelmed him.

2

The next day, he went to the Stadtpark alone. Thoughts of the head in the tree assaulted him. He remembered now in the green grasses of the park the unmistakable red line, blood, dripping a drop at a time, hitting his boot, rolling down the side of the shining brown surface in a small rivulet and pooling into the increasing rain, turning the water red. It startled him now into the past.

``I'LL see you soon, I'll send for you darling,'' he could hear her now, see her blowing kisses in her plum-feathered hat, her white gloves waving, his mother, vanishing into the oval window of a carriage.

She didn't drown, quite. She lay in the water too long a time, the people said, and when they returned her to Vienna she was no longer his mother. She looked like his mother but she moved in a strange, distant way, and she did not recognize her own child. "Gone out of her head," they said. And it served her right, the gossips said, the young beautiful woman who had married an older man, his father, and run off with a lover.

The Inspector remembered it now. His mother was disgraced. And when she returned he ran down the driveway to see her, and as she was led from the coach as if in a dream, held on either side by two nurses, her eyes looked right through him. He ran anyway and threw his arms around her, and it was as if he had embraced a block of stone. She did not know him. In a week she stopped moving at all and lay in the bed, staring at the ceiling. The doctors came and went. Vicious whispers circled the hallways. And then she was dead. When they came to remove the body they found his grief-stricken father in despair. No one had seen the terrified boy move from behind the closet door, to lie shaking under the bed. When they finally found him he was quiet and composed. He must be strong, and not cry, his father said, his mother said, and then she was gone.

It would take time, they had said. As the Inspector sat in the park staring at the trees he felt the weight of his long search lift, as a fog lifts off a bay. He remembered now as a boy they had said, "It will take time." It had taken nearly forty years.

He got up from the bench then and felt the old energy he used to feel beginning to move along his legs.

3

I think," Slotkin told him, slowly stroking his beard, "that the bodies were dismembered elsewhere and dumped at these various sites."

The Inspector looked at him carefully. In utter frustration he had insisted the unwilling and elderly Slotkin come to Vienna to assist in identification of the body parts. Slotkin had retired years ago, but he was brilliant.

Slotkin held up a portion of leg and pointed to its ragged edge. Then he took out a magnifying glass. "This piece, for example, if you look at it you think it was hacked off by a maniac. Indeed it may have been a maniac, but a highly trained one. You see," he said, pointing to the tissue beneath the glass, "it was originally surgically cut."

The Inspector looked through the glass.

"And then," Slotkin said, "for some reason, later on you see," he pointed to another section of muscle and bone protruding around a knee, "someone messed it up, battered it, I believe quite deliberately, as if to confuse things."

"Altered the evidence to protect the doctor?" the Inspector said quickly. "It is a surgeon you say, am I correct?"

Slotkin nodded slowly. "I believe so. Only a surgeon would choose to make the cut here. And the nature of it is horrible, of course, but the actual cuts, you see, originally had a kind of elegance." He went on, "Unfortunately, except for the Van de Vere samples, the others are too mutilated to be sure. But the assumption must be that it is the same method in all instances.

"And you are correct of course, Inspector. The two necks we have been able to identify indicate they died of asphyxiation, so the likelihood is that they were all strangled originally, and then cut up."

"Yes," the Inspector said. He was in a solemn mood. Slotkin was confirming what he had suspected for some time. In the midst of all this horror, he kept having thoughts of the Countess and how he might see her again.

4

I don't know whether it was the excitement caused by Cecily's infatuation with the handsome Russian soldier at the ball, or her evening at the theater with Mr. James, about which she originally had spoken quite a *lot,* or the Countess' illness, but since the Countess seemed more like her old self again I didn't think that was it. All I know was that during the next weeks everyone noticed Cecily seemed extremely preoccupied. She had become deathly quiet.

5

The Countess awoke with a start, feeling the fine cool silk of the sheets in the palm of her hand. Her fingertips touched the silk slowly, as if it were the fur of an animal, and she were attempting to calm it. Something had awakened her, some need, some disturbance within herself. She had been feeling so *well* and had resumed some work. She was excited by the designs she had completed only yesterday and had decided to bring some of them to Paris. Perhaps that was it.

She rose quickly in the dim morning light, went to the cupboard, and took out her Japanese robe, the silk one with red and black and gold dragons on it, the embroidery snaking a huge line across the back of the dragon. She wrapped the black sash around her, and, slipping into her slippers, moved quietly out the door and down the stairs. The servants were sleeping.

She knew the stairwell well, her hands moving along the walls, its curves and crevices, as if it were a body she were fitting, familiar in its shape and outline, although, she mused in the half-conscious mental life of the dark and early morning, if the walls were women they would change slowly and over the years there would be lumps and bumps where there were now only smooth, soft surfaces. But there would never be the sharp angled corners her hand slipped over now, the unyielding joint of wall to wall. Briefly she remembered fitting Lady Wolfe, who had, she thought, the most violent rib cage ever, having acquired no fat, but simply these firm, bony sharp protuberances, and fitting her she had wondered that Lady Wolfe's husband either had strange tastes or went unsolaced by his wife all his life.

She swiftly moved into the dressmaker's shop. The three cloaks the seamstresses had finished yesterday, one in ivory, one in dark green, and the third a brilliant scarlet, were hanging against the far wall. She shivered, for the shop was cold and dark at this hour. She had not come here at night for months. She used to come often, for comfort. In the half-light she stepped up to the first cloak, the dark green one hung in front, and as if she were looking for something, she stroked the cloak, fingering the silk of its lining, its heavy, thick velvet closures, then burying her face in the folds of the hood, breathed into the soft, sumptuous velvet, at once cool and warm, warm to her flesh, but cool from hanging all night in the unheated shop. And then untying the closures from the hanger, she slipped it over her shoulders and, moving to the window, sat in the chair, rocking, stroking the fine soft velvet, and imagining she was riding through the park. She began humming very softly to herself.

She was feeling quite content with this state of contemplation when she heard a noise not far behind her. A step. She did not move until the step was firm in her mind, then she sprang up, but two large hands held her shoulders lightly but firmly down. And a familiar voice, soft, reassuring said, "I did not mean to startle you, Bettina."

Her heart beat loudly in her chest as she reached up, before she knew what she was doing, reached up and touched the hands on her shoulders, and turned her head, breathless, "Maurice . . . whatever are you doing here?" As she turned to him in the dim light, and looked into that keen, crevassed face, that astonishingly handsome face, with its black moustache and piercing eyes, a face now only inches from her own, her heart beat more loudly than it had been beating from fear.

"Why are you here?" It was a plaintive question, a plea, a demand, an entreaty all at once.

"I have been waiting and watching for days, hoping you would come. . . . I am ashamed that I . . ." his voice, dark, half caught in his throat, "Bettina, can you ever forgive this?"

"I must ask you to leave, Maurice," the Countess said, quickly turning her back to him. "I need a place of safety, of refuge. I came here for that. . . . I cannot speak with you about . . . these matters. Please go."

"You must hear me out!" His voice implored her. She turned part way around. "If you cannot indulge me my confession for myself, Bettina, and I allow that you may not, you must hear me out for your own sake. There is no profit in refusing to hear what you have misunderstood. I have come here for myself, to be sure, but also," his voice was lower, softer, "also, Bettina, for you. You must hear this."

She still had not turned to him. After some minutes she said, "Say what you must and then leave!"

"I do not expect you can feel for me again what you once . . ." he paused, "felt. But I have learned many things, and I must confess I despise that I hurt you, that I was a coward."

"Maurice," her tone was not forgiving, but matter-of-fact. "It is, was, too much to expect you to understand." She turned to him and he saw her eyes begin to glisten. "But I thought you would," she said. "It was a terrible blow to see what I saw in your eyes, and I can't forget it. I saw your hatred, your contempt, for me." Her voice had dropped almost to a whisper.

"The contempt was there," he said slowly, "but it was not solely for you, Bettina. The rage was there. . . . I was overcome." He turned to her. His admission of this, which she thought she would find so horrifying, had the odd effect, quite suddenly, of comforting her. "It was there," he said, "but it was for myself. I was jealous you were ever touched by another man, this is so. Insane with it. I believed you would cast me aside, as you did Philippe, that I was nothing to you. The contempt was for myself. It was not from lack of feeling, Bettina, but from too much of it."

"So!" she said turning to him, her eyes bright with anger. "You ask me to judge you not by what my eyes saw, which was contempt, not by what my ears heard, which was contempt, not by your hateful action, which tossed me aside, like some malignancy. No, Maurice, you ask me to judge you by some invisible presence in you that, now, you decide was there. I suppose you will call it *love*." She spat the word at him with such vengeance it startled him.

There was a strained silence. "You thought you loved me, Maurice." Her voice was heavier now, and slow. "And you convinced me. But it was not true. It was a lie." Her eyes met his in a level, unforgiving gaze. He stepped back slightly, off balance, his hands up suddenly as if warding off a blow.

"Not," he said. Then, "Not a lie, no." He started to speak again, and faltered. His hands swept up and covered his face, and his body shook with emotion.

The Countess watching this felt a barely controllable impulse to flee. She wondered later that she should find pity so predatory.

"Forgive me," he said finally. She was no longer certain precisely what for.

"Please, listen to what I have to say." He reached forward to touch her arm, but she pulled away. He was urging her now with a new authority. "If you cannot forgive me Bettina, believe me, I know this, you will pay a high price. It is terrible for me to lose you," she heard his voice tremble again and its trembling moved through her like a wave, "but it will be unbearable for me to think I have caused you your own self-hatred, because you cannot forgive me."

"Who is the sophist now?" the Countess said, but he heard her crying.

"You said," she said finally, "you have come here every night, for days, why?"

"Oh," the cry was out of him before he knew it, "just to see you!"

She could not stop herself; she was gripped at the emotion in his voice. She was desperate for something, to help her understand.

"I . . . I went back," he said finally. She knew immediately what he meant and wondered at it.

"How long were you there?" she said, after some time.

And so they talked, long through the night and as the morning light appeared in the city he prepared to go.

"Well?" he said, finally, his voice taut with hope.

"I . . . Maurice, I . . . I don't know . . ." she stammered, looking up into his eyes. His eyes held her and she saw his grief as he stood quietly, and she moved then, the fatal inch, toward him, and took his hands in her own, and leaned her head against his shoulder and pressed her body into his. He had removed his coat, and only his shirt and her thin night dress were between them. She could feel his heart beating.

"This is . . ." She heard him struggling with a formality she felt he invoked to protect her.

"Yes . . . ," she said, ". . . how long have you been waiting?"

"For days now, I have come, hoping to find you."

"You have found me . . ." she said, raising her eyes to his, and pressed her lips against his, and then they were lost, as she knew, as he knew, they could be, and in the cold small room, where the light was slowly getting brighter they made love on the red, the green and white velvet fabrics, they made themselves warm with the furs hanging in the back of the shop, with the wolverines, the Russian sables, the furs of the aristocracy needing mending, they kept warm. They were consumed and quite beyond themselves.

They had finally to rouse themselves, for the dawn was full upon them now, the sunlight cascading into the shop. "We must go," he said, his lips across her brow. "We must."

"I cannot," she said, and she couldn't. He had to unleash her fingers from his, untwine her hand from his arm, she could not let him go and kept returning to him as if there were no light, as if there were no dawn, no city, no work, no husband, no family, no dress shop, no dressmaker, no cloth, no thread, no silk, no velvet, nothing except this devouring, magnificent presence between the two of them, this deli- cate dark and dangerous agreement that had wrenched everything from her and then returned it to her a hundredfold. She had, she thought, lost her fear of the world.

He kissed her tears, salting his mouth, traced her fingertips with his own. She kissed his face a hundred times, no, she thought later, possi- bly a thousand. He must come again, he would come again, sometime soon, in the morning, again, please somehow he must. He said he would. And she knew, she knew this by the feel of his mouth along her arm, her back, and down, that mouth that has pressed such warm kisses down her back would not lie, could not ever lie to her.

6

It was raining hard outside, so Henry James did not at first hear the insistent knocking at his hotel room door. The secretary he had hired was not due to arrive for another hour, and he was annoyed to have to interrupt his reading and go to the door. He opened the door, and to his shock there was Cecily, bright-eyed. She threw herself at him, put her arms around his neck and cried out, "*Je suis Karenina,*" and fainted dead away.

"Oh my heavens," said Henry James, startled, disturbed, concerned, and troubled all at once. He was obliged to carry the fainting girl in his arms, in what, he was aware, was a most unseemly manner, the entire time hearing himself cluck the most absurd drivel, "Oh dear, oh dear, oh dear." And then, "Maid! Maid!" He could no longer remember the wretched woman's name, but finally she came in, looking askance at him, which did not help at all, "Please, do something, she's fainted." The maid, being a practical woman, went for the smelling salts.

When Cecily came to, Henry James realized that his problem rather than being over, had only just begun. She looked at him with a disturbing earnestness and said, "My life is a tragedy. That is why I have come."

He knew indeed about the dramatic imagination of adolescent girls. But there was something else here as well that he did not want to deal with. He tried to placate her. "I am sure, my dear, after some tea, you will feel much restored. There can be times when life seems overwhelming, but really it is not. It can be managed, I assure you. Does your mother know where you are?"

Cecily's eyes narrowed. "Don't be stupid," she said. This shocked him.

"I'm sorry," she said, looking at the floor, "I, I should not have come, but I, I am in terrible straits," and she began to cry.

It took several hours of tea and conversation to calm her down. It seemed she had determined to go to Paris and wanted the names of some people in Paris who would befriend her. She asked him to say nothing to her parents about this, putting him in a dreadful position, so he advised her that perhaps the Countess could be of greater assistance since she traveled to Paris so often, but Cecily again shook her head. "It would put *her* in an impossible position," she said. *He* must do it, and he must promise to keep secret the names he gave her.

He agreed, in his panic, to write a letter for her, a letter of introduction, and assured her that these particular friends had a large house and would, at his urging, take her as a guest. Then he urged her not to make this unescorted trip to Paris as it could only cause her terrible trouble in the end. His persuasion was of no avail. Then, miraculously, by four in the afternoon he got her to agree to return to her parents. It had stopped raining, and he insisted on escorting her, which he noticed she welcomed. But they had not got within ten yards of the Countess' house when her entire body started to shake, and she turned quite pale.

"I cannot go in there." She turned to him utterly stricken, "Please, I beg of you," and she clutched his arm and began to sob. Then, just as suddenly, he felt her go limp once more, and it took all of his strength to gather her up and carry her to the door.

When I heard Mother scream, I ran to the door in time to see a stricken Henry James, carrying an unconscious Cecily in his arms.

"What is it? What is it?" Aunt Ida was saying as she and Father ran to take Cecily from Mr. James' arms. They lay her down on the sofa, and she began to moan.

"She just keeps fainting," Mr. James said, his face all red and strange. "I found her at my door this morning, quite early. She rang, and when I went to answer, she was standing there and then cried—you see, she is so suggestible—she cried out to me, *"Je suis Karenina,"* and swooned into my arms. I, I contacted a doctor I know who lives not far from me. When we revived her, I impressed upon her the necessity of returning here, only to have her," he looked up helplessly, "swoon again. She is quite distraught."

We were all in a dither. Mr. James declined to stay for dinner. No one knew quite what to do, but we all agreed we would say nothing more to Cecily until the morning.

But the morning, it turned out, was too late.

When I awoke the next morning Cecily's bed was empty. What alarmed me was that the bed was not open but folded and tidied up neatly, as if it were not to be slept in again. I had never seen Cecily do this. I sat up, and that's when I saw a note, tied to the pillow.

Dear Reader:

I know this is unexpected, but I must go away for a while. Do not worry for my safety. I have decided that I've reached a point in my life when I must take a journey. I am thinking things and meeting people I never imagined before. This is having a deep effect on me. Although I cannot disclose here the full workings of my heart, I must pursue this. I assure you I have friends and funds in Paris, and I will be fine. This is something I must do. I will contact you. Thank you for everything and much love.

Cecily.

Cecily was gone. Gone! And "Dear Reader," as if we were some anonymous public. Mother and Father were frantic and called the Inspector at once. Aunt Ida whispered to me that we must get in touch with Mr. James and Mrs. Wharton to find out what it was that an impressionable young woman who imagines she is a heroine in a novel, might do. Or where she might go.[1]

---

[1] The next portion of the manuscript is missing, although a few notes remain. Apparently Cecily ran away to Paris where she was taken in by a group of feminists, including a radical feminist doctor, Madeleine Pelletier. The Inspector, with the help of Henry James, went to Paris in order to locate her, finding her, according to the section I have been able to decipher so far, living with various women, including the rather notorious Natalie Barney. Barney was a close friend of the Fitzgeralds, to whom James had recommended Cecily. When Cecily arrived, the Fitzgeralds were on vacation, and the butler referred her to Natalie Barney, who was taking care of the two Fitzgerald dogs and their four cats. She then met Dr. Pelletier. Dr. Pelletier was one of the rare women to be granted a medical license at the end of the century. She grew up in poverty and was by all accounts sexually abused by her father. She became a fierce feminist, who insisted they accept her at medical school and managed to pay her way. She was a brilliant student and devoted her life to the medical care of women, particularly poor women.

7

Thereisaquestion," Captain Voll said, interrupting him in his office, "as to how to dispose of, the various ... uh, body parts."

"What do you suggest?" the Inspector asked.

"As we cannot identify any complete bodies," Voll said, "I suggest one grave. I have already made arrangements, subject to your approval."

"How many pieces are there, as of now?" the Inspector asked.

Voll returned with a list. "We have eight hearts, thirty pieces of livers, and portions of five brains. We have five hands, two left, three right, five left legs, and four right legs, no pairs, fourteen portions of temples, eye sockets included, and approximately fifteen undistinguishable pieces and bits of flesh and bone. All told," Voll continued, "we have eighty-six body parts. All female. The only exception is the body of the woman in the park, of course, which, has been returned to her family."

"That can't be the same murderer," the Inspector said, suddenly angry. "She never got cut up."

"I believe," Voll said, "as I told you. That he was interrupted. He knows we are looking."

I cannot tell by the manuscript if Cecily was pregnant or simply imagined this at the time. If so, it was very likely the result of her love affair with the young Russian cavalry captain she met at Baron Tedesco's Ball. In any event, Inspector LeBlanc knew all of these feminist women and was one of the few men that Pelletier respected.

How Cecily wound up staying in Natalie Barney's salon, which attracted radicals and lesbians, is sheer conjecture. Surely Cecily's mother would have fainted at the thought, although Barney was, of course, an enormously intelligent and sympathetic woman, and it is unlikely that Cecily could have found a safer harbor.

It is clear from the manuscript that she was there only a short time, until both the Countess and the Inspector were able to prevail upon her to return to Vienna. The incident was hushed up, and no one was the wiser. There is evidence, however, that Cecily's mother was treated by doctors in Vienna for an extreme nervous disorder which developed during this period.

"Perhaps," the Inspector said, weary. His head seemed to him quite suddenly insupportable, heavy, like a rock on his neck.

"Bury them," he said.

8

Cecily came back from Paris a different person. She had become a feminist and seemed to have changed her point of view on everything. She said that the feminists in Paris were much stronger than in Austria or Germany.[1] She was much more serious and, in a certain way, more lighthearted. Still, she had her sarcastic remarks, "Oh, no one," she told Aunt Ida, "takes Mrs. Wharton or Mr. James very seriously at all. They are really old fuddy duddies among the real cognoscenti."

"Among the real cognoscenti," Aunt Ida said, "there is always a great deal of competition about who is most 'real,' unfortunately."

"Well, all my friends in Montparnasse," Cecily said, "don't think they are very avant-garde at all."

"One can be avant-garde and uninteresting," Aunt Ida said, "although people don't speak of it."

I said nothing but watched this from afar. It reminded me of something I heard Mrs. Wharton say one evening when someone asked her about that same old provocative argument—if a "woman writer," were different from a "man writer." It had made her angry, and she said, "A writer is a writer, different subjects attract different individuals," or something to that effect. But when the woman, who was a photographer, asked the next question Mrs. Wharton seemed so surprised that at first she could not answer.

The woman asked, "If a man writer attempted a certain subject which had previously been the subject of women writers such as, for example, the interior lives of women . . ." At this Mr. James quipped, "Interior lives are, I should hope, the province of all writers." "I

---

[1] This was not, strictly speaking, true in every area. French women were, in fact, among the last to get the vote, which they finally were granted in 1945.

mean," the photographer persisted, "if a woman writer were to attempt something previously thought of as male, say, an adventure of the sea or even revealing a man's feelings, she'd be attacked, wouldn't you say?"

"If it were good, she wouldn't be attacked, if it weren't, she would," Mrs. Wharton had replied forcefully. And then the woman, leaning forward in a most insinuating way, said to Mrs. Wharton, "Now, really think about it. Do you think you would publish everything you might want to write? Would you be afraid of no subject, for example, a subject that would be less, shall we say, shocking for a man?" The woman's eyes had narrowed. To my surprise Mrs. Wharton's face turned red. She took a sip of ice water and then said very primly. "I believe I am free to pursue any subject of interest to me, and I do." Soon after this she excused herself, and I found her on the terrace where she was having a very loud and forceful argument with Aunt Ida, but when I asked Aunt Ida later what it was about, she simply said it was "very complicated," and she would explain it to me some day, which meant she hoped I would forget about it, but I did not forget about it. I thought about it again, just a few days later when Cecily brought up the subject of being in a woman writer's novel or a man's and then announced something which surprised us all.

I had noticed a striking change in Cecily, which was that Cecily seemed to me quite suddenly happy. Something had happened to her in Paris that made her much different. This was confirmed when she quite suddenly said, "I don't want to be a heroine in anyone's novel anymore. As much as I admire Mr. James and Mrs. Wharton. *I* want to decide what happens and who I am." When she had first announced this everyone seemed quite surprised.

"So you don't wish to be Isabel Archer, then?" Aunt Ida had asked.

"No," Cecily said. "Even though I now think that she went back to Italy only to *assist* Pansy and that she would have left Mr. Osmond eventually, so you see she was not condemned at all." We all thought this was a very interesting interpretation, and not one that would have occurred to us, and that we all had to discuss this further, but I envied Cecily her statements. She seemed to be free of some constriction that I still felt very mired in, although I did not wish to be a character at all, at least as far as I knew.

9

It had gotten unexpectedly warm, the way it sometimes does in the early spring, and the Countess had invited us to go on a journey to a place just outside Vienna, by the river. I was quite pleased to see that Sabina, who was pursuing her medical studies most successfully, had agreed to join us. I think it was this change in the weather, which made it seem like summer, as much as the conversation, because all of a sudden the Countess stood up and suggested that though it was late in the afternoon we should all go boating on the river.

We agreed and there was a lot of excitement as we made our way down to the boathouse. I thought it was something more than the weather, as Aunt Ida and the Countess had been arguing, as they usually did, about very controversial matters. This time it had been about women and history, and Sabina had also gotten extremely excited about it. Others in the restaurant had begun to look around at us; we were causing quite a scene. As we walked to the boathouse I asked Aunt Ida why she was so vehement that women, regardless of the historical circumstance, would not behave in the warrior-like ways of men. I said I thought maybe the Countess had a point.

"Don't tell me that," she said, her eyes flashing. "It leads nowhere. Nowhere. The Countess is wrong. She believes it is a question of the system. It is not. Women will never be as cruel as men, if they are running it." The Countess overheard this. "Oh Ida," she said, turning her face, "I wish what you were saying were *true*. I can't quite believe it, as you know. I think the responsibility is with the system, and of course we . . . oh, look." She pointed suddenly to another boat out on the river that was just coming in to the boathouse.

"You see," she said, skipping ahead of us, "they are renting already!" and then she dashed on so quickly we had to hurry to catch up.

10

There was a great deal of chatter as we made our way down the steep stairs to the boathouse. Outside were canoes, and rowboats and rather long, gondola-like boats.

"We can't take those," the Countess said, "they tip too easily. And the current can be quite strong." She turned to Sabina. "Can you row?"

"Oh, very well," Sabina said, and turning to Ida, "and Ida too, I am sure."

"Well, it so happens I have never done it but I am certain with instruction I can," Aunt Ida said, and Cecily and I both said that we were strong rowers indeed.

We were very disappointed when the man at the boathouse explained that he wasn't renting yet as there was still ice in the river; the boat on the river belonged to his worker. There was more chatter, and I saw that the Countess had soon talked him into it. He had us sign some papers and the Countess paid generously, and we left our purses and parasols in the small office. Sabina was about to bring her parasol for it was quite sunny, but the Countess said there was no point crowding the boat.

The boatman brought a small green boat around. We were soon seated safely in it, Sabina in the rear, with the Countess, and Cecily and myself in the center rowing, and Aunt Ida perched in front like a lookout.

"Oh this is so thrilling," Aunt Ida said. The boatman told us to watch out for ice chunks and to be back in an hour, while it was still light. We soon settled down except for Aunt Ida who had never been in a boat before and had to be advised not to move about so vigorously as she could tip us over. After that she sat so still the Countess told her she could relax as she resembled nothing so much as a masthead.

With little effort Cecily and I had rowed us out into the center of the river, where we noticed the current was much stronger than it had been along the shore, and soon we were swept quite swiftly down the river. It was after a few minutes that the Countess remarked that we should attempt to go closer to shore and we should not get ourselves so far down river that we might experience difficulty returning.

"There have been times, you know," she said, "when the current gets treacherous and we have been forced to put ashore and find someone to take us back to town."

Upon hearing this I said to Cecily that I wished to turn back now. I was surprised Cecily did not argue and supposed she must have been as alarmed as I was at how far from the boathouse we had already traveled. We first directed the boat across the current toward the shore, and then as we got close to it, we turned it around, with some difficulty, and with the Countess navigating who should row backward and who should row forward we avoided a near collision with the bank.

We found ourselves rowing very hard, even though the current was much slower closer to shore. The Countess and Sabina went back to talking in the rear of the boat, and Aunt Ida was looking forward, and Cecily and I were simply enjoying the difficulty of pulling the oars against the current. It was only a few minutes later, or so it seemed to me, that Sabina offered to change places with me and I gratefully accepted her offer. My favorite part of boating was to lie back, my head tilted over the side, and look at the reflection of my face rippling in the water. The Countess insisted that we bring the boat almost to the bank, as she was not confident we would make the switch without mishap, so we did and pretty soon I was relaxing in the back with the Countess as Sabina and Cecily, who seemed tireless, were rowing away in the middle.

We had not gone far on our return when we noticed a very large piece of ice suddenly floating by. Sabina was making an effort, but I noticed we were not moving much at all. When the Countess asked if she could relieve her, Sabina said no. It all seemed perfectly benign, until we felt the wind pick up and clouds covered the sun.

"Can you go faster?" the Countess asked worriedly. "We are losing the light."

Sabina, nearly breathless, put forth more effort and Cecily's face was very pink, but she refused to give it up. And then in minutes, the boat started to turn. I had closed my eyes and felt something of a jolt.

Sabina yelled, "Oh-h," Cecily cried out, and Sabina's oar was seen floating on the water not far from the boat. Cecily attempted to turn the boat back toward's Sabina's oar.

"We hit something," the Countess said worriedly, but Sabina was leaning quite far over the edge of the boat attempting to reach her oar. Just as her hand reached out to grab the oar, she let out a scream and fell forward as if reaching for something in the water. Sabina's face was only inches from the water, and had tipped the boat dangerously, which the Countess realized and threw her weight to counterbalance, and mine, grabbing me to the far side as she commanded Sabina to let go of whatever she had and get back into the boat. Cecily and Ida were desperately trying to pull her back by her skirts and finally they succeeded. But when we looked at Sabina's face it was white with shock. She sat staring and her mouth opened, but no sound came out.

"What is it?" Aunt Ida said, aghast at Sabina's expression. Then *she* looked into the water and cried out, "Oh my God!" and stood up just as Cecily yelled, "Get down!" The boat swung around again and the Countess and I were pitched nearly over the side, and that was when I saw it. Floating there, where I expected to see my own reflection, was a woman's face, with long blond hair, and wide-open, frozen eyes.

I shrieked, just as Aunt Ida stood up again and Cecily reached forward to pull Aunt Ida down to her seat and in that moment lost her footing and fell on top of Sabina, pulling Ida with her. Aunt Ida fell over the two of them into the water and the next thing I knew, the boat had capsized and we were all in the water, gasping and coughing, the boat's bottom floating upright and the freezing current pushing us. "Oh God, oh God," Aunt Ida was gasping, and Sabina seemed to come out of her shock and started yelling that we should all hold onto the boat, we must not let go of the boat. And then she urged us to kick, but our skirts were so heavy I did not know if I could kick, and she was yelling that we must hang on and try to push towards shore.

The water was very cold and I was quite terrified. I could feel how heavy my skirts were and I felt like something was pulling me under the water. I could feel myself going down, down under, and soon my face was so close to the dead woman that my lips touched her. I was not afraid, I felt quite warm and then I felt the Countess' arm, surprisingly strong under my own, pulling me back up as she yelled to me,

"You must hang on, my God, you must." Her voice yelled out, *"Help, help! Someone help!"* and it seemed forever before some fishermen were around us, hauling us up into their boat.

One of the men had taken off his clothes and had jumped into the water to help us. I could see now that he was almost naked as he stood next to us on the deck. By now there was a thick mist all around us, and our teeth were chattering. The fishermen ushered us below, saying we must get out of our wet clothes, and they gave us men's clothes, which they insisted we wear.

Some time later we marched back up to the top of the deck, and by then the men had found it. They were out there with lanterns. They had turned our rowboat over and lodged underneath was the frozen body Sabina and Ida had seen, and when I saw it lying there in the water, as I looked over the side of the fishing boat by the light of the lanterns, my heart stopped and I thought I would not breathe again. The Countess looking at the frozen face in the water shuddered and looked as if she might faint. Sabina, like a person in a trance, moved forward as if to touch it and had to be restrained by one of the fishermen. Cecily, white and still, stared as I did; the frozen face just under the water, the most terrifying sight I had ever seen. It was, at that moment, as if the water were a mirror and I saw my own face reflected in its surface as if my face were that of the dead woman floating still and cold beneath it. Aunt Ida was crying, and by now Sabina was sitting on the deck holding her head in her hands. I do not know what happened after that. There were suddenly police officials around us and I remember seeing the Countess coming off the boat behind me, which meant I must have been first, and she was dressed in pants and a man's shirt and cap, and so was Cecily, directly behind her, with her hair up under the cap, and Sabina too, in a long coat and a wool hat over her ears, and Aunt Ida, as if all of them were in shock and transformed and almost not real.

It is the kind of thing that happens and you think one thing, and then some time later when you are seated in the parlor and there is tea and cakes and you are in your own clothes again, that you think you could not have seen it. It could not have happened. You were not nearly drowned in the river with a dead woman swirling near your fingertips, a dead woman with your own face on hers, and a man nearly naked pulling you through the current and up the ladder, freezing and cold and terrified, and then looking in the mirror, warm now, and seeing yourself dressed like a man, as if it were all a dream and you did not know if this could be happening or even if it was happening.

It is later, later that it all changes. As the thing merges into your memory, it seems to merge equally into your forgetting, and it all becomes quite *nicer,* more presentable, so that when I found myself talking to Mother and Father, I said it was all quite horrible, but somehow it wasn't. It was suddenly my voice that was saying, "Oh it was quite a lovely afternoon and we were having a lovely row upon the water and then this dreadful thing occurred." And that was all I would or could say and the words "this dreadful thing occurred," were not words at all, but simply sounds, for they pretended to describe it and said nothing, nothing at all about my own face lying dead frozen and still in the water.

11

The only information the Inspector was certain of was that there was a near accident and some body had been discovered down by the river. He had gone as quickly as possible to the scene and saw by the time he arrived that a small crowd had gathered. He picked up his pace and hurried forward to the river's edge.

When he got there he found a pale-faced man yelling and bending over, and was surprised to see that it was the normally unflappable Captain Voll who called, "They have found a body in the river."

Then as the Inspector turned around he saw on a huge rope and grappling hook that had been flung over a beam for leverage, the body they had raised from the river shining in the lights, like a huge silver fish, a woman's body covered in ice, swinging and turning in the lantern glow. The hair was long and blond and stuck to the body like seaweed. As he approached he felt the coffee and cakes of the afternoon rise to his chest and a burning pain seized him. He looked at the face which, frozen, preserved by the cold, seemed to him disturbingly alive. He wondered if she could have been alive when she entered the river, so natural did her expression seem. The water had frozen her dress and the necklace on her neck so that she seemed as if she had been stopped in transit, eyes open, as if, when the ice melted she would step out and proceed to Demel's for tea. The combination of eerie life-likeness and morbidity in the figure caused the Inspector to shudder.

"No one who looks at it doesn't get bothered," the man with the grappling hook and the winch said to the Inspector.

"Who found this?" the Inspector snapped, turning to Voll. His voice had an odd metallic quality. Suddenly he was having trouble hearing. He kept hearing an echo in his head as Voll spoke, as if he were in a cave.

"Some women in a rowboat, capsized, picked up by a fishing scow. ... They've been sent home ... just in shock ... no injuries ... ," he heard it dimly as he studied the body.

"Who is this woman?" he said softly. "Do we know?" There was a pause. "The dressmaker," Voll said, "Mme. Pacquin." Voll turned away.

"Give me a torch," the Inspector said, one hand reaching out as he touched the frozen head. He held the lighted torch over her hair, the ice melting in thick chucks. "She must have been just below the surface in a shallow spot," he said. "The water runs too swiftly further out to freeze." The others watched the Inspector's hand moving through the frozen hair, lifting it delicately from the neck.

"It is unquestionably Mme. Pacquin," Voll said. "And unquestionably a suicide." He held up some jewels. "We found these, large stones in her pockets, in order to drown."

The Inspector ignored him, bent in a close examination of the body. Then he stood up.

"Not suicide," he said.

"Really, Inspector," Voll sounded impatient, "does a woman put stones into her pockets normally?"

The Inspector turned to him. "*She* didn't put them there. There is a small, distinct bullet hole in the base of her neck. She was murdered."

12

It is true that in the ensuing days I could neither eat nor drink. I moved about as in a fever. When people spoke, I looked away. For long hours I lay alone in my room, crying. Timothy insisted on a doctor. I refused. I had seen only the one body in the river. But many nights in my dreams I saw hundreds of them. When the ice broke, like dead fish in a stagnant stream, they washed ashore. I woke up screaming.

Cecily approached my bed and confronted me and I, to my utter astonishment, pushed her away, both of us surprised at the resources of my strength—I opened the door to our room and shoved her outside. Then I locked the door and spoke to no one. I wanted to sleep, only sleep, but never to dream. I was sick at heart.

Once, I heard whispers outside the door.

"It's that horrible thing she witnessed," Mother was crying. I heard the Countess softly imploring me to open the door. I could not move. Nor for Aunt Ida.

I do not know how much later it was, but I awoke to find Mother and a doctor sitting on the bed opposite me. Mother was quite calm and offered me some tea.

I was feeling much better and knew I had behaved quite disgracefully.

Sometime later I descended the stairs and ventured into the living room. The Inspector was there, waiting for me and I felt myself grow faint at the sight of him. I feared now more than ever that he would make me tell.

13

Then days passed. No one spoke further of it and I found I soon could not recall very much at all. Only the sunlight on the water and something about the boat tipping. Then I saw the Countess on the gangplank in a man's hat and coat. I forgot everything else. As far as I knew I had seen nothing. I forgot the woman's face, and to some degree, of course, my own. It is so strange now when I think of it that something so powerful and so terrifying is forgotten, as if it never occurred at all.

14

The Inspector turned sharply, his hand on his gun. He had heard footsteps and he had seen something move in the shadows. Was he being followed, or was it the footsteps of the invisible who followed him? The footsteps of his fears on nights like this could be loud. He turned again. Sometimes he heard footsteps. The footsteps were not too bad. The worst of it was when he heard the sound of the wings, large black wings, brushing against his hair.

15

Sabina had agreed, finally, to accompany the woman Carl called his grandmother, Olga, on one of her walks through the Inner City. Sabina knew the old woman was strong, but she did not know how long she could keep up this pace. They had started out early and briskly and maintained that pace for some time amid the winding alleys and streets. The sun was higher now and Sabina was feeling cheerful, even though tired. The old woman had a delightful sense of humor and seemed today to be in an altogether different mood than the last time she had seen her.

They had just entered the Ninth District and turned down a small, narrow street when the old woman suddenly stopped. She turned pale and leaned weakly against the side of the alleyway. "What is it?" Sabina said. The old woman said nothing, but pointed to a doorway —number 32. "There," she said, "I saw it there."

It took some minutes before Sabina could get her to tell the story of a scene the old woman had witnessed there many years ago. It seemed she had come upon a distraught woman who was beating a baby, screaming, "I wanted a girl!" to the point where she had to be restrained and the police were called. As the old woman spoke it was so vivid Sabina felt a chill run up her spine.

Soon Sabina was relieved to see a familiar cafe, the Schwartzspanier-hof, loom up at the next block and persuaded Olga to have a coffee.

As they entered the cafe, however, Sabina noticed the old woman became weak. Sabina, concerned, attempted to get her to eat some soup, but she would have none of it. She said in a quiet voice that she needed to go home. Sabina got up immediately and spoke to the manager to arrange a carriage for them. The old woman said very little as they waited. As they drove, the old woman sat in the corner of the coach, silent, her face drawn. Sabina knew it was here, in Vienna itself, that she had seen the red sky she had spoken about that weekend in the country.

"It's here, isn't it?" Sabina said. "The fire you saw, it is here in Vienna."

The old woman said wearily, "It is here. In Russia. Everywhere. I am looking for a safe place for you, somewhere, I will try to find it." She held her head in her hands then, and said no more. Sabina thought there was nothing to be done with this desperate subject. Whatever the nightmare was, what disturbed Sabina more was that the old woman saw no escape. . . . Some horror in Vienna yes, starting here, but one that spread out into the world? What kind of pogrom was this, a pogrom from mankind itself, an exile from the world?

16

SABINA'S DREAM

In the morning she would blame the dream on her exhaustion. But it unnerved her.

In the dream she was walking down a long narrow street. When she came to a house, the number 32 seemed to glow from a window over the door. She was afraid and walked quickly past the house to the corner store.

She entered the shop and felt her body go rigid.

There, not three feet in front of her, was a hideous woman with a long grey skirt and a kind of tri-cornered black hat standing in front of a baby carriage. She felt a signal of foreboding unlike anything she had ever known. What was it about this woman and the baby carriage? What strange omen was this? Sabina attempted to move away, toward the section where the fruit was kept in baskets, but the woman backed up suddenly and whirled around glaring, as if Sabina had interfered with her course. She was holding the baby in a long white christening gown and cap and the baby was screaming, its face red and distorted, its head monstrous. In the seconds it took for all of this to transpire Sabina also raised her eyes to the black-hatted face. This was also the ugliest woman she had ever seen. Her face was huge and bulbous, and full of creases and a sneering expression.

In a wrathful and contemptuous expression the woman shouted, "Watch where you're going, you fool!" As she snarled like an animal, the woman's spittle reached Sabina's face, and she drew back as the woman screamed, "Out, out, out of my way!" In that moment the baby's flying hand reached up toward the woman's upper lip, where a large boil was rising, and hit the crust of it so the pus streamed out and dripped down her chin. Sabina let out a small cry, an "uhh," as her revulsion registered on her face and she turned away, as if to hide in the celery stalks and carrots across the way while the woman, slapping and screaming, rolled the baby about in its white gown, whipping the ends of the gown up and over the tiny hands, binding it, as the baby cried. The woman in her fury now took the baby's cap from its head and stuffed it into its mouth, throttling it, screaming and hitting the baby with a stick.

"I wanted a girl, I wanted a girl, I wanted a girl!" she cried as a man, a doctor, rushed forward and grabbed the stick. He had blue eyes, like Carl, and a black beard like Freud. He struggled with the woman, but she pushed him down and then, with a large stick, began to beat the child. "I wanted a girl, I wanted a girl!" And then Sabina approached and the woman beat her, screaming.

The doctor now turned into a policeman. He had a pencil and pad and questioned the woman. "Do you have other children at home?"

The woman, suddenly docile, nodded.

"Well, then, any daughters?"

The woman nodded.

"So what matters then, this one. What possible difference could this make?" he asked.

"What possible difference could this make?" the policeman yelled, and Sabina woke up.[1]

---

[1] There is some question as to whether or not this was a memory or vision of Olga's, whether we are in the presence here of prophecy or coincidence. It so happened that Hitler's mother did see doctors in Vienna. Hitler was born in 1889. Whether Olga could conceivably have seen this woman, I do not know, but I find that degree of coincidence unlikely. Sabina's dream seems to be a reenactment of Olga's description to Sabina. Sabina was probably extremely agitated by the suggestion that she shared the old woman's "psychic" powers, and yet may have identified with her in some complex way. Whatsoever it was that Olga witnessed, Sabina's dream does raise an important question.

There are those who find this a specious if not trivial issue—the idea of reducing the horrors of the Third Reich to the simplicity of a mere transformation in a zygote. Certainly if Hitler had been born a female child he would not have risen to leadership of the Nazi party. That does not mean, unfortunately, that there would have been no Nazi party, nor does it mean there would have been no Third Reich. The fact remains that there were women manning, so to speak, the gas ovens in concentration camps. Certain feminists disagree with me and believe that is precisely what they were doing; i.e., "manning," that is to say internalizing male values and attitudes. I confess I do not find it specious or trivial. I regard the entire matter as most troubling. There is no easy answer to this question of gender and history as you yourself, dear reader, must know. For you yourself must have made judgments and assumptions about *my* tone, *my* knowledge, *my* expression, and these judgments have already described to you my gender, which is also my authority, is it not so?

17

On an excuse, Stekal had suggested he accompany the Inspector to his lodging because of the lateness of the hour. Stekal was a loyal policeman. He was assigned to the Inspector. He would protect him. The integrity of Vienna depended upon it. But the Inspector was difficult, he wanted no protection. "He thinks he is invincible," Stekal mused. But Stekal had heard the footsteps; he had seen the disappearing forms; on one occasion he had heard a shot. This was no imagined threat. The murderer was close on the Inspector's heels.

"Perhaps, sir," Stekal said when they arrived at the boarding house, "I should walk in with you."

"What?" the Inspector said, "to my room? Do you think I need a nursemaid?"

"Sir, there is someone—surely you have heard him?" He looked around. "Sir, someone was following us."

"I heard it," he said.

"What if he waits in your room?" Stekal said. "If he gets you sir, then he will get me."

"But I hear nothing now," he said. "No one has access to my room, Stekal," the Inspector said. "Not even the landlady." He pulled the key from his pocket. "You see, I am the only one with a key." Stekal stood there nervously.

"Go home, to bed," the Inspector said. "I will know if he is about." He patted his hip, "And I have protection. Besides," he said, "I have the dog. He waits inside for me." The Inspector nodded and Stekal walked off.

When the Inspector climbed the stairs he heard the creaking in the steps, and noticed the landlady did not appear to complain, as she so often did at late night entries. He listened at his door. Something was wrong. Normally the dog was at the door, barking and scratching. He turned the key quietly in the lock and pressed himself back against the wall, slowly letting the door swing open. Nothing. He crept in and then leapt back into the hallway, his heart racing.

No sound. No sound from the dog. Slowly, his gun in his hand he leaned around the doorjamb and lit the lamp. Nothing moved. All was still. And then his eyes crossed to the bed. The sheets and blankets were bleeding red where the black dog for solace had crawled into the Inspector's place, under the covers.

"Oh God," he said, not thinking, and rushed into the room. The animal was dead.

He banged on the landlady's door. To his relief, she eventually appeared, complaining about the hour. "My dog is dead," he said, "shot. This is important. Did you hear it?"

18

The Countess had urged Sabina to join Mrs. Wharton and herself at a cafe. The Countess found Mrs. Wharton an exhausting if inspiring companion. The woman was astonishingly well informed on architectural history and they had spent the morning looking at Adolf Loos' and Wagner's buildings and their plans for future constructions. When it came to architecture, the Countess thought, she had surprisingly avant-garde tastes.

Still, she was relieved to see Sabina enter the cafe, until she saw her expression.

"Why Sabina, whatever is the matter?" the Countess asked. "You look as if you had seen a ghost."

Sabina at first would say nothing and then she told both of them about Olga and the prophecy.

"Really," the Countess said, "you can't go around believing old women who make prophecies. It's disgusting in my opinion. When you remove free will from life you remove life. I am surprised," she said with annoyance at Sabina, "that you would support such rot, quite honestly."

"It . . . it isn't something I ordinarily would . . . or could accept," Sabina said quietly. "She said it is possible to avoid it, but, but she wasn't sure . . . then I had this dream." Sabina was trembling.

"You seem quite distraught," Mrs. Wharton said kindly. "It is, I must confess, difficult on occasion to be in Vienna. It is, in a way, too disturbingly stimulating."

"What do you mean?" Sabina said.

"Well," Mrs. Wharton said, looking at the Countess, "all this waltzing, all these balls, amid this Secessionist art, all these *individuals* who agree with Mach that there are no individuals, it's all well, rather contradictory, and then those dinner conversations! It is bad enough to be in Paris, but here . . . people like Kraus . . . one gets the sense no one believes in anything."

"Schnitzler was right," the Countess said. "What was it he said? We live in a time when no one believes in anything, not even themselves, and they are quite right not to do so."

"But it's not possible," Mrs. Wharton said, with mounting annoyance, "it is all sophistry. Of course people believe in things. Even nothing is something to believe in. It's a very dangerous fad, I feel, all this questioning about language. It leads to nihilism, which is always dangerous."

"I really don't understand you, Sabina," the Countess said. "Vienna has problems. Modern life has problems. I would be the first to acknowledge this. But this . . . this horror you speak of . . . Not here."

Edith Wharton was looking at the two of them. The fact was she didn't know exactly what was going on. Sabina was an impressionable young woman. And the Countess, she thought, in some profound way was new to hope, and would savagely defend it. As for herself, she wasn't so sure. Hope for a better future for herself and for mankind, surely was part of her. But you couldn't have hope, she firmly believed, without a profound sense of the individual, of personhood, of that very fundamental experience she felt in her own life that Morton Fullerton had released to her. Something was tossed up in the brilliant light of Vienna, and she herself was not sure what it was. She didn't understand the business about the Jews. She thought they made too much of it. But certainly something was in the air. Some assault on self, some assault on the individual, that could arise here, that could crush the single voice. Still, when she thought about it it did seem very unlikely. Not here, nor in Paris, surely, not in these places of such erudition and learning.

"My dear," she said to Sabina, "there are too many highly educated people here, *cultured* people, for things to go so terribly wrong, don't you think? I mean, look around you."

But Sabina could not look up. She was losing her mind, she thought. She must forget her dream, and work hard to think of more productive things. It must be all because of her powerful feelings for Carl,[1] she was not through with him; she had allowed herself to become too emotional again.

19

Captain Voll began to wonder more and more about the Inspector's methods. He knew he was upset about his dog, but his behavior seemed desperate.

"I hear," Voll had said, "that you have ordered another autopsy. I admit I was mistaken. It was not suicide, despite the note and the stones. But since clearly she was shot, what could possibly come from an autopsy?" He stood in the doorway. "It is so, so . . . illogical," he said. "I must tell you, Inspector, you seem driven to look for endless

[1] Although I am not sympathetic to Jung's writings myself, I feel I must point out that this manuscript constructs a rather unfair portrait of a man who made serious contributions to the understanding of the human mind. It is also important to note that when Spielrein went on to study with Freud she felt herself to be caught in a very difficult conflict between the two men. Aldo Carotenuto in his book *A Secret Symmetry* (Pantheon, 1982) believes she was central to Jung's concepts of male and female—i.e., animus and anima. She sent her dreams to Jung, who believed that Freud's theories were "overrationalizing."

In an interesting letter to Jung at a later time, Sabina felt an overwhelming need to attempt to synthesize the theories of the men. Sabina wrote to Jung: "You should have the courage to recognize Freud in all his grandeur, even if you do not agree with him on every point, even if in the process you might have to credit Freud with many of your own accomplishments. Only then will you be completely free, and only then will you be the greater one." (Letter, Spielrein to Jung presumably of 27–8 January 1918, Carotenuto, p. 189.)

Spielrein continued to study psychoanalysis with Freud and eventually became a psychoanalyst. She returned to Russia during the Russian revolution in 1917, firm in the hope that the promises of a "real revolution" would be contained in Freudian therapy. It is believed she was murdered in the Stalin purges.

clues." The Inspector looked up. Voll's logical mind was perplexed, the Inspector could see, which gratified him. He smiled to himself. Wait until Voll discovered the next move.

20

THE MUSHROOM FEAST

When the Inspector announced he was going on a picnic with ten of the suspects, Captain Voll had been open-mouthed. He saw now that he meant to go through with it. He looked wonderingly at the group the Inspector had gathered. The Inspector entered the police station and asked if Voll had seen the large picnic hamper he had prepared. He had gone to some trouble to be certain the hamper was packed with the proper wines, which included a magnificent white that he had bought for the occasion, and a variety of cheeses and breads, as well as Valentina's Zwetschkenknoedel, Alma's chocolate sacher torte and Lisette's mohnstrudel,[1] not to mention some of his own sugared harps.

He finally unearthed the hamper, which had been shoved into a closet in another room, and all went outside and got back into carriages. The Inspector and the Countess, Mrs. Wharton, Mr. Fullerton, and Mr. James were in the first, and we were in the second. The Freud family followed. Sabina and Carl Jung could not come, as they were already at Jung's country house. The spot he was taking us to, the Inspector said, was well known as a site for wild mushrooms. Although the Inspector had brought many delicacies with him, the plan was to gather wild mushrooms, and to bring them home for dinner in order to have a "mushroom feast." It was some time before we arrived at the spot, but when we did, we eagerly descended from the carriages and ran to put down our blankets and our bundles. The Inspector showed those of us who didn't know what to look for, and we all broke up into groups.

There was a very relaxed atmosphere, and everyone seemed quite

---

[1] Plum cake, a chocolate tart, and a poppyseed cake.

delighted to be there. No one was even talking about the murder; we were just running about gathering mushrooms. Mr. James was a scrupulously careful collector; he would bring each mushroom to the Inspector, asking, "Is this all right?" meaning was it safe to eat, and the Inspector would nod and Mr. James would put it in his sack. The only one who didn't check with the Inspector was Dr. Freud, who said he knew all about mushrooms.

Later when we had settled on our blankets, and broken out the cheeses, I looked up and saw that the entire outing had the most lovely air of absolute delight about it. There was Mr. Fullerton in a splendid white suit leaning against the tree, his straw hat cocked just so; and Mr. James, leaning back on one elbow, his long legs in brown tweed twill stretched out on Aunt Ida's pink quilt, with his hat off and his brown hair blowing just a little in the wind; and Mrs. Wharton, seated below Mr. Fullerton in a bright yellow dress, with a large hat full of veiling and blue roses, which had caused quite a sensation. She kept tilting her chin up to look at Mr. Fullerton, who bent down, on his haunches, and she kept laughing, and pushing the veil back and raising her hand across her brow to shield her eyes from the sun.

The late morning sun had come through the trees in long golden bolts, striking off of Mr. Fullerton's hat, which had on the side a bright brass button where the ribbon was clasped. I could see into Mrs. Wharton's eyes, and as I watched her I thought she was prettier than I realized. That chin, so redoubtable when you looked at it coming towards you, was now, tilted upwards toward Mr. Fullerton, another kind of chin entirely, ending in a soft, deliberate curve down her neck, like the wing of a bird in flight, that fine bone that bore the bird so elegantly was the bone, I knew, that also beat relentlessly five hundred times a minute in a high wind, a tireless formation of will and grace, borne now, I thought, by unexpected gusts. Sheer pleasure tilted that chin upward in precisely that position to bear, just then, the weight of imagined yet undared heights, and I remained fascinated by Mrs. Wharton in that bright light, and Mr. Fullerton who was, by far, the most handsome and beguiling man I had ever met, transfixed by this transformation, to see a woman of such unnerving composure suddenly blush, just a little, in the midst of her laugh and press her palms down the summery fold of her dress in sheer exultation of being, in that moment, the precise object of Mr. Fullerton's rapt attention.

So complete were she, Mr. Fullerton, the sunlight, Mr. James' legs, and Aunt Ida's pink blanket that I was transported, and saw them set against all the scurrying others, like so many colored chalk sketches, like little blots of blue and pink and red moving in and out of this canvas in the midst of which stood someone, something real and so splendid, my breath did catch at this, and I saw what the others did not see—Cecily sat to the side of Mr. James deep in thought, examining a leaf, and had just awkwardly pushed herself up on an elbow, and the Countess was looking at the Inspector—I saw in one glance why painters painted and why composers wrote songs and the rest of us just sat and stared; I saw it was this golden, hidden, treasured moment when the felt things leapt forth from behind the light dazzling your eyes as you saw it and did not see it, but you felt it like the wind on your skin, the smell of roses in the air, that sharp quickening when the shape of a chin and the feeling in your breast were all one grand and lilting flight.

It was that evening at dinner that it happened. The Countess' cook had prepared the mushrooms, which were to be served as a first course, according to the Inspector's recipe. There was a great variety of them, and only Cecily said she thought they were disgusting and she wanted no part of eating them. The rest of us were all served when the Countess raised her glass and holding it, twinkling in the candlelight, offered a toast, "To pleasure and happiness."

"Oh glorious thing!" Dr. Freud said, poised with the mushroom on the fork and holding it up to the light and then, just as he was about to put the mushroom in his mouth, the Inspector cried out suddenly and hurled himself across the table, crashing through the flowers in the centerpiece, spilling the water into the roast and vegetables on the table, knocking over wine glasses, and shoving the stricken doctor off his chair.

Mother screamed. Aunt Ida went oh, oh, oh. The Countess gasped as the Inspector's large bulk landed half sprawled across the doctor, who lay on his back beneath him, kicking like a crushed insect. As Dr. Freud yelled, "Get off, get off, come to your senses!" the Inspector climbed glumly off the table, brushed the gravy, flowers, and vegetables off his shirt and turned to us with a stern and savage look and said soberly, "*Do not* touch your food or your drink."

"What is the meaning of this outrage!" Freud glowered.

"Your life, my good doctor; you were about to eat *Amantis Canthraxis.*" He turned and reached for the mushroom and held it up. "It bears a dangerous resemblance to the most reliable chanterelle. Doubtless you were right to be confused. Fortunately, this purple bruise was visible to me or it would have killed you in an instant."

A strange silence fell on everyone. The doctor sat there stupefied. Then Dr. Freud picked up the mushroom. "I have eaten this many times. I do not believe . . . this is not . . . ," he hesitated.

"Smell it," the Inspector said.

The doctor held the mushroom to his nose.

"Do you smell it?"

The doctor looked at him, his fierce, black eyes full of astonishment. "Yes."

"The smell of death," the Inspector said.

"It is not possible," Freud said. "How . . . how is it it grows here? I have never . . ." The doctor was shaken.

"It is a fluke," the Inspector said, "a fluke of nature, like you, like me. The mushroom is to nature as we are to history. Unexpected. Only partially explained. Like our entire species, really, freaks of nature. There is much to be learned here. Natural calamities posing as the most innocent of pleasures. Dangerous resemblances. Imprecise knowledge. To take the imitation for the original has so many dangerous consequences."

There were many murmurs then, the kind of talk that erupts when everyone is recovering from a shock.

"I am grateful for your intervention, Inspector," the doctor said finally slowly and formally, "although I do not support your philosophy. I do not regard myself as a freak of nature. As for your own inclusion in that genre, I leave it to your self-knowledge. Nor do I suffer from imprecise knowledge. *Incomplete,* perhaps, in regard to human beings, but not, I hope, *imprecise.* In regard to mushrooms, my expertise is less than my passion, and so an error might be anticipated. It is not likely to find a poisonous mushroom growing in that forest, there must be an explanation."

"Follow me," the Inspector said, and we all followed him to the kitchen. The cook had not prepared all of the mushrooms as there were too many. He went to the mushroom basket and, emptying all the mushrooms onto the middle of the floor, motioned the rest of us to step aside. The mushrooms, brown and white and milky, and some orange, filled the air with a delicate damp fragrance. The Inspector took them one by one, held them under his nostrils, and tossed them into a pile. After a minute he took one, said, "Poisonous," and tossed it into another pile. We watched this ritual of separation until the Inspector had accumulated a large pile of poisonous mushrooms.

"Enough to silence an army," he said, pointing to one pile. "The way in which this mushroom works is particularly significant. No effects are noticed immediately. It is only upon its disintegration in digestion that the oils are released. It takes approximately four hours. Men have spit it out and lived. It has a pleasant taste so that would not be one's inclination. However," and at this he scooped all the poisonous mushrooms into the basket and left the good ones in the center of the table, "however, what is most significant is that these mushrooms are not ones that any of us have picked. My original mistake was in assuming they grew there. Freaks of nature. But it is another freak of nature that has produced them. These mushrooms are at least a day old. They are dry. They were picked much earlier and brought here for us, I believe. It is too neat to be an accident."

"Are you saying," the doctor asked, "that someone is deliberately trying to poison us?"

"Yes."

There was great excitement after this as we all wanted to know who was really intended to get the poisoned mushrooms and die.

The Countess was very upset, as was everyone else. The Freuds were very sober as they hurried to their coaches shortly after.

Just after they left the Inspector said suddenly to the Countess, "You first greeted Minna, Freud's sister-in-law, as Fr. Freud. What caused your error?"

"At the doctor's home, it is always she who lets me in."

"So you assumed she was his wife?" the Inspector said. The Countess seemed flustered. "No, the first time I met her she introduced herself that way," she said.

"At his home?" the Inspector asked.

"No," the Countess said, "I first met her when I was visiting an herbalist. Her name is Didi."

21

The next evening, when the Inspector arrived at the Countess' house, I thought he must have come early in order to contrive his efforts to elicit secrets from the cook. But that evening he had not come early to see the cook. He had come, it turned out, to see me.

"You must tell me," he said as we walked into the garden, "what you saw that morning and why you are ashamed to let me know. Your confidence is safe with me. I will reveal nothing and act only on what I must use to apprehend the murderer. I believe it is critical in solving the case—it may be the murder weapon as well as the murderer whom you have seen. I must implore you to recall it."

"I cannot," I said to him, a terrible fear rising in me, "as much as I wish to help you, I simply cannot," I said. He turned and saw that my face was pale with fear.

"Perhaps then," he said as we strolled a little farther into the garden, "you will permit me to use a technique in which you will feel very sleepy, and while feeling sleepy, you may remember something of importance and tell of it. And when you awake, you will have no memory of having told at all. How would that be?"

"I don't know," I told him.

"And what if Dr. Freud were to use this technique? Would you give him permission to obtain this information from you provided you knew nothing of it?"

I said again I did not know, and he put his hand gently on my shoulder and said he would give me several reasons that made it urgent that I do so.

He had something to tell me, he said, and I would feel ever so much better if I would hear him out. Trembling, I sat down as he told me of his plan, and I knew I must make certain decisions.

22

Where lies Madame Pacquin?
She's under the water
Because of her sin.
Her feet will be on land,
But her head will be in the sand.

"What is this?" the Inspector asked Voll.

"Another rhyme. It showed up just this morning. Apparently I owe you another apology, Inspector. These two murders are linked. The killer was intending to dismember her yet."

"I see," the Inspector said, "that the note appears to be identical." He looked up at Voll. "Now we have simply to prove this."

"I believe I have come close to a solution," Voll said. "Inspector, with your permission, may I show you something?"

23

The Inspector showed Didi, the herbalist, the photograph of the head in the tree. Her eyes turned away. Her voice was shaking.

"Her name is not Van de Vere," she said. "It is Suzanne des Champs. She came to me," Didi said, "because she said she needed to forget something . . ."

Didi turned to him, her voice quiet. "I have never seen a woman so desperate, and I have seen many desperate women. . . . I asked her, did she want to tell me . . . anything? . . . and she shook her head and said it was 'heinous, unspeakable,' and she broke down. Whatever it was," Didi continued, "apparently she had just discovered it. . . . Something had just happened. She was planning to run away."

"You have no idea . . . what it was?" the Inspector said.

"No, I could not get her to say anything," Didi said, looking at her hands. "I thought she might try to do something . . . to herself. I, I did not want the responsibility so I, I did speak to her husband about her condition. He was very upset. He thanked me."

"Her husband?"

"Yes. He is a distinguished doctor, Dr. Loeffler. The anatomy professor at the university. He was most concerned. I had assumed that the problem was solved. I never heard she was missing."

At this last response Didi was surprised to see the Inspector behave so rudely. He had turned on his heel and was out of her apartment before she could even finish the sentence.

24

As the Inspector was about to enter Dr. Loeffler's house at 91 Burggasse, the door opened and to his astonishment there stood Heinrich Voll.

"Good afternoon, Inspector," he said, "You are just in time to congratulate me on solving the murders. I have just arrested Dr. Eduard Loeffler."

25

It was late in the day when Mr. James and Mrs. Wharton were preparing to go out to dinner that the Inspector paid an unexpected visit to Mrs. Wharton's hotel. He carried a folder into the dining room and opened it.

"Oh, I had no idea a murderer would make the notes so *neat,*" Mrs. Wharton said.

"I see," Henry said. "They have all been cut from newspapers, and pasted."

"The notes appear to be the same," the Inspector said, "but I do not, for my own reasons, believe it is the same author. I would like, if you don't mind, your professional opinion."

"Oh, let us see," they both said, almost together.

"Well it's not really a nursery rhyme at all," Mrs. Wharton said. "It's not based on anything French, English, or German that I know, and I know many of them."

"And the rhyme schemes are totally different," Mr. James said.

"Yes," Mrs. Wharton said, "this one has no rhythmic sense at all."

"The accented and unaccented syllables fall in a totally different pattern," Mr. James said, "from the Van de Vere rhymes."

"So in all likelihood, they were not written by the same person?" the Inspector said.

"Well, one has an ear for rhythms and the other doesn't, so I doubt it would be the same person." They said this, again together, almost in unison.

"Henry," Edith said, "let us confer." They withdrew and asked the Inspector to wait.

Henry looked at the papers before him. Perhaps there was something here after all. He would certainly like to be of help in apprehending the murderer. And then he saw it.

"Look," he said to Edith, pointing to the scattered letters that had appeared at the bottom of the notes. It was curious—and from the police's point of view, meaningless—that the murderer had the habit of scattering a few additional letters around the page when he had finished compiling the words for his rhymes. Henry handed Edith the notes.

"I don't see what you mean," she said. "The rhyme schemes are different of course, which makes me think it was two different people."

"Oh definitely that," Henry said, "but even more, look at the extra letters."

Edith Wharton took the papers from him and studied the notes. At the bottom of the notes were the letters, scattered in exactly the same way. The most recent note had the letters *e, i, o, u.* Perhaps Henry had made them into a word, a word she'd never heard?

"I don't see what you mean," she said, feeling a bit disappointed that he might have discovered something which eluded her.

"Well," he said excitedly, "I don't know that it's definitive, or anything of the sort, but all of the scattered letters on the other notes, save this last one—the one that doesn't rhyme in the same scheme—why all those other notes have consonants on them, you see, *t, n, r, w, q,* all of that, and this last one, why it's only vowels."

Edith stared at him. "How extraordinary of you to notice," she said.

"Yes." He thought it rather was. He was quite proud of himself.

"Well, you see," he said, wanting to embroider on his victory, "I've always been rather interested in vowels. They say it was the Greeks who invented them."

"How clever of you to remember that," she said.

"Well," Henry said, "you can hardly forget it when you think about it, of course. I mean imagine that all those languages before Greek were nothing but consonants. I mean can you imagine the excitement of having a letter for a sound. Think of it!" he exclaimed.

"O," Edith Wharton said.

The Inspector stood up when they returned.

"In our opinion it's not the same person," Henry said, "most definitely. Even if you changed your rhymes, you wouldn't change your ear."

"Thank you," the Inspector said with a little smile, and giving a little bow and taking the papers from them, he bid them goodnight.

26

The next morning the Countess arrived at breakfast looking pale and thoughtful.

"The murder has been solved," she said quietly. "The Inspector has asked us all to come to Dr. Freud's house at ten o'clock to hear the solution to the crime."

We all thought it was most exciting, but the Countess looked quite grim. "Perhaps," Cecily said, "because it means the Inspector will return to Paris."

"Well," I said, "that isn't a problem, the Countess is forever in Paris herself."

27

There was an uproar in the police station. Loeffler had been taken into custody, everyone knew that. And now this. No one knew how he'd gotten it. But Loeffler had taken arsenic and killed himself. The Inspector's fury was a bellow, they said, that could be heard around the Ringstrasse.

28

At ten o'clock promptly the next morning we all gathered at Dr. Freud's house. Henry James and Mrs. Wharton were seated by the stair. Sabina was next to them. Dr. Jung, who was no longer speaking to Dr. Freud, was in Zurich. Leopold was standing behind the Countess. Dr. Fliess, and Emma Eckstein and her father sat on opposite sides of the room. Frl. Bernays and Fr. Freud were seated on the sofa. Mother, Father, Timothy, and I stood up, while Cecily sat on a stool near Aunt Ida.

We were all extremely tense as we awaited the Inspector's solution. The Inspector was sitting down, his shoulders slumped forward. We were rather surprised when the Inspector, looking very subdued, explained in a quiet voice that his talented associate, Captain Voll, had actually suceeded where he had failed, that Captain Voll was responsible for piecing together the final investigation, and therefore, it was to

Captain Voll that he was now yielding the floor. There was a small murmur, but we were all quite relieved that the murder had been solved after all.

Captain Voll was, I thought, almost savage with triumph. His eyes sparkled and his face was quite red. He stood before us all and recounted precisely what had happened. I looked over and saw Dr. Freud smoking his cigar.

Captain Voll explained that the body that had been found in the river had yielded an important clue. It was the body of the dressmaker, Mme. Pacquin, which had originally been thought a suicide. However, the Inspector discovered marks on her neck, and Captain Voll had then brilliantly linked this murder up to the events in Dr. Freud's study. He deduced that it was the same murderer who had killed and amputated and compiled the notes about the woman known as Gertrude Van de Vere, whose body parts had been sprinkled all over Vienna, and that he had murdered at least eight other women as well. There were murmurs all around, and I heard Mother sounding very upset until we heard Captain Voll say that the murderer was a doctor, a Dr. Eduard Loeffler, and he had already been arrested. There was a sigh of relief at this possibility because it meant none of *us* in the room was the dreaded murderer, although I confess I never really *thought* this. When we got over our excitement we were able to understand the story as follows:

Baroness Jessica des Champs, unmarried and pregnant with Dr. Eduard Loeffler's child before her marriage, went on a journey to relatives in Amsterdam. While there, she gave birth and gave the baby up for adoption, whereupon the child's name was changed by her new parents to Gertrude Van de Vere. Subsequently, Mlle. des Champs married Dr. Loeffler, who was told there had been no child. Meanwhile, upon reaching adulthood, Gertrude decided to become an actress and took the name Suzanne de Montezuma because it was exotic. She first worked as a waitress on the left bank in Paris. She became discouraged in her acting career but eventually was engaged as a dress model. On a visit to Paris, Jessica des Champs Loeffler saw her by coincidence and was struck by the striking similarity, despite the fact that des Champs Loeffler was sixteen years older. Gertrude Van de Vere, now Suzanne de Montezuma, was immediately hired as the "double," in the Paris dress shop that catered to Jessica des Champs, now Mme. Loeffler.

Eduard Loeffler, who was tired of his truculent, difficult wife, fell madly in love with her "double," Suzanne, who fell in love with him. He murdered Jessica, disguised it as an accident and persuaded Suzanne to marry him, a month later. He took her off to Vienna. But he became strange, from guilt over his murdered wife, and the alarmed Suzanne wrote and asked her parents to visit.

When her parents arrived, Suzanne, that is Gertrude, was out, so her parents spent the day talking to Dr. Loeffler. As fate would have it, during this time, the parents revealed the story of the child, who had been given to them at birth in the city of Amsterdam, whose original name was des Champs. Dr. Loeffler at this point had to realize he had married his daughter but said nothing.

Several months later Dr. Loeffler decided to tell Suzanne that she was in fact his daughter. He fully expected her to forgive him, and insist on maintaining the marriage. At first, she thought him simply mad, then she was naturally quite horrified and eventually ran away. During this time she sought help from both an herbalist and her dressmaker Mme. Pacquin. Loeffler was going mad; he stalked Suzanne and then murdered *her* in a fit of rage and guilt, and dismembered the body. Then he began to leave the notes and went on a rampage, murdering women throughout Vienna.

Voll then established that Loeffler became concerned that Suzanne's dressmaker, Mme. Pacquin, was suspicious of him, so he arranged that stormy night to murder Mme. Pacquin as well. He purchased a gun, for which Captain Voll had the receipt, intending to make it look like a suicide.

He shot her and arranged to have the body delivered to his home, 91 Burggasse, in order to dismember it. But due to an illiterate coachman the body was taken instead to 19 Berggasse. When the error was realized the coachman was ordered to return and retrieve the body, but as it was nearly dawn by then, Dr. Loeffler did not want the body returning to his *home,* where it would be seen, and so he sent it into the river where he intended it to sink. The only missing piece was the gun, which was never recovered.

There were incredulous murmurs all around as everyone said this was simply amazing and they were very impressed. Captain Voll looked very pleased.

"Heavens," Father said, "it's all very disturbing, and not anything I could even have imagined."

"And so a series of explanations have been presented which qualify as causes. Those of you who are satisfied are at liberty to go home now," the Inspector said, rising from his chair. And then he paused. "But those of you who would know the truth of this matter must remain. Although this explanation is both elaborate and logical, it is *wrong*. Dr. Loeffler did murder these women. But he did *not* murder Mme. Pacquin, whose body it was that was brought *here*. I have *proof* of *that*," and he looked at me. I blushed at this.

Captain Voll looked stunned as the Inspector said this and he stood up. The Inspector ordered him to sit down and both of the other lieutenants sat next to him.

"You see," the Inspector said, moving to the center of our group, "this murder was brilliantly planned and executed with a devotion to purpose rare in any circumstances. I could not understand what my difficulty was in solving this case, until the murderer himself made it clear to me. This matter is a very personal one for me. The murderer of Mme. Pacquin knows me, and our story is central to his crime.

"There was, when I was very young, another child on the estate on which I grew up. By happenstance, a troublesome nursemaid quite convinced him that he really belonged in the manor house, and that it was I who belonged in the gardener's cottage. We had been born on the same day, at approximately the same hour, but his mother had died. The nursemaid had persuaded the young impressionable boy that I had usurped his position. That, in fact, the babies had been switched.

"I had quite forgotten all of this as I was young at the time, although I was aware of his intense affection for my mother. This jealous child, aided and abetted by his father, got so out of hand that at the age of seven, in an insane jealous rage, he made an attempt on my life. I still block the event in my memory but I recall my father telling me about it. The boy had injured me to a point near death. I was discovered by my father only at the eleventh hour, and the boy and his father were expelled from the estate. He was at the time my only friend and I loved him like a brother. This event was quite shattering to me, and I totally forgot it, a circumstance, no doubt, he was counting on. For that child's name was Johann Heinrich Vollmann and he is none other than Captain Heinrich Voll, who has attempted, as his final revenge on me, to commit a crime he believed I could never solve, and more than that, to commit what he envisioned as the perfect murder."

There was much commotion and many exclamations at this. Heinrich Voll stood up, and yelled, "This is an outrage! An absolute outrage! You have no proof."

The Inspector stayed him with an outstretched hand, and two of the Inspector's other assistants sat Voll down in the chair, while we listened to the rest of the astonishing story.

"It was all very clever," the Inspector said, "exceedingly clever. But Captain Voll was not considering motive. Dr. Loeffler killed his wife and daughter in fits of passion. And then he went quite mad and went on a rampage through Vienna. The murder of the dressmaker would have to have been more calculated, although admittedly still possible since Loeffler was by then insane. But Captain Voll made a fatal error. You see, he had already solved the Loeffler murders prior to my arrival in Vienna. So that when he strangled Mme. Pacquin, he ordered her to be dumped in Loeffler's living room at 91 Burggasse which would be a perfect cover for him. But the coachman misread the streets, which differed by one letter. The illiterate carriageman misread the address and brought the body instead to 19 Berggasse, Dr. Freud's home, and put it on the floor. Captain Voll had Loeffler's fingerprints on the gun and intended to shoot the already dead body in order to frame Dr. Loeffler. He shot Madame Pacquin forty-eight hours *after* he strangled her, which the autopsy demonstrated. Upon seeing the horses around the Ringstrasse, passing Burggasse, he realized that the coachman had made an error, and raced to Berggasse, to the Freud house, where he met the carriageman in the street and instructed him to retrieve the body and place it in the proper house. Upon retrieving it from Freud's study, he shot it before putting it into the coach, to prove the gun was Loeffler's, but then because of the screams from the Freud house he lost his nerve, panicked and headed for the river. In his panic, he overcompensated on alibis. There he put stones in her pockets and threw some of her jewels on the shore. He decided to make the murder appear to be a suicide, but he knew that if the suicide was ever questioned, he still had the gun with Loeffler's fingerprints stored safely in the basement. But it was precisely this effort to cover it up that exposed him.

"Captain Voll is an astute police investigator himself. How odd, then I thought, at what he missed in his perusal of Mme. Pacquin's desk. It never occurred to him to look for another lover's letter as he could not bear the thought of the rival who had put him in a jealous rage.

But this rival did him in. Heinrich Voll had been Mme. Pacquin's lover, but she had tired of him, and was expecting her other lover the day after she committed "suicide." The other note confirms this. No woman expecting a lover commits suicide. So, why a strangulation, and a bullet hole and stones in the pockets of *one* body unless they had been deliberately put there?"

"You, you never told me," Voll spluttered suddenly.

The Inspector looked up. "Of course not," the Inspector said mildly. "I walked for several hours, trying to imagine the state of the woman's mind, decided to search the house myself, and found the letters.

"You have, Heinrich Voll, in many ways authored your own demise, for your composition is admirable in its attention to detail and its effort to imitate Loeffler's notes. And the rhyming note was composed with cut-out newspaper words to imitate Dr. Loeffler's notes. But Dr. Loeffler, although a bad poet, was not as bad a poet as *you,* which made me *very* suspicious." He nodded to Mr. James and Mrs. Wharton. "And my suspicions were confirmed. When you knew of my plan to have everyone hypnotized your response to me at the station was one of genuine horror. You had to act, as you would, under hypnosis, be discovered. You followed us to the mushroom feast and attempted to eliminate all of us at once if necessary."

Voll was silent—the Inspector turned to us. "He was desperate at this point and saw his opportunity. When I took Lieutenant Stekal to Captain Voll's house, after making certain that Captain Voll was not in, we found there the remarkable cane with a silver head, hidden most effectively under some garments in the basement. It was, of course, the cane that belonged to Sabina. How convenient that after searching Dr. Loeffler's chambers, we found no cane, but when Captain Voll searched it, he discovered the cane that he had planted but had in fact belonged to himself. He himself placed it in Dr. Loeffler's house!"

"It is a lie, all lies!" Voll exclaimed. "It was you, Inspector, who took the cane from Loeffler's house and hid it in my house, and then went there with Stekal to frame me!"

"More than that, Hr. Voll, more than that." The Inspector turned to me. I felt everyone's eyes upon me. "We have, besides Sabina, another witness," the Inspector said, pointing to me. "And further," he said, walking to the far end of the room and then, making a dramatic turn to me, "she has written down and drawn in her personal diary, made known only privately to me, a picture of a man who fits your description, Hr. Voll, and where, indeed, we were led to the gun."

There was a murmur of excitement and I saw Cecily's eyes bear in on me.

"It is a fantasy," Voll said quickly. "Haven't you learned, Inspector, about the words and thoughts of hysterical young women, women who need to be married? This is no *proof;* it is all conjecture. It is sheer imagining. All you have is a girl with a pencil; what you need is a man with a gun." He sat back.

"In this case a girl with a pencil is more than a match for a man with a gun. This sketch," the Inspector said, offering the small sketch I had taken from my diary and given to him, "is that too a fantasy? You can see she has drawn an extraordinary likeness to your face. And finally, she has drawn the gun, which, alas for you, you found necessary to retrieve and hide in your basement, where we discovered it wrapped in the red cloth she has pictured here. You had thoughtfully organized everything in one box. It is very clever," the Inspector said, "because the gun has Eduard Loeffler's fingerprints, a fact you arranged as proof to frame him. It also, of course, contains *your* fingerprints. You attempted to use that gun, *one more time,*" he turned to us, his face grim, "on me."

He threw the shells on the table and they rolled across the floor.

"Fired at me on April 2nd," he said to Voll, "by an excellent shot." At this Voll threw back his arms and ran straight for the Inspector crying, "I'll kill you!" He lunged for the Inspector, throwing off the two lieutenants, and pinioned him to the floor, his hands around his neck, everyone screaming except Mr. James, who suddenly picked up a stone statue from the desk and saved the Inspector by knocking Captain Voll on the head. He collapsed, moaning, to the floor. They handcuffed him immediately. But Voll was not done. As they dragged him from the premises he suddenly recovered.

"You just *wait,* Inspector," Voll said, suddenly roaring, his bleeding face lifting from the floor. "You have not solved the murder after all. You the Great Inspector, hah!" The venomous tone surprised us all. "You have solved nothing . . . oh yes, I admit I did murder Mme. Pacquin. She was *filth,*" he spat. "She threatened to go to my wife, and then I did hire a coachman to place her body in the river. But Mme. Pacquin was never *here.*" The hiss in his voice, like a whisper, created a shudder through the house. "You, Inspector, *great* Inspector," he turned to the Inspector, "have let them all down, Hah! Hah! Hah!" he laughed suddenly and I saw Cecily, who was seated nearest him, grow quite pale. "Because the murderer who placed that body here still walks free and you can never *catch* him." I heard a gasp then. "It is not I who had the coachman bring the body here. . . . No, Inspector, it was another coachman altogether. A night for bodies, was it not then? Hah! Hah! Hah!"

"It was you," the coachman said, entering suddenly from the other room, "I remember the beard . . ."

"Look hard, man, it was not I," Voll said.

"But the cane, you have the cane!" the coachman said. "I remember the cane well."

"Precisely," Voll bellowed forth, "and go yourself, Inspector, great Inspector, to the pawn shop. I will bring you the ticket and you can see I have purchased the cane myself, only two days ago—Hah!" Voll's voice was shrill, high, shrieky.

"Why would you purchase this cane?" the Inspector asked, his face drawn.

"Because I knew it would lead to the murderer," Voll said, "and I wanted him *free*. You alone are not so clever. I too have interrogated Miss Spielrein. I, too, know the significance of the cane. Oh, yes, it was *I* myself who placed the fingerprints on the gun of the woman in the park you thought was a suicide. I was always *first* at the scene of the crime to make sure you were misled in *precisely* the way I wanted you misled. It was *I* who laid the clues you in your arrogance imagined you *discovered*. It was *I* who placed the head in the tree! You have failed Inspector, and *grandly."* Voll was screaming now.

"But, but, Slotkin," he said, "Slotkin confirmed the body parts were surgically *cut*. Would you have us believe there was a *second* mad doctor?" There was tension and uncertainty in the Inspector's voice.

"Slotkin only saw Van de Vere!" Voll laughed hysterically. "I saw to it!"

"But the notes . . ." the Inspector said, "they were composed in the same way, all of them—the Van de Vere rhymes."

"More!" Voll screamed. "Hundreds. He compiled hundreds." His face had blown up now red like a balloon, "I *placed* them there to mislead you!" His horrible laugh broke through the air.

"But . . . but why?" The Inspector's face was drawn and white. Someone, I'm not sure who, was crying.

"Why?" The Inspector's voice was hoarse.

"Because," Voll's voice cut through the air with a horrid, etching squeal, like a razor against glass. "So that you see your murderer still walks and kills and there will be *many* other bodies in the river! Unrecovered bodies! And he has vanished into the night, like the fog itself and you have only a confused coachman with an error in an address. The murderer runs free! Hah! Hah! Hah!" I ran out of the room at this point, my hands over my ears trying to shut out the sound of his terrible laugh.

29

MY DREAM

That night I dreamed about Aunt Ida.

"So it's the story then; what we tell, how much we tell, if we tell, that makes us well then?" Aunt Ida asked quizzically, her head cocked to one side, her hand on her umbrella posed for the weather, just like a revolutionary, I thought, waiting at the ramparts.

As long as I dreamed of Aunt Ida, I was quite reassured. But I dreamed many dreams that night. And although I knew there were many of them, in the morning I could not remember any. Only the ones about Aunt Ida. I knew I was dreadfully worried that in fact if we all had these other selves, why any one of us might have done the terrible murders, in one of our other selves, and that self might be the very one that Hr. Voll said was walking the streets unchecked. I know there were many because they had to keep waking me up, I was screaming so.

30
HENRY'S DREAM

Words, turning and burning under the dark lake of consciousness. Black swans rising now with the bait, sated, to the surface. And then they were gone. Shadows. Perhaps they weren't birds at all. Shadows. Perhaps not even shadows. And amid all this, Nietzsche could rejoice. He was a braver man than I, Henry thought, moving closer to Freud, who sat next to him. They were sitting on a bench, by a lake, and they were both throwing bread. It scattered on the water. It scattered on the ground. And in the morning he could no longer remember if they had been there, the two of them, like Hansel and Gretel casting a path out of the forest, or if they were simply there, watching shadows, feeding swans.

He had had a fitful night. He had not expected things to turn out as they had. Such an odd sort of story about the Inspector and Voll, and the murders, the poor women—all of it. He was relieved it was over. He was eager to go to Italy. But there was this nagging sense within him of something quite unsatisfied. He realized what it was: he had not expected this, that evil such as this could be embedded in something as seemingly remote as the frustrations of a childhood plot.

31
THE INSPECTOR'S
FIRST DREAM

Voll was speaking to him. "You are quite correct. I have shot Mme. Pacquin, but it was not her body which was in Dr. Freud's study. The mystery remains unsolved, Hr. Inspector. A murderer is at large whom you can never find. Hah! Hah! Hah!" The laughter echoed around the room, stealing his sleep.

The Inspector woke up. It had become a nightmare he could not escape. Was it possible, was it true that Voll was right? That he had in fact purchased a cane from the pawnshop that had been left there by a murderer, an *additional* murderer to Voll and Loeffler? A madman slaughtering at will? Or had Voll, in fact, planned to have the cane sold to the pawnshop, and arranged to have himself buy it back, simply as part of some insanely diabolical plan to foil any and every investigation?

The clock read three A.M. Fitfully he got up, and prepared to dress. He would sit again, this night, in the chair, reading Baudelaire. Something to take his mind from it.

He was on his way to the armoire when he slipped, quite suddenly and fell unexpectedly to the floor, bringing a piercing pain along the side of his neck. His reaction upset him utterly, as tears streamed quite suddenly from his eyes, and he sat, overwhelmed by a wrenching, unbearable grief.

It came to him, then. The memory of Voll. He saw him now, the child Johann Vollmann, with such stunning clarity he did not see how he could ever have forgotten.

I T was that child of seven who was above him now, pinning him down with a startling strength. It had started as a game. A simple game. The Inspector remembered the soft summer day, and his friend Johann jumping playfully on him from behind, pulling him to the ground, the Inspector laughing and then suddenly not. He could not move. He was pinned by the force of Johann's knee against his neck, his other hand weighting his shoulder. But it was his eyes, child's eyes against the bright sun behind him, it was those eyes the Inspector had refused to see that he saw now, the hatred bare and unmasked as the ferocious boy took the large sharp rock and brought it down across the Inspector's head, once, twice, in stunning blows as the child Johann screamed his scream of jealousy and rage, "Meine mama, meine, meine!"

The Inspector stayed still for some time, trying to calm himself before the vivid release of that summer day, forty-three years away.

32

Henry James got out of the bath, shaking and shivering in the draft. He didn't know why, but he absolutely hated being cold. Sometimes he thought he was the coldest person ever born. Gratefully he wrapped the towel, warm from the heaters, around him and then dressed as quickly as possible. Cecily would be at the Countess' tea, later today, he felt sure. He brushed his hair and adjusted his tie. It had haunted him, utterly haunted him, the business of someone writing about him. And now suddenly he thought he rather *liked* it. He felt the old pain cut through him, and in another minute it left. He felt heartened. Why perhaps if they wrote about him, they might invent the very thing for him to do that life, by its proscription, had failed to. He went down to breakfast, his feet jumping the last two stairs.

"Oh Mr. James," the startled housekeeper said, "it didn't sound at all like you." He was smiling and ordered his coffee, having a new sense of his possibilities. No longer the observer, free at last, to act.

33

All the next morning, the Countess had been trying to convince us that Voll had pulled off a terrible trick—he was trying to torment us all by terrifying our imaginations. "He not only did it, but placed the body there, I am sure of it," she said, smiling brightly, and the look of conviction on her face made us all feel much better.

She told us that she had had word from the Inspector that the emperor had ordered the case closed, and that the Inspector would be returning to Paris. Cecily whispered to me that she thought it was strange that the Countess seemed happy about this, and I said that I was sure the Countess would go to Paris somehow too, although how I did not know precisely. There had been a kind of glow about the Countess of late that everyone noticed; a happiness, and not even the terrible events of Voll and the murder had seemed to take this away from her.

We were all pleased when the Countess told us she had invited everyone who would be leaving the city—that is, Mr. James and Mrs. Wharton—to come to her atelier for tea. She had been designing beautiful dresses for the upcoming "Blumencorso," a parade through the Prater, with the emperor, and carriages, and everyone in the city carrying bouquets of flowers.

Mother was surprised at the invitation, she said, because although she knew about the sewing shop, she also knew that the Countess had had to keep it secret from her husband. The Countess, smiling, had said that Leopold had learned of it some months ago; she had in fact, told him and he had ordered it closed. "But," she said with that mysterious smile, "he has no longer any influence over me."

Then the Countess excused herself, because the Inspector had arrived at her atelier, where, she said, she had something special she was eager to show him.

34

It was spring now. The beautiful citizens of Vienna paraded and strolled, cavorted, and displayed themselves along the Kärntnerstrasse, through the Burggarten and along the Prater. The Inspector stopped to watch them. As he strolled along the Ringstrasse, he admonished himself that he had quite forgotten how magnificent Vienna could be. How was it that it had oppressed him so when now, strolling along its boulevards, looking at the delicate beautiful Votivkirche, the gleaming gold dome of the Secessionist building, the gardens before the Rathaus, the statues of Schiller and Goethe, listening to the melodies drift along the streets—the world of Brahms and Beethoven, Strauss and Schönberg—he felt only its celebration? How could he not have responded more fully and appreciated the joy of such a place, where the best is thought and displayed, in art, music, painting and sculpture? How could he have been so blind to the dazzling beauty that now, in the spring, seemed to burst into life through every street and chestnut tree? He moved a little more quickly, now, sensing as he passed the cafes—the Viennese arguing, Czechs, Germans, Croats, Slovaks, Poles, and Magyars gesticulating, that this great confluence of humanity had in its future the very best that could be thought and said. The very best! A new confidence suffused him then and he sported a jaunty stride.

As he crossed the bridge toward his boardinghouse in the Prater he looked back and saw the Ringstrasse as a huge horseshoe, and he imagined he could see as far as the statue of Maria Theresa at its center, arms opening wide, embracing the city. As he turned toward the Prater he saw children playing, and a wonderful orchestra had started up near this entrance to the park. It was Schubert and he stopped to listen.

That night however, after he boarded the train, amidst the clack of the wheels, when he tried to sleep, his fears came back to haunt him.

He was standing high, where he did not know, on a parapet that did not exist, looking down across the city and it was as if his arms, extended, were the Ringstrasse itself, embracing the golden domes and winding streets of the center of Vienna. His arms, like the Ringstrasse, were reaching wide, as if to reach out for something, and as he cradled the city in his embrace, as he saw the Rathaus and the Staatsoper, the Hofburg, the Parliament, the Volksgarten, the Stephansdom, the buildings got smaller and smaller, faded and reappeared, and the pageant of history that had been the Rathaus and the Burgtheater now was the Louvre, the Isaaskyevskaya in Leningrad, St. Peter's and the Colosseum, the Ringstrasse now was circling Paris and Prague, Berlin and Budapest, Leningrad, Moscow, Sarajevo, Rome. The Ringstrasse stretched out around these cities as their monuments rose and fell before him like so many tiny, mirage-like dioramas. His arms began to ache as they reached out, and then the Ringstrasse was turning red, running with blood, his arms broke off from his shoulder, and the statue, his statue of himself, fell down.

And then he was only a man, running. He was a man running through the bloodied streets of the Ringstrasse and a carriage with six black horses was careening down on him. Faster and faster they galloped, aiming for him as he tried to twist and turn, when his feet, heavy with fear, pulled him down. He looked up and saw the Countess, reaching for him.

"Where are you?" he called to the Countess in the dark.

"Here," she said, her voice light, as if she were singing, "We are over here. Come over here, with us." And as the light came up he saw he was now in a room full of women, and they were talking and humming and sewing. The room was full of heads and arms and bodies, and the women, chattering, as they were sewing beautiful garments, were sewing the arms back onto the bodies, as if life were a large doll they had the magic to restore. As he walked among them, he saw that some of the women were making clothes, beautiful clothes, fabrics of gold and silver, for the bodies—clothes of satin and wool and silk and taffeta, with lace and ribbon as delicate as a spider web, and as they worked they began to sing, their fingers moving in and out of the cloth they sang louder and louder, and pretty soon the room was filled with ribbon and song. And Wharton and James came in then and sat down and listened. And Freud was there, holding an arm and head in place, consternation on his brow, while Jung and Sabina stood outside—on the threshold, beckoning. And yet they did not stop, the women singing and sewing until their voices got louder and louder and went out the window in a mighty song, and spilled onto the streets until the room itself seemed to rise from the ground with their effort. It was the most beautiful singing he had ever heard. He floated then, into its current as they drifted all of them, out into the country sky, over the lakes and valleys to a land he did not know.

35

I was happy for any excuse to go into the Countess' shop, and I saw the same was true for Mrs. Wharton and indeed Mr. James as well and even Sabina, for that afternoon we wandered around looking at all the fine cloaks and dresses, feathers and sequins. And while we were in the front of the shop, we could hear the seamstresses in the back, talking and laughing and occasionally humming. I remembered then when I had been in the shop before and I had said to the Countess how happy I thought the women were working there, and I said impulsively that I too wanted to have a dress shop where people were happy and making beautiful things.

"Do not be so romantic," she had said to me. "They are well taken care of here. But there are workshops where their fingers bleed and they go blind at a young age. It is, as I have maintained," she said to me, "a question of how the system is employed."

I was surprised to see that Dr. Freud arrived, along with Minna and Martha, and they all complimented the Countess on her coffee, her tea, and her cakes. Minna was trying on a cloak, and when I turned she seemed to be blushing at her reflection in the mirror. The cloak was red, a color called claret, and I don't know if it was a reflection from the glass, or the light, but her cheeks were very pink and she looked quite lovely.

Martha gazed at her with interest. "Why wherever would you wear *that?*" she said.

Mrs. Wharton and Mr. James were discussing a ball gown of the Countess' own design. They were full of admiration.

The Countess had agreed to model it, and she asked me to help her into it. When I could not fasten the waist she turned to me, her eyes all excited, "Really?" she said. I nodded. I hesitated, knowing what pride the Countess took in her figure, and did not want to say that she had gotten *fat,* but, "It's much too small," I said hopelessly, and the Countess jumped up off of both feet and clapped her hands and spun around as if it were the best thing that had ever happened to her. I was puzzling over this when we went back into the shop and the Countess excitedly explained that she had still to make some changes before she could model the dress. Mrs. Wharton was eyeing her carefully.

I was feeling a little sad because I knew this was probably the last time we would all be together, although the Inspector had already left. Suddenly, out of nowhere, Minna said, staring into the mirror, "It makes you wonder. An evil man like that Voll, it makes you wonder, you know, about it all."

I felt a shiver go through the entire room and then Mrs. Wharton said suddenly, "Why Henry, what is it?" and we all turned to see Henry James sitting there with a very studied expression on his face. He looked up, startled.

"Oh," he said, "I am only listening." His head was cocked to one side.

"For what?" Mrs. Wharton asked. Her voice was tremulous. Mr. James' face was poised, so still, as if he were a photograph. Henry leaned forward then, desperate, hoping for a sound, a word, a promise, some means of grasping the sickening abyss. He strained. There *was* something. The words died in the air. The voiceless voice inquired, but he could not hear.

"I'm listening for the song," he said. I don't think anyone knew what he meant at first, at least I didn't, but the Countess and Dr. Freud and Mrs. Wharton looked at him for a long moment as if they knew.

"I don't hear anything," Martha said, staring into the mirror at Minna's back. "I suppose we could have imagined it," she said softly.

"All of it?" someone said. "Everything?" and no one knew then. Nothing for certain. The only evidence fragments, pieces of papers, cries torn from a box.

Editor's Postscript

This is how one pictures the angel of history. His face is turned toward the past. Where we perceive a chain of events, he sees one single catastrophe which keeps piling wreckage upon wreckage and hurls it in front of his feet. The angel would like to stay, awaken the dead, and make whole what has been smashed. But a storm is blowing from Paradise; it has got caught in his wings with such violence that the angel can no longer close them. This storm irresistibly propels him into the future to which his back is turned, while the pile of debris before him grows skyward. This storm is what we call progress.[1]

Walter Benjamin
Illuminations

That was the end of the manuscript. It left me wondering if there might be more. Somehow I felt there were chapters missing, and although I endeavored to find them, as I said earlier, all efforts to locate the source of this document were unsuccessful.

I still do not know why it was sent to me, or indeed how it arrived. As

---

[1] The parallels between this story and our own time, particularly the questions of separation and assimilation, as well as the ever-present search for definitions of "identity" and "self" seem almost uncanny. It is such concerns, that made me think that Walter Benjamin's image of the angel was a fitting one for this postscript.

I said in my introduction, I am a medieval scholar and I believed originally that the manuscript was sent to me because of my expertise in
deciphering handwriting. And because, of course, the book was bound
and written as if it were a manuscript from the Middle Ages. That is to
say, it observed some curious conventions of the period. It was written
on skin—what kind I could not readily discover. It was neither goat nor
calf. It was like no vellum I had ever seen. It was white on both sides.
There did not seem to be a "hairy side," as we medieval scholars
are wont to say. And then there was the problem in the binding. It
was a convention during the medieval period to distribute the body
parts of kings, queens, saints, and martyrs to various parts of the
kingdom, thereby making "holy" the places where the relics were
buried.

It was also a convention to place relics—pieces of bone and hair—
inside the bindings of the books. And what was disturbing to me about
this book I had been sent was that I clearly heard the presence of bones
in the binding, and I wondered what would be the purpose of relics—
gross samples of hair and bones—in this book? This was, after all, no
Bible or holy book. No one had been martyred here. I finally had no
choice but to take the cover apart and to discover somewhat to my
surprise that there were in fact no relics. What was it then that I heard?
I refastened the binding with the greatest care, and still when I opened
the book to read, I would hear a sound trickling down the binding—a
chilling slide.

I did not know if the sounds I heard were the ghosts of bones past or
those yet to come. I wondered then, was it possible that the old woman,
Jung's grandmother, had been prophetic, or that it only seems so, now,
after the events of this terrible century. In my own life, and my own
career, these anti-Semitic matters have been of no small consequence.
I suffered the loss of my entire family. Professionally the anti-Semitism
of medieval studies prevented there being any Jewish medieval scholars
between 1920 and 1940.

I have many unanswered questions. My reason still prevails, but my
heart, thinking on these things, grows heavy. And I hear now, on dark
and lonely nights, the sound of the horses—once again—the stamp of

hooves, the jangle of bells. Their breath grows warm on my neck and I hear a crackling in the bindings. Is it something waiting to be let out? And if so, what? And the question haunts me—will I, can I, after my knowledge of these things, still hear the sounds of song?

ABOUT THE AUTHOR

Carol De Chellis Hill is the author of *Jeremiah 8:20, Let's Fall in Love,* and *The Eleven Million Mile High Dancer.* She lives in New York City, where she teaches writing at New York University.